The Republic of China

THE REPUBLIC
OF CHINA

1912 to 1949

Xavier Paulès

Translated by Lindsay Lightfoot

polity

Originally published in French as *La République de Chine. Histoire générale de la Chine (1912–1949)* © Société d'Édition Les Belles Lettres, Paris, 2019

This English edition © Polity Press, 2023

Laboratoire d'Excellence

tepsis

Transformation de l'Etat
politisation des sociétés
institution du social

This work has received funding from UMR Chine Corée Japon, from the Laboratoire d'Excellence Tepsis (ANR-11-LABX-0067), and has been supported by the Programme d'Investissements d'Avenir.

Polity Press
65 Bridge Street
Cambridge CB2 1UR, UK

Polity Press
111 River Street
Hoboken, NJ 07030, USA

ISBN-13: 978-1-5095-5257-3

A catalogue record for this book is available from the British Library.

Typeset in 11.5 on 14 Adobe Garamond
by Fakenham Prepress Solutions, Fakenham, Norfolk NR21 8NL
Printed and bound in Great Britain by CPI Group (UK) Ltd, Croydon

The publisher has used its best endeavours to ensure that the URLs for external websites referred to in this book are correct and active at the time of going to press. However, the publisher has no responsibility for the websites and can make no guarantee that a site will remain live or that the content is or will remain appropriate.

Every effort has been made to trace all copyright holders, but if any have been overlooked the publisher will be pleased to include any necessary credits in any subsequent reprint or edition.

For further information on Polity, visit our website: politybooks.com

For Aliénor

Contents

Illustrations

Title-page calligraphy by Toshiko Yasumoto-Martin.

Maps

All the maps were created by Noël Meunier.

Acknowledgements

Firstly, I would like to thank the editorial director of the 'Histoire générale de la Chine' series, Damien Chaussende, for the confidence and honour shown me when he entrusted me with this book. I would also like to thank my French publisher, Les Belles Lettres, and, in particular, their director, Caroline Noirot.

The publication of this book is the culmination of a long journey, begun during my two postdoctoral years with the Japan Society for the Promotion of Science (2005–7) at Tokyo University. The complete freedom accorded me then allowed me to read extensively outside my specialist field and to begin reflecting on the republican period. My profound thanks are also due to Professor Takamizawa Osamu for his help throughout my stay in Japan.

The seminar 'New Historical Approaches to Republican China', which I have led at EHESS (The School for Advanced Studies in the Social Sciences, Paris) for almost ten years, with my two colleagues Delphine Spicq and David Serfass, has been the vital crucible in which many ideas have been formulated, discussed and matured in an atmosphere of benevolence and friendship. I think David and Delphine will be pleased to see, on reading this book, how much it owes to this shared experience. I am also grateful to all the seminar's students and speakers, unfortunately too numerous to mention here.

I have been fortunate, in writing this book, to be able to make use of a remarkable facility, the China Centre Library, the fruit of several generations of librarians' work. Special thanks are due to our two current librarians, Monique Abud and Wang Ju.

A further source of pleasure and inspiration came from exchanges with my colleagues at the Centre for Modern and Contemporary Chinese Studies. The help, support and confidence of its successive directors – Christian Lamouroux, Élisabeth Allès, Frédéric Obringer and Anne Kerlan – have been invaluable.

During my own years as Director of the Centre for Modern and Contemporary Chinese Studies, I was fortunate to be able to rely on a strong team of two managers, Soulia Bentouhami and Laura Vernon, who have always shown a rare patience and competence.

I would also like to thank my students Dominique Biehl, Martine Breton, Victor Gaumé, Maxime Giraudon, Sammantha Ho, Victoire Rouis, Tobit Vandamme, Li Wei and Xie Lingqiong. They have given me much – probably more than they realize.

For her careful translation of this book, I express my deepest thanks to Lindsay Lightfoot. I would also like to thank Elise Heslinga and the team at Polity for their meticulous editing service.

Finally, my thoughts go to my family, my wife Chunyi and my children. This book is dedicated to my daughter Aliénor, born during the long years it took to write.

Introduction

From 1912 to 1949, the ruling Chinese regime was the Republic of China (*Zhonghua minguo* 中華民國). The period was named after it and, in China as in the West, the thirty-seven years from the fall of the Qing Empire (1912), up until the declaration of the People's Republic of China (1949), are known as 'the republican period' (*minguo shidai* 民國時代).

This republican period is particularly important in history because it put an end not merely to the reign of the Qing dynasty, but also to the thread of successive dynasties which had run through Chinese history for 2,000 years.

For a long time, researchers remained nervous of this chaotic interval, with the rising influence of the Chinese Communist Party (CCP) as its common thread. This teleological perspective was not peculiar to Chinese historians. Fascinated by China's shift to socialism in 1949, their counterparts in the West adopted a similar approach over subsequent decades. The demands imposed on them as teachers also made this necessary – by giving the CCP the major role, they were able to confer some overall coherence on a complex and energetic period, which was additionally characterized by a weak central power and the assertiveness of numerous centrifugal forces.[1] However, this perspective runs up against simple facts: the Communist Party, founded almost ten years after the fall of the empire, in 1921, only ceased to be an insignificant group of intellectuals in the mid-1920s. And not until very late on, around 1944, was it able to challenge the supremacy of the Guomindang (國民黨, Nationalist Party),[2] which had been in power since 1928. Moreover, as this book will attempt to show, the CCP's victory was the result of a combination of particularly fortunate factors. Unquestionably, the party was skilful in taking advantage of them, but in the final analysis they were not of its making. Under these circumstances, it is no longer legitimate to read the whole period in the light of the CCP's ultimate victory.

Therefore, we will not give the CCP its customary place in overviews of the republican period. This is a difficult choice, obliging us to reconsider the general significance of the period. It is also a questionable choice, since you might think that it hardly does justice to the enormous quantity of work, often of very good quality, that has been devoted to the CCP. It was, nonetheless, a necessary choice if a more balanced interpretation of the period was to be achieved, and the importance of political actors outside the revolutionary movement, such as the warlords and the technocrats of the Guomindang, was to be re-established.

Also, we will move away from an interpretation that, for over twenty years, has emphasized the concept of modernization instead of examining the narrative of the revolutionary saga. After all, however we define it, modernization was a phenomenon that took place in a much broader time frame than just during the period 1912–49.

Furthermore, the fascination with the dynamics of modernization leads to the neglect of whole sections of society and the economy, such as the traditional service sector and cottage industries, despite their enormous intrinsic importance. Finally, we will try to dispel certain negative propagandistic views of the period and, following the lead of other recent historians, show that, even in the absence of a strong central power, the country made significant progress, particularly in the fields of state-building, economic development, education and intellectual life.

Sources

The first wave of historians (from the 1950s to the 1970s) based their research on printed material and archival collections of Western and Japanese origin because the political context of the Maoist period deprived them of access to China's archives (and even of access to China itself). The British, American and French diplomatic archives were the most widely used. These major powers were both the most eager for detailed information about the country, and the only ones able to afford the luxury of a close-knit network of diplomatic representatives. There were, in addition to the arsenal of diplomatic sources, the remarkable investigations carried out by the South Manchurian Railway services.

Since the 1980s, access to archives and libraries in China has been widely opened up and historians have faced the opposite problem: the overabundance of sources. In a recent article, Endymion Wilkinson estimates that the period 1912–49 has furnished as many sources available to historians as the three millennia of Chinese history that preceded it.[3] Experts on the Republic can draw on traditional printed sources already familiar to historians of earlier periods, such as local gazetteers (*difangzhi* 地方志), literary works such as notebooks (*biji* 筆記), and family genealogies (*zupu* 族譜). The dramatic increase in printed material available is due to the huge development of the press and publishing. There were at least 3,000 daily newspapers and tens of thousands of periodicals during this time.

The unprecedented growth of bureaucracy, together with the fact that the period is close to us in time, explains why there is also an enormous amount of archival material. From the early 1950s, a repository was set up specifically for archives produced during the republican period: the Nanjing Second Historical Archives (the First Historical Archives, located in Beijing, are dedicated to Imperial China). The Second Historical Archives mainly contain central government documents. Local archives throughout the country are stored in a network of provincial and municipal archives. It should be mentioned, however, that the archives of the Communist Party and those of the People's Liberation Army remain inaccessible. While the long-term trend was towards increasingly open access to archives, nothing can be taken for granted: while the Second Historical Archives have been largely open to them for the past two decades, for several years now researchers have seen the doors of this institution close on various pretexts. The situation in the Shanghai archives is very similar.

Qualitatively speaking, some sources, such as photography, film and radio, use techniques invented or perfected during the period. However, their use by historians remains too unsystematic as they raise tricky methodological issues. The corpus of sources produced under the Republic also includes the first statistics and surveys that can be considered scientific by today's standards. Major sociological surveys were initially carried out by foreigners (those coordinated by the agronomist John Buck during the late 1920s and early 1930s have remained justly famous), and also, increasingly, by the Chinese. The work of folklorists (in particular, Japanese) also deserves the full attention of researchers.

Historians of the republican period may also draw on oral history. However, the number of books in which oral history surveys represent, if not the main source, at least a significant contribution, is remarkably small for a period so close to us.[4] It must be emphasized in explanation of this surprising fact that the witnesses of the time went through terrible ordeals during the Maoist period after 1949, when your life or death could depend on personal and family history (woe betide the descendants of social categories vilified by the communist regime, such as landowners). The reluctance of witnesses to entrust researchers with their memories of the republican period is therefore more than understandable, as is their tendency to cautiously restrict themselves to verbatim transcripts of the communist discourse about the period.[5] These difficulties are somewhat eased for witnesses living abroad. Current and future historians can draw on transcripts of interviews conducted as part of major oral history surveys, such as the one led by Martin Wilbur at Columbia University in the 1960s and 1970s with former senior Guomindang officials in exile in the United States or Hong Kong.

In terms of sources, the famous 'historical and cultural materials' (*wenshi ziliao* 文史資料) are one of the great original sources for the republican period.[6] They are the result of a considerable effort by the communist government in the early 1960s to collect evidence from the pre-1949 period. The radical originality of the approach lay in excluding the heroes of the communist chronicle and instead giving a voice to those who were not part of it, or who were even opposed to it. Contributors included businessmen, journalists, low-level Guomindang officials, local government officials and warlords – in short, people who had responsibilities – some small, some greater – at the time. This unequalled editorial and historiographical enterprise has produced a huge collection of volumes published in China at different administrative levels (with an interruption due to the Cultural Revolution), which continues to grow each year.

Like the *wenshi ziliao*, the mass of sources available to historians continues to grow at a steady pace, and the discovery of new ones regularly leads to radical reassessments. For example, access to Soviet archives in the 1990s significantly transformed Chinese historiography. More recently, the availability to scholars of the enormous diary kept by Chiang Kai-shek throughout his adult life has helped to renew our understanding of his character and, more broadly, of the policies he pursued as the country's leader for over two decades. The next major turning point in research may come with the development of mega-data processing linked to the recent availability of huge documentary databases, or from archaeology, which is still in its very early stages.

The general approach in this book

In this overview, I have chosen to focus on historical China (known as 'China proper' to historians), which is also called the 18 Provinces (Anhui, Fujian, Gansu, Guangdong, Guangxi, Guizhou, Henan, Hubei, Hunan, Jiangsu, Jiangxi, Shaanxi, Shandong, Shanxi, Sichuan, Yunnan, Zhejiang, Zhili/Hebei). This is the area that has been dominated for a long time by the Han people and was incorporated in the empire's administrative structure. It does not include the vast areas which were all under the rule of the Qing dynasty prior to 1911, though in widely differing ways: Northern Mongolia, Southern Mongolia, Turkestan/Xinjiang, Manchuria, Tibet and Taiwan. These territories shared the characteristics of having a predominantly non-Han population and a lack of integration into the standard administrative network of the empire, reflected in the wide delegation of power to local elites. The affairs of these parts of the empire were in general handled by ad hoc administrative departments in Beijing. Chinese suzerainty was asserted in markedly different ways, such as through ties of allegiance to the emperor, the presence of one of his representatives or sometimes a modest garrison. The last decades of the Qing showed a desire to further integrate this periphery by imposing a link that could legitimately be called colonial.[7] Efforts were made to establish Chinese administrative and legal norms. Settlers from the Han population were encouraged, along with the promotion of Chinese culture and language.[8]

Despite its obvious military and political weaknesses, under the Republic the Chinese central government continued to pay close attention to these regions. Whether successive governments were based in Beijing, Nanjing or Chongqing, it is worth noting that they took care to claim a form of tutelage over these regions through the various channels at their disposal. Thus, Yuan Shikai managed to maintain the principle of Chinese suzerainty over Mongolia through an agreement that concluded long and arduous tripartite negotiations between China, Russia and Mongolia on 7 June 1915. To counter the Dalai Lama, who was pursuing a clearly pro-independence policy, the Beijing government, dominated at the time by the Zhili clique, tried to take advantage of the ninth Panchen Lama's flight to China in the winter of 1923–4. At the beginning of 1928, while the Guomindang were tearing themselves apart in internal struggles and the military reconquest of North China was still to take place, Chiang Kai-shek nevertheless took the trouble to set up a commission for Mongolian and Tibetan Affairs (*Meng Zang weiyuanhui* 蒙藏委員會) in the government he was organizing. Over a decade later, in February 1940, when his withdrawal to Chongqing following a series of military defeats by Japan made the situation equally critical, Chiang sent one of his relatives, Wu Zhongxin, to the enthronement ceremony of the new Dalai Lama, in an attempt to reassert the fact that Tibet was China's vassal.[9]

These efforts contrasted with the reality of the situation in these regions under the Republic. Not only were they completely emancipated from Chinese tutelage, but their ties with China were often less close than with other neighbouring powers. The most obvious examples are the cases of Taiwan, a Japanese colony from 1895, and Manchuria, which was a fully satellite state of Japan's from 1932. It should also be noted that today's region of Xinjiang[10] looked to Moscow, for example, as much – or more than – to Beijing or Nanjing under the Republic.[11]

It was neither the great diversity of the various components, nor the relative scarcity of research devoted to these fringe regions, that made me decide to leave them out of this volume, but an observation that is as simple as it is far-reaching: the linking of these peripheral regions to the Han bloc after 1949 was by no means inevitable (and, in fact, did not happen in the cases of Northern Mongolia and Taiwan). Clearly, it is questionable whether these regions belonged to what should be called 'China' under the Republic.

This is all the truer given that China in the years 1912–49 was culturally, economically and in terms of its people much more intimately connected to its overseas communities than, for example, to Tibet or Mongolia. I have therefore tried to capture the importance of the role of overseas Chinese communities during the republican period. Their profound influence in China must be emphasized: until 1924, for example, the driving forces of the Guomindang were located overseas. Equally, it has not been sufficiently emphasized that, conversely, the diaspora spread Chinese influence around the world, and particularly in the region where its numbers were greatest: South East Asia.

Like the other volumes in the *Histoire générale de la Chine* series, this book is organized in two parts. The first, divided into five chapters, offers an unfolding of the events over the period according to a classic periodization, to which we will return briefly below. This is followed by four chapters organized around broad themes: the economy, state building, society and intellectual life. With these nine chapters, the book will provide a convenient basis for university studies focused on the republican period. The first chapter is devoted to the political earthquake of the 1911 Revolution, which put an end to the bimillennial rhythm of successive dynasties. It concludes in 1916 with the death of Yuan Shikai, the dictator who had succeeded in turning the revolutionary shock wave to his own advantage. Yuan's project was essentially one of centralization: his death represented the culmination of a recentralizing initiative that straddled the turning point of 1911, since it was started under the Qing in 1901 with a wave of far-reaching reforms known as the New Policies (*xinzheng* 新). The year 1916 marked the transition to an era of disintegration of central power and the rise of local provincial strongmen, whose power resided in a military force connected to their person: the warlords (*junfa* 軍閥) whom I describe in Chapter 2. In the early 1920s, under the leadership of one of the most prestigious revolutionary leaders, Sun Yat-sen, amid a tumult of power struggles between the warlords, there emerged in Guangdong a new political force – the Guomindang. Supported by funds and military advisors from the Soviet Union, the Guomindang reorganized themselves along Bolshevik lines. It also included members of what was then little more than a group of intellectuals – the Chinese Communist Party. Taking full advantage of the disunity among the main *junfa* (warlords), and by allying themselves with some of them, the Guomindang managed to reunify the country in 1928. The third chapter is devoted to the Nanjing decade (1928–37), the linchpin of the republican period. During this time of comparative respite, the efforts of the Guomindang government in Nanjing to undermine the warlords and modernize the country were largely successful. Dealing with the increasing threat from Japan in the north of the country was a different kettle of fish. The fourth chapter deals with the major turning point represented by the long Sino-Japanese War (1937–45). Beyond the human and material cost, the war represented a completely new throw of the dice, largely benefitting the CCP, which was on the brink of collapse in 1937. The last chapter of this part, devoted to the civil war that began shortly after the Japanese surrender, shows that, despite the weakening of the Guomindang during the war against Japan, their defeat at the hands of the CCP was anything but a foregone conclusion. The latter's victory owed more to Chiang Kai-shek's strategic errors than to the supposed collapse of the Guomindang.

You only need to browse the history shelves of Chinese bookshops to see that no other period (by far) attracts such keen interest from the general public. What is true of popular works is equally true of scholarly literature: the period, both in China and in the West, has given rise to a superabundance of books and articles. Just thirty years ago, it was still possible to write a book on republican China without resorting to publications from China. Apart from factual data, Western scholars had little to gain from venturing into the vast continent of Chinese historical publications, frozen in the permafrost of Maoist orthodoxy. Equally, Western historiography remained unknown to Chinese historians, because of ideological conformity, and also language. The times have changed and there has been a slow but significant improvement in historical writing in mainland China for a good twenty years now. Consequently, some books, such as Wang Qisheng's history of the Guomindang, have become essential reading. One of the main obstacles in writing this volume was therefore the great quantity of publications devoted to the Republic. This explains my somewhat regretful decision to exclude Japanese documentation. Apart from the fact that Japanese historiography is not so indispensable for this period of Chinese history as it is for others, the pressing need to reduce the mass of scholarly literature from which the substance of this book is drawn to proportions that a single author could cope with was overriding.

It is a necessary but difficult exercise to balance the achievements of the most recent specialized research with the expectations of a fairly wide public, who you hope are interested in understanding modern China better, in the light of its recent history. The aim is to make your subject accessible by simplifying, without sacrificing too much of its complexity.

While many historians have successfully carried out this task, few have achieved as much as Georges Duby in his second book, *Rural Economy and Country Life in the Medieval West*. This masterpiece, which reads with equal pleasure more than half a century after its publication, was my model and has scarcely left my desk.

ONE

The 1911 Revolution

Let us recall that in the mid seventeenth century, China was conquered by invaders from the north, the Manchus, who founded the last dynasty – the Qing. Unlike their Ming predecessors (1368–1644), they were of non-Chinese ethnicity, but nonetheless the Qing adopted the traditional dynastic model in its entirety. They therefore considered themselves the custodians of the Mandate of Heaven (*tianming* 天命) that made the emperor the Son of Heaven. Although they hardly touched the administrative organization and – even less – imperial symbolism, the Qing emperors maintained for themselves and the Manchu people an identity distinct from the Han majority, and perpetuated the domination they had exercised since their conquest. The administrative and military organization of the Banners was crucial in this respect. A Banner division included not only soldiers, but also their families and servants. Although initially the Banners were not necessarily composed of Manchus (there were also Mongol Banners and Chinese who rallied early to the Manchus), there was a tendency to confuse the Banner population with Manchus. In the main Chinese cities (and, above all, in the capital, Beijing), the Banners settled in areas reserved for their exclusive use. Their members enjoyed several privileges – in particular, they received cash and food distributions. Also, the system known as diarchy gave equal rank in the political–administrative organization to the Manchus and the ethnic Han Chinese (who outnumbered them by almost a hundred to one). Despite the existence of the privileges and favours, the Han population accepted Manchu rule well during the eighteenth and first half of the nineteenth centuries. At the same time, the Manchu yoke was made lighter by the fact that the Banner populations underwent a noticeable assimilation, as evidenced by the marked decline of the Manchu language in favour of Chinese. The dynasty was severely weakened by several major revolts (Taiping and Nian) which marked the third quarter of the nineteenth century. A series of defeats and setbacks inflicted by the Western powers (the Opium Wars, wars against France, then Japan, and finally the Boxer Rebellion) seriously undermined its prestige and forced it to grant foreigners important privileges (extraterritoriality and territorial concessions, for example). In this context, at the end of the nineteenth century a revolutionary opposition emerged that was active in reviving anti-Manchu feeling. The founding of the United League (*tongmenghui* 同盟會) in Tokyo on 20 August 1905 by Sun Yat-sen, Liao Zhongkai and Wang Jingwei represented a significant step towards unifying the revolutionary movement. Although a loosely integrated organization, the United League developed a revolutionary ideology that promoted virulent anti-Manchu nationalism and advocated the establishment of a republican regime with socialist overtones. The United League organized various uprisings in the following years, particularly in Guangdong. All of them were, in fact, suppressed without much trouble. There was therefore no indication that the seemingly minor, largely improvised revolt in Wuhan on 10 October 1911 would signal the end of the Qing dynasty.

The flashpoint in Wuhan

Despite the development of the revolutionary movement from the 1890s onwards, the Manchu dynasty was not condemned to collapse under the weight of its own inadequacies and weaknesses. The idea of a sclerotic dynasty succumbing to its own inability to reform should be rejected. As is now well known, the Qing dynasty succumbed in 1911 because of a set of measures – the New Policies (*xinzheng* 新政) – so bold that it is no exaggeration to call them revolutionary.[1] Implemented in just a few years, starting in 1901, they included an overhaul of the law, the creation of new armed forces (*xinjun* 新軍) and the abolition of the imperial examination system. The institutional reforms were just as radical – planned to achieve a parliamentary monarchy in several stages, the first of which was the election of provincial assemblies (*ziyiju* 諮議局) by censal vote in 1909.[2] These rapid and far-reaching structural reforms undermined the traditional political, social and intellectual basis of imperial power. Worse still, some of the institutions that the dynasty created with the New Policies would turn against it and become, as we shall soon see, the spearhead of the revolution.

Regardless of their social or political impact, the New Policies placed a heavy burden on already fragile public finances. Military reforms, like educational reforms, were very costly. Forfeiting the taxes from opium, following the adoption of an ambitious plan in 1906 to eradicate the drug, did not help. All in all, during the first decade of the twentieth century, the Qing demanded a sizeable fiscal effort from the country, which did much to fuel discontent.[3] This was undoubtedly a necessary evil, but it might have been better spread out over time.

Finally, the last years of the empire were marked by an unwelcome attempt at recentralization, coupled with a strengthening of Manchu political control.

After the death of Empress Dowager Cixi in November 1908, the regent Zaifeng, a confused and mediocre character, exercised power in the name of his son, Puyi. Yuan Shikai, a senior Han official who had been Cixi's right-hand man and a major architect of the New Policies, was removed from power in January 1909. Yuan Shikai was opposed not only as a Han, but also for having concentrated too much power in his own hands. In particular, having established the major component of the new military forces, the Beiyang Army, he had very close ties to its principal leaders.

In Beijing in October 1910, the regent adopted an intransigent and uncooperative stance when faced with the hostile National Assembly meeting (another political stakeholder resulting from the New Policies), which sought to impose the principle of the ministry's responsibility before it. The formation of the first cabinet of ministers on 8 May 1911 was an important moment. It engendered deep disappointment in the ranks of the reformist elites, the vast majority of whom remained loyal to the Qing (they wished to maintain the dynasty while moving the regime towards a constitutional monarchy). These constitutionalists noted with bitterness that in the first cabinet Manchus and princes of the blood took the lion's share of seats, as in the choice of Yikuang as prime minister.[4] A wave of protests swept the country and gradually became endemic. But it was the central government's plans to nationalize the local railways that provoked the first open revolt in Sichuan province in September 1911. In addition to the drive for centralization, in this instance there was the need to set to rights a business that was in a poor state because of the haphazard management of the funds that had been raised. Unhappy with the method of compensation put forward by Beijing, the local elites organised a protest, presenting the nationalization project as the first step towards the concession of their railway to foreign powers. The disproportionate violence of the repression tipped the provinces towards a revolt, which was contained and then effectively suppressed by the Qing. It would be simplistic to see the Sichuan revolt as a mere false start to the 1911 Revolution: it was one of the factors that triggered it. By diverting troops, it forced the government to clear garrisons from certain cities, creating favourable circumstances for a second spark to ignite in Wuhan.[5] More specifically, the revolution began in Wuchang, capital of Hubei province, one of the three parts (along with Hankou and Hanyang) of the urban area that made up the city of Wuhan. The troops of the New Army (*xinjian lujun* 新建陸軍) had been worked on there for several years by the revolutionaries.[6] The accidental explosion of a bomb on 9 October revealed a plot in the making and forced the revolutionaries (mostly rank and file) to act without delay. Governor General Ruicheng panicked and fled on 10 October. Hankou and Hanyang fell to the revolutionaries over the following days. The city's progressive elites joined the uprising on 11 October. One of the top brass, Li Yuanhong, was (reluctantly) appointed military governor (*dudu* 都督), while the chairman of the provincial assembly, Tang Hualong, became the civilian governor.

From Beijing, the regent Zaifeng responded swiftly, sending troops who succeeded in regaining control of Hankou (27 October – 1 November). On the political front, pressed on all sides to make concessions, he sacrificed the Yikuang ministry (1 November) and promulgated a 'new charter with 19 fundamental articles' (*shijiu xintiao* 十九新條), which seriously dented the privileges of the Manchus in the sphere of government.[7] But in the meantime, the revolt spread to other provinces. The political vacuum in government was glaring in the face of this serious crisis. Yuan Shikai was subject to more and more appeals from the regent. But Yuan was aware that he was indispensable and worked hard to leverage his price for returning to the political scene. The strategy paid off: he was made supreme commander of the army, then prime minister (7 November). Over the following weeks, it became clear that his manoeuvres were aimed less at saving the dynasty than at consolidating his personal position. He placed his men in all the key posts and finally obtained the resignation of the regent, Zaifeng (6 December). He also took action militarily, though in moderation. Indeed, an immediate crushing of the revolt would not have suited him. After the initial success of the recapture of Hankou, he ordered the troops under his command

1 Li Yuanhong in 1911.

to stand down. During the period in which the dynasty's power was wavering, Yuan's strategy was to place himself in the advantageous role of arbitrator, which explains why he took the initiative of opening negotiations with the revolutionaries at that time.[8]

The last dynasty's unorthodox downfall

The empire was a political construction that was all the more robust because it had the unique feature of incorporating a principle that ensured its own continuation. According to an idea developed as early as the Zhou dynasty (eleventh to third centuries BCE), the Mandate of Heaven could be withdrawn from a dynasty that deviated from the principles of good governance, and the fallen dynasty made to give way to a new one. The empire remained in existence. The loss of the celestial mandate was said to manifest itself in climatic anomalies and natural disasters. Without denying that certain dynasties may have undergone a process of institutional disintegration, these climatic and natural hazards were an integral part of the process leading to dynastic change. Floods and droughts caused famines, which led to revolts and a budgetary crisis for the state resulting from a drop in tax revenue and an increase in spending on relief for famine victims. A typical dynastic succession scenario would take several years, or even decades. Widespread and deadly uprisings, driven by starving peasants, swept the country. It was not uncommon for China's neighbouring powers to use the opportunity to join the fray as well. The incumbent dynasty would struggle to cope as its own military forces were weakened by the shortage of tax revenue. Victory would raise the leader of the revolt to the imperial throne, where he then founded a new dynasty.

Does the fall of the Qing follow this pattern? Not at all – 1911 was not marked by climatic disasters triggering famines that led to revolts. There was no climatic ill fortune at the end of the Qing (certainly nothing like the succession of terrible years that go a long way to explaining the fall of the Ming). Nor was there any encroachment from neighbouring powers either. As for the course of events, it was extremely rapid, as barely four months elapsed between the first shot fired at Wuchang and the emperor's abdication. It was also an urban movement, in which the rural population took no part. Another feature distinguishing the 1911

Revolution from earlier revolts was that there were virtually no pitched battles (except for the recapture of Hankou). This was reflected in the low cost to human life. The main military operations took place during the first weeks of the revolution in Wuhan (in particular, the slaughter by imperial troops during the recapture of Hankou in the last days of October). During this period, there were several thousand deaths (5,000 in the ranks of the revolutionary troops in October).[9] It should not be forgotten, either, that the Manchu Banner populations of certain cities in the country (Fuzhou, Zhenjiang, Xi'an, Nanjing) were purely and simply massacred.[10] But, in total, the losses were at most in the tens of thousands. This is certainly not a negligible number, but in the light of Chinese history, and, clearly, unlike all other episodes of dynastic transition, the revolution was not a bloodbath.

To use a medical metaphor, instead of being (as was usual) a slow-developing infection spreading to the heart of the empire, the 1911 Revolution was more like a virulent cancer whose metastases spread in a few days by means of the telegraph.

Indeed, the events of 1911 vindicate the Qing, in retrospect, for their reluctance to use the telegraph in the period 1860–80, which, as Zhou Yongming has shown, was not based on geomantic or religious considerations but on well-founded fears around the political role that this communications tool might play.[11] The 1911 Revolution was clearly stirred up by the telegraph. In the months immediately prior to the revolution, the provincial assemblies had swiftly developed the habit of using it to coordinate their action and provide mutual support, by regularly threatening to dissolve themselves. The rapid spread of news that it allowed (the press being responsible for further promulgation) explains how different provinces could almost simultaneously declare themselves in favour of the revolt and proclaim their independence (see Map 3).

The first two provinces to declare independence after Hubei were Hunan and Shaanxi (22 October), soon followed by Shanxi (29 October), Jiangxi and Yunnan (31 October).[12] Declarations of secession then followed during November. The provinces remaining under the control of the dynasty at the end of 1911 were those closest to the capital – Zhili, Henan, Shandong and the three provinces of Manchuria, plus Qinghai and Gansu.

There was a semblance of a political alternative facing the empire in 1911, even if it was rather poorly organized – the United League. The latter had two strengths: its establishment among the overseas Chinese communities, which brought it men and capital; and the prestige of its leader Sun Yat-sen, a veteran of revolutionary struggles. Born in the Guangzhou area in 1866, educated in Hawaii and Hong Kong, where he obtained a medical degree in 1892, he began travelling the world in the mid-1890s to propagate his revolutionary and anti-Manchu ideas among the overseas Chinese communities. At the time, the headquarters of the revolutionaries were in Tokyo, where the United League was founded (August 1905), and the unsuccessful uprisings in south China were organized from. However, the United League, entirely unconnected to the Wuhan uprising, did not in any way plan the revolution. If anything, the fact that Sun was in Denver at the time is proof of that.

One of the fundamental characteristics of the revolution was its multi-faceted nature, which makes it difficult to describe as a whole. As we have just seen, the revolutionary movement spread and matured simultaneously in the different provinces. There was thus a series of revolutionary centres that were relatively independent of each other and followed different dynamics. Despite the variety of local situations, certain constants could be observed in the way the revolutionaries organized themselves to seize power. Even if the peasant masses could occasionally serve as an auxiliary force for the revolutionaries, the revolution was above all an urban phenomenon. In an ironic twist of history, during the process it had initiated that was supposed to lead to a parliamentary monarchy, the dynasty created three of the institutions that would trigger its own downfall. Firstly, the provincial assemblies, although elected by less than 1 per cent of the population, were endowed with a certain legitimacy from their tax-based voting system (censal). The men who had emerged in their midst would soon be, if not the leaders of the revolt, at least those to whom, very soon and almost everywhere, the revolutionaries naturally turned. Next, the chambers of commerce (*shanghui* 商會), more than 900 of which were established across the country between 1904 and 1912, had existed somewhat longer and they also played an important role. They were generally well organized and, moreover, each one's influence was multiplied by a network of local branches. Endowed with substantial financial resources, they were often the first to give loans to the new authorities in the days following the latter's installation. To cope with the disintegration of the existing administration, it was not uncommon for them to take over running matters. The last – but not least – important stakeholders in the revolutionary process were the new military forces (*xinjun*), organized on the European model from 1895 onwards, and then much more systematically after 1901.[13] Almost everywhere, these troops spearheaded the revolution, with many of their officers becoming leaders.

A more ancient protagonist in the fall of many dynasties was added to this trio – the secret societies.[14] Since the end of the nineteenth century, they had been associated with the revolutionary forces and they maintained this position, often acting as the armed wing of the revolt against the Qing authorities. The situation in Shaanxi reflects this connection. A formal alliance was concluded in July 1910 between three partners – the revolutionaries of the local branch of the United League, the New Army, and the leaders of the region's major secret society – the Elder Brothers' Society (*Gelaohui* 哥老會).

The multifaceted nature of the revolution accentuated the division between the revolutionary forces, which were far from an orderly phalanx. Their motley composition stemmed from, amongst other things, ideological differences (which predated the revolution). Due to the diversity of the revolutionary centres, which manifested themselves and developed quite independently, local leaders of the revolution emerged in the role of political leaders and came to nurse national ambitions. In simple terms, the initial focus in the Hubei/Hunan region gave them a particular importance as they were at the origin of the revolutionary process. Although the revolution took its first steps almost completely independently of the United League, the latter nevertheless succeeded – thanks especially to the energetic Huang Xing – in setting up a revolutionary centre in opposition, based in the Lower Yangtze River valley. The province of Guangdong was also taken over by Hu Hanmin, a Sun Yat-sen loyalist, in the first weeks of the revolution.

In these conditions, it is not surprising that the revolutionaries experienced difficulties in building a unified organization, a necessary condition for conducting negotiations from a position of strength. Li Yuanhong took the initiative by asserting, on 7 November, the need to organize a government. The revolutionaries of the Lower Yangtze River valley proposed forming one by gathering together in Shanghai delegates from all the provinces. Li Yuanhong was against this and managed to get the Assembly held in Wuhan. On 2 December, at a meeting in the British concession of Hankou, the delegates decided to elect a provisional president by a two-thirds majority of provincial representatives. But the counter-attack by Yuan Shikai's troops in Wuhan changed the situation and forced them to move to Nanjing to set up the Assembly and their government. In the first weeks of December, two candidates for the position of president emerged clearly: Li Yuanhong and Huang Xing. However, it was Sun Yat-sen, just returned to China, who was elected (by a very large majority) president of the Provisional Government on 29 December, and who proclaimed the Republic in Nanjing on 1 January 1912.[15]

Sun Yat-sen was not (as Chinese historiography would have it) elected for his prestige and his position as the undisputed leader of the revolutionary movement. He was elected by default, primarily to preserve the unity of the revolutionary camp. The priority was to close ranks for negotiations with the Qing. None of the protagonists harboured any doubts: in the long run, the post of president could only be held by Yuan Shikai, if he were to come out in favour of the Republic.

The dynasty was desperate and tried to take advantage of the fact that the revolutionaries did not offer a united front. It must be emphasized that there was no deposition of the emperor, but an abdication, and this abdication was the result of negotiations in which the dynasty obtained several concessions from the revolutionaries. The area and the troops it still controlled were far from negligible. The case of Shandong province, which declared its independence on 13 November before rallying once more behind the dynasty on 30 November, showed that the revolutionary impulse was not necessarily irreversible.

The dynasty agreed to the abdication following tense negotiations (after a long argument about which word to use for the act of abdication, *ciwei* 辭位, which has a nuance of voluntary acceptance, was chosen). Why did the Manchu government, which still held some strong cards, give in? There are several factors to consider. There had been a distinct lack of leadership since 1908. The great servants of the dynasty with the stature of statesmen, such as Li Hongzhang, Zhang Zhidong and Liu Kunyi, all died in the first decade of the twentieth century. There was indeed a person with sufficient influence and stature to command the obedience of the country's main military forces as well as the upper echelons of the administration, and who, by rallying the constitution-alists, could save the dynasty. But – sadly, for the latter – it was Yuan Shikai. Instead of saving the dynasty, he would be its gravedigger. Moral considerations may have played a part on the Qing side: retaking control of the country would have entailed enormous military operations, at considerable human cost. But it is important to note that the agreement reached with the revolutionaries had plenty of substance. The emperor remained with his court in the Forbidden City and retained his title. Reformers and revolutionaries at the time had their eyes on Japan, where the preservation of an emperor had accompanied the success the country had enjoyed since the Meiji period. Subsidies for the Banner population would continue. This agreement was honoured, despite the considerable financial burden it entailed, probably because the very presence of the emperor in Beijing continued to empower the faction that controlled the capital.

1912, the year of many possibilities

Once the abdication was announced on 12 February, Sun Yat-sen immediately offered his resignation in favour of Yuan Shikai, who had declared his support for the Republic. The transition proved to be long and somewhat confusing, although the decision was ratified by the Assembly on 15 February.[16] Yuan was sworn in on 10 March, but Sun remained in office until 1 April. During this period, the predominant issue was whether to move the capital to Nanjing. This was the option chosen by Sun Yat-sen and his entourage, who argued that Nanjing was the capital of the Ming (the last ethnic Han dynasty) until 1420. Beijing might indeed embody some continuity with Manchu rule. However, tactical considerations were primarily responsible for their preference for Nanjing. It was a matter of weakening Yuan (whose military base in the north was feared by everyone). But, once again, the revolutionary factions were not unanimous. The view that Beijing alone could be considered the true capital had many supporters.[17] Also, it is too simplistic to juxtapose a North China that would side with Yuan Shikai against a South China that would support the revolutionaries and Sun Yat-sen. The former constitutionalists of the late Qing era from the Shanghai region, such as Zhang Jian (president of the Jiangsu provincial assembly), Zhao Fengchang and Huang Yanpei, rallied to Yuan Shikai and to the choice of Beijing. Yuan prevailed through skilful manoeuvring, going so far as to stage a rebellion among Beijing's troops to justify the indispensability of his presence in the north. The political revolutionary staff and the Nanjing Assembly packed their bags and arrived in Beijing in April.

Parallel to debates over the capital, the foundations of a republican order were laid down by the provisional constitution, which was adopted in March 1912 by a (similarly provisional) parliament composed of representatives of the various provincial governments. It was substantially inspired by that of the French Third Republic. The prospect of the powerful Yuan Shikai becoming president of the Republic encouraged members of parliament to reduce as much as possible the powers associated with this office, in favour of their own legislative power. In the months that followed, Yuan gave every impression of playing along with the parliamentary republic. The first administration (1 April – 17 June 1912) led by Tang Shaoyi, a relative of Yuan, was duly approved by the provisional parliament in Nanjing and was pluralistic. It included leading figures from the ranks of the revolutionaries, such as Cai Yuanpei (Education) and Song Jiaoren (Agriculture). Over the following months, although Yuan found it difficult to accept real autonomy for the parliament, on which he exerted a lot of pressure, he never went so far as to break with it. The revolutionaries' pact with Yuan was reinforced by the friendly visits to Beijing of the two main figures from the United League, Sun Yat-sen and Huang Xing, in the summer of 1912. The apparent naivety of the revolutionary leaders might seem surprising. But it is important not to ignore Yuan's skilful approach, in which he made pledges of adherence to the Republic's principles. Nor should everyone's preoccupation with maintaining unity in a climate dominated by fear of foreign intervention be underestimated. In view of all this, it is quite logical that the revolutionaries chose to bet on the next elections, in which everyone was preparing to do battle.

The United League reshaped itself into a political party called the Guomindang in a bid to win the elections (August 1912). It was not Sun Yat-sen who orchestrated this transformation. Indeed, he devoted most of 1912 to making himself, like Gambetta in France in the 1870s, the travelling representative of the Republic (and of the Guomindang) throughout the country. Song Jiaoren, a 30-year-old rising star, established himself as the party leader during this period. His strategy was to bring other political parties on board. With great skill, Song Jiaoren eliminated the most radical aspects of the United League's revolutionary programme. In this way, he managed to integrate Wu Jinglian's Unity Party (who were reluctant to accept talk of social change) and the Citizens' Party led by Cen Chunxuan (who felt the same about gender equality). As a result, the Guomindang programme became much more moderate.[18] Similarly, despite his personal convictions, Song Jiaoren agreed to inject a certain amount of federalism, which was bound to appeal to the local elites.

Centralized power began to fragment during this period. Taxes were no longer received centrally, and the appointment of local officials was also decentralized. However, while this dynamic diminished Beijing's power, it benefitted the provincial administrations, avoiding further political fragmentation.

The year 1912 was a year of many possibilities, but it was also a year of many administrative experiments by provincial elites, which historians have viewed in various lights. Xiaohong Xiao-Planes sees the period November 1911 – September 1913 as a short golden age of fiscal and administrative efficiency for Jiangsu province.[19] Under the leadership of its military governor, Tan Yankai, Hunan made a considerable effort to promote primary education and showed a strong drive towards industrialization. In Chengdu, on the other hand, the impressive advances made during the New Policies period were visibly dwindling. The degree of development of the proto-bourgeois stratum (known to be more advanced in the large coastal cities) seems to be the variable that determined these differences.

Intellectual animation was widespread; newspapers and magazines proliferated, in the absence of censorship (the Constitution of March 1912 guaranteed freedom of expression). In Beijing, no less than fifty daily newspapers were launched. Associations were also multiplying across the country. Although they had very different aims, they were all driven by the same nationalistic impulse. In Shanghai, there were more than thirty political parties and groups, including a Chinese Socialist

Party, as well as numerous feminist leagues.[20] The leading intellectuals of the time engaged in intense political debates, particularly on the form the state should take. But the commitment of intellectuals went much further. Thus, Zhang Binglin, a highly skilled linguist, founded his own party. As for the greatest of them, the exceptional writer Liang Qichao, in April 1913, he founded a large conservative party, bringing together the former constitutionalists. It was called the Progress Party (*Jinbudang* 進步黨), with which he aimed to break the Guomindang's dominance in the Assembly.

In the winter of 1912–13, elections were held (the most democratic to that date in China). Even if the suffrage was still based on tax, the conditions of enfranchisement were considerably relaxed. The 1.6 million voters in the 1909 provincial assembly elections increased to around 40 million, or about a quarter of adult men. This was considerable progress. The percentage of the population registered to vote was much higher, for example, than in Japan at that period.

The years under Yuan Shikai (1913–1916)

The elections in the winter of 1912–13 were a triumph for the Guomindang, which obtained a majority in both houses. Song Jiaoren set his sights on running for prime minister as the winner of the elections and according to the logic of a parliamentary regime. His assassination on 20 March 1913 brought the process of establishing a Western-style democracy to an abrupt close. Was Yuan behind the murder? He denied it, but in the eyes of the vast majority of his contemporaries, he was the prime suspect. Nowadays, opinions are more divided amongst historians. Whatever the case, the following weeks showed that Yuan was utterly opposed to accepting any limitation to his power. On 27 April 1913, he took out a massive loan from foreign powers, without bothering to obtain the approval of parliament, as the Constitution required. This aroused indignation amongst Yuan's opponents, not only because the latter monopolized the funds obtained and strengthened himself, but also because the terms of the loan included placing the Salt Tax Administration under foreign guardianship as a guarantee. In April, the first sessions of the newly elected parliament had shown that it was not prepared to openly oppose Yuan. The latter increased his adroit manoeuvres, intended to weaken and divide the Guomindang in parliament, including a generous use of corruption. Sun Yat-sen pushed for an uprising of the revolutionary forces but the other Guomindang leaders were reluctant, aware of their military inferiority. Nor was the country ready to follow. Indeed, the merchant elites, who had been one of the driving forces behind the 1911 Revolution, made no secret of their hostility. Desperate for some stability, they would not consider running the risk of a new civil war. A further consideration came into play, that of putting national unity first. Supporters of a political solution were in the majority (including amongst the Guomindang).

It was not until July 1913 that the so-called Second Revolution began, when Yuan dismissed the governors of the Guomindang-held provinces (Guangdong, Anhui and Jiangxi). Jiangxi declared its independence (12 July) on the initiative of its governor, Li Liejun. Guangdong and Anhui followed suit, soon joined by other southern provinces (Hunan, Fujian, Sichuan).[21] But Yuan's military superiority soon carried the day. The clashes between the southerners and Yuan Shikai's troops, where they took place (especially in Jiangxi and the Nanjing area), turned to the advantage of Yuan. By the beginning of September, the die was cast. With the subjugation of the provinces that had escaped his control, Yuan's power was strengthened by the Second Revolution, whose leaders, headed by Sun Yat-sen, went into exile.

In the first months of 1914, Yuan eliminated, one by one, the last obstacles to his power: parliament was dismissed in January, and the local assemblies were dissolved the following month. A new constitutional pact (*xinyuefa* 新約法) replaced the provisional constitution of March 1912 and provided a lifetime presidency for Yuan (1 May).

The opposition was considerably weakened. The main leaders of the Second Revolution regrouped in Tokyo around Sun and were far from inactive. But the establishment of the Chinese Revolutionary Party (*Zhonghua gemingdang* 中華革命黨) on 8 July 1914 did not pose much of a threat. Sun, stung by his experience of the 'first-wave' Guomindang as a parliamentary party whose control had escaped him, intended to base this new organization on his person alone, imposing an oath of personal allegiance on each member. Even some of his oldest lieutenants, like Hu Hanmin or Liao Zhongkai, were displeased by this move and were slow to join the new party. Others, who were among the great revolutionary figures (Huang Xing, Wang Jingwei, Li Liejun, Chen Jiongming) refused to do so.[22] The Chinese Revolutionary Party therefore took on the appearance of a minor grouping, inconsistent, and with a poor following. In the months that followed, the activity that he instigated (a 'disorganised terrorism' according to M.-C. Bergère) did not help to make him the hub of a credible opposition to Yuan. Even worse, Sun's heavy use of Japanese subsidies helped to destroy his credibility by giving the impression that he was working for Japan. Furthermore, amnesty measures introduced in May 1914 for the exiles of the Second Revolution met with some success (though the main leaders were not initially included, the amnesty was subsequently extended to them). Returnees from Tokyo increased in number.[23]

Thanks to his extended powers in the new constitutional pact, Yuan now had the power to dismiss the highest-ranking civilian and military officials in the different provinces, reflecting the effective ascendancy of the central government. He thus succeeded in placing loyalists at the head of almost all the provinces. In the summer of 1914, for example, he replaced the governor of Shanxi, a liberal, with the head of his own secret police, Lu Jianzhang (nicknamed 'the Butcher' for having had many revolutionaries executed). Even famous participants in the 1911 Revolution who had not joined the Second Revolution had to give up their positions – such as the military governor of Hubei, Li Yuanhong.[24]

The political individuals who rallied to Yuan included prominent intellectual figures, many of whom were leaders of the 1911 Revolution. The famous cabinet of talents (personified by Zhang Jian and Liang Qichao) is a particularly striking testimony to this. Taxes started flowing into Beijing from the provinces again. The government also managed to take out its first domestic loans in 1914 and 1915. The plan to abolish the administrative level of provinces, even if it was not implemented, testifies to a concern for a profound reorganization of the country's administration. A mistrust of entities large and rich enough to embark on the path of autonomy, or even independence, was part of this concern. The administrative structure inherited from the revolution reflected the crucial role played by the army. It was notably characterized by the pre-eminence of provincial military governors (*dudu* 都督), whose powers extended, to a greater or lesser extent, beyond that

2 Yuan Shikai in 1912.

of the army. The restructuring aimed to give less importance to military power. In the provinces where it had not previously existed, the post of civilian governor was created to counterbalance the military governor, whose powers were being reduced. The intellectual effervescence and freedom of speech which the Revolution of 1911 had allowed, and which had continued until the Second Revolution, suddenly receded in the face of a policy which was, on this level at least, indisputably reactionary.

We have seen how cleverly Yuan Shikai was able to subvert the revolution for his own benefit. Having done so, he would confirm his ability as a statesman. His efforts to reform the central government's tax administration reflected both his modernizing aims and his need to equivocate and adapt to circumstances. Initially, from 1912 to 1914, Yuan's aim was to continue the Manchu government's efforts to bring the organization of central government finances into line with the Western model. This involved the organization of a general budget managed by a Ministry of Finance centralizing all tax revenues. As this proved too ambitious, he redirected his efforts, from 1915 onwards, towards a more traditional reorganization of land tax, based mainly on simplifying the conditions for its collection and updating the land register.[25] In any case, behind his efforts lay a desire to regain control of tax sources that had been appropriated by local authorities. But Yuan had a much broader vision: in the economic sphere, for example, he brought about a coherent reform of the banking system, including the establishment of a central bank by Zhang Jian, an accomplished scholar with the highest degree of imperial qualifications who had developed a powerful textile business. Zhang was placed at the head of a large Ministry of Agriculture, Forestry, Industry and Commerce.

Yuan's unscrupulousness and all-consuming ambition have been emphasized again and again. His capacity for work, as well as his exceptional wholehearted efforts, deserve to be highlighted more. But, above all, the charisma he exuded has been overlooked. Testimonies express admiration, from figures differing as widely as Wellington Koo, a brilliant Westernized, cosmopolitan diplomat, and Yan Xishan, the strongman of Shanxi, a thick-skinned military man of modest birth. Nevertheless, this asset of charisma could be turned against him if his personal reputation were seriously damaged.

The international context and the influence of the war in Europe

The danger for Yuan was to come from the field of foreign relations. It is an understatement to say that the 1914–18 war had a strong effect on China. Of course, the latter did not align itself with the Franco-British allies until late in the day, on 14 August 1917 (see next chapter). But the war had significant consequences that would be felt throughout the republican period. In the first place, competition from European industries disappeared as they ran at full capacity to feed the war effort. It was therefore a favourable period for Chinese industrialists (see Chapter 6). In the longer term, the war weakened the European powers demographically and economically. It also created a strong pacifist mood amongst the European public: there was greater aversion to spilling their soldiers' blood, which considerably reduced their governments' latitude for resorting to the gunboat diplomacy of the past in China.[26] Finally, due to the ostracizing of Germany and then Soviet Russia, the foreign powers ceased to present a united front against China, which had been a key to European dominance.

However, geopolitics, like nature, abhors a vacuum. By mobilizing the main European powers, the Great War ensured the rapid ascendance in East Asia of two rising stars – the United States and Japan. The United States' primary concern was to make the most of emerging trade opportunities.

Japan, for its part, soon discerned in the European war – so conveniently prolonged – an unexpected opportunity to advance its pawns into China. In the name of its alliance with Britain, it began by seizing German possessions in Shandong, without much difficulty (the garrison of Qingdao capitulated on 7 November 1914). China was presented with a fait accompli. Japan would not stop there. On 18 January 1915, the Japanese government sent Yuan Shikai a list of Twenty-One Demands. Clearly, their acceptance would make China nothing more or less than a Japanese protectorate. In the months that followed, Yuan tried to play for time while his diplomats worked hard making repeated, though discrete, appeals to the Western powers. The latter were reluctant to allow the Japanese to establish their hegemony over the Far East. Japan was therefore forced to pull back somewhat, but the demands they made on 7 May 1915 remained exorbitant and were accompanied by an ultimatum. Yuan had his back to the wall. Public opinion was strongly inflamed against Japan and ready to rally to him. But Yuan was too clear-sighted not to conclude that he was militarily inferior and diplomatically isolated. On 9 May, he decided to accept Japan's humiliating terms. The Twenty-One Demands crisis had a far-reaching effect. Firstly, this humiliating climbdown undoubtedly undermined Yuan's personal prestige. But, beyond that, the Demands delegitimized his efforts at centralization because they made it clear his efforts had no impact on China's strength on the international stage.

The fall of Yuan Shikai

The humiliation of the Twenty-One Demands would obviously have required some time to digest. A few months later, however, Yuan embarked on a very dangerous initiative. Having let some of his close circle prepare the ground since August, on 12 December 1915 he announced his intention to re-establish the empire (in the form of a constitutional monarchy). The rebellion against Yuan's monarchist ambitions was not long in coming. It took the now classic form of a provincial declaration of independence: that of Yunnan in late 1915. A prominent figure in the 1911 Revolution in Yunnan, Cai E led the units of the New Army in Yunnan and, together with the province's military governor, Tang Jiyao, called on all the other provinces to rise up. Soon backed by forces from neighbouring Guizhou province, a National Protection Army (*huguo jun* 護國軍) launched an assault on Sichuan, which was held by Yuan Shikai loyalists. There, the former did battle with the forces loyal to Yuan. In the meantime, Liang Qichao increased his published incitements to revolt against Yuan. Other important provinces, such as Zhejiang, joined the rebellion. The Yuan camp, however, was breaking apart. Many of Yuan's most loyal lieutenants made little secret of their hostility to his imperial ambitions and turned their backs on him. Following the well-established practice of diplomatic illness, Duan Qirui, Xu Shichang and Feng Guozhang withdrew from the political scene, citing sudden health problems.[27]

The rather sad gesture of definitively abandoning the return to an empire on 22 March 1916 facilitated a ceasefire in Sichuan. However, it had become clear that the rejection was as much one of Yuan himself as about his project to strengthen central power. The sudden (but natural) death of Yuan Shikai on 6 June 1916 removed from the chessboard a figure who was central, but whose considerably diminished political power augured ill for the future. The political division that already existed in the south and west of the country now extended to the north. The era of the warlords now began.

How did Yuan come to make such a disastrous decision? How can we explain this move when he was already exercising almost absolute power as president? We should not rule out the hypothesis that the certainty or presentiment of his imminent death prompted him to give a hereditary turn to his personal power. This must be interpreted less as the product of personal megalomania than as a political move (inspired by his advisor Frank Goodnow), intended to thus enable him to further push the recentralization project, embarked on in 1913, or perhaps even at the end of the nineteenth century.

His reading of the 1911 Revolution and the Second Revolution of 1913 is probably also to blame. For the former, he seems to have overestimated the anti-Manchu resentment – which was only one of the components of the revolution – and thus underestimated the rejection of the imperial institution itself among the country's elites. In the second instance, he did not see that the rallying of the constitutionalists to his personal power was circumstantial. They had not truly embraced abandoning the principle of ministerial responsibility before parliament. In any case, we have perhaps focused too much on the failure of the attempt to re-establish the empire (admittedly fraught with consequences) without dwelling enough on the forms it took. Some aspects of the strategy employed may, of course, raise a smile. These included, for example, the 'spontaneous' organization of petitioning groups among categories of the population, such as rickshaw pullers or beggars, for whom it is doubtful whether the restoration of the empire to Yuan was ever a matter of intense concern. If these manoeuvres are pretty transparent, they nevertheless reflect a deeper plot: the plan to stage the reintroduction of the empire by popular will, with Yuan on the throne. On the other hand, the date chosen, 1 January, echoes Sun Yat-sen's proclamation of the Republic four years earlier. It is in any case a declaration of modernity, just as the chosen reign name, *Hongxian* 洪憲 'Great Constitution', is in itself a political programme with direct reference to constitutional monarchy. Clearly, the imperial restoration did not take the form of a return to the model of the empire based on the Mandate of Heaven, thus testifying somewhat paradoxically to the irreversible character of the political turn taken in 1911.

In any case, Yuan's misfortune underlines the extent to which the 1911 Revolution constituted a profound rupture, putting an end to the imperial model that had been perpetuated for over 2,000 years. It introduced not only new institutional structures, but also a crucial change in basic assumptions. The theory of heavenly mandate was replaced by a legitimacy based on the consent of the people.

In the short term, the revolution did not metamorphose into what was the ultimate goal of all the actors, well beyond the rejection of the Manchus and regime change: the strengthening of China's power. An analogy might be drawn with the French Revolution. As Tocqueville noted, over and above the seemingly unfathomable rupture of the Revolution, a work of centralization was made good. In the case of the 1911 Revolution, no one personifies this centralizing dynamic better than Yuan Shikai. In the following decade, although Beijing's power would be challenged by powerful centrifugal forces, the political project of a strong, centralized state, apart from a few years of interest in federalism, would continue to be a matter of consensus. The tendency towards recentralization re-emerged during the Nanjing decade, and developed with even greater force after 1949.

TWO

Cliques and Warlords (1916–1928)

In contrast to the Nanjing decade which followed it, the period
1916–28 is unanimously regarded as lost years for China. The verdict
in communist and nationalist historiographies is particularly harsh.
They see it as a period of anarchy from which only the May Fourth
Movement (1919) and the period of the first United Front, between the
CCP and the Guomindang (1923–7), stand out. Although exceptionally
fertile intellectually, since it witnessed a real cultural renaissance,
discussed in Chapter 9, this decade was essentially characterized by the
powerful disintegration of central power and by the warlords' stran-
glehold on the country. Beginning with the death of Yuan Shikai and
ending with the Northern Expedition, it is often referred to as the era
of the warlords.

The narrative of this period generally focuses on the rise of the
Guomindang, which reorganized along Bolshevik lines and equipped
themselves with their own military apparatus, against a background of
rising nationalism. This traditional version is not without its virtues: in
particular, it has the advantage of providing a reading grid for a period
characterized by the extreme complexity of its events. Its weakness is its
teleological approach: the Guomindang, until the mid-1920s, were not
very significant. At best, and uncertainly, it presided over a very small
base, since it was limited to the central part of the single province of
Guangdong. Its takeover of the whole province came very late indeed,
only effective after Hainan Island's capture in January 1926. The
trajectory of the Guomindang should not be overemphasized and an
effort should be made to focus the narrative of this period on the most
important phenomenon: the general dominance of the warlords. They
should not be written off as a mere accident of history. They are worth
studying and had their own way of doing politics, even if this meant a
multitude of conflicts, alliances and changes of alliances of dismaying
complexity. Only after drawing up a sufficiently precise picture of the

32

warlords' control of the country is it possible to grasp the radical nature of the renewed political offer made by the reorganized Guomindang from 1924 onwards. This will then allow us to understand how, against all expectations and all military logic, they managed to defeat the major warlords of northern and central China during the Northern Expedition of 1926–8.

The rivalry amongst North China's major cliques for control of the government

To understand the political life of the period that began with the death of Yuan Shikai, a clear distinction must be made between the phenomenon of cliques (*xi* 系) and that of warlords proper (*junfa* 軍閥). In northern China, three main cliques aspired to a role in central government and sought, when it was still sitting, influence in parliament. Control of Beijing was essential in this struggle between them. The government in Beijing, together with the parliament, embodied republican legitimacy; as such, it represented China on the international stage. Accordingly, the government in Beijing had privileged access to loans from foreign banks. In addition, dating from agreements concluded in 1912–13, the Maritime Customs and the Salt Tax Administration, two important fiscal bodies whose revenues were put towards the repayment of China's debt to foreign powers, transferred their surpluses to the government in Beijing.[1] Thus, Beijing was not only symbolically, but also financially, important.

When Yuan Shikai died, Duan Qirui and Feng Guozhang (members of Yuan's inner circle) took over the leadership of the two emerging camps, the Anhui and Zhili cliques, respectively. The names of these two cliques are not derived from their geographical base, but from their leader's province of origin. They competed for control of the Beijing government and the direction of its overall policy. After Feng Guozhang's death in 1919, the Zhili clique was led by Wu Peifu and Cao Kun. A third clique, emerging slightly later, also arose. Taking advantage of the Anhui/Zhili rivalry during the late 1910s, Zhang Zuolin consolidated his power in Manchuria: he led the so-called Fengtian clique (named after the most important of the three north-eastern provinces that made up his base).[2]

The cliques included a civilian element, with men who did not aspire to military command but to positions of power and enrichment.

33

Ministers switched with each reworking of alliances and power relations between the three cliques. In a letter to his wife in 1917, Victor Segalen, who witnessed these confused episodes in Beijing, spoke of 'whirling ministers'.

Cliques should not be viewed as perfectly structured groups. A clique was a little more than a mere alliance. They comprised a fragile architecture of networks of personal loyalties, possessing nevertheless a certain coherence. The analogy with clans, kin or lineages[3] (which the Chinese term *xi* suggests) is particularly relevant. A clique was organized around a relatively stable core of direct heirs of the clique's 'ancestor' (in these cases, Duan Qirui and Feng Guozhang), on to which elements more or less directly associated with this core were grafted. Finally, free agents joined as well. Thus, the Zhili clique in the first half of the 1920s was built around the duo Wu Peifu and Cao Kun, with their subordinates, while the support of elements such as Feng Yuxiang remained much more precarious.[4]

When Yuan Shikai died, and in accordance with his deathbed provisions, Li Yuanhong became the new president on 7 June. Li recalled the parliament that Yuan had dissolved in 1913 and reinstated the 1912 Constitution. Rather characterless and easily swayed by events, Li Yuanhong did not have sufficient political standing. He was not a Beiyang Army insider, unlike the two powerful figures who were emerging: Duan Qirui and Feng Guozhang. This pair had remained as leaders of the Beiyang Army after Yuan's forced withdrawal from politics in 1908. Duan became prime minister, and Feng, vice president.[5] Although Li was nominally head of state, the real master of the political game was Duan. Nevertheless, Li Yuanhong often obtained parliament's support in obstructing Duan's notoriously pro-Japanese policies. After various skirmishes, a major crisis broke out in the spring of 1917 over China's entry into the war against Germany. This was supported by Duan. The issue had implications beyond the realm of foreign policy. With Li Yuanhong's support, parliament voted against entering the war and then approved Duan Qirui's removal. The latter immediately mobilized all his supporters to secure Li Yuanhong's resignation. Li Yuanhong, having no armed forces, tried to launch a counter-attack by appealing to Zhang Xun, the governor of Anhui. This choice reflected Li's weakness, as Zhang Xun made no secret of his loyalty to the Qing.

Zhang took advantage of his presence in Beijing to organize a *coup d'état* and declared the restoration of the imperial regime (summer 1917) by placing Puyi back on the throne. Having run out of tactics, Li fled (3 July). Zhang Xun's forces were no match for the general coalition that immediately formed against him and were swept away in less than two weeks.

With Li Yuanhong out of the picture politically, the cards were redealt. Feng Guozhang took over the presidency, with Duan Qirui as prime minister. By the autumn of 1917, the common ground between the Zhili and Anhui cliques, which mainly consisted of agreeing to eliminate Li Yuanhong and then Zhang Xun, no longer existed.[6] However, for the moment, they confined their confrontation to the elections for a new parliament, which in turn determined the installation of a new president (Feng's term of office expired in November 1918).

It seems that Zhang Xun, whose political skill was not his strong point, was manipulated by Li Yuanhong's opponents.[7] His power grab was less anecdotal than it appears, particularly because it led to Li Yuanhong's proclamation of the dissolution of parliament on 12 June. Fresh elections were organized, for which the Anhui clique set in motion an impressive electoral machine called the Anfu club. However, five southern provinces (Guangdong, Guangxi, Yunnan, Guizhou and Sichuan) contested the legitimacy of the elections and refused to hold the vote in their territory. This was the origin of the so-called Constitutional Protection Movement (*hufa yundong* 護法). This movement incorporated the temporary convergence of three political forces: firstly, there was Sun Yat-sen, the early anti-Manchu revolutionary and first president of the Chinese Republic. Marginalized, he had been racking up political errors since the mid-1910s and saw this as a perfect opportunity to get back on track. Secondly, there were the members of the 1912–13 parliament, dissolved in June 1917, who, judging their chances of re-election to be very slim given the context of the elections, went to Guangzhou, where they declared themselves to be in 'extraordinary session' (*feichang huiyi* 非常會議). Lastly, we come to the warlords of southern China (Lu Rongting and Tang Jiyao). These two were certainly part of the 1915 Constitutional Protection Movement, but their intentions were less to defend the Republic than to take advantage of a superb opportunity to emancipate themselves from central power and consolidate their nascent satrapies.

Two years later, their aim was little changed: they intended above all to take advantage of the union between the five provinces to form a bloc, whose unity was admittedly very precarious, but which could dissuade the forces of the North from imposing a reunification by force.

The elections were held in May–June 1918 with a reduced electorate (less than 33 million). They are best known for the massive fraud and vote buying that took place. The resulting parliament was widely renewed, unsurprisingly, very much in favour of the Anhui clique. On 4 September 1918, it elected Xu Shichang as president. He was a civilian with neither a military force nor a territorial base. At 64 years old, he was significantly older than the other protagonists and had made a great number of friends among them during his long and brilliant career in the Qing administration. While Xu was thought of as an affiliate of the Anhui clique, he also represented an acceptable alternative for Feng Guozhang. Furthermore, his moral stature and various personal ties also gave him the advantage of being an acceptable candidate for the South.[8]

Despite the elections that had taken place, the Guangzhou government continued to rally the support of the members of the parliament elected in 1912–13 (whose ranks were swelled in 1919 for good measure) and proclaimed itself the repository of republican legality. It was nevertheless unsupported by Sun Yat-sen, who, having recognized his inability to impose his leadership in Guangzhou, returned to Shanghai in the spring of 1918. Obviously, the presence in Beijing and Guangzhou of two governments, each claiming legitimacy, and the de facto dislocation of the country into a powder keg of local powers, did not satisfy anyone. Negotiations were held almost continuously in Shanghai between delegations from Beijing and Guangzhou, up to May 1919, when it became clear that neither side was prepared to compromise on the issue of the two rival parliaments (each demanding the dissolution of the other). Xu Shichang, who had personally put a lot into a peaceful reunification with the South, was weakened politically and was also affected by the discredit that his government incurred from the May Fourth 1919 Movement. Xu was also, thanks to his prominence, the only individual capable of being, if not an arbiter, then at least a skilful negotiator capable of achieving compromises between the Anhui and Zhili cliques.

Thus ended a period when clashes between the major cliques that emerged after the death of Yuan Shikai were fought with gloves on. It was the prospect of Anhui hegemony that triggered a short war between the Zhili and Anhui cliques (14–18 July 1920), more than opposition to Duan's pro-Japanese policy. The Zhili clique won, thanks to the alliance it had managed to arrange with Zhang Zuolin's forces on a second front to the enemy's rear. The Zhili clique, now led by the Cao Kun/Wu Peifu duo, dominated the Beijing government in the following years. The defeat of the Anhui clique also marked the end of a period when Japan, taking advantage of the power vacuum left by the European powers, had been trying, since 1916, to make a satellite of the central government, by backing Duan Qirui and granting massive support to the Anhui clique. Japan completely altered its strategy after the defeat of its puppet. From then on, it lost interest in the government in Beijing and sided with Zhang Zuolin's regional power based in Manchuria – the main region in which Japanese interests were concentrated. Since the Western powers, returned once more to the Far East, were against China falling under the exclusive influence of Japan, the latter focused on strengthening its influence in Manchuria, while also discouraging the national ambitions of Zhang Zuolin. This strategy also reflected the increasing weakness of the Beijing government. It was no longer a realistic strategy to try and gain power throughout China by securing the Beijing government.

The clear defeat of the Anhui clique in 1920 left the Zhili clique face to face with its ally, the Fengtian clique (see Map 4). With President Xu now confined to a ceremonial role, the government of Prime Minister Jin Yunpeng was principally limited to handling day-to-day business. Everything else, including essential matters, was settled between the two allies. The Zhili/Fengtian compromise was eventually shattered by Zhang Zuolin's growing ambitions. Thwarting the latter's attempt to push south, Wu Peifu defeated him at the end of the first Zhili/Fengtian War (April–May 1922), but without being able to annihilate his forces or drive him from his stronghold.

Having repulsed their enemy in the north, the Zhili clique then set out to finish off Sun Yat-sen's government in the south. The latter, once again established in Guangzhou, had been elected there in April 1921, with the title of President. In a move towards reunification, the clique

3 Wu Peifu in the mid-1920s.

put forward what appeared to be a compromise solution: the return of Li Yuanhong and the recall of the 1912 parliament to Beijing, in exchange for the simultaneous resignation of the two competing presidents, Xu Shichang and Sun Yat-sen.

The attempt fell apart due to Li's clumsiness, which torpedoed his own ministry, and Sun's stubborn refusal to resign. Cao Kun was then elected president on 5 October 1923, in return for large bribes.

The Second Zhili/Fengtian War began in September 1924 with the struggle for control of Shanghai between Qi Xieyuan, allied to the Zhili clique, and Lu Yongxiang, supported by the Fengtian. The Zhili won the first round, taking Shanghai. The head-on collision between the two cliques came a little later. The main battle took place in the Shanhaiguan area (a key position controlling access to North China from Manchuria) on 19 September. Just as the situation seemed to be developing favourably again for the Zhili clique, the betrayal by one of Wu Peifu's main allies, Feng Yuxiang, disrupted everything. On 23 October, Feng, who had secured the support of Yan Xishan, lord of Shanxi province, threw his troops against Beijing, where he took Cao Kun prisoner. Cao was the incumbent president of the Republic. This is sometimes called the 'Beijing coup' – *Beijing zhengbian* 北京政變. Feng's treachery was bought (for a huge sum) through the mediation of Japanese officers anxious to avert the threat of their protégé Zhang Zuolin's defeat and the ensuing invasion of Manchuria by Zhili troops. In the days following his coup, Feng Yuxiang got off lightly, making himself look like a champion of the republican cause by renaming his forces *Guominjun* 國民軍 (the People's Army) and then expelling Puyi and his retinue from the Forbidden City (5 November). Meanwhile, caught off guard by Feng Yuxiang's betrayal, despite his efforts, Wu Peifu's forces were irretrievably dispersed. This left Wu with only one option: to leave the theatre of operations in North China and move to the Yangtze River valley to try to rebuild his forces with the help of militarists who, like Qi Xieyuan, remained loyal to him.[9]

In Beijing, where Feng's power grab had rolled the dice once more, parliament was dissolved again. The new allies Feng Yuxiang and Zhang Zuolin agreed to bring Duan Qirui (the former head of the Anhui clique) out of retirement and give him the office of provisional chief executive (24 November). Duan's efforts to re-establish forms of legality by convening a Reconstruction conference on 1 February 1925 may seem rather derisory. Nevertheless, Sun Yat-sen saw an opportunity and went to Beijing in the hope of establishing himself as an arbiter, or at least becoming involved in an improbable reform. His famous political will (see Appendix 1), written on his deathbed, evokes this chimera when it mentions the need to convene a National Convention as soon as possible.

Feng Yuxiang and Zhang Zuolin pretended to perpetuate the forms of a central government, placing Duan at the head of an executive that no longer executed much. But the substance of power relations remained military more than ever: the status quo between the victors would not last. In the months that followed, the two did their utmost to expand their respective areas of influence – one pushing his pawns towards Henan, the other in the Shanghai region.[10] The open war between them began at the end of 1925. This time, Zhang Zuolin won the alliance of Wu Peifu, still resentful of Feng Yuxiang.

Feng and his generals suffered defeat after defeat and Feng had to flee to the USSR. Zhang's victory established his hegemony across North China. While the first two wars between the major northern cliques (the 1920 Anhui/Zhili War and the 1922 First Zhili/Fengtian War) had been affairs of a few days' duration confined to a limited theatre of operations, the Second Zhili/Fengtian War (1924) and the subsequent Guominjun/Fengtian War were terrible struggles lasting several months, involving large numbers of troops on different fronts.[11] They resulted in a weakening of the protagonists' forces and a drain on already precarious finances. As a result, they created a strong vacuum which the Guomindang were able to take advantage of in the months that followed.

All these clashes between the three major northern cliques were aimed at control of the Beijing government and, in the longer term, the reunification of North China (north of the Yangtze River). These cliques were able to form blocks of provinces, some amounting at their peak to as many as a dozen. Thus, the political end point of the struggle between them remained that of the country's unification.

Meanwhile, south of the Yangtze River, less powerful – if no less pugnacious – warlords were asserting themselves. Geographically isolated, with more distinct identities, the southern provinces (Sichuan, Yunnan, Guizhou, Guangdong and Guangxi) were not directly involved in the major clashes between the Anhui, Zhili and Fengtian cliques. This did not make them havens of peace. Conflict was just as fierce as in the north, the main difference being that the opponents had no ambitions to reunify the country. In 1918, the strongman of Yunnan, Tang Jiyao, managed to extend his influence to the two neighbouring provinces of Guizhou and Sichuan, for a short term.[12] Lu Rongting and the old Guangxi clique extended their hold over Guangdong and Guangxi. For the large cliques in the north, these forces only came into consideration as a strategic alliance opening a second front (but actual concerted action was rare). In the case of the most divided provinces, the big northern cliques tried to advance by choosing a champion from among the competing rivals. Thus, Wu Peifu tried to interfere in far-off Guizhou by supporting Yuan Zuming, and similarly in Sichuan, he backed Yang Sen.[13]

Who were the warlords?

The dissolution of central power in the second half of the 1910s benefitted those who began to be called the 'warlords' (*junfa*). It is worth looking a little more closely at them. In his masterful study, *Crimson Rain*, William Rowe has shown that Chinese society had numerous formenters of violence.[14] If the situation became even slightly favourable, they spread beyond the sectors of society and geographical areas to which they were formerly limited during periods of stability. The weakness of central government from 1916 onwards, combined with a surfeit of weapons available at very low cost following the end of the 1914–18 conflict, provided a particularly favourable context for their unleashing. Local big shots, bandits and disaffected soldiers could, by dint of daring, energy and luck, become warlords.

It is not easy to define the term *junfa*, of Japanese origin *(gunbatsu)*, which Chen Duxiu introduced into the Chinese language relatively late, in 1918.[15] Nevertheless, it can be argued that a warlord was someone who managed to gain control of a certain land base through his military strength (otherwise he was no different from the itinerant bandit chiefs who plagued many areas). No warlord would think of using this highly pejorative term (which remains so today) to describe himself. *Junfa*, in fact, is a term always applied to other people: a rule that the Guomindang's propaganda fully espoused. The definition of *junfa* became even more complex after 1926: the term was used ad nauseam in nationalist propaganda during the Northern Expedition to refer to the Guomindang's enemy military leaders. But this ceased to be the case for those rallying to its cause, who were dubbed 'revolutionaries', with a wave of the wand. On the other hand, as soon as a Guomindang general distanced himself from them and assumed some independence, a relatively frequent phenomenon in the 1930s, he became (once more) a *junfa*. This labelling, taken up by nationalist and communist historians in the following decades, led to the classification of resolutely progressive figures as being among the *junfa*. The case of Chen Jiongming is probably the most typical: his particularly advanced democratic ideas did not prevent him, once he dramatically broke with Sun Yat-sen in 1922, from being inflicted with the infamous title of *junfa*.

The implausible identikit portrait

There is a tendency to highlight some particularly colourful warlords, such as Zhang Zongchang, the notorious 'Dogmeat General'. His role, which was quite modest (master of Shandong province from 1925 to 1927) does not justify his being so well known. His fame stems from the fact that it is hard to find a better example for attracting ignominy amongst the warlords: brutal, rapacious, unscrupulous, an opium user and gambler (contrary to what one reads everywhere, his nickname does not come from any taste for canines, but from an expression associated with a game of chance which he particularly enjoyed). And, finally, with a feature peculiar to him alone, and of the sort to fuel fantasies, this ladies' man amassed a true harem for himself. Contemporaries enjoyed relating the antics of this bogeyman, and these are readily repeated by modern historians.

If the warlords seem a very heterogeneous group at first sight, the profile of the great warlords of the north was indeed quite similar: they were often former senior officers of the Beiyang Army, the main military force of the country at the end of the Qing period, and belonged to roughly the same generation. They often had a more than respectable intellectual background. Among them were included many prize-winners from the highest level of imperial examinations (Feng Guozhang, Wu Peifu), as well as from the second level (Yan Xishan).[16] Wu Peifu in particular liked to present himself as a scholar. During campaigns, he would ostentatiously compose poems on the battlefield. Zhang Zuolin, an illiterate former bandit, was an exception.

In the west and south of the country, the warlords had much more varied profiles. Many of those who became *junfa* relied from the start on an armed force to serve their ambitions: they included former Qing soldiers, militia leaders, as well as bandits. But this did not apply to everyone: there were also former civil servants from the late Qing, and revolutionaries driven by personal ambition. Some figures fell more or less into all these categories. This was the case of Lu Rongting, a leader who dominated Guangxi between 1912 and 1921. A former bandit on the borders of Indochina[17] and Guangxi, he was co-opted into the Qing military forces, where he quickly rose in rank and became, in 1911, an occasional revolutionary, the last step before earning his *junfa* stripes.

The warlord was not necessarily a native of the area under his control, and this was the case for many of the great warlords of North China. Again, Zhang Zuolin, who ruled over Manchuria, from which he originated, was the exception. There was a much clearer trend towards the emergence of locally born provincial governors in the south and west. Local origin was one of the factors that favoured the longevity of a warlord, who could use his personal and family networks to establish his power base. Some warlords had short careers; others ruled their territory for many years, even decades. In the latter case, geography often came to their aid. The most notable longevity belonged to Yan Xishan, who remained invulnerable in Shanxi throughout the republican period because of the isolation of the province, protected as it was by mountains and rivers. But there are other examples, such as Jing Yuexiu, who was impossible to dislodge from his northern Shaanxi base, from 1917 until his death in 1936.

Notwithstanding some exceptions, however, short careers were the norm and help to explain the absence of warlord dynasties. It was singular for a son to succeed his father. The case of Zhang Xueliang, who managed – though with great difficulty – to regain control of Manchuria after his father's death, remained unique.

The driving forces behind *junfa* power

To recap, some warlords in northern China controlled several provinces and cherished ambitions for occupying Beijing (and thus taking over what remained of central power). The situation in southern China was less clear. A province such as Sichuan, which was heavily subdivided, offered a very favourable habitat for the proliferation of minor local rulers. Only late in the day did a stronger ruler emerge to impose a semblance of unification on the province. Far from comparable to the great beasts of northern China, some *junfa* were small fry, holding just a few dozen villages to ransom. Near Guangzhou, Li Fulin (remembered for his support of the Guomindang in the early 1920s) was master of a single large island in the Pearl River Delta.

Generally, though, it is quite clear that warlords sought to control as much territory as possible. But in the main they were eager to control the most prosperous regions, which promised abundant tax revenues. From this point of view, certain strategic areas were particularly coveted, either because they contained mineral resources or were granaries, or because they were traversed by major communications routes. The control of the main rivers, roads and especially railways offered many advantages: apart from the taxes that could be collected and the ease with which troops could rapidly be moved, extortion associated with the railways was a very regular activity for various warlords.

The big cities, with their concentrations of wealth, were further appealing targets. Whether it was a question of levying taxes on commercial transactions, consumer goods or landed property, or of 'inviting' banks to give loans, it was the cities that had to be secured. Liu Xiang's pre-eminence over the half-dozen warlords who shared Sichuan after 1927 was mainly because he managed to secure control of Chongqing, one of the province's two main cities. Among the most coveted were the cities that housed the two great arsenals, legacies of the Self-Strengthening period (1861–95) – Shanghai and Hanyang. Zhang Zuolin, with Japanese assistance, also built a large-scale arsenal in Mukden[18] in the early 1920s. In the mid-1920s, Feng Yuxiang's Russian military advisors clearly pointed out Feng's Achilles heel. He had no arsenal worthy of the name – a shortcoming further aggravated by the landlocked nature of the territories he controlled. No warlord could hope to play a leading role without securing control of these means of power.

Fully aware that they could not rule by force alone, and anxious to root their power in local society, the *junfa* were careful to associate themselves with local elites. They were greatly concerned by the matter of their legitimacy. James Sheridan perceptively observes the extent to which warlords were eager for official titles to cloak their personal dominance, and imaginative in inventing new ones when these proved inaccessible.[19] Moreover, they not only kept a close eye on the press in their region to ensure that no unfavourable articles were published, but also, for example, financed various publications to highlight their philanthropic activities.

A general survey is enough to counter the totally simplistic idea of warlords using only brute force to impose their law. That said, what values did warlords present to legitimize their power? At first sight, the impression of a rather confusing patchwork emerges: of hostility to the Qing regime, with a corresponding proclaimed loyalty to the Republican regime; an authoritarianism blended with Confucianism; and the promotion of regionalist identities.[20] It is also noteworthy that the warlords were the only political actors during the Republic to seek the support of religion as a basis for their legitimacy. This recourse could take several forms. The most widespread tactic adopted by the warlords to patronize popular religion was building, restoring or protecting temples. They also tended to promote the cult of ancient military heroes who righted wrongs – models of courage and virtue such as Yue Fei and Guan Yu – as a way of exalting the military element of society (and enhancing their own prestige in the process). Others, such as Tang Jiyao in Yunnan, ostensibly patronized well-known religious figures of good repute (in this case, Xuyun, one of the greatest Buddhist masters of the time). In the early 1920s, federalism became fashionable. For the warlords, it was a blessing in disguise, offering a justification for their vague hopes of independence. The start of the Northern Expedition prompted those who opposed it to strike up a chorus of anti-communist rhetoric (Zhang Zuolin made a speciality of this).

The key point, however, was that the warlords proved impervious to the rapid renewal of political ideas in the mid-1920s. Thus, with few exceptions, they remained reluctant to promote the ardently nationalist rhetoric that the Guomindang and the Communist Party shared. The rallying cries of organization and mobilization of the population in the name of a nationalist and revolutionary ideal, the idea that society should be considered not as a given but as the object of a demiurgic recon- struction, were so many new views that would remain alien to the *junfa*.[21] Being out of step with the radically renewed political offering proposed by the partners of the first United Front, and to which the population increasingly subscribed, was one of the causes of their ousting from the political scene.

Conflicts, alliances and viscosity

The conflicts between warlords can give the false impression of a simple violent outburst, but they were, however, governed by some unwritten rules. Certain moves were proscribed. Political assassination, in particular, was an indelicacy that remained very rare (at least between rivals of equal standing; they were less shy about inferiors). It was also customary to give a defeated opponent a way out. Chinese political life during the Warlord period not only had its rules, but also had its behind-the-scenes activity. Hong Kong and the foreign concessions (especially Shanghai and Tianjin) were settings for this. Some of the imposing mansions the warlords built there can still be seen today, such as that of Sun Chuanfang in the British Concession of Tianjin. Many defeated warlords or disgraced politicians retired there in peace with the money they had accumulated, or perhaps they were waiting patiently in the hope that the wind would change and they could try to make a comeback. At the time of his death, Sun Yat-sen's only significant possession was his house at 26, rue Molière in the French Concession in Shanghai. However, Sun's probity was quite exceptional for his time: despite the immense sums of money that passed through his hands, he was the only one of the leading men of power who died poor. Therefore, the very fact that he acquired this house shows that, during the Republic, a refuge in a concession was an indispensable tool in a political career. It was here that Sun worked on the necessary intrigues to retrieve his situation during the less auspicious periods of his political career, such as his time in the political wilderness from the spring of 1918 to the autumn of 1920 and the uncertain period from August 1922 to February 1923. During the latter, after being chased out of Guangzhou by Chen Jiongming, he negotiated the terms of an alliance between the Guomindang and the USSR.[22]

The existence of unspoken rules governing the clashes between warlords points to another important element: in reality, the independence of a lord was never absolute and the survival of each one depended on alliances. For example, a small *junfa* often tried to secure the support of a powerful person from outside the province in which they had carved out a domain, in order to have room to manoeuvre when dealing with the warlord who controlled most of their province. Nor was it uncommon for warlords to seek the support of a foreign power. This was particularly true of peripheral areas where material aid from territories under the control of an external power could more easily reach. In Yunnan, which bordered Indochina, the warlord Tang Jiyao and his successor Long Yun were supported materially, under French rule, by the French Tonkin[23] Railway for arms deliveries and on the same railway for exports. At the other end of the country, in his north-eastern stronghold, Zhang Zuolin received significant support from Japan, which had made a colony of Korea from 1910.[24]

The ceaseless conflicts between the warlords were also characterized by the inability of any of them to emerge victorious for more than a decade, until the Guomindang upset the balance in their own favour in 1928. Here we have an example of what has been called a situation of political viscosity, a notion used by Dominique Barthélemy to characterize the era of the first Capetians.[25] The term 'viscous state' implies that any significant thrust produces opposing forces whose combined effects tend to slow it down and cancel it out.

In this instance, two main dynamics were at work. The first was set in motion as soon as a warlord achieved significant successes. Concern about his rise to power caused other potentates to unite against him. Thus, in the spring of 1923, a coalition composed of Zhang Zuolin, Sun Yat-sen and Lu Yongxiang was formed (a 'relic' of the past greatness of the Anhui clique, the latter still holding the province of Zhejiang). This motley coterie, called 'the triangular alliance' (*sanjiao tongmeng* 三角同盟), had no other reason for its existence than to bring together all those whose interests lay in blocking the pressing threat of hegemony from the Zhili clique.[26] The second dynamic was a centrifugal force that permanently worked on the cluster of loyalties that constituted the very substance of a warlord's power. They certainly made every effort to consolidate this by entrusting commands or civil responsibilities to members of their family. A widespread and very interesting phenomenon, which would certainly merit a study in its own right, was that of the brothers of the *junfa*, who were especially deeply involved. Cao Rui, Cao Ying, Long Yuguang, Chen Weizhou and Liu Xianzhi are not the best-known names from the republican period. What these men had in common was that they were brothers of warlords and were placed in strategic positions by them.[27] But, despite any precautions taken, it was very common, especially when the military forces and possessions of a warlord significantly increased, for the ambitions of their subordinates, who might wish to carve out their own independent satrapy, to assert themselves. These men were often the recipients of active and self-interested support from a neighbouring warlord who was only too happy to weaken a rival.[28] Two of the greatest warlords of North China had to face betrayal from one of their top men when they reached the peak of their power: Wu Peifu, against whom Feng Yuxiang turned during the second Zhili/Fengtian War, on 23 October 1924; and Zhang Zuolin, who was betrayed, in turn, the following year (November–December 1925), by one of his main lieutenants, Guo Songling.[29]

Was national unity in jeopardy?

The decade of the warlords was an era of extreme division, a situation that was widely felt by contemporaries to be unsatisfactory and temporary. Historiography itself continues to judge the period largely through the prism of the threat to national unity. Apart from the fact that the warlords reigned supreme without being accountable to the central power in Beijing, it has been repeatedly pointed out that some of them had no hesitation in helping foreign powers, who, in turn, tried to extend their influence through them. Successive leaders in Yunnan or Manchuria were bound to seek the support of the power on the other side of the border. But the docility of these lords towards their foreign allies should not be exaggerated. Zhang Zuolin, for example, was never the compliant puppet of Japanese dreams.

There is also a tendency to focus on manifestations of disunity rather than those that reflect, against all odds, the resilience of a national framework. In reality, China was not dismembered and was never in danger of it. People and goods continued to circulate freely. It is true that the *junfa* had their own armed forces and raised their own taxes. The importance of some circulating their own money should not be overestimated. This would be to forget that, in China, minting money had never been, directly or indirectly, a sovereign privilege. But none of them ever tried to found an independent country and, as such, to have state-to-state relations with foreign powers. Furthermore, as Henrietta Harrison points out, each *junfa* perpetuated the republican liturgy in the part of the country under its rule, including the display of the national flag.[30] This was, of course, a way of affirming their legitimacy, but it also expressed the primacy of national unity.

The powerlessness of Beijing should not be exaggerated either. Despite the weakening of central government, the decisions of ministries such as those of Justice and Education were implemented throughout the provinces. Some administrations continued to function effectively on a national scale, such as the Salt Tax Administration or the Post Office, whose imposing network of 12,000 agencies covered the entire country, unaware of the warlords' wishful thinking about independence.

Ultimately, the warlord era continued to be dominated by the consensus around preservation of national unity, as well as, in practice, by the highly partial 'independence' of the warlords.

The diplomatic context, the May Fourth Movement (1919) and the rise of nationalism

The term 'May Fourth Movement' has two facets. In a broad sense, it was an intellectual movement that started conventionally with the founding of the magazine *Xin Qingnian* 新青年(*New Youth*) in 1915. This movement lasted until the mid-1920s. It was characterized by its iconoclastic approach, which undertook a systematic critique of the very foundations of Chinese culture in the name of science and progress. It will be dealt with in detail in Chapter 9 on intellectual life.

In the narrower sense of the term, which will interest us here, it refers to the wave of protest that started on 4 May 1919, provoked by the news that the rights and advantages enjoyed by Germany before 1914 in the province of Shandong would pass to Japan instead of being returned to China.

To understand the bitterness with which the news of this transfer of German rights to Japan was received, it is necessary, on the one hand, to consider the context of diplomatic history, marked by a spectacular recovery that began in the last decade of the Qing dynasty, and, on the other hand, to note, within a shorter time period, the existence among the population of hopes aroused by the fact that China belonged to the winning side when the war ended.

Two decades of spectacular diplomatic recovery for China (1906–1926)

As early as 1906, China had signed an advantageous treaty with Great Britain regarding Tibet. Then, through a series of agreements in 1907 and 1911 with the same administration, and with skill and tenacity, it had obtained an end to opium imports from India. Of course, China had to endure the humiliating Twenty-One Demands from Japan in 1915. But as soon as China entered the First World War in August 1917, it began to recover, cancelling the extraterritorial rights of the Germans and Austro-Hungarians. It also obtained from its allies a five-year suspension of the Boxer Indemnity payments. Participation in the Versailles Conference was a victory in itself.

The beginning of the 1920s was the start of a triumphant period for Chinese diplomacy. The agreements with Germany and the Soviet Union in 1920–1 confirmed that the two great powers were renouncing their privileges in China: their nationals no longer enjoyed the right of extraterritoriality, and the payment of compensation for the suppression of the Boxer Rebellion ended.[31] But it was at the Washington Conference

(November 1921 – February 1922) that the Beijing government, which continued to represent China diplomatically, could claim the most remarkable success. It benefitted from very favourable arrangements proposed by American diplomats, which set up the conference, and aimed to put an end to the rival imperialisms and conflicting spheres of influence in China. Its other objective, which was not presented explicitly, was to challenge the advantages – considered disproportionate and detrimental to the balance of power – that Japan had secured in China since the Twenty-One Demands episode. China obtained commitments to renegotiate treaties. Finally, on the conference fringes, Japan renounced its rights over Shandong, within the framework of bilateral negotiations between itself and China. The next step was the Tariff Conference in Beijing on 26 October 1925. Chinese diplomats skilfully used the emotion generated by the May Thirtieth Movement of 1925 to demand that Washington's promises of a return to customs autonomy be swiftly fulfilled. This was agreed to, in exchange for the abolition of internal customs (foreigners had long considered such taxes to be a major obstacle to the development of their exports to China). This would come into effect on 1 January 1929.

Disappointed expectations following the Versailles negotiations

China had declared itself neutral at the beginning of hostilities and entered the war against the Central Powers rather late, on 14 August 1917. One of its aims was to retrieve the advantages acquired by Germany. From a strictly military point of view, China's contribution was zero, but it did provide several hundred thousand workers to the Allies in support of the war effort. These Chinese worked mainly in factories or ports, often in difficult conditions. After the armistice in November 1918, they made a major contribution to reconstruction in the battle zone. Altogether, around 3,000 of them lost their lives in Europe (mostly from disease).

At the end of the war, China not only stood on the winning side but could rightly claim to have made a significant contribution to the final victory. It was counting on the support of the United States, whose president, Wilson, had set himself the goal of ushering in a new era of justice, collaboration and equality in world diplomacy, and whose

Fourteen Points were outlined in January 1918. The Chinese delegation therefore arrived at the Versailles peace conference with high expectations, aiming to challenge the system of unequal treaties that kept the country in a state of semi-subjugation. One of its members, Wellington Koo, made a remarkable speech to this effect in January 1919. With such a horizon of expectation, the news of the transfer to Japan of Germany's rights in Shandong was therefore felt by public opinion to be a bitter humiliation.

A movement without precedent

Beijing University, which Cai Yuanpei had made into a place where intellectual freedom was combined with excellence, was the central focus of the unrest. The first student demonstration took place on 4 May 1919. From the start, new forms of political expression were set in motion. The mobilization of students in the capital was not the main innovation. They had already protested against the signing of a secret military agreement with Japan a year earlier, in May 1918. But the action taken then consisted mainly in going (on 21 May 1918) to the presidency of the Republic to submit a written protest, in keeping with the tradition of reproval exercised by the literate elite towards the political power. In contrast, the demonstration of 4 May 1919 was aimed at the people of Beijing and, through them, the entire Chinese people. It was therefore a demonstration in the strictest sense, like those of today – that is, a form of organized collective action intended both to put pressure on the authorities and to sway public opinion. It was orchestrated, with participants shouting slogans and displaying banners in order to influence the people watching them march.[32] The demonstration resulted in the ransacking of a pro-Japanese politician's residence, and a police crackdown that led to the arrest of several dozen students. The May Fourth Movement was also spawned by the evolution of the early years of the Republic. On the one hand, the evolution of the political situation after 1912 engendered widespread disillusionment; on the other, the absence of a strong state provided the conditions for freedom of debate and expression, and allowed the movement to spread. Indeed, although the first student demonstration took place on 4 May 1919 in Beijing, the movement was not confined either to the capital or to student and intellectual circles. It spread swiftly to all the major urban centres in China. The workers mobilized, through their traditional organizations (guilds). In Shanghai, 60,000 workers held a five-day strike. The population's participation, in its broadest sense, took the form of boycotts. M.-C. Bergère has clearly shown how, in the case of Shanghai, different urban classes coordinated their actions and shared the same nationalist ardour.[33] Mostly spontaneous, with the political class trailing in its wake, the May Fourth Movement first and foremost demonstrated the rapid development of a national consciousness. The idea of a community of citizens transcending not only social strata, but also regional affiliations, was established in this way. The Shaanxi Students' Association in Beijing (*Shaanxi lüjing xuesheng lianhehui* 陝西旅京學生聯合會), for example, became the Common Progress Society (*Gongjin she* 共進社) in 1918, broadening its perspective immeasurably, to the point of becoming one of the linchpins of the May Fourth Movement in the capital.[34]

4 Arrest of Beijing University students (June 1919).

Demonstrations, strikes and boycotts were organized throughout the country with the backing of local warlords, many of whom expressed support for the Beijing movement, condemning its repression, and providing aid and shelter. This was the case, for example, in Jiangxi, then ruled by Chen Guangyuan, where 3,000 students demonstrated in the streets of Nanchang on 12 May against the repression of the movement. Sichuan's military governor, Xiong Kewu, allowed two demonstrations to be held on 25 May and 8 June. While taking the necessary measures to ensure that the movement did not get away from them, protecting those who marched, the warlords hastened to present themselves in a good light by bombarding the Beijing government with indignant telegrams. It was as much due to their actions as to the popular pressure expressed through strikes and boycotts that the Beijing government was prompted to dismiss its three most pro-Japanese ministers on 10 June. The Chinese delegates at Versailles refused to sign the treaty.

The mobilization resulted in a mainly symbolic victory (the Japanese remained firmly established in Shandong). The importance of the movement lay rather in its marking the beginning of new responses: large urban strata were invading the political scene in the name of nationalist ideals. These new actors were to play a full role in various crises in the years that followed, such as that of 30 May 1925.

The rise of the Guomindang (1917–1926) and the Guangzhou decade[35]

During the last eight years of his life, Sun Yat-sen strove to make Guangdong the launch pad for his plan to reunify the country. As we have seen, as part of the movement to defend the Constitution, on 17 July 1917 he arrived in Guangzhou, then ruled by Lu Rongting, the leader of the old Guangxi clique. Sun's strategy was to oppose the Beijing government and claim republican legitimacy, relying in particular on the members of the 1912 parliament who had taken refuge in Guangzhou. But finding that Lu Rongting was unwilling to support his nationwide ambitions, Sun left Guangdong in the spring of 1918.

Two years later, in October 1920, Chen Jiongming, one of the former leaders of the 1911 Revolution in Guangdong, managed to oust Lu Rongting. It was with limited enthusiasm that he in turn welcomed

Sun, who had just re-founded the Guomindang the previous year on the highly symbolic date of 10 October.[36] On the surface, Chen, a progressive who was genuinely committed to the republican cause, might seem politically much closer to Sun than Lu Rongting had been. But he favoured a federal China: in the short and medium term, his priority was to develop Guangdong province into a model for the rest of the country. This did not sit well with Sun Yat-sen's ambition to use the province (even if it meant crushing it with taxes) as a springboard for military reunification. In reality, the Chen Jiongming – Sun Yat-sen partnership was like trying to mix oil and water as Chen was a federalist and Sun dreamt only of marching to Beijing to reunify China. For two years, the two men pursued pretty contradictory policies. In June 1922, Chen broke off all ties and attacked Sun's headquarters. The latter narrowly escaped death and managed to reach Shanghai. Once again, Sun was able to observe that the last word goes to whoever has the military power.

Six months later, Chen Jiongming was driven out of Guangzhou by a motley coalition of militarists funded by Sun. Many of them were troops from other provinces, carried there by the tides of the constant wars of the period. They were euphemistically called 'guest armies' (kejun 客軍). Some of these forces, such as the 23,000 Yunnanese commanded by Yang Ximin, were strong enough to pose a threat to the Guomindang. Sun returned to Guangdong on 21 February 1923. He was more in control than in 1920, even if his situation remained extremely precarious. Indeed, the Guomindang had to jostle for position with their new uncontrollable allies (who shamelessly squeezed the population and competed to raise taxes in Guangzhou) as well as against yesterday's enemies (Chen Jiongming, in particular, remained a threat in eastern Guangdong).

These issues persuaded Sun that it was essential for his party to have an army that was not an ally, but one over which he had complete control. He also became convinced that playing the hand of republican legitimacy no longer made much sense: from 1923 onwards, Sun gave up waving the banner of the defence of the Constitution and republican institutions as he had been doing for five years to justify his opposition to the North. The new government he founded in Guangzhou at the beginning of 1923 could count on the help of the USSR, with which he had negotiated the Sun–Joffe Manifesto in January 1923. For Sun Yat-sen, the alliance with the USSR was a decision made with the head rather than the heart. It should be noted that, despite the agreement, both sides were trying to keep other options open. The Soviet Union continued to support Feng Yuxiang in the north-west, while Sun was still willing to listen to other powers.

Nonetheless, the alliance with the Soviet Union was a turning point. The impressive figure sent by Moscow to advise Sun Yat-sen, Mikhail Borodin, played an important role in its successful implementation. The choice of the Soviet alliance was far from unanimously popular in the ranks of the Guomindang, so much so that on several occasions Sun had to use all his personal prestige to keep it going. The United Front tactic was supported by the left wing of the Guomindang (Wang Jingwei, and in particular Liao Zhongkai, who was one of its main architects). On the other hand, it immediately aroused open hostility from the right wing (Hu Hanmin). Among the moderates, distrust was less acute, but would increase as the Russian advisors grew in importance and the CCP developed. The most heated debates concerned the place to be given to communists in the party. One of the main provisions of the Sun–Joffe Manifesto was the dual membership of communists in both the CCP and the Guomindang, which stirred up strong reservations. However, it is important to underline the imbalance of the allies: the Guomindang, with 50,000 members (200,000 including those overseas), was gigantic compared to the CCP in 1923. The latter, founded in 1921, had only a few hundred members. Certainly, its secretary general was Chen Duxiu, an intellectual of great stature. But he was not an apparatchik and, moreover, he was personally reluctant to accept the United Front credo imposed by the Third International: it was therefore Borodin who settled the details of the alliance with the Guomindang and smoothed out the innumerable difficulties to which it inevitably gave rise on a day-to-day basis.

The First Party Congress (20–30 January 1924) was a major turning point for the Guomindang and, by extension, for the entire political chessboard of the period. This congress provided the party with a much more coherent and hierarchical organization, largely modelled on the 1919 statutes of the Russian Communist Party.[37] In addition, the Guomindang set up an organization capable of orchestrating systematic propaganda on a vast scale. The period 1924–6 saw an energetic development of propaganda, targeting especially the army and schoolchildren. However, there was no pure and simple alignment on the Bolshevik model. The Guomindang retained some original features from their past. First of all, they confirmed Sun Yat-sen's special status. The January 1924 Constitution provided for a national congress and a central executive committee, but placed both under the authority of the *zongli* 總理, who was mentioned by name: Sun Yat-sen. Another foundational text, the *Fundamentals of National Government Construction* (*Guomin zhengfu jianguo dagang* 國民政府建國大綱), adopted in April 1924, reflected a certain influence of the federalist theses that were flourishing in 1920–3: it took up the idea of political construction that should begin with local autonomy at the level of the districts and provinces. It was up to a national congress to combine the latter two into a coherent whole.[38]

From a military point of view, the Guomindang managed to win over some very valuable allies at this time: the triumvirate of militarists of the new Guangxi clique (Huang Shaohong, Li Zongren, Bai Chongxi), who had just reunified the province of the same name for their own benefit. They secured the western flank from the dangerous expansionist intentions of the powerful warlord of Yunnan, Tang Jiyao. But they were also very capable military leaders who would make an important contribution to the Northern Expedition.

The first attempts at state-building took place in the Guangzhou base under the impetus of Liao Zhongkai (1923–5), and especially the young Song Ziwen, who took over the rationalization of taxes from him.

Until then, Sun had relied on alliances (with secret societies or warlords) to obtain troops, but he now intended to provide the Guomindang with an army that was entirely subordinate to him. To this end, the opening of the Huangpu Military Academy (still fairly well known today by its Cantonese pronunciation: Whampoa) to the east of Guangzhou represented a major step forward. This Academy received considerable support from the USSR, and its organization was directly inspired by the model of the Red Army training schools created by Trotsky in 1918. In addition to intensive indoctrination (courses on demism[39] were given by Hu Hanmin), the cadets received high-quality military training under the supervision of Soviet advisors led by Blücher.

The founding of the Academy was also a fantastic opportunity for

5 16 June 1924, inauguration ceremony of the Huangpu Academy. The figures on the platform are, from left to right, Liao Zhongkai, Chiang Kai-shek (director of the Academy), Sun Yat-sen and his wife Song Qingling. The flag on the left is the prototype national flag put forward by the Guomindang (it would become the official national flag after the Northern Expedition), the one on the right (white sun on a blue background), is the party flag. The imposing man dressed in white standing at the foot of the stage is Morris Cohen, Sun's personal bodyguard.

Chiang Kai-shek. Just returned from the USSR, where he had been sent by Sun Yat-sen, he was appointed director of the Academy on 3 May 1924, the starting point of his meteoric rise. The graduating classes of cadets from the Academy were to play a major role in political life for the next half-century. They spearheaded the Northern Expedition and later provided political support for Chiang (although a small minority, such as Lin Biao, joined the communist ranks). The entry of the Huangpu cadets into the political arena took place on 15 October 1924, when they massacred the Guangzhou merchant militia on Sun's orders. This bloodbath (hundreds of deaths and considerable destruction in the Xiguan 西關 county) revealed the precariousness of Sun's situation in Guangzhou itself. The details of the circumstances that led to the tragedy (arms purchased by the militia abroad with all the necessary authorizations, but whose delivery was delayed by order of the government, which intended to levy a very high tax) are not essential. What led Sun to order the killing was that the merchants' organizations were likely to give tangible form to the general discontent, especially as they were headed by an energetic and popular leader, Chen Lianbo. In particular, the Cantonese, already burdened with taxes, showed no enthusiasm for financing the military expedition to the north, which, at the time, might have seemed, if not a whim, at least a particularly risky undertaking.

The consolidation of the Guomindang base continued over the next two years. The fragile Cantonese bridgehead was once again threatened in June 1925 by a revolt under Yang Ximin and Liu Zhenhuan, two of the main warlords who had put their armed forces at Sun's disposal to enable him to regain a foothold in Guangdong at the beginning of 1923. It was put down with some difficulty. But, in the meantime, a major event occurred: the death of Sun Yat-sen.

1925: the death of Sun Yat-sen and its aftermath, the May Thirtieth Movement

The death of Sun Yat-sen in March 1925 was an important event for the Guomindang, who found themselves without a clear leader. It completely redealt the cards, not only because the statutes of the Guomindang guaranteed him strong personal power, but also because nothing was planned for his demise. The question of leadership was therefore immediately debated by a government that proclaimed itself as 'national' in July and reorganized itself accordingly. Chiang Kai-shek, the latest addition to the Guomindang's top circles, was not initially considered a potential successor. But the assassination of Liao Zhongkai (30 August 1925) changed the situation because it led to the dismissal of the main representative of the right wing of the Guomindang, Hu Hanmin, who was accused of having ordered it. Two of the great historical leaders of the Guomindang were thus abruptly eliminated from the race to succeed Sun. In October–November, the threat that Chen Jiongming continued to pose from the eastern part of Guangdong, where he had taken refuge with his supporters, was annihilated by Chiang Kai-shek at the cost of a very difficult campaign. This increased both his prestige and his political stature. In the following months, there was fierce rivalry between him and Wang Jingwei. The latter, having identified the threat that Chiang now posed, increased the plots aimed at isolating him. In particular, Wang threw his weight behind the postponement of the Northern Expedition, which not only represented a military make-or-break that the Russian advisors themselves considered premature, but was likely, if successful, to give the main military leader, Chiang Kai-shek, an inordinate degree of importance.

The emotion following Sun's death helped to distract public opinion from the many episodes in his career that were entirely out of tune with the Guomindang's new revolutionary rhetoric denouncing imperialism and unequal treaties (Sun had assiduously courted imperialist powers for funding throughout his career). In this context, the May Thirtieth Movement 1925, which began before the shock wave caused by his death had subsided, was to elevate him to the status of an icon of nationalism and anti-imperialism.

The May Thirtieth Movement 1925 was also part of the swell of nationalist agitation that emerged at the beginning of the year, and of the intense activism amongst workers, where unionization was progressing rapidly and strikes were increasing. On 30 May 1925, British policemen from the Shanghai International Concession opened fire on a large anti-imperialist demonstration, killing 13 people. These deaths, providing the movement with its martyrs, gave it a new impetus. In the following months, strong patriotic feeling manifested itself in cities across the country. While the students were still in the vanguard, they were joined by the workers, who had acquired a new importance. The general strike declared in Shanghai was three times as well supported as the one which had accompanied 4 May 1919 (200,000 workers). The wave of strikes spread throughout the country in the following months.

Unlike the May Fourth Movement, the warlords (who were one of the targets of the movement this time) had only one response to the nationalist demonstrations and the workers' movement: repression. A demonstration organized in Beijing on 18 March 1926 to demand, among other things, the abrogation of the unequal treaties, ended in a massacre in which 47 people were killed. Conversely, the Guomindang stirred up and encouraged the May Thirtieth Movement. A large anti-imperialist demonstration organized in Guangzhou on 23 June 1925 resulted in the death of 52 people, killed by Franco-British forces entrenched in the Shamian concession. The great Hong Kong strike that followed, carried out in the name of anti-imperialism, represented the peak of

Guomindang activism directed at the working classes that had been manifested since the beginning of the alliance with the CCP. Between June 1925 and November 1926, over 100,000 Hong Kong workers left the colony. They were supported by the Guangzhou government, which armed some of them to form pickets to enforce a boycott of British goods and a blockade of the colony, which was paralysed as a result. In reality, popular mobilization remained very limited in Guangzhou itself, and the authorities there quickly distanced themselves from the organization of the strike, which threatened to create a state within a state. But this does not detract from the main fact: the Guomindang were able to present themselves, in the eyes of public opinion, as the standard-bearers of the struggle against imperialism.

The Guomindang promoted the idea that their planned military operation, the Northern Expedition, would provide the answer to the country's ills. They deployed particularly aggressive and clever propaganda, publishing a series of posters likening the *junfa* to ferocious beasts complicit with the imperialists, from whom the Guomindang would deliver the country. In the Lower Yangtze River valley, memberships took off even before the arrival of the Northern Expedition troops: in Jiangsu, the number of Guomindang members increased eightfold (from 3,225 to 27,872) between October 1926 and April 1927.[40]

However, the Guomindang were not the only group to benefit politically from the May Thirtieth Movement 1925. Their ally, the CCP, which had consolidated its organization since its 3rd Congress in June 1923, took advantage of it to broaden their recruitment, particularly in working-class circles. Its membership soared from 1,000 in January 1925 to 10,000 a year later. The influence of the communists grew at an even more impressive rate, to the point of arousing growing concern among the Guomindang's right wing. The famous incident with the gunboat *Zhongshan* on 20 March 1926 testifies to the atmosphere of fear that this rise in power inspired. This episode is particularly confusing and difficult to interpret. Chiang Kai-shek, fearing (or pretending to believe) that there was a power play against him, had the communist leaders arrested, before, all danger having been averted, backing down and releasing them. In the following weeks, he successfully manoeuvred to weaken the left wing of the Guomindang.

The Northern Expedition

The Northern Expedition refers to a series of military operations in which the Guomindang, from their base in Guangdong, succeeded in defeating the major warlords and installing a national government in Nanjing. Three phases stand out during the Northern Expedition. The first phase (July 1926 – March 1927) corresponds to the defeat of the two great warlords of central China: complete and definitive for one, Wu Peifu; partial for the other, Sun Chuanfang. There followed a second phase: a pause as a result of internal dissension in the Guomindang, in particular the split in the United Front. The third phase took place from April to June 1928, when Zhang Zuolin was defeated (see Map 5).

Phase 1: the defeat of Wu Peifu and Sun Chuanfang

After removing Wang Jingwei following the *Zhongshan* gunboat incident, Chiang Kai-shek managed to overcome the reservations of the Russian advisors. The launch of the Northern Expedition in July 1926 was due to the favourable context. The rallying of a warlord from southern Hunan, Tang Shengzhi, was a piece of good fortune for the crossing of the rugged regions that commanded access to that province.[41] Of greater bearing was the fact that the Northern Expedition benefitted from the power vacuum produced by the conflagration between the two dominant powers of the time. The Zhili/Fengtian and the Guominjun/Fengtian wars of the mid-1920s had drained both the military forces and, even more, the finances of the opposing sides. The Northern Expedition would benefit from the void created by these military operations.[42]

Nevertheless, on the eve of launching the expedition, the disproportionality of forces was still too striking for success to be ensured. The Guomindang's armies came down to 100,000 men, almost ten times fewer than the troops of the warlords it intended to defeat. Qualitatively speaking, however, the comparison was certainly in their favour: the combativeness and discipline of some of the forces they would face were very weak.

In reality, the Guomindang's greatest asset in the summer of 1926 was the profound division among their opponents. The defeat and break-up of the Zhili clique, soon followed by Zhang Zuolin's victory over Feng Yuxiang, had raised the threat of Zhang's hegemony. This was a real boon for the Guomindang: even after the first Guomindang victories, their enemies still believed that, ultimately, the main threat lay in the north. During 1925 and the first half of 1926, intrigues, skirmishes and reversals of alliances between the four strongmen of the moment followed one upon another. These leaders were Zhang Zuolin, Feng Yuxiang, Sun Chuanfang and Wu Peifu (the latter having regained, if not his former splendour, at least some military means thanks to the support of former subordinates in Hunan and Hubei). This was particularly favourable to the Guomindang as it prevented any possibility of a coalition against them. On the other hand, they could count on allies: in addition to the new clique in Guangxi already mentioned, there was Feng Yuxiang, the USSR's second iron in the fire in north-west China. Initially, the designated target was Wu Peifu. Carefully isolated, he lost his footing militarily. The conquest of Hunan was easily accomplished (July 1926). That of Hubei, marked by the difficult siege of Wuhan, was completed in October. Wu Peifu, focused on his operations against his mortal enemy Feng Yuxiang to the north, constantly underestimated the danger posed by the Guomindang. When he finally decided to turn his elite troops against them, it was too late.[43]

With Wu Peifu at bay (he was busy reorganizing his remaining forces in Henan province), the nationalist army's offensive turned to a new, even more formidable target – Sun Chuanfang. His was the main force in central China and he held the provinces of Fujian, Jiangxi, Anhui, Zhejiang and Jiangsu. Sun Chuanfang had watched Wu Peifu's defeats but had not got involved. Chiang Kai-shek had orchestrated this by repeatedly assuring him that the Northern Expedition was directed against Wu Peifu alone. But once victory was achieved in Hubei, Chiang turned all available forces against him without delay or hesitation. After two months of hard fighting, Jiangxi province was conquered. At the same time, Guomindang troops stationed in eastern Guangdong province and commanded by He Yingqin went on the offensive against Fujian province. Its capital, Fuzhou, fell on 9 December. Then Sun Chuanfang's troops were driven out of Zhejiang province (January–February 1927). Substantially helped by the defection of Chen Tiaoyuan, the conquest of southern Anhui in February–March opened up the road to Shanghai. When the vanguard of the Northern Expedition troops entered on 22 March 1927, the workers' unions were holding the city following the insurrectionary strike they had called the day before.

Up to that point, the successes of the Northern Expedition could be explained as much by the qualities of the Guomindang army as by the fact that it had been able to divide its opponents. Above all, they quickly became past masters at approaching and convincing enemy generals to betray and turn against their commander. Every means was used to achieve this result: cash, of course, and promises of promotion, but also personal ties and common regional origins. Donald Jordan astutely observes that it was often military leaders from the south of the country who betrayed Wu Peifu and Sun Chuanfang. They retained command of their forces, which were incorporated, unmodified, into the Guomindang army.

However, as early as November 1926, an agreement was reached between Zhang Zuolin, who felt that a new wind was blowing, and Sun Chuanfang (their alliance took the name of *Anguojun* 安國軍: National Pacification Army). Of course, it did not take shape immediately, and there were still many second thoughts between the allies. The fact remained that the Guomindang, instead of facing their opponents one by one, now had to confront an alliance.

Wars between cliques of warlords were operations combining political manoeuvres and purely military operations, and the populations remained spectators. The Northern Expedition differed in that it was also a political operation in which the Guomindang mobilized the active forces of society for their own benefit. For a long time, acts of sabotage and the support of the workers' unions were given undue importance in explaining its military successes. It is true that the action of the railway workers, who by various means blocked the transport of material and troops in the territories held by Wu Peifu, represented very useful assistance, for example. However, Donald Jordan's detailed analysis concludes that, on balance, the assistance thus provided was not a decisive factor. It is nevertheless true that the advance of the nationalist armies was accompanied by propaganda work and the mobilization of the population through the formation of trade unions and peasant unions.

On the other hand, what the Northern Expedition had in common with military operations between warlords was that the fighting was at least as important as the skilful manoeuvring in persuading the officers of the enemy forces to defect. There was, however, one significant difference – the one-sided nature of the defections. The Guomindang could count on the loyalty of their generals.

More generally, the Guomindang also benefitted greatly from the resentment caused by the domination of two northerners (Wu Peifu and Sun Chuanfang) over southern provinces.

The first part of the expedition gave rise to disputes with foreign powers concerned with protecting their interests and worried about the clearly anti-imperialist slogans. But, at this stage, they did not take on significant proportions, and remained localized clashes (even if in Nanjing, in March 1927, several foreigners were killed and gunboats deployed). Thanks to their careful and moderate handling of these incidents, the Guomindang achieved the desired result: the foreign powers stayed neutral.

Phase 2: the time of divisions

The Guomindang took great advantage of the divisions amongst their enemies in the first phase of the Northern Expedition. But soon, in their turn, they were weakened by serious and lasting dissension. There were two main bones of contention within the Guomindang. Firstly, Chiang Kai-shek's military successes increased his political clout and that of his supporters, which caused much resentment. Secondly, there was growing hostility to United Front policy from a broad right wing.

In January 1927, the Guomindang government had left Guangzhou, which was now too remotely located, and moved 800 kilometres farther north to Wuhan. The Wuhan authorities were dominated by the CCP and by the left wing of the Guomindang (Xu Qian and Deng Yanda), who took revenge for the serious blow inflicted on them by Chiang Kai-shek in March 1926. A leftist wind blew through the city of Wuhan, where strikes, meetings, parades and demonstrations occurred one after another. It was also the only time in the Guomindang's history when militant feminism took centre stage and real advances were made: the first female county chief took office in Hunan. Borodin and the left wing of the Guomindang had a common goal: the political elimination of Chiang. And over the following months, the Wuhan authorities increased the number of decisions designed to undermine Chiang Kai-shek's power. The latter was then based in Nanchang to coordinate the main military operations in the lower Yangtze region. Increasingly concerned about the growing influence of the communists in Wuhan, the right wing of the Guomindang joined him. Chiang was also able to enlist the support of Shanghai's business community, which was concerned about the rapid progress of communist activism among the city's workers. The good offices of two of the largest bankers in the area, Zhang Jia'ao and Chen Guangfu, gave him access to considerable financial resources.[44]

Exchanges quickly became heated between Wuhan and Nanchang, which anathematized each other while trying to attract the undecideds to their camp. These internal conflicts had a detrimental effect on the funding and logistics of the troops. The consequences on the front were serious: in April 1927, the North recaptured much of the ground it had lost on the left bank of the Yangtze River in Jiangsu and Anhui provinces over the previous weeks. The Guomindang armies crossed the Yangtze River again and were put on the defensive.

The rift between Chiang Kai-shek and the left of the party became even more pronounced when Chiang decided to put an abrupt end to the United Front with the Shanghai coup. On 12 and 13 April 1927, Chiang Kai-shek's troops, with the help of the Green Gang (*qingbang* 青幫) gangsters under the orders of Du Yuesheng and with the complicity of the Western powers, proceeded to disarm and massacre communist militants and trade unionists.[45] A period of mass violence spread throughout the areas controlled by Chiang and his supporters in the following days. The ruthless hunt for communists lasted all summer. Being a committed follower, or even just suspected of sympathy for the communist cause, led to execution. At least 40,000 people were killed, including Li Dazhao, one of the main communist leaders. The CCP membership, which had been around 60,000 before April 1927, fell to 10,000 in a few months, due to executions and defections. The massive purge caused a haemorrhaging within the Guomindang of young members who had joined in previous years and who often leaned to the left, as well as members from amongst the workers and peasants.

In the days following the Shanghai coup, Chiang Kai-shek formed a government in Nanjing. Wuhan retaliated by barring him from the Guomindang. Although it was now headed by Wang Jingwei, Chiang's main rival, who had returned from abroad, the Wuhan government only held three provinces (Hubei, Hunan, Jiangxi) in its ambit. Furthermore, unlike Chiang Kai-shek, who enjoyed the financial support of the Shanghai business community, the Wuhan regime's financial base was very fragile. This weakness cost them Feng Yuxiang's alliance. The latter, helped for years by the Soviets, should logically have rallied to Wuhan. Weary after raising the stakes – a process in which he excelled – Feng opted for Nanjing, which guaranteed him more substantial financial aid, on 21 June.

In the areas under its control, the Wuhan government also had to deal with the excesses of the peasant movement. Incited by communist militants, peasant unions were particularly developed in Hunan and Hubei. Their actions rapidly became more radical. The unions attacked the homes of landowners, seizing their land and property and redistributing it to poor peasants. The traditional dignitaries were quick to react and raise militias, which further increased the violence. Although they tried to contain the excesses of the peasant unions, the communists were increasingly distrusted. Many of the leaders (foremost among them Wang Jingwei) were also aware that the CCP, a useful ally at that point, was nevertheless a potential rival. This situation displeased the officers, many of whom came from the landowning class. In the months that followed, Wuhan's main military supporters withdrew, one after the other. In an attempt to stem the losses and retain the support of the few military leaders still attached to their cause, the leaders of the Wuhan government decided to break with the communists (July).

Taking advantage of this schism between Wuhan and Nanjing, the Northerners rallied and took the initiative again: the city of Xuzhou fell into their hands on 25 July. This was the moment Chiang Kai-shek chose to announce (on 13 August) that he was leaving office. Making a show of complete disinterestedness, he said he was leaving in the hope of restoring unity. However, at the age of 40, he had no intention of giving up his ambitions. Taking a calculated risk, his aim was, on the contrary, to demonstrate that, without him, chaos and defeat were certain, and so to prepare for his return with a strengthened position.

Confusion reigned in the weeks that followed. Militarily, the army was near to being routed and the military commanders had the greatest difficulty in repelling an audacious counter-attack by Sun Chuanfang, who had crossed the Yangtze and threatened Nanjing (Battle of Longtan, 26–31 August). Politically, they had reached deadlock. At the very moment when general negotiations intended to put an end to the schism finally began, Wang Jingwei discredited himself by endorsing a surprise attack by his supporters (Zhang Fakui) on Guangdong province on 17 November. This low blow provoked such general indignation that Wang had no choice but to go back into exile. Without its leader, the days of the Wuhan government were numbered.

Chiang Kai-shek, whose supporters were busy preparing his return, took advantage of this period to enhance his political stature by making a trip to Japan, where he was accorded the respect due to a head of state. By December, the situation was ripe and Chiang was recalled. He returned to his duties, furthermore, in the position of arbitrator and peacemaker. The only survivor of the 'Wuhan spirit' was a group of people in favour of a middle way between the CCP and the Guomindang. Led by Deng Yanda, it was the origin of the Third Party (*disan dang* 第三黨), which was to grow somewhat in the years following its creation in December 1927. Deng's arrest and subsequent elimination in August 1931 dealt it a fatal blow. The search for a third way was to remain a recurrent feature, until the communists' final victory. But attempts to launch a political organization capable of providing a consistent alternative to the Guomindang and the CCP would fail, time after time.

Phase 3: Zhang Zuolin's defeat

The third phase of the Northern Expedition began on 7 April 1928. Talks had been going well in the preceding months. They were productive for the Guomindang, which not only confirmed their alliance with Feng Yuxiang but also secured the important cooperation of Yan Xishan (the master of Shanxi). Zhang Zuolin was now isolated, against this coalition.[46] He could count on the single, rather mediocre support of the remnants of Sun Chuanfang's armies, which aligned themselves under his banner.

In the spring of 1928, the Guomindang's armed force was utterly unlike the 100,000-strong expeditionary force to which it had been reduced in July 1926. Their ranks were swollen not so much by the raising of new recruits as by the incorporation of enemy troops whose generals changed sides as Phase I progressed. In February 1928, with their two allies, Feng Yuxiang and Yan Xishan (each bringing 100,000 men), Nanjing's forces reached 1 million.

Shandong was conquered in a single month (April). Thanks to sufficient coordination, the Guomindang and their allies overcame the bulk of the enemy troops (half a million well-equipped soldiers) in just a few weeks, on the northern plains. Although Zhang died on 4 June, his generals fought on. On 8 June 1928, Yan Xishan's troops entered Beijing. A month later, the fall of Tianjin marked the end of operations.

This third phase of the Northern Expedition was, like the first, characterized by large-scale offensives. But after the Guomindang broke with their former ally, the CCP, and made a strong move to the right, the strategy of stirring up popular movements to make use of them had ceased to be employed. Furthermore, the victories won no longer owed anything to the defection of enemy officers. These were not now needed, because the Guomindang had greater military strength than their opponent. On the other hand, the mechanisms of regional solidarity that allowed the temporary assignment of generals from the South were no longer in play, as the Guomindang forces were now confronting Northerners.

As mentioned, major clashes with foreign powers had been avoided, albeit with some difficulty, during the first phase of the Northern Expedition. Although Tanaka's Japanese government was concerned about the Guomindang's advance into North China, which brought it closer to Manchuria – Japan's main area of influence – it was determined to use only diplomatic means. The presence of many Japanese residents and of troops to protect them made Shandong fertile ground for an incident. It finally happened on 3 May 1928, when nationalist troops invaded Jinan, the capital of Shandong, only just abandoned by the Northerners. The situation quickly escalated. In the following days, the Japanese forces received reinforcements and attacked the Chinese forces. More than 3,000 people were killed in the fighting, mainly from the ranks of the Chinese. The main lesson to be drawn from the Jinan incident was that it revealed the inability of the Japanese civilian authorities to impose de-escalation on the military forces on the ground and even on the general staff in Tokyo. This tendency was to continue and would have serious consequences. For the time being, the flashpoint in Jinan had been contained, but its memory remained. It was partially responsible for preventing a rapprochement between the new Chiang Kai-shek government and Japan, which was still a possibility in the late 1920s.

Zhang Zuolin was, of all the leading militarists, the one who came closest to the aspiration of reunifying the country for his own ends. His death therefore had a symbolic impact, marking the end of the era of the warlords. His assassination also had another significance. Japanese diplomacy was not determined to obstruct Guomindang reunification of the country at all costs. The Japanese resolved to make the preservation of their interests in Manchuria the cornerstone of their diplomatic approach to the Guomindang. Their aim was to keep Manchuria safe from invasion, especially if it was followed by a reunification of China under the Guomindang. They managed to convince Zhang Zuolin to withdraw to Manchuria, having obtained a guarantee from the Guomindang that they would not try to dislodge him. This was an accommodation that

6 Zhang Zuolin circa 1924.

was acceptable to everyone (even if Zhang did not willingly give up his ambitions to expand southwards). His assassination on 4 June 1928 was carried out by officers in the Guandong Army (*Kantōgun* 関東軍).[47] This was the name given to the Japanese forces occupying the eponymous territory (ceded by China to Japan in 1905), who were also responsible for protecting the rail tracks of the South Manchurian Railway Company. Their aim in removing Zhang was apparently to stir up unrest that could lead to their taking direct control of Manchuria.[48] This assassination heralded many similar actions by officers of the Japanese forces, on their own initiative. These initiatives were almost always ratified after the fact by Tokyo, where the influence of the Foreign Ministry on foreign policy became increasingly weak in the 1930s. Japan's policy towards China was now dependent on ultra-nationalist hotheads who would proliferate power plays for narrowly local issues, or even just to further their careers.

Although far from a military walk in the park, the Northern Expedition, like all civil wars since the fall of the empire, did not represent a demographic bloodletting. Nor did it cause widespread destruction, although locally, as in Wuhan, damage could be significant. Its consequences are not comparable to those caused by the gigantic revolts of 1850–65, or, as we shall see, by the operations associated with the Second World War.

Beyond the symbolic, the capture of the capital, Beijing, the former centre of gravity of the Beiyang power, led to the recognition of the Guomindang government as the Chinese representatives on the international stage. A few months later, on 29 December 1928, Zhang Xueliang, Zhang Zuolin's son and successor in Manchuria, declared his allegiance to the Nanjing government after months of prevarication and negotiations.[49] To all appearances, the triumph of the Northern Expedition was complete.

This was, of course, a major military and political success for the Guomindang. The comparison with what they had been only two years earlier is more than flattering. However, the Northern Expedition contained the seeds of the serious weaknesses that would undermine the future Nanjing government. In this way, at the end of 1928, behind a facade of unity, the Nanjing government only really had control over the three provinces of the Lower Yangtze valley: Jiangsu, Zhejiang and Anhui. Its two main allies since the beginning of the Northern Expedition had greatly expanded their influence: the new Guangxi clique controlled not only its home province, but also Hunan and Hubei. And Feng Yuxiang ruled over the provinces of Shaanxi, Henan and Shandong. Yan Xishan had a firm grip on his traditional stronghold (Shanxi) and the Beijing–Tianjin region. Finally, Manchuria remained Zhang Xueliang's bastion. They all retained most of their autonomy through a formal recognition of allegiance.

7 Chiang Kai-shek (middle) and the two main warlords allied to the Guomindang in the final phase of the Northern Expedition – Feng Yuxiang (left) and Yan Xishan (right).

THREE

The Nanjing Decade (1928–1937)

The Nanjing decade lasted from the end of the Northern Expedition to the outbreak of the Sino-Japanese War. The period takes its name from the capital chosen by the new regime, a choice that reflected the desire for a fresh start politically.

Nanjing was primarily a rejection of Beijing. The Guomindang could have had two capitals like some of the dynasties. But the wish to conspicuously strip Beijing of its capital status is clear. This is also reflected in the change of name. In June 1928, it was no longer Beijing, the 'capital of the North', but Beiping, the 'peace of the North'. At the same time, the province in which it is located, Zhili (meaning 'the metropolitan province', reflecting the fact that it was directly under the central administration), was renamed Hebei (a purely geographical term). We saw how much keeping the government of the young Republic in Beijing at the beginning of 1912 represented a setback for the revolutionary camp. And in 1928, Beijing embodied not only the fallen dynasty, but also the Beiyang governments led by the large cliques of warlords, who were anathema to the Guomindang. So, for the Guomindang, taking Nanjing as their capital was to repudiate any continuity with the central power of the early years of the Republic. Furthermore, Nanjing was the opportunity for the new regime to give substance to its project for political renewal, by developing its capital in stone, tarmac and concrete. In terms of urban planning, Nanjing was a blank page. Almost razed to the ground following the repression of the Taiping rebellion, the city had only been partially rebuilt. As a result, very large areas were available for construction.

The choice of Nanjing also ensured firmer control of the Lower Yangtze River valley, the economic centre of gravity of China, whose importance had been further reinforced by the spectacular development of Shanghai since 1842. Finally, it also expressed an evolution within the Guomindang. The victors of the Northern Expedition were generally men from the south. But if the Guomindang veterans from the heroic days of the United League were mostly of Cantonese origin (Hu Hanmin, Wang Jingwei, Gu Yingfen, Zou Lu), this was not the case for the young guard of thirty-somethings who emerged from the mid-1920s onwards. Both the civilians (Song Ziwen, Zhu Jiahua, Chen Guofu and his brother Chen Lifu) and soldiers (Qian Dajun and Chen Cheng) in this new generation of politicians, like Chiang Kai-shek himself, were largely from Zhejiang and Jiangsu.

Unquestionably, the Guomindang established themselves as the main actor during the Nanjing decade. They would try to take advantage of the relative peace to implement their programme of modernization and centralization. But the calm that had set in should not be exaggerated: the Guomindang never really had a free hand. Up until 1931–2, the warlords were the main menace they faced, while over the subsequent five years the threat from Japan became more and more pressing.

1928–1932: troublesome former allies

The unrest and revolts that followed, from 1928 until early 1932, should be interpreted as a series of aftershocks from the major political earthquake created by the Northern Expedition. Indeed, it completely redealt the cards in two senses. Firstly, it put the Guomindang, a previously very marginal political force, at the centre of the political arena. At the same time, the balance within the party itself was upset, with the rise of the military element and its main manifestation – the affirmation of Chiang Kai-shek's leadership.

Chiang's control of the Guomindang in 1928 should not be exaggerated, however. He had to deal with rival forces throughout the Nanjing decade. The early years of the Nanjing government were based on a modus vivendi between Hu Hanmin and Chiang, which was more of a non-aggression pact than an enthusiastic collaboration. The other great historical leader of the Guomindang, Wang Jingwei, remained in the background, looking for an opportunity to return to the forefront and even to supplant Chiang.

Historians are yet to pay Hu Hanmin the attention he deserves. Endowed with an acute intelligence and formidable stamina for work, a fine scholar (he was notably a remarkable calligrapher), he had proved himself as a statesman when governing Guangdong from 1912 to 1913. The main figure on the Guomindang's right wing in the early 1920s, he was excluded from succeeding Sun Yat-sen in 1925 because of his probable involvement in the assassination of his rival Liao Zhongkai. Although he returned to the political scene at the end of the Northern Expedition, he remained relatively isolated. This situation, which considerably undermined his political influence, is partly explained by his personality. Many people suffered as they bore the brunt of his biting sarcasm. More generally, Hu Hanmin displayed the extreme coolness that often accompanies too much intellectual superiority.

The government formed in October 1928 gave significant positions to two of the main warlords allied to the Guomindang: Feng Yuxiang (vice president of the Executive Yuan and Minister of the Army) and Yan Xishan (Minister of the Interior). But the first tensions between Chiang and his allies at the end of the Northern Expedition arose immediately,

8 Hu Hanmin in Paris on 27 April 1928.

74

over the reorganization of the military, which was overstaffed and costly to maintain. Not without cause, the warlords who had rallied to the Guomindang saw in the demobilization conference organized in January 1929 a predictable manoeuvre on the part of Chiang Kai-shek, who intended the demobilizations to apply to all military forces except his own. The conference ended in failure, heralding the revolts that were to follow between the beginning of 1929 and the end of 1930. The warlords became aware of the risk that the Nanjing government would succeed in eliminating them and establishing a total hegemony.

Operations began with the revolt of the Guomindang's two oldest allies: first that of the new clique in Guangxi (March–April), then that of Feng Yuxiang (May). These two uncoordinated revolts did not really endanger Chiang, who made them see reason quite easily. The Central Plains War (*zhongyuan dazhan* 中原大戰), as it is called, was a far more serious matter. It pitted Chiang's troops against a broad coalition of warlords.[1] It involved 1.4 million soldiers, and more than 400,000 of them were put out of action (dead or wounded). This ruinous and deadly war lasted from May to October 1930. Yan Xishan and Feng Yuxiang (who obtained an alliance with the new Guangxi clique in the south, which in turn attacked Hunan) matched Chiang Kai-shek's forces. Worse still, these allies were active on the political scene and reached out to the malcontents in the Guomindang. In the summer of 1930, a government was founded in Beijing which included Wang Jingwei among its members. This government was quick to claim the heritage of the Guomindang, and to use Sun-Yatsenian rhetoric to denounce the dictatorship of Chiang Kai-shek.

It seemed quite clear, in these conditions, that the last heavyweight not to have thrown himself into the fray, Zhang Xueliang, could act as referee. Aware of this, Chiang Kai-shek made it his priority to grant him a huge sum of money. In a sacrifice for the greater good, he even agreed to relinquish de facto control of the Beijing and Tianjin region to him. The allies surrendered in October 1930. The Guangxi clique and Yan Xishan were weakened, but not out of the game. In fact, they were able to count on rear bases in Guangxi and Shanxi that were difficult to access and that had been consolidated by their dominance there for many years. The same could not be said for Feng Yuxiang, who, once his military forces had been wiped out, disappeared from the political stage.[2]

The last major crisis of the period 1928–32 sprang from a controversy within the Guomindang over whether to adopt a provisional constitution (*yuefa* 約法). This controversy ended the alliance between Chiang and Hu Hanmin that had been formed in 1928. Chiang was in favour, while Hu Hanmin, who saw himself as the repository of Sun's intellectual legacy, was strongly opposed. This was, of course, a clash between two rival ambitions, as Hu never accepted Chiang Kai-shek's pre-eminence. But this was anything but a trivial dispute since it concerned the promulgation of an interim constitution. According to Sun Yat-sen's ideas, China was in the transitional phase known as 'political tutelage', the aim of which was to teach the people to exercise their suffrage. The drafting of a constitution should take place later, once the representatives of the people had been elected. It touched on a crucial issue, namely the role of the party. Hu wanted to defend the Guomindang (where he retained his main supporters) and refused to see their role disappear: this provisional constitution seemed to him to be an artifice intended to hasten the end of the political tutelage phase. Chiang, whose hold on the party remained relatively weak, tried hard to play down his role.

Chiang chose to settle the disagreement by intimidation and had Hu Hanmin placed under house arrest (28 February 1931), a decision that had a very explosive effect. In the months that followed, Chiang's political opponents organized themselves. A dissident government was set up in May 1931 in Guangzhou. The importance of the political figures who composed it gave it a certain political weight. A fairly substantial group of respected figures assembled behind Sun Ke, Sun Yat-sen's own son, and (again) Wang Jingwei, including Gu Yingfen and Tang Shaoyi, as well as two leading Guomindang diplomats, Chen Youren and Wu Chaoshu. It was no mere chance that this rebellion chose to establish its government with Guangzhou as its capital. We have already noted that a split had appeared within the Guomindang between the older members, among whom the Cantonese were notoriously over-represented, and what we might call the 'new guard', often from Jiangsu and Zhejiang. Well, the 1931 revolt undeniably had a strong Cantonese accent. Its driving force was made up of Guomindang veterans unhappy with their marginalization following the rise of Chiang Kai-shek. What made it more worrying was that it relied not only on the considerable military resources of General Chen Jitang in Guangzhou itself, but also on Cantonese forces stationed in other parts of the country.[3] Moreover, the Guangzhou government not only denounced and inveighed against Chiang, but also actively sought alliances. Having secured one with the new Guangxi clique, it tried to link up with those defeated in the Central Plains War. Military operations began on 13 September 1931 with the entry of Cantonese troops into Hunan.[4] Their objective was to dislodge Chiang Kai-shek by force. However, two factors soon averted the threat of a full-scale civil war and led to an accommodation: Japan's assault on Manchuria (September 1931), which was soon followed by the Battle of Shanghai (28 January to 5 May 1932), and the manifest impossibility of the Cantonese setting up a credible government without Chiang. The latter, as on several previous occasions in times of crisis, seemingly withdrew from the political scene, on 15 December. The attempt to form a government around Sun Ke fizzled out. Chiang Kai-shek quickly made his return at the end of January 1932.

The period of stabilization: 1932–1935

If there is a golden age during the Republic, it is these three years without large-scale military operations. Indeed, during this period, Nanjing's struggle to curb the local potentates took a more discreet turn and a different route. The period of open revolt was over. The single exception was Fujian. The 19th Route Army, which distinguished itself in the Battle of Shanghai in early 1932, as will be seen later, had quickly secured control of Fujian province where it had been garrisoned. Its leaders (the main figures were Cai Tingkai, Li Jishen and Chen Mingshu) rose in revolt in November 1933. They adopted a clearly left-wing programme and called for the joining of forces hostile to Nanjing. However, the rebels committed many political blunders, such as openly questioning the quasi-divine status of Sun Yat-sen. As they failed to win allies, their revolt was easily contained by January 1934.[5]

The regime resisted the various blows of 1928–31 by relying on its geographical base: the lower valley of the Yangtze River, an area that it controlled closely, from which it drew most of its fiscal resources and which also offered the advantage of a central position. But the regime also had a social foundation. The thesis of Marxist historiography, which saw the Guomindang as the defender of the interests of the big entrepreneurs and capitalists against the proletariat, does not stand up to examination of the facts. Although the Guomindang found their support primarily among the urban middle classes, it was faithful to Sun's political project in which the revolution should not espouse the interests of one class at the expense of others. Its only declared enemies were the imperialists and the warlords (together with the communists after 1927).[6] Certainly, the March 1927 coup and the break with the CCP brought the Guomindang closer to the Chinese bourgeoisie. However, the latter became disillusioned in the following years when the Guomindang began to restrict the autonomy and room for manoeuvre of the organizations it dominated. Rather than an alliance, we should therefore speak of cohabitation between the bourgeoisie and the Guomindang. Industrial circles and governmental spheres intermingled, as in the case of one of the main entrepreneurs of the period, Liu Hongsheng, who took on political responsibilities to ensure the preservation of his private interests.

In early 1932, the warmongering option, embodied by the nonentity Sun Ke, did not survive the fall of his cabinet. A new equilibrium was needed, based on a more pragmatic approach to Japan and the alliance between Chiang Kai-shek and Wang Jingwei. The two men managed to reach a sustainable agreement because they shared the same conviction that the time had not come to confront Japan in open warfare: China was still too weak. They differed on how to remedy the situation. Chiang favoured building a strong military force, while Wang saw building a sufficiently solid economic and industrial base as the essential requirement for vying with the enemy. While there was inevitably competition for the allocation of scarce fiscal resources to different goals, the two policies were by no means irreconcilable.[7] During these years, Chiang Kai-shek remained the dominant figure in the government. He focused on strengthening the army and building a powerful war industry. Wang Jingwei, on the other hand, held the position of president of the Executive Yuan (equivalent to that of prime minister), except for a few months between October 1932 and March 1933. Wang concentrated on diplomacy and the economy. He was the architect behind the policy of compromise with Japan. During these years, he allied himself with Song Ziwen, Chiang's brother-in-law, who enjoyed powerful support amongst Shanghai's banking and upper-middle-class circles. One of the most significant products of this alliance was the Cotton Control Commission, which was created in 1933. This body was intended to improve the entire cotton chain, from the production of raw material to the textile industry, to compete with foreign (especially Japanese) competition.[8]

The alliance between Chiang and Wang lasted, with many difficult periods, until 1 November 1935. On that day, an attempt was made on Wang's life, apparently at the instigation of a coterie of warmongers connected with the 19th Route Army. Seriously injured, Wang resigned from his various positions in December to go to Europe for treatment.[9] However, the strategy of appeasement, although based on a clear grasp of the state of the military forces, came up against a growing unpopularity, including within the Guomindang, as illustrated for example by the resignation of Song Ziwen from all his governmental responsibilities on 25 October 1933. A hardliner in the face of Japan's increasingly blatant encroachments, he had been the initiator of a much more protectionist customs tariff that had provoked Tokyo's ire.[10]

In the ranks of the Guomindang as well as public opinion, opposition was also about the autocratic nature of power. Yet, although he benefitted greatly in political terms from the Northern Expedition, Chiang's power remained precarious. Despite managing to become part of one of the most powerful families in the country, the Song, through his marriage to Song Meiling in December 1927 (see Appendix 4), his in-laws planned to use him as much as he used them. The same was true of the powerful Green Gang, the secret society that had liquidated the Shanghai communists in 1927. For Chiang Kai-shek, it was more of a troublesome ally than a docile auxiliary. Chiang was a very difficult character, and the circle of his closest friends did not include political heavyweights, but those like Dai Jitao (whose son, Jiang Weiguo, he adopted), Dong Xiangguang, Huang Fu and Zhang Qun. He could also count on the unconditional support of the so-called Huangpu clique: a group of officers who trained at the Huangpu Academy when he was its director and with whom he maintained a master–disciple relationship.

Within the Guomindang, he had to deal with factions such as that led by Wang Jingwei. Behind the facade of a single-party state, the reality of the political scene in the Nanjing decade was largely one of muted but incessant struggles between cliques (see Chapter 7). Things were even more complex because of the entwined interpersonal relationships and family networks (see Appendix 4), not to mention the links

9 Sun Ke (Sun Yat-sen's son) and his wife in Paris on 27 April 1928.

created by common regional origins. To maintain control and remain the strongman of the regime, Chiang was forced to perform a balancing act between several competing groups.

The organization of the secret services during the Nanjing decade is a telling illustration of Chiang Kai-shek's strategy. He tried both relying on personal ties and provoking competition between different organizations so as to consolidate his power. From the end of the 1920s, the intelligence organization was characterized by intense rivalry between different services. That did not change over the following years. In 1938, the division into two organizations was formalized, one of which had authority in matters of military intelligence, and the other in civilian. The *Juntong* 軍統 (abbreviation of *Junshi weiyuanhui diaocha tongji ju* 軍事委員會調查統計局 – Investigation and Statistics Bureau of the Military Affairs Committee) was under the authority of Dai Li, and the

Zhongtong 中統 (short for *Guomindang zhongyang dangbu diaocha tongji ju* 國民黨中央黨部調查統計局 – Investigation and Statistics Bureau of the Guomindang Central Committee), was controlled by the brothers Chen Lifu and Chen Guofu.[11] In reality, there was perpetual rivalry between the *Juntong* and the *Zhongtong*.

The Guomindang's achievements

However, the internal divisions did not paralyse the Guomindang, which must be credited with important achievements during these ten years.

Its diplomats, most of whom were already in place in the Beiyang governments, made significant progress in abolishing the unequal treaties. Between 1927 and 1931, they negotiated the restitution by the United Kingdom of its leasehold territory of Weihaiwei (treaty of 18 April 1930), and of its concessions in Hankou, Jiujiang, Jinjiang and Xiamen, not to mention the return of the Tianjin concession by the Belgian government.[12] The de facto takeover of the administration of the Post Office, for which the Washington Treaty had mandated co-management with the foreign powers, was another notable advance. The Salt Tax Administration and the Maritime Customs, two institutions that had been under foreign control as guarantees for the repayment of Boxer compensation, came under the control of the Ministry of Finance in 1927–8. The Nanjing government also obtained the restoration of customs autonomy. A new customs tariff was introduced in February 1929, followed by a second one in May 1933, which set particularly high tariffs for those goods competing most with Chinese production.[13]

On another front, Chinese diplomats defended tooth and nail the (highly questionable) idea that the borders of China as a nation-state should coincide with those of the multi-ethnic Qing Empire. For example, they got the international community to recognize the 'indisputable' nature of Manchuria's affiliation with China.[14] They were able to play on the threat of Tokyo's hegemony over the Far East, which worried the Western powers and encouraged them to take up China's cause. It can be said more broadly that, throughout the time of the Republic, China excelled in turning its relative weakness into strength. With great skill, it managed to present itself as an atavistically peaceful country.

This was the period when the Great Wall was put forward as the symbol of an essentially defensive state.[15] Sun Yat-sen had already set the tone on 5 January 1912, in a manifesto addressed to foreign powers: 'We, the Chinese people, peaceful and law-abiding, have never waged war except in self-defence.' The multi-centennial expansion of the Chinese Empire is portrayed as the result of a kind of miraculous and benign cultural subjugation, to which the force of arms remained alien.

The New Policies reforms had run up against the need to increase tax revenues. In this respect, the Guomindang obtained significant results: tax revenues more than doubled during the decade (870 million in 1937 against 334 million in 1929).

This (comparative) windfall strengthened the regime's base and was one of the reasons why it was able to successfully negotiate the consolidation of public debt. Moreover, the debt was now underwritten first and foremost on the Chinese market, a strategic choice which had mixed effects. Unlike borrowing from foreign banking consortia, it was a guarantee of independence. However, in the context of a credit market characterized by a shortage of available capital, it ran the risk of making access to credit much more expensive and thus hampering investment (see Chapter 6). However, the advances in taxation made during the Nanjing decade had their limits. Furthermore, taxes were an excessive burden on the modern sector of the economy. In a country still dominated by the enormous preponderance of countryside, the overhaul of the land tax was an indispensable step in establishing the regime fiscally. However, this was a daunting task which would involve, among other things, dispossessing the local administrations of their control and a large share of the benefit, and reconstituting a land register. At a very early stage, Nanjing renounced this and decided to leave the collection and benefit of this tax to the provinces and districts. Furthermore, the development of direct taxation (on income, but also, for example, on inheritance and property), planned since the beginning of the 1930s, was slow to materialize despite the creation of a Direct Taxation Office (*Zhijieshui shu* 直接稅署). This office was still a fledgling structure. The war with Japan meant it would remain so.[16] If, despite notable advances, Nanjing never really had the means to fulfil its ambitions, it was largely due to its inability to generate sufficient fiscal revenues. State expenditure, even considering the regional administration levels, never exceeded 6 per cent of domestic product in the period 1931–6, whereas, for example, this indicator reached 14.3 per cent in the United States in 1933.

Other crucial action fronts for the Guomindang were monetary and banking systems, which were completely reorganized. In 1935, the government, using the good offices of the gangster Du Yuesheng, took over the country's main banks (including the Bank of China, *Zhongguo yinhang* 中國銀行, and the Bank of Communications, *Jiaotong yinhang* 交通銀行).[17] At the end of the same year, Du managed to create a fiat currency, the *fabi* 法幣, whose issuing monopoly was entrusted to four government-controlled banks. It was a great success. The delicate operation of getting private banks to surrender their silver reserves in exchange for denominations of the new currency was carried out with great adroitness.[18] This reform had many advantages: it put an end to the fragmentation of the money supply which, under the influence of the warlords, had reached a critical point in the 1920s, when almost thirty different currencies were able to coexist.[19] The sharp rise in world silver prices had led to massive silver exports and a pronounced deflation in which the economy had been trapped since 1932–3. The government thus provided itself with the means to curb this deflation (and ultimately to bring an end to the crisis) by issuing money.

Taken together, the banking and monetary sector reforms greatly increased the government's ability to intervene in the economic sphere. The group of large private bankers in Shanghai, who had previously maintained a strong political influence by cultivating relations within certain government circles, no longer cast its shadow.

Infrastructure was another area of major achievements. The inauguration of the Guangzhou–Hankou line in 1936 completed a veritable backbone of railway linking Beijing to Guangzhou via Zhengzhou, Wuhan and Changsha. The opening up of the north-west made decisive progress thanks to the opening of a radial line which reached Xi'an at the end of 1934. The length of the network, which had attained almost 13,000 kilometres in 1924, was of the order of 20,000 kilometres in 1937 (but 40 per cent was concentrated in Manchuria).

We have only touched on some of the main aspects here of the work accomplished, which had a true coherence because it advanced a long-term project: the centralization and, in the long run, the strengthening of Chinese power. It was also lasting: many of the reforms would leave an enduring mark, such as the astute law of July 1928 which managed to impose the metric system as the national frame of reference by, among other things, redefining certain traditional units so that they fell neatly within the metric system. For example, one pound (*jin* 斤) was equivalent to 500 grams, as is still the case today. This was a decisive step towards a much needed unification and rationalization of weights and measures.[20]

While all these achievements are to the credit of the Guomindang, it should be noted that some of them had been under preparation since the New Policies period, and under the Beiyang regimes. The best example was the reworking of the law, which will be discussed in Chapter 7. But the development of the system of phonetic transcription and romanization that the Guomindang implemented from 1928 onwards was also the product of efforts pursued by the Beijing governments from the beginning of the Republic.

The looming Japanese threat

Japanese imperialism was clearly the most serious threat to the Nanjing government from the early 1930s onwards. In Tokyo, times had clearly moved on since the democratic Taishō period, set in motion in 1912. Ultra-nationalist military circles presented expansionism in Manchuria as the only possible way out of the economic crisis that was hitting the country. However, if the case for expansionism towards Manchuria and then North China had been developed, its implementation did not follow from any pre-established plan. Improvisation ruled the day and military forces on the ground held the initiative. In fact, the main drive behind Japanese expansionism in China was the Guandong Army. After the assassination of Zhang Zuolin in 1928, its officers took the initiative in various surprise attacks from 1931 to 1937. The general staff and the government in Tokyo, who were much more cautious, only lent their support and ratified actions after the fact.

The Japanese threat materialized in September 1931. The Guandong Army staff organized a mock attack on the South Manchurian railway on 18 September 1931 (the Mukden incident) and accused 'Chinese bandits' of being responsible. In the weeks that followed, the Guandong

Army forces advanced southwards, easily repelling the mediocre troops of warlord Zhang Xueliang who stood in their path.

The conflict took an even more dramatic turn when it spread to Shanghai. As China's main industrial centre, Shanghai was home to major Japanese economic interests, including spinning mills that employed almost 60,000 Chinese. There were 20,000 Japanese nationals in the city. Many Japanese navy ships, jealous of the success of the army in Manchuria, were at anchor there. It had also been a hotbed of anti-Japanese activism since the start of operations in Manchuria. Shanghai was the epicentre of a major boycott of Japanese products launched in July 1931 in response to the massacre of Chinese nationals in Korea, which was further reinforced by the start of military operations in Manchuria. Inevitably, agitators on both sides of the issue found this fertile territory. The Japanese navy added fuel to the fire by issuing an ultimatum to the mayor, Wu Tiecheng, demanding he condemn anti-Japanese movements. Following instructions to compromise, Wu complied. But it was becoming clear that Japan was seeking military escalation and had no hesitation in stirring up incidents to achieve this. On 28 January 1932, large Japanese marine infantry forces went on the offensive in the northern suburbs of the city. Just when they thought they could achieve a quick victory, they hit a snag. The three divisions of the 19th Route Army responsible for defending the sector put up a fierce resistance. It was a mini-Stalingrad for the Japanese troops. The urban setting and the determination of the Chinese defenders allowed them to hold their ground against an enemy with very superior firepower (it had total supremacy in artillery). The Japanese soldiers were stalled for several weeks, despite heavy reinforcements. The 19th Route Army continued to hold out, supported by reinforcements sent by the central government. The months of February and March were moments of great patriotic excitement throughout the country: the tenacity of the soldiers who resisted in Shanghai aroused the enthusiasm of a population that followed their feats of arms day by day in the press. The leaders of the 19th Route Army (notably Cai Tingkai, whose keen feel for communication was not unrelated to his sudden popularity) achieved heroic status. Following a ceasefire on 3 March, an agreement was signed on 5 May 1932. It resulted in relative failure for the Japanese side, which found itself diplomatically isolated and unable to obtain the demilitarization of the Shanghai region. This partial victory came at a cost to China, nonetheless. The already scant public finances were now drained. Moreover, the main battlefield was the northern suburbs of Shanghai, particularly Zhabei, where there was a very large concentration of industry. All that remained was a field of ruins.[21]

Meanwhile, the Japanese had a much easier time militarily in Manchuria. Rather than proceeding with an outright annexation of the conquered territories, the preferred option of the Guandong Army, the choice to bring about the creation of a state was a concession to the qualms of the general staff in Tokyo by the former. On 1 March 1932, the creation of Manchukuo was declared, bringing together the three north-eastern provinces of Fengtian, Jilin and Heilongjiang. The choice of its capital was Changchun, which was highly symbolic, and it was swiftly renamed Xinjing, 'the new capital'. This was, in fact, the city that had sprung up due to the activity of the (Japanese) South Manchurian Railway Company. At this point, the Japanese played a card they had held in reserve: the former emperor, Puyi, whom they had taken under their protection in 1924. Puyi was at first appointed chief executive (*zhizheng* 執政) of a state that then took the form of a republic. The League of Nations made known its hostility to any recognition of Manchukuo, and Japan withdrew from the League. So the interest in maintaining a republican facade, which was intended to encourage the Western powers to recognize the new state, had disappeared. Two years later, this republic gave way to an empire, with Puyi on the throne. But there was no question of any real autonomy. Manchukuo quickly signed agreements that ratified its continuation under the supervision of the Guandong Army. At every level, the administration was run by Japanese civil servants. The economy was placed entirely at the service of Japan's strategic interests. Finally, 1 million Japanese settlers moved into Manchuria during the 1930s.[22] For China, the loss of Manchuria was of obvious strategic and military importance. But it also contributed to aggravating the economic difficulties of the country, which had already been damaged by the great floods of the Yangtze in the summer of 1931, as it represented a very important outlet for Chinese industry and crafts.

Shortly afterwards, in early 1933, the Japanese added the province of Rehe to Manchukuo. Between skirmishes and ambushes, operations were moving closer to Beijing. The beginning of 1933 was marked by heavy fighting near the Great Wall. The Tanggu Truce of May 1933 put an end to this. It stipulated that Japanese troops must remain behind the Great Wall, south of which a demilitarized zone was established. Although much desired by Chiang Kai-shek, who wanted to have a free hand to liquidate the communists, this respite proved short-lived. The whole period 1933–7 was marked by provocations and skirmishes. These years were punctuated by a series of agreements that were humiliating setbacks for China. Between the end of 1934 and 1935, Chahar and Hebei in turn were steadily drawn into Manchukuo's orbit. Southern Mongolia declared its independence on 12 February 1936, which meant little other than allegiance to Japan.[23]

The military situation in the north-east was a confusion of negotiations at both local and governmental levels, against a background of surprise military attacks, not to mention the actions of the secret services, which resulted in an abundance of assassinations and incitements.[24] To complicate matters, the Japanese and Nanjing governments were constantly negotiating with those who claimed to be theirs on the ground, but whose allegiance was highly unreliable. The Guandong Army dug their heels in when the Tokyo government appeared willing to make a lasting peace. Capitulation in the face of Japan took forms other than territorial losses. It included the dismissal of officials deemed to be anti-Japanese in the central government (Song Ziwen was the most notable example), and the banning of anti-Japanese publications, demonstrations and boycotts. A 3 July 1934 tariff represented another major concession on the part of the Chinese government. This trouncing over the matter of Customs meant lowered tariffs for goods imported en masse from Japan, competing directly with Chinese products (such as cotton fabrics), while it increased them for capital goods (machines) and various raw materials (raw cotton and fuel) which had in common that they were indispensable to the development of Chinese industry and crucial for its competitiveness.[25] Between capitulations and humiliating compromises, the Nanjing government paid dearly politically. Their policy of appeasement and compromise provided opponents of all kinds with ideal grounds for denunciation of the government. Hu Hanmin lost no opportunity to pillory Chiang Kai-shek in his review *Sanminzhuyi yuekan* 三民主義月刊 (*The Three Principles Monthly*). Nor was Feng Yuxiang to be outdone either in the exercise of portraying Chiang

Kai-shek as inclined to surrender. But this should not obscure a positive fact – the emergence of a nationalist resistance. In the years up to 1937, it was a thorn in the side of Chiang Kai-shek. But it finally proved to be a crucial asset during the first years of the war, enabling him to successfully mobilize the population against the invader.[26]

Warlords on the wane

Although the warlords were no longer the real masters of the game, especially after 1932, they remained significant players throughout the Nanjing decade. On their own, none of them was any longer a match for Chiang Kai-shek. But an alliance between several of them could pose a credible threat. We have seen how some potentates, and not the least of them, were brought down or even annihilated between 1928 and 1931. However, these successes were counterbalanced by the emergence of a new breed of warlords: military leaders from within the ranks of the nationalist forces themselves, who cut loose and came to the fore in the province where they were in charge. Chen Jitang was among the key ones. In 1931, he managed to take advantage of the national crisis caused by the arrest of Hu Hanmin to remove the rich province of Guangdong from Nanjing's control – the very province that had served as a base for the Northern Expedition.[27]

He Jian gradually did the same with Hunan after he was appointed governor between 1929 and 1936, as did Han Fuju with Shandong.[28]

Nevertheless, in terms of the balance of power with the warlords, an appraisal of the Nanjing decade remains undeniably positive, especially after the recapture of Guangdong province in the summer of 1936. From this perspective, the advance of the Japanese army into the north of the country was a lesser evil for Nanjing because it took place in territory controlled by the warlords. The outline of the state of Manchukuo corresponded more or less to the former territory of Zhang Zuolin (then, after his assassination by the Japanese, that of his son and successor, Zhang Xueliang). Warlords controlling several provinces were still numerous at the end of the Northern Expedition (Feng Yuxiang held control of Henan, Shaanxi and Gansu, as just one example).[29] On the eve of the 1937 war, none of the warlords controlled several provinces. One last coalition of militarists with some breadth and coherence remained in the

10 The great warlord Chen Jitang, overlord of Guangdong between 1931 and 1936.

mid-1930s: the one that linked Guangdong, Yunnan and Guangxi. It too was brought to heel in 1936.

As a result, there were fewer warlords left, and among them there were two endangered species: the colossi and the minor figures. At the beginning of the 1930s, one or more warlords began to assert themselves in various provinces that were still very divided. In Sichuan, the quintessential fragmented province of the 1920s, five warlords cleared out the opposition around 1927, until Liu Xiang took charge in the early 1930s (though he did not manage to dispatch the others completely).[30] The hard work of eradicating the multitude of small local satrapies in Shaanxi was carried out by Feng Yuxiang's forces between 1927 and 1928 and completed by Yang Hucheng in the 1930s. Han Fuju became the sole overlord of Shandong in 1932, after defeating Liu Zhennian, who still controlled most of the eastern part of the province.[31]

In most cases, whilst the warlords remained independent, Nanjing succeeded in clipping their wings by various means. Mention has already been made of Chiang's initiatives to demobilize their troops, which they unsurprisingly resisted to the end. Attempts to bring the purchase of arms under central control had limited results, to say the least (none, for example, in Sichuan). Other methods proved more effective. One was to weaponize the danger posed by the communists. Armies loyal to Nanjing moved to provinces facing a communist threat to assist local forces. Once stationed there, these troops remained and allowed Chiang to bring the province concerned under the sway of Nanjing. This was the case in Guizhou in 1935, where the two main satraps, Hou Zhidan and Wang Jialie, were removed. A whole range of other means were employed with the intention of directly or indirectly weakening the warlords in another way – namely, by diminishing their financial resources. Thus, the success of the monetary reform of the mid-1930s and the progress in the circulation of central government money (*fabi*) considerably weakened the currencies issued locally by the warlords, who were then deprived of important leverage.[32] To drain the finances of the new Guangxi clique, Chiang Kai-shek resorted to another method, which was to divert the routes of opium produced in Yunnan (the best in China) to the north, thus depriving the clique of the duties it levied on opium shipments passing through the province. Less subtle, but scarcely less unusual, were the schemes designed to get one or more subordinates to defect: this is how Chiang Kai-shek managed to overcome Feng Yuxian in the spring of 1929, by securing the defection of his lieutenants Han Fuju and Shi Yousan.

Although they were enemies, there were constant exchanges and negotiations between the various warlords and the central power. Unthinkable a few years earlier, one practice became widespread in the mid-1930s: that of Chiang Kai-shek's inspection trips to the warlords' fiefdoms. From March to October 1935, he divided his time between Sichuan and, to a lesser extent, Yunnan and Guizhou.[33] During this period, he made numerous public appearances, speeches and inspection tours. And even if, in the struggle that was being waged, there were many low blows, it would be wrong to believe that everything was permitted: Chiang was not afraid of resorting to political assassinations, but the warlords were never targeted. The only two warlords of any significance to be assassinated during the Nanjing decade were one by the Japanese (Zhang Zuolin), and the other, Sun Chuanfang in November 1935, by a young woman, Shi Jianqiao, in personal revenge for the death of her father, whom he had killed. Similarly, Chiang usually left a way out for the defeated adversary reduced to helplessness by the loss of their army and their territorial base. The new retiree went to live out their life, usually in peace, abroad or in a foreign concession.[34]

It is also important to take a firm stand against an excessively schematic vision that would draw a radical opposition between the lower valley of the Yangtze River (in particular, Jiangsu and Zhejiang) – closely held by the Guomindang and where they were, as it were, ruler of their kingdom – and the rest of the country, which only recognized their dominance in a purely nominal way. The reality was more complex. There is no reason to question the idea that the Guomindang's power base was in the Lower Yangtze River valley (except to qualify it a little).[35] On the other hand, it must be emphasized that the degree and form of its control over the rest of the country could be broken down into a very wide variety of forms. For the sake of convenience, historians usually state that many warlords remained 'semi-independent' during the Nanjing decade. While they back up this claim with many examples, they fail to analyse a fact that is at least as significant – namely, that they were equally 'semi-dependent'.

Nowhere is this clearer than in the area of taxation. The Nanjing Ministry of Finance administration had good coverage of Zhejiang, Anhui and Jiangsu, and managed to generate very large tax revenues. Most other provinces accepted the presence of some of its components to varying degrees, but the revenue from them was (proportionately) less. Others, such as Sichuan, which are too often portrayed as completely independent, certainly tolerated the presence of the Maritime Customs and the Salt Tax Administration, which had been in place for a long time, but had fallen into the hands of the Ministry of Finance at the end of the 1920s.[36] Similarly, in Shandong, Han Fuju returned some of its tax revenues to Nanjing, while the railway revenues were completely outside the latter's control.[37]

Nonetheless, Nanjing's reach extended into the provinces through major consensual reforms that were driven by the central ministries. This was the case for prisons. Directives issued in Nanjing (like those issued in Beijing under the Beiyang governments) were applied throughout the country, while reports from the local penitentiary services were transmitted back up the chain of command to the capital.

The successful marginalization of the Chinese Communist Party

It would be wrong to overestimate the extent of the threat posed by the Chinese Communist Party (CCP). However, one thing prevented the CCP from being completely overlooked. Less than its own strength, what made it a potential threat was that it was part of a worldwide revolutionary movement supported by a power, the USSR, which shared with China a border several thousand kilometres long. The Chinese communist revolution was indeed linked to its Russian predecessor by an umbilical cord called the Comintern. The latter sent advisors and provided financial assistance, and Moscow offered a safe haven where Chinese communists could take refuge and receive medical care and training. The protective wing of the Comintern, however, did not afford only advantages. For the Chinese communists, it had the disadvantage of imposing strategic options which, in general, served the short-term interests of the USSR – and, as we shall see, of Stalin – more than those of the Chinese revolution.

Following the violent break-up of 1927, and after having tried to continue to play the United Front card with the Wuhan government (see Chapter 2), the CCP went underground. Chen Duxiu, blamed for the setbacks following the break-up of the United Front, was removed from office. Qu Qiubai succeeded him as Party leader. The latter, whose main merit was his knowledge of Russian, applied a strategy based on Stalin's view that China was in a revolutionary situation. This diagnosis (and especially the need for Stalin to assert its validity in the face of Trotsky's criticisms) justified the multiple attempts to rouse the popular masses.[38] The communist uprisings of late 1927 varied in nature, but not in outcome. All of them led to quick and bloody failures. At the beginning of August 1927, in Nanchang, a mutiny in the regular army, led by officers won over to the communist cause (Ye Ting and He Long), misfired. In December 1927, the Guangzhou commune relied on the support of the urban lumpenproletariat (notably the rickshaw pullers). It was crushed in two days. But the most famous insurrection in the series was the Autumn Harvest Uprising in Hunan (9–19 September

1927), led by Mao Zedong. After this failure, he made it to the Jinggang Mountains, on the borders of Jiangxi and Hunan, with a few hundred survivors. He managed to survive in this poor and very remote region by allying himself with bands of local brigands.[39] Reinforced by Zhu De's 2,000 men (May 1928), then 700 with Peng Dehuai (November 1928), he gradually extended the area under his sway. Jiangxi Soviet became one of the main communist rural bases in the early 1930s. The development of rural soviets only took place in the south of the country. There were none in the North, which had remained impervious to peasant movements in the 1920s (with the exception of Henan province).

In November 1931, the Jiangxi base became the Chinese Soviet Republic. The hierarchy of the CCP from 1931 to 1935 was a group trained in Moscow, the 28 Bolsheviks, whose main figures were Bo Gu, Wang Ming and Zhang Wentian. They sought to impose their authority on the various bases that were developing. Determined to bring the local leaders to heel (first and foremost Mao), the hierarchy sent Zhou Enlai to Jiangxi in October 1931. The latter demonstrated his manoeuvring skills with success. Mao's marginalization seemed to be a foregone conclusion after the Ningdu conference in the summer of 1932.[40] The Central Committee (then led by Bo Gu), fleeing Shanghai, settled in Jiangxi in January 1933. This move was an admission of the terrible weakening of the CCP in the cities, the result of the reckless strategies (largely directed from a distance by Moscow) of its leaders and effective repression by the Guomindang. It was also a confirmation of the central role that the Jiangxi Soviet was now called upon to play.[41]

This new importance of the soviet could not fail to attract the attention of the Guomindang. Crushing it became a priority objective. Naturally, Chiang Kai-shek had not failed to react to the development of the Jiangxi Soviet, which from 1930 onwards was the target of several annihilation campaigns. They all failed because of a lack of resources, or because the troops involved had to be urgently redeployed to higher-priority theatres. The strategy employed must also be questioned. In particular, the Guomindang had sought to kill two birds with one stone by combining the elimination of communists with the domination of local rural elites. This error was remedied in 1933 when the Guomindang collaborated with the latter instead of trying to supplant them. The fifth campaign would be the last. Supported by the local militias (reorganized and reinforced by the efficient Xiong Shihui, appointed governor of Jiangxi in December 1931), the nationalist troops followed a methodical encirclement tactic. The use of belts of blockhouses allowed them to gradually penetrate to the heart of the territory held by the communists. In order to break the fatal encirclement that was taking shape, the communists were forced to flee in October 1934. Propaganda subsequently magnified the Long March (*changzheng* 長征) that followed.[42] Far from being an epic saga, however, it was above all a succession of completely improvised manoeuvres, an arduous journey towards the west and then the north to escape annihilation. The very term 'Long March' was not applied to this operation until the end of December 1935, by Mao.[43] At that time, Mao tried to rewrite the history of this desperate flight in two ways: on the one hand, by making it a tactical manoeuvre directed by him, and on the other, by setting aside the fact that there were in reality several long marches. Fighters from various other communist bases also sought salvation towards the west.

In October 1934, 100,000 people left the Jiangxi base, but their numbers fell by two-thirds in six months, not so much because of skirmishes and battles as because of desertions and disease. Having changed its objective many times, the Long March finally ended in October 1935. What remained of the CCP's central military and political apparatus, a meagre phalanx of 10,000 people, found refuge in an extremely remote and desolate region, where a very new communist base existed: northern Shaanxi.

The Long March was not only a military disaster. The party continually tore itself apart in internal struggles. Mao emerged victorious by succeeding in two operations which enabled him to assert his pre-eminence (though not at that point making him the undisputed master). First of all, he made the most of his opportunity: sidelined since the summer of 1932 from the leadership, and therefore from decisions on the strategy to be followed, he seized the opportunity at the Zunyi conference (January 1935) to reject responsibility for the disastrous loss of the Chinese Soviet Republic. His second masterstroke was to successfully remove the threat posed to his dominance – just secured in Zunyi – by Zhang Guotao. A founding member of the CCP, the latter was a veteran of revolutionary activity, having led a Marxist study group since 1920 with Li Dazhao. In April 1931, he had been sent to take charge of a base, second only in importance to the Jiangxi Soviet at that point: that of Eyüwan 鄂豫皖, on the borders of Hubei, Henan and Anhui. Dislodged by nationalist offensives in early 1933, Zhang's forces hunkered down in a corner of northern Sichuan, taking advantage of the weakness and disunity of the local warlords. But this respite was only temporary, and, under pressure from nationalist troops, they set off back to the west. They linked up with Mao's forces on 14 June 1935. At that time, Zhang had military forces that were not only five times greater in number than Mao's, but also much less worn down.[44] Disagreements with the Mao-dominated Party leadership increased immediately. Two months later, there was another split. Mao led his troops, without too much trouble, into northern Shaanxi where he set about consolidating a new base. Zhang headed south with his men but encountered hardened nationalist forces in Sichuan. Then, confronted with hostile populations, he tried in vain to establish a base in Tibet. These military operations resulted in his forces melting away in a few months. At the end of 1936, he returned to northern Shaanxi in defeat. The CCP established its capital in January 1937 in Yan'an and Zhang Guotao understood that his time was up and that he was no longer in a position to challenge Mao's leadership. In April 1938, he was the first (and last) high-ranking CCP official to defect to the Guomindang.

In the precarious shelter of Yan'an, the CCP bandaged its wounds and tried to rebuild its forces, starting with its army. Moreover, during these years, the other small and scattered communist bases struggled to survive, facing the onslaught of Guomindang troops with varying degrees of success.[45] Most eked out their survival on a very meagre level, like so many scattered seeds biding their time, which would soon come. Indeed, they would regain all their importance when the time came for war against Japan and the second United Front, and for the development of bases in areas conquered by the enemy.

While the CCP was marginalized during the Nanjing decade, it was an intermittent process. April 1927 was obviously a crucial date for the communists, who could no longer develop under the Guomindang umbrella. Fierce and effective repression followed the break-up of the first United Front: the Party's membership melted away. In the subsequent years, the CCP failed to significantly restore its position in the cities, especially among the working class. If, however, it gradually rebuilt its

11 Mao Zedong and Zhang Guotao, spring 1938.

forces, it was by following a completely different tactic, along the double axes comprising the construction of rural soviets, and an independent armed force. We must stop equating the 1934–5 period with the Long March, an interpretation developed and promoted by Mao himself as part of the wider project of modelling the history of the CCP on his personal actions. In reality, in 1934–5, a wider movement developed to systematically eliminate the rural soviets embedded in the south of the country, resulting in a clear success for the Guomindang: from 300,000 members in 1933, the membership of the Communist Party had fallen to 30,000 by the beginning of 1937.[46]

The run-up to the Sino-Japanese War: 1935–1937

The attack on Wang Jingwei on 1 November 1935 heralded a new phase. Indeed, Wang fell because he bore the brunt of the growing unpopularity of the policy of appeasement towards Japan. The pressure of increasingly anti-Japanese public opinion was mounting. On 9 December 1935, tens of thousands of students demonstrated in Beijing, demanding a firmer approach towards Tokyo. The movement spread, and in the following months public salvation associations (*jiuguo hui* 救國會) were organized throughout the country.

In May 1936, they united in an All-China Federation of National Salvation Societies (*Quanguo gejie jiuguo hui xiehui* 全國各界救國會協會), which organized a huge anti-Japanese demonstration on the occasion of the funeral of the famous writer Lu Xun. Greatly scandalizing public opinion, the Guomindang responded by arresting the seven main leaders of the Federation (from then on known as the 'Seven Gentlemen', *qi junzi* 七君子) on 22 November 1936. Among the leading figures hostile to the policy of prioritizing the elimination of communists over the fight against Japan was Zhang Zuolin's son, Zhang Xueliang. Although he had to retreat in the face of advancing Japanese troops in the north-east of the country, he retained control of substantial military forces. Together with another local military leader, Yang Hucheng, he was responsible for the so-called Xi'an incident. This episode has been the subject of widely differing interpretations and remains shrouded in some mystery.[47] Chiang Kai-shek travelled to the Xi'an area, then controlled by Zhang Xueliang, in order to ascertain on the spot the measures taken to eradicate the communists from Shaanxi. Zhang, who had lately drawn considerably closer to the communists, had Chiang arrested on 12 December 1936. At first, Chiang feared for his life. But, very quickly, Stalin gave precise orders, relayed by the CCP, that no harm should come to him. Since the 7th Congress of the

Communist International in July 1935, the Comintern's strategy had been to form anti-fascist popular fronts, which in China implied seeking a rapprochement with the Guomindang. Stalin and Chiang Kai-shek also had a common enemy: Japanese expansionism. On this basis, secret negotiations for an alliance had already been going on for several years. Stalin needed a China that was, if not strong, at least not abandoned to anarchy – and, above all, anti-Japanese.

As soon as the news of Chiang's arrest became known, an unexpectedly large wave of sympathy swept through public opinion. Everyone suddenly realized that, with the threat of war against Japan looming ever larger, the disappearance of Chiang Kai-shek would surely plunge the country back into chaos. Two weeks after his arrest, Chiang was released (under continued pressure from Moscow) without the nature of the verbal commitments made to his captors being very clear. There was even a spectacular reversal of events: Chiang Kai-shek returned to Nanjing with Zhang Xueliang (who remained his prisoner for the rest of his life). Chiang's descent from the plane was triumphant: he was acclaimed by a huge crowd, while spontaneous demonstrations of support took place throughout the country. Unquestionably, Chiang emerged stronger from the incident.

In fact, the most recent research suggests that the influence of the Xi'an incident on subsequent events has been considerably overstated. Negotiations for the formation of an anti-Japanese United Front were opened, it is true, but they dragged on. After a few months, Chiang dismissed Yang Hucheng, placed loyal troops in southern Shaanxi and began to threaten the communist base again. It was definitely the outbreak of war with Japan that saved the communists from the promised annihilation, not the Xi'an incident.

Xi'an was not a turning point in explaining Chiang Kai-shek's decision to resist Japanese pressure. Having established this fact, does the explanation lie in the pressure of public opinion? This is, for the most part, the view of communist China's traditional historiography. There is a much broader problem – engulfed in a Manichean reading of the Guomindang's actions, this historiography sometimes has to overcome a most uncomfortable issue: how to account for the fact that the Nationalist Party and its leader can be credited with certain 'good' decisions? The trick is simply to claim that these decisions were only taken 'under pressure from the masses' (the latter, it goes without saying, being duly enlightened by the CCP). This approach has led to a significant overestimation of the role of public pressure. As we shall see in the next chapter, Chiang Kai-shek's decision probably had primarily to do with coldly considered political, military and strategic considerations.

FOUR

The War against Japan (1937–1945)

The Sino-Japanese War was a turning point for the republican period. It decisively redefined the regional geostrategic balance by removing the threat from Japan. But its length meant its domestic consequences were even more important. The eight years of terrible hardship interrupted the process of consolidation of centralized power that had characterized the Nanjing decade. By weakening the Guomindang and opening up new prospects for the CCP, the war completely rearranged the balance of power.

The war was divided into three periods: two episodes of war of movement, in 1937–9 and 1944–5, framed five years during which the front remained more or less stable.

The war of movement: 1937–1939

The war was triggered by a trivial incident. Following manoeuvres by Japanese troops around the Marco Polo Bridge (*Lugouqiao* 盧溝橋) south-west of Beijing, one of their soldiers was reported missing. The search for him led to a clash with Chinese troops on 7 July 1937. In this region, Japanese pressure had been constant since the aftermath of the Tanggu Truce, fuelled by the competition between the different components of the Japanese army present there. In August 1937, the Guandong Army and the troops stationed in Tianjin were renamed the 'North China Area Army'. In this context, the Marco Polo Bridge incident was no more serious than many others, after which an accommodation was reached. And, indeed, in the three weeks that followed, there was no sign that the consequences would not be resolved through negotiation. Chiang Kai-shek's policy from 1931 to 1936 had been to equivocate with Japan. This was the result of an accurate assessment of the balance of power, Chiang being aware of the clear inferiority of his armed forces. What were the factors that made him reconsider and not give in this time?

Why did Chiang Kai-shek choose confrontation?

As we have said, neither the pressure of public opinion nor the spoken commitments made by Chiang Kai-shek at the time of the Xi'an incident can explain why he decided in mid-1937 to accept the risks of an open war against Japan. Unquestionably, a favourable wind had been blowing since the outcome of the Xi'an incident. The country was beginning to reap the benefits of the Nanjing decade, and the power of the Guomindang had never seemed stronger. The threat of the warlords was fading, with Nanjing having seen the return of the rich province of Guangdong to its fold (without a fight) in the summer of 1936. The Communist Party was considerably weakened. On the military side, well-equipped divisions trained by German instructors began to be operational. The first major manoeuvres involving these new forces took place in November 1936. It is true, however, that the over-optimistic views of Alexander von Falkenhausen, Chiang Kai-shek's chief military advisor since March 1935, may have led him to believe that his forces were now ready to take on the Japanese army.[1]

12 Japanese infantry in combat in the suburbs of Shanghai, 30 October 1937.

On the other hand, if the concessions he had agreed to since 1931 could be seen as an expedient to buy time, it seems that Chiang was determined not to capitulate over Beijing and Tianjin. In fact, it was in the days following the capture of these two cities by Japanese forces (28–31 July) that his resolution to run the risk of war took shape.[2] On 13 August 1937, Chiang Kai-shek took the step of extending hostilities to a second front that he believed to be more favourable – Shanghai. This choice of Shanghai was based on a diplomatic and strategic calculation. Diplomatic, because Shanghai was the place where the interests of the Western powers were concentrated, and Chiang hoped, one way or another, that they would intervene in the conflict. Strategic, because this urban terrain was the most favourable for the Chinese army (as opposed to the North China front, whose great plains constituted a theatre of operations where Nippon's material superiority was clear). The memory of the glorious resistance of Chinese troops at the Battle of Shanghai (early 1932) probably also helped to convince Chiang Kai-shek that it was in his interest to bring Japan to fight on a terrain that was, if not ideal, at least more favourable to his troops. On the other side, the Japanese took up the gauntlet and stepped up their efforts, lining up over 200,000 men in Shanghai.[3]

Japan's first victories

Chiang Kai-shek chose to align his elite divisions on the Shanghai front. For three months of fighting, these troops showed remarkable valour, only giving in inch by inch, at the price of heavy losses. But after a landing of Japanese troops farther south threatened them with encirclement, Chiang made the mistake of ordering a retreat too late, which was carried out in confusion. On 12 November, Shanghai fell into Japanese hands.

In the abundant historiography of the war, one question keeps coming up – did Chiang make a mistake by committing the best troops available to him to Shanghai on a long-term basis? The answer is yes, when you consider that he was calculating first and foremost on dragging the West into the war, in one way or another. The Japanese were careful to spare the foreign concessions and the West remained unmoved. More importantly, Chiang lost the best of his army and many of his best officers.

It should be noted, however, that, in terms of domestic politics, Chiang Kai-shek showed his willingness to fight Japan, thus helping to establish his stature as the country's leader. The commitment – and, to some extent, the sacrifice – of the best of his forces prompted warlords to stop vacillating, join the fight against the Japanese forces and agree to put their troops under his command. This was the case of the military from the new Guangxi clique, who remained loyal throughout the war. Yan Xishan did the same, almost immolating his army in the fierce defence of his province, Shanxi. The warlord of distant Yunnan, Long Yun, also responded to Chiang Kai-shek's call and sent 160,000 men to the front. Bringing warlords of the calibre of Long and Yan under his banner, and getting them to actually participate in the war, was a clear success for Chiang Kai-shek. However, success was far from complete. In December 1937, the loss of Shandong took the wind out of his sails. General Han Fuju, the master of this province, despite very strict orders and the military means (100,000 men) to carry them out, did nothing to halt the advance of the Japanese troops. He fell into the hands of Chiang Kai-shek on 4 January and, after a summary trial, paid for this inaction with his life.

After the Battle of Shanghai, the Japanese troops moved on Nanjing, the capital, evacuated in the autumn by the Guomindang government. The capture of the city (13 December) was followed by a large-scale massacre of civilians and prisoners. Estimates of the number of victims are variable and controversial. They range from 50,000 to 300,000.[4] The abuses by the Japanese troops led to the exodus of millions of civilians trying to escape them. The foreign concessions in Shanghai were flooded with refugees in the first months of the war.

The second United Front and Soviet aid

The second United Front had this in common with the first: the Guomindang only accepted it because it gave it access to indispensable aid from the USSR. Since the early 1930s, China had maintained close ties with Germany, who supplied it with military advisors and weapons. The diplomatic rapprochement between Germany and Japan (the anti-Comintern pact signed in November 1936) obliged the Guomindang to renounce an alliance that geographical distance made irrelevant anyway.

From then on, the USSR became the only power ready to counter-balance the Japanese threat. For Stalin, the worrying developments in Europe and the diplomatic rapprochement between Germany and Japan made the threat of a war on two fronts increasingly clear. It was therefore in the USSR's interest to avert the threat of a Chinese collapse that would leave it face to face with a fiercely anti-communist Japan.

The principles of the United Front were laid down in agreements concluded between the CCP and the Guomindang in September 1937. Among other things, they stipulated that the communist troops were under the command of the Guomindang, which is why the bulk of them officially took the name of the 8th Route Army (*balujun* 八路軍). But the CCP, beyond declarations of intent, refused to actually place its soldiers under the command of Chiang Kai-shek, and contented itself with carrying out a few attacks whose lack of scale contrasted with the abundant exploitation for propaganda purposes that it drew from them. This was not the main focus of the Guomindang, however. Between October 1937 and February 1938, the USSR sent 297 military aircraft, 290 cannons, 82 tanks and 400 motorized vehicles. Between March 1938 and June 1939, China obtained three loans from the USSR which Chiang immediately used to acquire, at particularly advantageous prices, Soviet weapons, including 900 aircraft. In addition, as many as 5,000 Russian instructors, advisors and technicians served in China between 1937 and 1941. Soviet aid to China was channelled through Guangzhou (until its conquest by the Japanese in October 1938) and, by road, through Xinjiang to Lanzhou.[5] This support, crucial during the early years of the war, declined somewhat in 1940–1 after the start of military operations in Europe. Following the non-aggression pact concluded between the USSR and Japan on 13 April 1941, and especially after the start of the German invasion in June 1941, it ceased completely.

Beyond the Guomindang–CCP alliance itself, the early years of the war were characterized by an atmosphere of national unity. Some significant gestures were made – notably the release by the Guomindang of political prisoners such as Chen Duxiu and the Seven Gentlemen on 9 July 1937. China was enjoying an atmosphere of intellectual freedom, particularly during the months when the government was based in Wuhan. At that time, there was even a certain degree of political pluralism emerging. The People's Political Council (*Guomin canzhenghui* 國民參政會) was established in June 1938. It was a consultative assembly, with representatives of all the political groups, as well as independent figures; 5 per cent were women. Edmund Fung sees in it – perhaps with a little exaggeration – an embryo of a parliament. Nevertheless (at least in the early years), the People's Political Council was a real forum for adversarial debate, with its leading members often critical of people in the government.[6]

1938, the difficult conquest of the Middle Yangtze River basin

After the loss of Shanghai, Nanjing and the lower Yangtze, the issue was now Wuhan, the key to the middle Yangtze and now the provisional capital.[7] Observers at the time did not give much for the chances of Chinese resistance. However, it would take the Japanese army almost ten months and the commitment of considerable reinforcements to achieve this objective. This was a turning point in the war. Despite the fall of Wuhan, the Chinese troops, among whom desertions remained a marginal phenomenon, showed their fighting spirit. The period was also marked by an awareness of the importance of propaganda for world public opinion. Orchestrated since the beginning of the war by the skilful Dong Xianguang, who was well connected in the world of foreign journalists and correspondents, the reorganization of propaganda activity bore fruit during the government's presence in Wuhan. Thanks to centralization, the recruitment of a very competent staff and a substantial budget, the objective was achieved. Western media relayed an increasingly positive image of the Chinese resistance. The idea that aid to China was both morally and strategically necessary made great strides in public opinion, especially in the United States, during 1938.

Chiang Kai-shek chose to fight at Xuzhou, a stronghold and strategic railway junction that commanded Wuhan while offering advantages to the defence. The victory at Taierzhuang, a city north-west of Xuzhou, in April 1938, the only significant one of the entire war, sparked national fervour throughout the country. But Taierzhuang, despite putting 20,000 Japanese soldiers out of action, remained a local success. It was barely made use of and did not prevent Xuzhou from falling shortly afterwards.[8] In order to delay the Japanese advance, Chiang Kai-shek then took the decision to blow up the Yellow River dykes at Huayuankou in June (while igniting a propaganda campaign in counter-attack attributing the destruction of the dykes to Japanese bombing).[9] The aftermath was cataclysmic. The effects of flooding on a vast scale would be felt for many years. The course of the river shifted by several hundred kilometres: it flowed into the sea not to the north but to the south of the Shandong peninsula. One estimate puts the number of victims at over 800,000. Millions of refugees were driven onto the roads. At the end of October 1938, Wuhan in turn fell to the Japanese armies. The retreat of the Chinese troops throughout the ten months of operations was orderly and without untoward consequences.[10]

Major operations were still taking place on a front opened up by the Japanese in Guangdong province. There was a successful landing on 12 October near Huizhou, and after only a few days the provincial capital, Guangzhou, was occupied, without serious resistance. In Hunan, Changsha was set on fire by its own defenders in November 1938, a move as devastating as it was premature, rendered unnecessary by the fact that the Japanese soon halted their advance on this front.

The lessons from fifteen months of war were clear. Japanese military superiority was overwhelming, particularly in the field of tanks, aviation and artillery. According to the Russian advisor Cherepanov, the Japanese army's artillery was four times more powerful, and its air force had thirteen times more bombers.[11] The Guomindang lost 'useful' China, and after the fall of Guangzhou and Wuhan, all the country's largest cities (apart from Xi'an) were in enemy hands.

Chongqing became the new capital of Free China for seven years. This city of 260,000 inhabitants in eastern Sichuan was chosen for strategic reasons. Located at the confluence of the Blue and Jialing Rivers, downstream from areas that remained under Guomindang control, it could be supplied by water. Its climate was far from pleasant, but the fog had the advantage of shielding it from aerial bombing for part of the year. Finally, it was surrounded by mountains which protected it from land invasion.

1939, settling in for a long war

In 1939, it became clear that the war would be a long one. A prolongation of hostilities seemed the logical result of the Guomindang's desire to continue the war and the impossibility for the Japanese to win the final victory due to the vastness of the Chinese territory.

But we can see that this might not have been necessarily the case. Numerous efforts to find a diplomatic solution were made during the first months of the conflict, by both Japan and the Guomindang. At first, attempts were made officially. The main one, through the German ambassador to China (the Trautmann mediation of October 1937 – January 1938), initially raised some hopes. But the Japanese side set such tough conditions that failure was inevitable. Thereafter, secret negotiations continued, particularly through Kong Xiangxi, Chiang Kai-shek's brother-in-law and chief minister.

Japan, in fact, had no clear line of strategy for the conduct of the war. Usually, Tokyo only endorsed initiatives taken by the general officers on the ground after the fact. Due to anti-communism, but also to the conviction that the USSR posed the real threat, the Guandong Army wanted to direct Japanese expansionism towards the north, which also corresponded to the views of some of the general staff. The effect of the 1937–8 purges on the resistance capacity of the Red Army was largely overestimated by the Japanese. During the summer, Japan undertook major military operations on the borders of Manchuria and Northern Mongolia in an attempt to draw the latter, which had signed a treaty placing it under Russian protection three years earlier, into the orbit of Manchukuo. But a limited Japanese offensive in July–August 1939 (the Battle of Khalkhin Gol for the Russians, Nomonhan for the Japanese) soon came up against a vigorous defence by Russian troops under the command of a young 43-year-old divisional commander, Georgy Konstantinovich Zhukov. The Soviet troops went on the offensive on 20 August and won a clear victory, which resulted in the almost total destruction of a Japanese division. Japan concluded that the USSR did not intend to dismantle the defence of the Eastern Front and that it was dealing with too strong an enemy. The German–Soviet treaty signed at that time (23 August 1939), in defiance of the 1936 anti-Comintern pact between Berlin and Tokyo, was another source of disillusion. Japan and the USSR agreed in the following months to respect the status quo before a formal non-aggression pact was signed (Matsuoka–Molotov agreements of April 1941). The USSR undertook to stop helping China. Japan's expansionism was now purposefully directed towards South East

Asia. There, new perspectives soon emerged following the collapse of two of the major colonial powers in Asia in the European war – the Netherlands and France. The United Kingdom, for its part, was majorly preoccupied from June 1940 onwards with defending its territory against a German invasion.

In China itself, Chiang Kai-shek ordered two counter-offensives during 1939. The first one in the spring failed. Instead, it was the Japanese who took Nanchang (Jiangxi) in May. But when they attacked Changsha, the capital of Hunan province, in August 1939, they were met with effective resistance from General Chen Cheng.[12] Interpreting this success as a manifestation of the weakening of his enemy's military forces, Chiang decided on a larger offensive for the winter of 1939. This was another failure, resulting in significant losses. Not only did Japanese troops contain the Chinese attacks with relative ease, but in November they also captured Nanning (in Guangxi), an important new city. The Chinese forces would not choose the offensive again right up to the end of the war. They settled into the strategy of a war of attrition (*chijiuzhan* 持久戰), advocated by one of the most influential Chinese military thinkers of the period, Jiang Baili.[13]

The war of position (1940–1944)

Stabilization of the front

During these five years, the war took a different turn. No major offensive was launched, while the belligerents sought to change the course of the war by other means. Aviation played an important role in this context. With huge superiority in this field, the Japanese regularly bombed the main cities. Chongqing was targeted more than 200 times and other major cities also paid a heavy human and material price. The most intense years of Japanese bombing were 1938–41. In 1939, 2,600 raids were carried out. After 1941, there was a relative lull in bombing. On the ground, operations continued, although no longer on the same scale. Japanese forces continued to lock down the southern coastline with the intention of completing the isolation of the area controlled by Chongqing. The main ports were taken (Fuzhou and Ningbo in the spring of 1941), and the Leizhou peninsula was conquered in early 1943. Already attacked in 1939, Changsha was attacked again on two occasions in 1941. The city, tenaciously defended by the talented general Xue Yue, nevertheless remained in the hands of the Chongqing troops.[14]

The secret services of both sides waged a merciless struggle.[15] In the occupied zone, despite the close protection they enjoyed, the life expectancy of high-ranking collaborators was short. Fu Xiao'an, the mayor of Shanghai, was assassinated in October 1940, and the governor of Guangdong province, Chen Yaozu, suffered the same fate in April 1944. Nor were the small fry overlooked. Thus, Shanghai businessmen (such as Gu Xinyi, killed in June 1938) who stayed to look after their businesses paid with their lives when they found themselves involved, often against their will, in a public life orchestrated by the collaborators.

In the Japanese-occupied part of the country, zones of guerrilla fighting were organized wherever the geographical configuration allowed. Almost all were held by the communists. It was not that the Guomindang deliberately denied themselves this option. On the contrary, from the spring of 1939, Chiang Kai-shek included guerrilla warfare behind enemy lines as part of his overall strategy. But it soon became obvious that the CCP were far better organized in this capacity. Clearly, this was an area where they could make the most of the know-how they had accumulated since 1927. In contrast, the Guomindang guerrillas were faltering and undermined by divisions. The Japanese, as well as the collaborating governments, were not inactive, and regularly carried out actions to 'clean up' the guerrilla zones. But, unremittingly, after each such operation, the communist bases were reconstituted and began to expand again. This situation worried the Guomindang, which saw the simultaneous growth of CCP forces and areas under their control, in which it had, in fact, no say.

The early 1940s were therefore also a turning point for the United Front. Although officially still current, it was increasingly no longer a reality. The so-called New 4th Army incident made this clear. It followed an ultimatum from Chiang Kai-shek, in October 1940, requiring communist troops south of the Yangtze to return north of the river again within a month. He was not obeyed, and in January 1941 a pitched battle occurred in southern Anhui. It resulted in several thousand deaths among the communist troops. The year 1941 was also marked by the beginning of the Guomindang's economic blockade of communist areas. Thereafter, the most important efforts to save the United Front were made by those who wanted to give substance to a 'third force'. They were behind the formation of the Comrades' Association for Unity and National Construction (*tongyi jianguo tongzhihui* 同意建國同志會) established in November 1939, which in 1941 gave rise to the famous Democratic League (*Zhongguo minzhu tongmeng* 中國民主同盟). If the League's membership was small, it still included some very influential figures, such as Liang Shuming and Zhang Junmai.

Population movements

The importance of population movements during the first year of the conflict has been mentioned. During the years of the war of position, they were less significant than the exodus of 1937–8. The highest estimates put the number of refugees between 1937 and 1945 at 95 million, but a comprehensive study of population movements during this period has yet to be carried out. It would probably confirm what some evidence suggests – namely, that population movements were not only restricted to those from the occupied zone to the free zone (this is the well-documented case of people who chose out of patriotism to leave to join Free China or the communist forces).[16] Movement was also recorded in the occupied part between areas where the Japanese presence was felt to a greater or lesser degree. The return to the occupied zone of refugees who had fled the Japanese advance is still a taboo subject in the historiography of the war period. It suggests that the Chinese were motivated by practical and economic concerns in this instance. Nonetheless, these movements were, in all likelihood, significant.[17] Thus, the population of Hangzhou, a city of half a million inhabitants on the eve of the war, which had fallen to 100,000 following its capture by Japanese troops on 24 December 1937, had already risen to 320,000 by 1940. Suzhou had returned to its pre-war population by the end of 1939.[18] In fact, it appears that it is inadvisable to focus excessively on members of the intellectual and urban elite who made very long journeys to settle in the cities deep within the free zone. Most of the professors and students from the major universities in Beijing and Shanghai refused to remain in the occupied zone, so a unified south-western university (*Xinan lianda* 西南聯大,

THE WAR AGAINST JAPAN (1937–1945)

usually abbreviated to *Lianda* 聯大) was founded in Kunming (Yunnan province) from Beijing, Qinghua and Nankai universities. For these elites, patriotism and the wish to resist were undoubtedly the driving forces behind the exodus. But in the case of the great mass of refugees, of much lower status, flight was simply motivated by fear of fighting and abuse. Instead of a distant exile (often beyond their means), the peasants preferred a distance of a few dozen kilometres so that they could return home as soon as the most pressing danger had passed.[19] The authorities in the collaborating regimes made every effort to convince them to return home to 'live in peace and work in joy' (*anju leye* 安居樂業), with some success.

China and the Allies

We have seen the importance of the aid given by the USSR in the first phase of the war. The baton was gradually taken up by the United States (supplemented, to a much lesser extent, by the United Kingdom). A first loan was granted by Washington in December 1938. Others followed in subsequent years. At the same time, increasing restrictions were being imposed on trade between the US and Japan. In July 1941, a total embargo was decided upon. Even before Pearl Harbor, Roosevelt resolved in November to provide more substantial financial and material aid.

In his *Memoirs of the Second World War*, Winston Churchill describes the feeling of absolute certainty of final victory that overcame him when he heard the news of Japan's surprise attack on Pearl Harbor on 7 December 1941, as this assured him of the unconditional support of the world's leading industrial power.[20] At the same time, Chiang Kai-shek, and with him the entire Chinese population, evinced similar sentiments. It is a fact that Pearl Harbor fundamentally changed the situation. Equipment and advisors would flow into Chongqing until the end of the war. However, even though the USA was the world's largest economy, its production capacity was not unlimited. For China, the challenge was to influence a major strategic decision: on which front of a war that was more global than ever would the bulk of the American effort be focused? To counteract the views of Stalin and Churchill, for whom the priority front could only be in Europe, Chiang Kai-shek tried to arrange for a much larger part of the American war effort to be directed to the Asian theatre. Chinese diplomacy applied two forms of pressure. The first, which they repeatedly cited, was the risk of the military collapse of Chongqing. By handing over China to the invading Nippon, it would enable Tokyo to redirect all its military forces against the United States on the Pacific war front. The second means of pressure, which was not explicitly formulated, was the threat of China concluding a separate peace with Japan. Chiang Kai-shek's wife, Song Meiling, repeatedly travelled to America (where she had received most of her education) to win over the political class and public opinion to China's cause. Her speech to Congress on 18 February 1943 had a particularly important impact.

Despite these efforts, Chiang Kai-shek never managed to challenge the priority of the European front for the US war effort. Although American military aid was crucial to maintaining resistance, it paled in comparison to the amount of aid received by, for example, the UK (the ratio was about 1:20). It should also be noted that the scale of American aid was similar to that provided by the USSR from 1937 to 1941. The last year of the war, marked by a sharp increase in American supplies, was an exception.

So, while China had become an ally, two incidents tell us clearly that it remained a second-level associate. Two operations that were carried out in Burma, a British colony, illustrate this. Chiang Kai-shek agreed to send a large number of his elite troops to fight on terrain which, while not without strategic importance (since American aid flowed through it to China), was not at all vital. The operations, which took place in April–May 1942, ended in disaster. Their implementation left Chiang feeling very bitter, since the Chinese divisions placed under the command of the American officer Joseph Stilwell were abandoned by him to their fate. Although the second Malayan campaign, two years later, ended in victory, Chiang again had to commit many of his best divisions at a particularly critical time, just before the start of the great Japanese Ichigō offensive.

The Chongqing government also actively sought help from the diaspora. Its pleas for help were heard and the Chinese communities organized themselves to send material aid and (especially) cash. In October 1938, a congress of overseas Chinese aid committees was held in

Singapore to better plan aid and, in particular, to organize the placement of national defence bonds.[21]

1940: the beginning of the Guomindang state's disintegration

The diagnosis of Guomindang mismanagement throughout the war, which was still being made in the early 1980s by Lloyd Eastman, has not survived research in recent decades.[22] It is now generally accepted that the Guomindang responded satisfactorily to the daunting challenge of waging a war against the subcontinent's greatest power virtually single-handedly. The evacuation of a significant portion of the factories in the Shanghai area to the interior was a significant achievement. This was a complex process, carried out in several stages: factories were often first evacuated to the Wuhan region, before being transferred farther up the Yangtze River to Sichuan. Arms factories were the first, but entrepreneurs in certain sectors considered strategic (metallurgy, chemicals and mechanics) were subject to incentives, coercion and financial aid. The enormous logistical and financial difficulties were smoothed out thanks to a fairly friendly collaboration between the entrepreneurs and the different parts of the administration involved (first and foremost the Resources Commission, *Ziyuan weiyuanhui* 資源委員會). The relocation of higher education institutions, and the less frequently mentioned relocation of some secondary education institutions, also proceeded in satisfactory manner, under the circumstances.

If the Guomindang state held up well during the first three years of the war, 1940 was a real turning point. The consequences of the attrition produced by the length of the conflict have to be taken into account. Conscription, by emptying the countryside, jeopardized agricultural production while also weighing heavily on public finances. The reserve supplies that had been sent to the interior of the country at the beginning of the war were running out. More circumstantial factors came into play: in Sichuan, the granary of Free China, a poor harvest (after two good years in 1938 and 1939) caused an inflationary surge. At the same time, the Japanese strategy of cutting off Free China from its sources of external supply achieved significant success when they occupied northern Indochina. Subsequently, the difficulty of importing weighed heavily on supplies. Inflation in the first two years of the conflict remained at levels that could still be described as reasonable: higher than in the pre-war period, but not exceeding 50 per cent per year. But from 1940 onwards, an inflationary spiral set in. It was unhalted until 1949. Together with increasingly unpopular conscription, it was the main cause of the erosion of public confidence in the government.

The Guomindang's diminished capacity for action was evident in one of the greatest famines of the first half of the twentieth century, in Henan in 1942–3. The effects of the drought were compounded by the fact that the province was bisected by the front line, so that it provided most of the food for the two confronting armies. When the scale of the disaster was known, disorganization of transport prevented the effective delivery of aid. The death toll was between 1.5 and 2 million.[23] There were other famines with lesser consequences in different regions.

However, the state adopted various measures, the most important of which was the reform of the land tax. This tax had been allotted to the provinces in 1928. The situation was becoming untenable because, by force of circumstance, this tax was now the main fiscal resource. It was decided that, from 1941 onwards, it would be paid into the central government's coffers. On the other hand, following a trial judged conclusive in the province of Fujian in 1940, the collection of land tax in kind (that is, in grain and no longer in cash) was extended the following year to the entire free zone. This was both to ensure that the authorities had stocks of grain and to protect against the effects of inflation. The creation of a Ministry of Agriculture and Forestry in June 1940 shows that agricultural production had become a major concern of the government. Over the following years, this ministry worked, with limited means, on the improvement of cultivation methods.[24]

The CCP, a new force

Within the Communist Party, Mao Zedong's strategy (strengthening of the CCP had to take precedence over all other considerations) quickly won out over a line favouring close collaboration with the Guomindang and conforming to Moscow's instructions, as embodied by Wang Ming. During the first years of the war, the communist forces fought only one major battle against the Japanese troops, the Hundred Regiments' Offensive led by Peng Dehuai from 20 August to 5 December 1940 in

Shanxi and Hebei. After initial successes due to the effect of surprise, the Japanese counter-attack was not long in coming and resulted in heavy losses in communist ranks. These would, however, be offset by the propaganda use made of them. Thereafter, the communist forces would cautiously settle for a few local skirmishes in order to preserve their strength.

Beyond the military sphere, the Party was working to improve its organization, and increase its strength and reach.

Internally, it exerted ever tighter control over its members, and from that time onwards displayed a clearly totalitarian aspect. In Yan'an, young people who joined the communist cause were subjected to military training and methodical indoctrination in cadre schools before being sent to harden and prove themselves in the various bases. If the Party recorded significant growth in its membership during the war without losing any of its iron discipline or doctrinal coherence, it also owed this to the launching of real purges from 1942. Under the guise of 'rectifying the Party's style of work' (*zhengdun dang de zuofeng* 整頓黨的作風), of combating 'dogmatism' and 'subjectivism', the aim was no more and no less than to eradicate all freedom of expression and all forms of ideological pluralism in order to impose an orthodoxy that now had a name: 'Mao Zedong Thought' (*Mao Zedong sixiang* 毛澤東思想). Within the Party, violent purges were certainly not a novelty. However, an important innovation appeared: they were carried out according to methods that were as much intended to punish and subjugate those who were their victims as to bring about the latters' true ideological remodelling. Long and humiliating sessions of public criticism became common at this time, as did the writing of endless self-criticisms in which the accused confessed and analysed their past mistakes. Woe betide those reckless few who, like the writer Wang Shiwei, refused to submit. They were crushed without mercy.

With regard to the general population in areas under the CCP's control, moderation prevailed. There were campaigns against landowners, but their stated aim was not land redistribution. Landowners were put in the dock because they were accused of being traitors (*Hanjian* 漢奸). But the main concern was to mobilize local resources to strengthen the army. Apart from that, the population remained relatively free to organize itself. The Party did not rush things regarding secret societies, bandit groups, self-defence militias and religious organizations. But if it tolerated them, it worked very hard to co-opt their leaders and infiltrate them. Once the Party's position was consolidated in a given area, repression could be brutal, as in the case of the Huaibei base in 1944, where the CCP apparatus set about ruthlessly removing its former allies: the self-defence associations and the secret societies.[25]

For the people in the cities, the theses of the 'New Democracy' (*xin minzhu zhuyi* 新民主主義) were promulgated. Mao outlined the major guidelines for this in January 1940. He took a moderate line, according to which the CCP's vocation was to take the lead in an alliance between all the progressive classes of society (the bourgeoisie thus having its place in the revolutionary process alongside the peasants, workers and intellectuals). A pragmatic approach dominated the economic programme: to reassure the bourgeoisie and small-business owners. It included the retention of the private sector. Lastly, the Party championed freedom of expression and political pluralism.

To appeal to students and young people from the urban elite, the CCP managed to present itself as the only real opposition force to Japan. This is the key to how nationalism can explain the rapid progress of the CCP. But, contrary to the thesis of Chalmers Johnson, who saw the CCP's ability to channel the anti-Japanese nationalism of the peasant masses to its advantage as one of the keys to its success, nationalism above all played a major role in attracting the urban youth and intellectual elites to the CCP.[26]

Finally, the Party presented a friendly face to the outside world. Edgar Snow, author of the 1937 bestseller *Red Star over China*, did much in the West to spread a romantic and idealized view of Yan'an. Throughout the war, others followed suit. Like Snow, every foreigner who visited Yan'an was closely monitored. Every effort was made to convince them that egalitarianism, freedom and justice prevailed in Yan'an, and that the communists were the only ones really fighting the Japanese. The naivety with which all these observers allowed themselves to be fooled would be astonishing if it did not foreshadow that of our European Maoists visiting China thirty years later, kept carefully isolated from reality, who were also captivated by the communist paradise that China was supposed to be during the Cultural Revolution.

Mao Zedong and Chiang Kai-shek, the crossed paths of destiny

If the strengthening of the political, state and military apparatus that occurred in Yan'an contrasted with the growing dissolution of the Guomindang, the two underwent a very similar evolution in one respect: the war produced a strengthening of the personal power of both Mao and Chiang Kai-shek.

The time has come to make a short but necessary detour into the biography of these two figures who dominated not only the republican period, but the entire twentieth century in China.

Adversaries for most of their lives, Mao and Chiang had points in common, especially in the early part of their trajectory. They were both from the south, from Hunan and Zhejiang respectively. Their social origin was just above that of the populace, from the circles of very small local notables who could not claim to be even slightly associated with the state hierarchy. They belonged roughly to the same generation – those who were in their twenties at the time of the fall of the Qing. In their adolescence, both saw and painfully felt the reality of a humiliated and dominated China – a common starting point for their political lives. Although they were equally enthusiastic about the 1911 Revolution, they were only secondary players. Mao, although resistant to any academic discipline and largely self-taught, proved to be a great writer (having worked in journalism). His anti-intellectual bent was confirmed as early as 1918–19, when he was an assistant librarian at Beijing University. This episode, in fact, left him deeply scarred, proving to him that he would never have a place amongst leading intellectual circles. Within the Communist Party, of which he was one of the founders, Mao proved to be a leader of men, served by a charisma as indisputable as his physical courage, assets that allowed him to bring to fruition a consummate skill for dividing his opponents. His scruples about resorting to their physical elimination disappeared from 1930 onwards. Mao also knew how to play another lesser-known asset: men from Hunan (and, to a lesser extent, from the neighbouring province of Hubei) strongly dominated the heights of the CCP organization. Not very comfortable in Mandarin, Mao, who retained his strong Hunanese accent throughout his life, benefitted from this informal network of men united by speaking the same dialect. In later years, he helped to maintain the predominance of Hunan natives himself by promoting the careers of men such as Liu Shaoqi and Ren Bishi.

Chiang Kai-shek followed a more traditional path. His military studies in Japan gave him the opportunity to gain experience abroad and to acquire command of a foreign language – something Mao always lacked, as he left China for only the first time in his life at the age of 56 (in the winter of 1949–50, to meet Stalin). A rather dull personality, Chiang was neither a strategist nor an intellectual. It must be said that his rise to prominence was marked by both skill in intrigue and luck. After the revolution, Chiang moved in the troubled waters between two closely entwined circles: the underworld of Shanghai's organized crime, and revolutionary circles. He played a winning poker hand in June 1922 when he risked his own life coming to the rescue of Sun Yat-sen, who was in mortal danger in Guangzhou. In gratitude, the latter sent him to Russia (August–November 1923) before making him director of the Huangpu Academy. Chiang was therefore in the right place (at the head of Huangpu) at the right time, when, with Russian help, the Guomindang were building up their military force, of which the Academy would form the backbone. He benefitted from the eclipse of Xu Chongzhi, who, backed by a powerful sibling group, was the party's main military leader in the mid-1920s. But Xu, guilty of a few mistakes as well as some notorious antics, quickly faded into the background, joining the ranks of those who have been consigned to oblivion because they loved a life of pleasure too much and power not enough. We have also seen how Chiang took advantage of a fortunate combination of circumstances in the months following Sun's death, with the assassination of Liao Zhongkai and the subsequent sidelining of Hu Hanmin.

The conclusion reached by the many biographical works devoted to Mao, notably the book by Alain Roux,[27] is that he was helped in his rise by his intellectual brilliance and charisma. On the other hand, it is likely that Chiang Kai-shek took advantage of the fact that his rivals, unimpressed by his personality, underestimated him. The fact that Mao was a man of much higher calibre than Chiang was of enormous importance as their personal power asserted itself during the war within both parties.

It is clear that the remnants of collegiality that remained in the functioning of the Guomindang faded away in the first months of the conflict. The Extraordinary National Congress of March–April 1938 enshrined Chiang Kai-shek's leading status by conferring on him the title of *zongcai* 總裁, president. Shortly afterwards, Wang Jingwei's defection rid him of the last figure from the Guomindang's past likely to overshadow him. They closed ranks around a leader who was the personification of resistance. The Cairo Conference (November 1943), where it was decided that Japan's surrender would be followed by the return of Manchuria, Taiwan and the Pescadores Islands to China, gave Chiang Kai-shek the chance to appear as a war leader dealing on an equal footing with Roosevelt and Churchill.[28]

At the same time, Mao also managed to increase his dominance. The final person in a position to question his leadership was Wang Ming, a brilliant theoretician who returned from the USSR in November 1937. Wang Ming was the main architect of the United Front policy, in his role as the transmitter of Moscow's directives. Considerably weakened by the end of 1939, Wang was ousted from the party leadership in 1941 (although he was not formally excluded until 1945).

However, Mao's ascendancy was not simply due to his lust for power. It was also a public relations operation orchestrated by the Party for the benefit of the outside world, to make sure that Chiang Kai-shek was not the face of China. This necessity helped to overcome any remaining doubts amongst some of the top-ranking leaders.[29] Increasingly, the CCP promoted the figure of Mao to the stream of Western journalists making the pilgrimage to Yan'an. One of the obstacles to Mao's assertion of his pre-eminence was his lack of status as a theorist. He worked as hard as he could to fill this gap. His writings began to be studied by Party cadres, and the term 'Mao Zedong Thought' (*Mao Zedong sixiang*) appeared in early 1941.[30] Children were taught to sing 'We are all Chairman Mao's good little children.' It was also during the war that the CCP acquired an authorized history: the 'Resolution from the Central Committee of Certain Issues in the History of the CCP' was adopted in April 1945. Although this text is essentially the work of Ren Bishi, its gestation, which began four years earlier in 1941, was collective. The Resolution (which only covers the history of the Party between 1921 and 1935) makes Mao the central figure, emphasizes the events over which he had control and castigates his main rivals (foremost among them Li Lisan, Bo Gu and Wang Ming).

Mao did not just succeed in becoming the head of the CCP. He also placed men of proven loyalty at the top of the Party hierarchy, such as the efficient Liu Shaoqi, who worked tirelessly to weaken Wang Ming from 1937 to 1938 and was already his no. 2.

One fact also deserves attention, because it is full of significance: Zhou Enlai's choice in mid-1939 to link his political destiny indissolubly to that of Mao (whom he had opposed several times previously). Thoroughly politically astute, Zhou saw clearly that Mao's ascendancy was irreversible. In the years and decades that followed, he even became a model of submission and devotion to Mao.

Occupied China and the collaborating governments

The history of China at war is also the history of the areas occupied by the Japanese: 900,000 square kilometres, with a population of over 180 million. In the early months of the conflict, several collaborating governments were set up at the instigation of the Japanese armed forces. The 'Provisional Government of the Republic of China' (*Zhonghua minguo linshi zhengfu* 中華民國臨時政府) was founded in Beijing by Wang Kemin in December 1937. It was soon followed in March 1938 by Liang Hongzhi's 'Reformed Government of the Republic of China' (*Zhonghua minguo weixin zhengfu* 中華民國維新政府), based in Nanjing.[31] But Wang and Liang were, politically speaking, second-rankers. The credibility of the governments they embodied was immediately undermined. As for the political staff they managed to attract, they were not very impressive. The Japanese fell back on Wang and Liang for lack of anything better, after having courted in vain men of a different stature, notably two former grandees from the 1910s–1920s: Wu Peifu and Tang Shaoyi. The discreet Japanese requests to these two continued until their deaths (Tang was assassinated on 30 September 1938, and Wu died at the end of 1939).

However, the main hopes of the Japanese would soon rest on Wang Jingwei. The man clearly had a complex personality. Able in his early years to cross swords with Liang Qichao over the philosophy of J.-J. Rousseau, his talent was such that in 1917 Cai Yuanpei asked him to take up a professorship of Chinese literature at Beijing University and thus take his place among the cream of the Chinese intelligentsia.[32] His revolutionary record was equally impeccable. In his youth, he had undertaken, with a courage bordering on recklessness, to assassinate the regent Zaifeng (April 1910). A founding member of the United League, he was from the outset one of the most prestigious leaders of the Guomindang. The death of Hu Hanmin in 1936 made him the last great 'historical' leader.

Wang's defection was effected over several stages. Hostile to the alliance with the communists and a supporter of appeasement with Japan before the war, he conducted negotiations with the Japanese through some of his deputies from early 1938. In exchange for a number of commitments from the Japanese side, the most important of which was the promise of a withdrawal of Japanese troops, he left Chongqing and flew to Hanoi on 18 December 1938. From then on, his position weakened very rapidly. None of the warlords who retained a certain autonomy – not even the powerful Long Yun, master of Yunnan, whose support Wang had particularly hoped for – came out in his favour. Similarly, apart from two fairly significant figures, Zhou Fohai and Chen Gongpo, no Guomindang heavyweight, including Chiang's most determined opponents, took the plunge. Wang probably made the mistake of underestimating the strength of the resistant nationalism we have already mentioned, which made the Guomindang leadership close ranks behind Chiang. Even among Wang's closest associates, many remained loyal to Chongqing, such as the economist Gu Mengyu.

Nevertheless, in early May 1939, Wang reached the occupied zone and began direct talks with the Japanese. Aware of his political weight and the fact that he could represent a very significant asset in Japan's hand of cards, Wang tried to negotiate for the government he wanted to set up to benefit from a real margin of manoeuvre vis-à-vis Japan and its authority to be exercised over the entire occupied zone. The result was disappointing: the Japanese side refused to concede these two points. Mortified by the harsh terms of the emerging agreement, Gao Zongwu and Tao Xisheng, two of Wang's main collaborators involved in the negotiations, defected in early January 1940. Wang Jingwei nevertheless inaugurated a reorganized national government (*gaizu guomin zhengfu* 改組國民政府) in Nanjing on 30 March 1940.[33]

It would be a mistake to put this government in the same category as those set up at the beginning of the war by the Japanese. They certainly shared the same virulent anti-communist stance and relayed the Japanese slogans of 'New Order in East Asia' (*Dai tōa shin chitsujo*

13 Wang Jingwei in 1925.

大東亜新秩序), and then that of the 'Greater East Asia Co-Prosperity Sphere' (*Dai tōa kyōeiken* 大東亜共栄圈), which appeared in the summer of 1940. According to Japanese propaganda, the Co-Prosperity Sphere was supposed to defend and promote a common culture among East Asian countries and free them from the domination of a West depicted as being mired in the vilest materialism. However, while the other collaborationist governments were fundamentally hostile to the Guomindang and their doctrine, Wang Jingwei's regime claimed on the contrary to be heirs to Sun Yat-sen's legacy. His choice of Nanjing as the capital reflected his desire to embody the legitimacy of the Guomindang. The flag it adopted was identical to the one flown in Chongqing; it differed only in the addition of a yellow pennant bearing the six characters *heping fangong jianguo* 和平返工建國 (peace, anti-communism and national construction).

But the outline agreement (*jiben tiaoyue* 基本條約) that was signed a few months later, on 30 November 1940, reflects how little autonomy Wang had under the Japanese. In the years that followed, Wang Jingwei certainly obtained some results, such as the retrocession of foreign concessions, but, in general, his manoeuvres failed on two counts that irremediably undermined the legitimacy of his regime. No evacuation of Japanese troops took place, even if he was given the possibility of forming his own army. Furthermore, he also failed to get rid of the system of Japanese 'advisors', such as the powerful General Kagesa Sadaaki, who exercised real administrative supervision of his government.

Wang Jingwei, who had not fully recovered from the wounds sustained in the attempt to assassinate him in 1935, went to Japan for treatment in early March 1944. He died in Nagoya on 10 November 1944. Zhou Fohai, who already controlled Finance and was the privileged interlocutor of the Japanese advisors, became the main figure of the collaborationist regime and remained so until the end of the war.

1944–1945: return to the war of movement

From the Ichigō offensive to the surrender

The last two years of the war were paradoxical: China came close to disaster with the Ichigō offensive, before finding itself a few months later on the winning side thanks to the victory of its American ally in the Pacific War. In May 1944 came a blow that was as unexpected as it was devastating – the vast Japanese offensive known as *ichigō sakusen* 一号作戦 (Operation No. 1) (see Map 9).[34] Although its objectives have not been fully elucidated, it seems that in launching this offensive, the Japanese general staff was pursuing two main goals. First of all, it was a question of obtaining control of a continuous zone between Manchuria and Indochina, in order to mitigate the American domination of the seas, which paralysed its communications. The other objective was to annihilate the American air bases established in Guangxi (Guilin and Liuzhou). The importance of these bases lay not only in their role on the Chinese front, but also in their usage for bombing operations in Japan. Operations began in the north, in Henan. In April and May, Japanese troops advanced easily and swept away nationalist troops in the west of the province. But it was the south of China that provided the terrain for the main confrontations, and in particular Hunan (a province that was all the more 'useful' because it had a large surplus of rice). The two main cities, Hengyang and Changsha, fell to Japanese troops. The Chinese armies also beat a miserable retreat on the Guangxi front.

Ichigō was highly successful for the Japanese. It plainly revealed the advanced state of wear and tear of the totally unprepared nationalist army, which in a few months found itself on the brink of complete collapse. At the beginning of December 1944, the American General Wedemeyer estimated that the fall of Guiyang was only a matter of days away and predicted that Kunming would fall in early February. Drawing up an unequivocal assessment of the performance of the Chinese troops, he wrote: 'The situation has grown steadily worse since June. The Chinese have not offered resistance worthy of the name since the defense of Hengyang where they fought creditably.'[35] In mid-December, at the exact moment when the very survival of the Chongqing regime appeared to be in jeopardy, the offensive, which had achieved its objectives, was halted on the initiative of the Japanese themselves.

In the course of the Ichigō campaign, Japanese troops inflicted very heavy losses on Guomindang forces. The financial effort required to deal with this offensive also increased the Chongqing government's fiscal difficulties and destabilized the economy.

Although no further significant operations took place until the end of the war, 1945 brought a final setback for the Guomindang. In February 1945, at the Yalta Conference, Stalin had pledged to declare war on Japan three months after the end of the fighting on the European front. On the night of 8–9 August 1945, the USSR entered the war against Japan. Contrary to what one might think, it was not just an anecdote in military terms. The campaign lasted about ten days. Indeed, even if the terms of the surrender were announced by Hirohito on 14 August, the ceasefire was not concluded in Manchuria until the 19th. Some units even continued to fight until 26 August. Soviet troops invaded Manchuria (reaching some objectives that were 800 kms – or 500 miles – behind the original front). They inflicted very heavy losses on the Guandong Army (around 80,000 dead). The political consequences of this campaign were even more significant, as the USSR now had a say in the affairs of north-east China.

The war's outcome

The toll the war took on China was terrible. Due as much to a glaring material inferiority as to the failure of its health services, the Guomindang army suffered much greater human losses than its opponent. Roughly 2 million soldiers, including 84 nationalist generals, died. Civilian losses were much higher, with the total number of victims numbering around 10 million.[36] But this bloodletting was spread over a period of more than eight years, which somewhat diminished its impact. Furthermore, not only young men were involved, because the civilian population was widely affected as well. And, unlike the great revolts of the third quarter of the nineteenth century, which had created localized voids in certain parts of China (the Lower Yangtze valley), the war did not lead to major interregional imbalances. Also, the war of 1937–45 certainly had an impact on the birth rate, but not to the point of causing the emergence of 'hollow classes'.[37] It would take a much worse catastrophe, the Great Leap Forward, for China to experience this phenomenon. China had not yet begun its demographic transition and had a vigorous birth rate that promised to quickly compensate.

The Chinese theatre of operations rivalled other Second World War fronts in horror, not only because of the number of casualties and the massacres of civilians such as those in Nanjing, but also because the means employed had changed. Japanese forces developed bacteriological experiments on human beings on an unprecedented scale. They also spread the plague by means of bombing, for example in the cities of Quzhou and Ningbo in October 1940.[38]

The material toll was no less heavy and is reflected in the difference between the pre- and post-war periods in the field of industrial production. Some cities were obliterated, such as Changsha and Wuhan (destroyed by American bombers in December 1944). The large-scale dismantling of industrial facilities in Manchuria (the counterpart to that at the other extreme of Eurasia, in East Germany), by Russian troops in the immediate post-war period, was a disaster of a different kind. This methodical looting had the effect of virtually wiping out one of China's major industrial regions. In 1947, Manchuria's steel production was about one-hundredth of what it had been in the Japanese era.[39] Communication routes also suffered. In addition to this destruction and looting were added the consequences of eight years of under-investment in the infrastructure that still existed. Although less visible, this also seriously compromised the future.[40]

On the eve of war, Wang Jingwei believed that an all-out war against Japan would only play into the hands of the communists. He was therefore prepared to make significant sacrifices to keep the peace with Japan. Chiang Kai-shek saw things differently. He had been certain for years that there would eventually be a war between the West and Japan in Asia. The West was thus destined to become China's ally and to enable it to triumph over Japan.[41] With curious irony, both were right: Pearl Harbor and the Japanese surrender in 1945 would initially prove Chiang right. But four years later, Wang Jingwei's prediction would come true: the war, by greatly weakening the Guomindang, had prepared the way for the CCP.

For it can be stated unequivocally that the real winner of the war was the CCP. A comparison between its pre-war situation and that of 1945 speaks for itself. Its 92,000 km² enclave (approx. 35,520 mi² – the size of Portugal) with 1.5 million inhabitants, had grown tenfold to 900,000 km² (approx. 348,000 sq. mi. – the size of Pakistan) with a population of over 100 million. The Party now had more than 1 million men under arms (there were 40,000 in 1937). It was then that its troops took on the name of 'Liberation Army' (*jiefangjun* 解放軍). The CCP went from a tightrope walker that had danced on the edge of the precipice during the Nanjing decade to a powerful wrestler, ready to go head to head with the Guomindang in the final act of the republican period.

This particularly outstanding performance from the CCP is the result of two factors: a clear strategy, and incredibly favourable circumstances. Indeed, it was not a certainty that the war would favour the CCP to this extent. A quick survey of operations may help us to see more clearly how much events resembled a succession of happenstances exceptionally favourable to the communists.

First of all, after the reprieve of the Xi'an incident, the outbreak of war saved the CCP, thanks to the imposition of the United Front. The Long March could have been even longer and ended in total annihilation. The first months of the Japanese offensive and the choice to resist inch by inch in Shanghai broke the back of the nationalist army, killing many of its elite troops. Although plausible at the end of 1937, the scenario of a capitulation, by allowing the invaders to set up a government of collaboration which would necessarily have had strong anti-communist overtones, certainly presented a great danger for the CCP. This did not come to fruition, however. Instead, China settled down to an eight-year war, which was another lucky break for the CCP. The length of operations made it possible to pin down the Guomindang troops, undermine the country's economy and disorganize the Nationalist Party. The fact that the Japanese only had a very imperfect grip (and even less so after the start of the Pacific War operations) on the area from which they had driven the Guomindang opened up immense opportunities for the CCP. Despite the Guomindang's efforts, by the end of the war there was, in addition to the main base in Shaanxi–Suiyuan, a string of some fifteen communist bases that had become entrenched behind enemy lines throughout the east of the country, from North China to the mountainous centre of Hainan Island (see Map 8). As for the powerful Ichigō offensive launched in May 1944 – luckily for the communists – it concerned mainly southern China. Its assaults were directed almost exclusively against Chiang Kai-shek's troops. The Guomindang lost military forces in the offensive, saw the destabilization of the economy increase, but above all, and most detrimentally for the future, they seriously damaged their credit with the main asset it had up its sleeve – the American ally.

The suddenness of the surrender, a consequence of the atomic bombs dropped on Hiroshima and Nagasaki, surprised the Guomindang, who were ill prepared for the consequences of a Japanese defeat that everyone knew was inevitable, but no one had foreseen as being so rapid. Paradoxically, the war ended too soon for the Guomindang to have been able to prepare for peace, and also to hope to take advantage of the Japanese weakening in the Pacific War and thus, if not to regain all the lost ground, at least to obtain some successes that would restore its image. The USSR's entry into the war against Japan at the very end was of great consequence from a political point of view. It gave the USSR a leading role in north-eastern China. Even though Soviet troops often had a rather tense relationship with the CCP, they nonetheless favoured the latter's military reinforcement by handing over to them, in the months following the surrender, a large part of the equipment seized from Japanese troops.

In 1972, Mao told Tanaka Kakuei, the acting Japanese prime minister, that the CCP should be grateful to Japan for its aggression, because without that they would never have come to power. As provocative as this statement may have been, it reflected the fact that the 1937–45 war radically altered the balance of power between the Guomindang and the CCP, and ultimately allowed the CCP to prevail during the 1945–9 civil war. We could go even further and say that Japan was, from the CCP's point of view, the ideal enemy – strong enough to inflict a litany of defeats on the Guomindang and to dramatically weaken them in a war of attrition, but not strong enough to win a total victory or to hold on to the vast territories it conquered.

FIVE

Civil War (1945–1949)

The short four-year period between the end of the Sino-Japanese War and the proclamation of the People's Republic of China is generally treated by historians as the chronicle of a death foretold (that of the Guomindang's hegemony over mainland China), whose deeper and more contingent reasons have been reviewed. We will take the same approach. However, it is appropriate to emphasize at the outset that not only was the defeat of the Guomindang not inevitable, but it could legitimately be considered highly unlikely in the aftermath of Japan's surrender.

A very favourable situation for the Guomindang

The political and symbolic dividends of victory

It has been shown how the war benefitted the CCP above all, to the point of opening up a new political horizon. Nevertheless, the 1945 victory brought very substantial benefits to the Guomindang as the legitimate government of China.

On a strictly military level, in accordance with the terms of the surrender, Japanese troops surrendered only to the Guomindang forces. The military potential of the latter was strengthened by the huge quantities of material that they recouped.

At the end of the war, the Guomindang could justifiably claim to have made China a great power. This status was manifest in the allocation to China of one of the five permanent seats on the UN Security Council, with Chinese becoming one of the five official languages of the UNO. As early as 1943, the Chongqing government had obtained another measure highly symbolic of China's new status. This was the repeal by the United States of all laws restricting Chinese emigration to its soil since the first exclusionary measures of 1882 (Magnuson Act, 17 December 1943). Among other things, Chinese emigrants were now able to acquire US citizenship.

The territories successively occupied by Japan were returned to China (including Taiwan). The retrocession of the Guangzhouwan leasehold territory by France was somewhat delayed, but nevertheless took place. (The Leased Territory of Guangzhouwan was on the coast of Zhanjiang, leased to France in 1898 and administered by French Indochina.) Only the two oldest European possessions, Hong Kong and Macao, escaped the changes. The last vestiges of the 'unequal treaty system', concessions and extraterritoriality, were no more than painful memories. The terms of Japan's surrender also allowed Chinese forces to launch themselves abroad for the first time since the Qing.[1] General Lu Han's 200,000 men occupied Indochina north of the 16th parallel from late August 1945. They indulged themselves by setting up their headquarters in Hanoi, in the palace of the governor general. Up until their withdrawal in May–June 1946, these occupation forces tried to promote the rise of moderate political parties to block the Viet Minh, without much success. Within China, the nationalists scored another notable victory by putting an end to the relative autonomy that Long Yun continued to enjoy in Yunnan. He could be considered (along with the various Ma scattered around the north-west) as the last specimen of a now almost extinct species – the warlords. Long was neutralized by a clever coup at the end of 1945, and his province came under the control of the central government.

The Guomindang could therefore envisage capitalizing on the prestige gained from the victory: Chiang Kai-shek's visit to Beijing on 16 December 1945 was a triumph, during which he was cheered by 100,000 enthusiastic young people in Tiananmen Square.

The economic rebound in the immediate post-war period

Japan's defeat and the end of the privileges enjoyed by foreigners opened up opportunities in another area, that of the economy. The disappearance of the very strong competition from Japanese products in China itself, as well as in South East Asian markets, represented a tremendous opportunity for Chinese industry. Similarly, competition from foreign manufacturers in China was also virtually eliminated as a result of the war. For example, foreign cigarette manufacturers, who accounted for more than 60 per cent of production before the war, represented a maximum of around 15 per cent in 1946–7.

14 Chiang Kai-shek a few days after the Japanese surrender.

The conditions for a powerful economic recovery were thus present and it manifested itself during the first two years of the post-war period. This is a fact generally ignored by Western historians; as for the Chinese, they only want to see in this recovery a 'deceptive prosperity' (*xujia fanrong* 虛假繁榮).[2] In doing so, they make the mistake of projecting the shadow of the (very real) economic slump of the following two years on to 1946–7.

In the main industrial sector (textiles), once the supply of raw materials had been re-established, the years 1946–7 were a brief but truly golden age. In Shanghai, cotton yarn production returned to and exceeded pre-war peak levels by 1947. Optimism reigned among entre-preneurs, who reinvested their profits massively.[3] Another indication of a climate of optimism conducive to the revival of the economy was the resumption of investments by overseas Chinese in 1946–7.

There is a lack of general statistical data on industrial production or gross domestic product in the post-war years.[4] However, electricity production data is available and can provide an acceptable indicator of the general level of industrial activity. At first glance, the national figures may seem very unimpressive (+5.6 per cent between mid-1945 and mid-1947). But this modest result is explained by a staggering drop in electricity production of 61.4 per cent in Manchuria, a region that accounted for almost three-quarters of electricity production at the end of the war. This was the result of the Soviet occupation. Russian troops systematically dismantled industries and electricity generating facilities. Taking these factors into account, the disastrous data from Manchuria clearly detracts from extremely strong growth in the rest of the country.[5]

Similarly, in the field of public finances, which had been damaged by eight years of war, the opportunities for recovery were undoubtedly there. The rampant inflation had at least one advantage: it made it possible to liquidate the domestic debt relatively easily (the external debt was expressed in foreign currency). This was done in mid-1946, when the Chinese government announced the liquidation of its loans at their nominal value. This operation was *ipso facto* equivalent to a cancellation of the domestic debt at a derisory cost to public finances. This sleight of hand, which resulted in the ruin of Treasury bill holders, naturally carried a political cost. The state also acquired a powerful boost with the general confiscation and then nationalization of Japanese assets in China. It should be noted that this nationalization was carried out without taking into account the claims of any former Chinese owners. In Tianjin, for example, Japanese forces had confiscated the vast majority of indus-tries at the beginning of the war. But at the end of 1945, instead of being returned to the despoiled former Chinese owners or their descendants, they fell directly into the hands of the state.[6] At the same time, Song Ziwen nationalized all the ex-Japanese mills and brought them together to form the Chinese Textile Construction Company (*Zhongguo fangzhi jianshe gongsi* 中國紡織建設公司), the first major state-owned group in the Chinese textile industry.[7] The Guomindang thus had available considerable advantages in assets at the end of the war. But it failed to make them bear fruit. Its management of the aftermath of the 1945 victory incorporated major errors that quickly weakened its position.

Immediately post-war: 1945–1946

The role of the USSR and the USA

The civil war played out against a Cold War background. Each of the protagonists, the Guomindang and the CCP, received help from one of the new superpowers. US logistical support was crucial in September and October 1945, in airlifting troops from former Free China to the occupied areas to disarm the Japanese troops. Apart from one interruption, there was no lack of American material aid. But it is clear that it came at a cost: the CCP was free to portray Chiang Kai-shek as a puppet of American imperialism. In Manchuria, communist troops recovered weapons from Japanese forces via Marshal Malinovsky's Soviet occupation troops. And when Russian troops left Manchuria (March–May 1946), the Chinese communists took control of most of the region.[8] But it would be quite wrong to see the CCP's victory as the fruit of Stalin's realpolitik, which would contrast with the excessive scruples of the United States, all too quick to deem its ally, the Guomindang, unpalatable. The Soviet Union's support for the CCP blew alternately hot and cold. Stalin was far from enthusiastic about the CCP. Up until very late, he thought it possible, and even desirable, to get along with Guomindang China, from which he had obtained a major concession on 5 January 1946 with the recognition of the independence of Northern Mongolia.[9] At the beginning of 1949, the USSR still seemed to be attached to the Guomindang's cause, which appeared to all other eyes to be almost lost. One episode is significant: the nationalist government, faced with the approach of the communist armies, asked foreign diplomats to close their embassies in Nanjing and move them to Guangzhou. Of all the powers, the USSR was the only one to comply, while the others kept their representatives in Nanjing in order to prepare the transition to the new communist power. Stalin was therefore very, very cautious, concerned as always to put the interests of the Soviet Union first, at the expense of all other considerations. All in all, while the role of the USSR and the United States should not be ignored, the CCP's victory did not come down to that.

Locking of horns for the first time

Although both protagonists were striving towards the same goal of remaining in sole control of the country (the idea of a partition was equally repugnant to Chiang and Mao Zedong), the façade of the United Front was maintained for a little over a year. Indeed, in the face of public opinion eager for peace, neither the CCP nor the Guomindang could afford to give the impression of being at the origin of the rupture. The two sides handled the first phase of their confrontation with kid gloves.

Negotiations to form a coalition government opened in Chongqing immediately after the Japanese surrender. Apart from the joint declaration of good intentions known as the Double Ten Agreements (*shuangshi xieding* 雙十協定), which was signed on 10 October, they did not lead to any tangible results. Above all, they were used by Mao to promote, with the help of Zhou Enlai, the image of a Communist Party championing democracy, unity and peace. During the months he spent in Chongqing, he met many important people, Western diplomats, politicians of various stripes, occasionally writing poetry with men of letters. His charisma worked wonders, contrasting favourably with the pallid Chiang who, over the next four years, demonstrated that he did not have the stature to be China's absolute master.[10]

General Marshall, one of America's most prestigious officers and statesmen, was sent to China in December 1945 to mediate and help form a coalition government. A political consultative conference, at which all the political forces were represented, met in Chongqing at the beginning of 1946. It set out the main political guidelines: establishment of a coalition government, adoption of a constitution, ceasefire and reduction of the armed forces. One of the crucial steps laid down was the convening of a National Assembly, with representatives from the Guomindang, the CCP, the Democratic League and other smaller parties. But these were mere pipe dreams: neither the CCP nor the Guomindang wanted a peaceful compromise. The Guomindang knew they were the strongest, and, soon strengthened by military successes, did not intend to give up on exercising sole power. As for the CCP, there was no question of it giving up an autonomous armed force, nor the territories it administered without being accountable to others.

The Guomindang's post-war failure

If there was an imbalance between the two parties, the Guomindang began to redress matters through their numerous errors. The former Japanese-occupied territories were subjected to what was tantamount to wholesale looting by newly arrived officials from the former free zones. Above all, the conversion rate of the currency put into circulation in the wartime occupied areas was set at an extremely low level. As a result, millions of people saw their savings evaporate. At the same time, the Guomindang opted for a minimal purge. Thus, among the civilian and military leaders of collaboration governments, about 2,700 were executed (the most notable among them were Chen Gongpo and Liang Hongzhi) and 2,300 (among them, Zhou Fohai) sentenced to life imprisonment.[11] Although the purge was less botched than has been thought, and for the most part involved trials that respected legal forms, there was a clear desire to spare the cadres of the collaborating regimes' military forces with a view to the coming war against the CCP.

The regime proved unable to eliminate another legacy of the war – hyperinflation. In contrast to the wartime period, when a certain inertia prevailed, the authorities took a succession of initiatives. The last of these was the creation of a new currency unit, the gold yuan, accompanied by an attempt at authoritarian price suppression orchestrated in Shanghai by Chiang Kai-shek's son, Jiang Jingguo. While this action was undoubtedly dynamic, it nevertheless came far too late.[12] Adding to the deleterious effects of inflation, were the effects of increasingly unbridled speculation, which took place at the expense of investment.[13]

Another mistake of the Guomindang was to alienate the intellectual elites through unnecessary brutality. Lianda University, which had remained a sanctuary of academic freedom during the war, was brought to heel in November–December 1945, with four deaths. In July 1946, two important members of the Democratic League were liquidated – Li Gongpu and Wen Yiduo.

The National Assembly did meet in November–December 1946, but without the communists and their allies in the Democratic League. On 18 November, Zhou Enlai, the main negotiator for the communist side, left the negotiating table for good. The following January, Marshall, having seen the futility of his mediation efforts, returned to the United States. From then on, weapons only would do the talking.

The military era: 1946–1949

The first military operations of 1946 were limited in scope and generally benefitted the Guomindang. In May, General Du Yuming won an important battle at Siping in Manchuria against the troops commanded by Lin Biao. Around 40,000 communist fighters were killed, and the retreat became a stampede. The ceasefire imposed on 6 June 1946 by American mediation was accepted very reluctantly by the Guomindang, as it offered a salutary respite to the beleaguered communist forces. To claim that without this providential ceasefire the outcome of the civil war would have been different is pure speculation. The fact remains that the communists received crucial support that enabled them not to lose what would become the main battleground: Manchuria.

Military operations began on a large scale in early 1947 in northern China following the final breakdown of negotiations. The Guomindang's numerical and material superiority (particularly in the fields of aviation and tanks) appeared overwhelming. It also occupied almost the entire country at the beginning of the operations. An offensive by General Hu Zongnan in March 1947 led to a largely symbolic victory: the capture of the communist capital, Yan'an.[14] It was a success in name only because thanks to the effectiveness of its military intelligence, the Communist Party had been aware of the plans for this operation. So, if the fall of its capital was unavoidable, at least its evacuation was well organized.

Important in all conflicts, intelligence played a particularly crucial role in this one because the communist secret services quickly gained a decisive ascendancy.

During the war, the *Juntong*, led with an iron fist by Dai Li, had grown impressively, to the point where, at the end of the conflict, it completely eclipsed its competitor the *Zhongtong*. It had tens of thousands of agents, its own prison system and a whole parallel administration. This worrying intelligence behemoth was far from ineffective during the Sino-Japanese War.[15] Its success in spreading terror and death among the collaborators in the occupied zone had been demonstrated. But Dai Li was also able, for example, to keep Chiang Kai-shek informed of the precise content of the deliberations of the Japanese government's Council of Ministers. The death of this irreplaceable executor of Chiang's dirty work (in an aeroplane accident in March 1946) was a very hard blow for the Guomindang. He had undoubtedly concentrated too much power in his own hands, so that his disappearance led to the disorganization of the *Juntong*. True, the nationalist secret services were still capable of some brilliant actions. For example, a perfectly targeted raid on Mao failed by the skin of its teeth on 18 May 1948. However, it is clear that the ability of the communists to turn high-ranking Guomindang officials during the civil war was not matched by the nationalists. General Liu Fei, a member of the general staff, is a particularly spectacular case of a spy in the pay of the communists at the highest level of the nationalist command.[16] The CCP thus had the enormous advantage of being able to read its opponent's game. And the first large-scale military operations soon showed that they had other important assets. The weight of the population's (more or less spontaneous) support for the communist forces has probably been exaggerated. Lucien Bianco rightly points out that, while the workers had given significant support to the troops of the first United Front during the Northern Expedition through strikes, sabotage and insurrections aimed at disrupting the enemy's rear, they no longer played such an important role during the civil war.[17]

More importance should be placed on the stronger motivation of the communist troops as a result of a constant drive for political indoctrination. At the command level, the communist military chiefs on the ground (Chen Yi, Liu Bocheng, Nie Rongzhen) proved superior to the Guomindang generals who opposed them (Chen Cheng, Du Yuming, Wei Lihuang). The Guomindang were not without good leaders, but Chiang Kai-shek made one of his greatest mistakes in this area. As loyalty to his person took precedence over any other consideration for him, he systematically dismissed the most capable leaders, preferring less competent men as close associates. According to a British intelligence report of April 1948, high command positions in the nationalist army were given to those who had close personal ties

15 January 1949, communist troops and their propaganda organization march in Beijing.

to Chiang Kai-shek or political clout in the Guomindang. The author of this report points out that it was exceptional for officers with only military excellence to be given important command positions.[18] The most obvious example was the sidelining of Bai Chongxi, the former Guangxi warlord, for whom Chiang felt a strong personal hostility, seemingly mixed with jealousy.

But the civil war was probably played out at the level of the supreme command. On one hand, while Chiang Kai-shek struggled to get his general officers on the ground to obey him, the chain of command worked very well in the Red Army. But, above all, Lin Biao took himself in hand after the serious mistake at Siping. His strategic genius was confirmed in battle after battle against Chiang Kai-shek, whereas the latter proved on various occasions that he was a great strategist.

The balance of power between the two armies was thus reversed following a major strategic error by Chiang, who let his best troops be surrounded and then capitulate in Manchuria (November 1948). The siege of Changchun (May 1947 –October 1948) was a particularly atrocious episode in a civil war that was not lacking in such episodes: 200,000 civilians, more than half the city's population, died of cold and hunger.[19] At the same time, the Battle of Huaihai 淮海 was being fought, whose theatre was bounded to the south by the Huai River (Huai he 淮河) and to the east by the coastal city of Haizhou 海州 in Jiangsu (hence its name). Altogether it pitted 1.8 million men against each other between November 1948 and January 1949. It was the last chance for the nationalists to turn the tide of the war and it ended in complete disaster for them.

The People's Liberation Army crossed the Yangtze River without any problems on 21 April. Nanjing and Shanghai fell with scarcely any resistance. It must be emphasized that, in addition to the mastery with which the PLA conducted military operations, the CCP planned the takeover of the cities carefully. Two contributions to a recent collective work illustrate this phenomenon well, whether it concerned protecting the production machinery of factories and workshops from destruction (which implies – paradoxically to say the least – curbing the enthusiasm of certain advance working-class groups), or ensuring the maintenance of order.[20]

The Guomindang side lost all hope. Military operations were aimed essentially at covering the withdrawal to Taiwan. The nationalist collapse was accelerated by the defection of several Guomindang leaders, who went over to the enemy with the men under their command – such as the governor of Hunan province, Cheng Qian, in August 1949. When Lu Han, the governor of Yunnan, became a turncoat in December 1949, he put an end to Chiang Kai-shek's hopes of making this province a last anti-communist bastion. The CCP appointed all these last-minute new comrades to sinecures, with all the necessary honours. But none of them was to play a real political role in the new regime.

The People's Republic of China was declared on 1 October 1949 in Beijing, in a well-orchestrated ceremony attended by 300,000 people in Tiananmen Square. Meanwhile, conquest of the south of the country continued. Guangzhou fell two weeks later, on 14 October. The island of Hainan was taken in April 1950. The new state, whose recognition by the USSR and populist democracies came not long after, set up its

16 Execution of communists by the Guomindang, circa 1948.

capital in Peking (renamed Beijing at this point). The red flag with five yellow stars (still used today) was adopted. Displayed for the first time on 30 September, it was the direct representation of the New Democracy's policy. A large star represents the Communist Party, surrounded by four smaller ones representing the social classes with which it is allied (workers, peasants, petty bourgeoisie and national capitalists). The arrangement of the stars and their difference in size clearly show the dominant role of the Party.

Sclerosis of the Guomindang

The defeat of the Guomindang cannot, however, be seen as purely resulting from military factors. In an important book, Lloyd Eastman diagnosed a rotting Guomindang in 1945.[21] He pointed to corruption, in particular. This diagnosis needs to be qualified and put into perspective.

The issue of corruption

Certainly, there is no shortage of examples of corruption in the final months before the defeat of the Guomindang. In memoirs of his youth, linguist Charles Li describes how a fire broke out in the building he lived in with his aunt. Having rushed outside, its inhabitants watched helplessly as the flames advanced. They started to hope again when the fire brigade arrived. But the latter then asked, as if it were quite normal, how much the occupiers were prepared to pay them to go into action.[22] It is understandable that such dramatic examples stuck in people's minds. Nevertheless, much of the corruption is explained (classically) by the fact that civil servants' salaries were being undermined by inflation to the point where they were unable to survive.[23] It is true, however, that corruption was not just about the small-fry civil servants who could no longer make ends meet. It also affected the highest level of the political hierarchy. For example, the powerful and opulent Kong family were shamelessly diverting American aid. The general 'every man for himself' of the last few months led to striking scenes such as that of the flight of Yan Xishan. The former Shanxi warlord, who had allied himself to the Guomindang, abandoned his bodyguards to an almost certain death on the tarmac of the airport, in order to be able to take off in his plane, too heavily weighed down by his personal hoard of gold.[24]

Whether manifested in military indiscipline, corruption or bribery, it must be emphasized that the increasing certainty of complete defeat could only incite those in power to put their personal interests above those of service to the state. It is reminiscent of the French army in disarray after the Battle of Waterloo, as depicted by Stendhal in *The Charterhouse of Parma*. In other words, the widespread and odious corruption was probably more a symptom of the party's failure than one of its causes.

Lack of renewal within the Guomindang

The Guomindang's sclerosis was manifested above all in a fact that has remained surprisingly neglected by historians: the absence of renewal within its leadership. From 1945 to 1949, it is clear that the people at the head of the hierarchy were the same as they had been for two decades. Young, efficient and energetic men had been at the helm during the Northern Expedition and the Nanjing decade; twenty years later, the same men seemed worn down by an over-extended political career. There was no fresh blood, for example, among the seven successive heads of the Executive Yuan between 1945 and 1949 (whose function was equivalent to that of the prime minister). There was no brilliant 40-year-old comparable to Chen Yun, Deng Xiaoping, Gao Gang or Peng Zhen (all born between 1902 and 1905), who rapidly climbed the ranks to the top of the CCP hierarchy during the 1940s. Studied by Lloyd Eastman, the *Gexin* 革新 movement, initiated within the Guomindang in 1944 by Liang Hancao, Xiao Zheng and Gu Zhenggang, was supposed to be directed against corruption and nepotism, but it must be interpreted above all as an expression of the deep malaise of the Guomindang's middle-level cadres, who faced the impossibility of gaining access to the highest-level posts.[25] The congestion was all the more fatal because it affected the very large cohorts of Guomindang members who had joined in the mid-1920s, in the flower of their youth, when the party was at the height of its prestige and revolutionary momentum. Not only was the impedance in their careers a symptom of the lack of renewal at the top of the state, but also it had a very pernicious effect, as it encouraged the men concerned to focus on their personal interests alone. This was another path to corruption within the Guomindang.

However, one young man joined the learned assembly of the most important leaders during the period of the civil war. The problem was that this was Chiang Kai-shek's son, Jiang Jingguo (born in 1910).[26] So, far from contradicting the diagnosis of a blocked ascendancy, this single exception actually reinforced it. Jiang Jingguo's qualities are not in question: honest, determined, gifted with a sharp mind and hard-working, he had proved his worth when his father entrusted him with the administration of the southern part of Jiangxi province, which remained under nationalist control, between 1939 and 1944. However, his rapid rise after 1945 was primarily a reflection of the fact that Chiang, who was approaching 60, was preparing his succession in an autocratic and quasi-dynastic manner (the transfer of power, in fact, would take place in Taiwan two decades later).

Furthermore, Chiang Kai-shek's now uncontested pre-eminence did not mean the end of the struggles between rival cliques beneath him. On the contrary, the latter were increasing in intensity, in particular because of the prospects opened up by the takeover of the occupied territories.

We see them fighting for control of Shanghai, notably through trade unions and secret societies, from the very first months following the Japanese surrender.

The impossible democratic transformation

Given the state of the Guomindang, it is hardly surprising that its democratic transformation proved impossible. The plans to move from the political tutelage stage to the constitutional stage, which had been aborted by the war, were back on the agenda. This corresponded not merely to a respect for the road map imposed by the writings of Sun Yat-sen. There was both internal and external pressure on the Guomindang. Faced with a Communist Party for whom the pretence of championing democracy came at little or no cost, as well as the need to present itself in a more favourable light to the American ally, whose help was more necessary than ever, democratization of the regime was essential. At first, it was mainly a question of show: thus, successive governments were supposed to be 'coalitions' because they brought in a few leading figures from outside the Guomindang. However, the true power remained firmly in the latter's hands. The long-awaited Constitution was adopted on 25 December 1946 and promulgated on 1 January (it is known as the 1947 Constitution). Largely inspired by Zhang Junmai, it is a pretty liberal text, which stipulates freedom of association, religion and expression. In terms of government, it provided for a semi-presidential regime, with an elected parliament exercising control over the executive.[27]

Elections for parliament were held in the winter of 1947–8 (late November – early January). Despite the considerable enlargement of the electorate and the adoption of direct universal suffrage, they were not a model of their kind since they featured, in particular, a system of official candidacy somewhat reminiscent of the French Second Empire. Immediately after, Chiang was elected president of the Republic by the deputies with an overwhelming majority. The surprise election of Li Zongren as vice president (against Sun Ke who had the support of Chiang Kai-shek) is deceptive. Moreover, a few weeks later, on 10 May 1948, the normal functioning of the institutions was suspended, and the president of the Republic was granted full powers.[28]

With the prospect of total defeat looming, Chiang resigned as president on 21 January 1949 and was succeeded by Vice President Li Zongren. In the following weeks, Li opted for the only alternative left to a chess player who can no longer hope to win because his forces are too weakened compared to those of his opponent: to seek a draw – a stalemate. Li knew better than anyone that the Guomindang's armies had been weakened and demoralized by a succession of defeats, and that all hope of military victory had vanished. But the Guomindang had a firm hold on the country south of the Yangtze, an area where the communists had no troops and very few partisans. Li's plan was to opt resolutely for the defensive by securing the front along the great natural defence line of the Yangtze. Faced with the communist North, the southern part of the country could thus remain in the hands of the Guomindang, with increased aid from the United States, to whom it tried to give pledges of liberalism.[29] This strategy, which remained the single alternative, could never be implemented, because many military leaders continued to take their orders from Chiang alone. The latter never gave up running things covertly, depriving Li Zongren of any capacity to act with the forces that remained at his disposal. In particular, Chiang would not hear of partitioning the country, and sabotaged the project to fix the border at the Yangtze. The so-called transfer of power in January 1949 was a charade, the ultimate manifestation of the Guomindang's inability to move away from autocratic practices.

Sclerotic, divided, corrupt, headed by a mediocre leader, the nationalist party had clearly failed. Nevertheless, it must be emphasized that the Guomindang did not collapse under the weight of their own inadequacies alone. Nor did the CCP just build a political and military organization that outperformed that of its enemy. It also knew how to weaken its opponent, by disseminating skilful propaganda (which denounced, for example, Chiang's subjection to the American ally) and by infiltrating agents at all levels of the Guomindang's administrative and military organization. For example, some of the excesses of Guomindang policy, particularly concerning repression of the press, appear to be the work of communist agents infiltrated into the censorship authorities.[30] In other words, the Guomindang's weakness was also largely due to the strength and skill of their opponent.

The CCP's policy

As noted, during the Sino-Japanese War, the CCP's strategy of moderation had been a fundamental factor in its progress. In the civil war too, as writers have correctly pointed out, victory was the fruit of the 'New Democracy' and not of socialism, which was then only a distant and uncertain prospect.[31] And even when it became clear that victory could no longer evade the communists, Mao Zedong reaffirmed that collaboration with the bourgeoisie (renamed the 'national bourgeoisie') remained more than ever on the agenda. Many foreigners in China were fooled into believing that they were in the presence of a 'so-called Communist party', as a Portuguese diplomat wrote in a report in 1946.[32] They were not alone. Leading liberal intellectuals such as Zhang Dongsun or Luo Longji (then one of China's leading human rights theorists) were also convinced of the benign nature of the CCP.[33]

Even if a more radical note was emerging, especially during 1946–7, the policy in rural areas remained dominated by pragmatism and adaptation to the diversity of local situations.[34] The CCP was well able to bend ideological considerations to the imperatives of military victory. Moderation was the order of the day in the recently conquered areas: only the reduction of tenant farms and the cancellation of debts were granted. A more pronounced radicalism was emerging where they had been the administration for longer: it was reflected in a redistribution of land, or even the beginnings of collectivization. As seen in Manchuria, local Party cadres gradually tightened their grip on the rural elites' class (through confiscation of their property, destruction of their prestige and physical elimination).

The CCP, which for the first time in its history found itself in control of territories of significant importance, managed to exploit them to a single end – military victory. The method used to recruit soldiers took the form of a successful combination of coercion and inducement. Well-practised propaganda extolled the role of soldiers fighting for the CCP's cause, but its effectiveness was reinforced by the tangible benefits provided to their families (material aid, education and free healthcare). As long as the extent of CCP-controlled areas remained limited (until the end of 1947), the drain on them was particularly heavy. Peasant farmers who had benefitted from land redistribution were particularly called upon. In a county in eastern Heilongjiang province with a population of 60,000, no fewer than 5,000 men were called up. Even if, later, the conquest of new territories made it possible to distribute the effort more evenly, the fact remains that the rank-and-file infantrymen from the ranks of the peasantry in the north were the primary instrument of the CCP's conquest of China.

Does this mean that the communist forces should be portrayed as a homogeneous, well-trained, disciplined and carefully indoctrinated mass? The reality was more complex. The men trained during the war against Japan certainly formed a core group of highly trained, hardened troops and fitted this model. Soldiers were better treated, which limited the extent of desertions. But the recruitment procedures could be quite expeditious and did not differ much from those employed by the Guomindang. In Manchuria, in the months following the Japanese surrender, a very wide range of men were recruited: 75,000 men were drawn from the exceedingly mediocre troops of the former Manchukuo, and a quantity of brigands were also recruited. Later, during the first big advances, speed took precedence over all other considerations in the newly conquered areas. In addition, the first major victories brought with them masses of prisoners. Special attention was paid to them and, once properly indoctrinated, they joined the ranks of the communist army. Moreover, it is a distortion to claim that communist victories resulted only from a superiority of numbers and political conviction. The Soviet advisors provided indispensable expertise that is still too often underestimated.

If, as we have seen, the spiral of defeats and the ensuing 'every man for himself' contributed to blackening the image of the Guomindang, in reverse – but similarly – the victorious impetus that spurred on the communist forces tended to conceal weaknesses that were nonetheless very real. Corruption and favouritism were not absent from the bureaucratic organization of the Party. In the military sphere, in addition to the absence of an air force and a navy, there was occasional but ill-timed interference by Mao Zedong, which was deplored.[35] And although Lin Biao's strategic talent is undeniable, he also made mistakes, especially at the beginning of operations. The main one was to fight a conventional battle in April–May 1946 to retain the newly acquired major cities of Manchuria.[36] This misstep could have had serious consequences had it not been for the much worse strategic mistakes made by the command of the nationalist forces, which we have already stressed sufficiently.

A third force gone missing

As we have seen, the Democratic League was founded in 1941. The League was both a coalition of small political parties (such as Zhang Junmai's National Socialist Party) and associations (Huang Yanpei's Society for Vocational Education), and a nebula of personalities, often very prestigious, who belonged to it on an individual basis (Luo Longji, Wu Han). The League would remain a loosely structured organization that was important mainly due to its moral authority. In the early 1940s, the League was able to hold out hope that the Guomindang state would evolve into a constitutional and democratic regime. In the last years of the war and the immediate post-war period, the new power of the CCP changed the situation entirely. It was now clear that democratization could not merely take the form of an institutional reform but must also involve the formation of a coalition government. However, the analysis made by intellectuals, as well as by the American mediator, was that the CCP/Guomindang confrontation constituted an insurmountable obstacle to any attempts in this direction. But all their efforts to form a credible third political force *in extremis*, which would be the indispensable cement of a coalition government, came to nothing.[37] Indeed, the pledges of democratization (Constitution of 1 January 1947, election of a National Assembly) were deemed insufficient by the already disillusioned intellectual elites. Like the Democratic League, which leaned more and more towards the communists (to the point that the Guomindang decided to dissolve it in October 1947), the rejection of the Guomindang, combined with the power of attraction of the CCP, condemned this third force to remaining merely virtual.

The withdrawal to Taiwan, a victory for the Guomindang?

In the months following the Japanese surrender, the Guomindang's takeover of Taiwan, although prepared for a long time, was particularly clumsy. Taiwan's elites, the overwhelming majority of whom were not fluent in Mandarin, were ostensibly excluded from responsibilities. The administration of the island was taken over by officials from the mainland. On the economic front, the situation deteriorated very quickly, and the population had to endure hardships that were new to them: supply difficulties, unemployment and inflation.[38] The desire to eradicate the very widespread use of the Japanese language raised tensions even further in October 1946, as it provoked strong opposition. The situation was becoming explosive. The spark was ignited on the evening of 27 February 1947 in Taipei. After police intervention in a routine smuggling case that went wrong, a riot broke out. The commotion did not subside and the next day violence against mainland people increased. The uprising quickly spread to the whole island while taking a clear secessionist turn. The governor, General Chen Yi, lost control of the situation and reinforcements were sent from the mainland (8–9 March). The takeover of the island did not take long and ended in a bloodbath. Estimates vary, but it is probable that 10,000 people were killed.[39] A veritable straitjacket was extended across the island.

Of course, much of the blame must be placed on the personal clumsiness of Chen Yi, who was resentful of a population that showed little admiration for its 'liberators' and even less willingness to disown the legacy of the Japanese period. The disproportionate nature of the reaction suggests that, for the Guomindang, there was no question of running the slightest risk of losing control of the situation. This is an indication that the option of retreating to the island in the event of defeat on the mainland was already on the table. This hypothesis is consistent with one of Chiang Kai-shek's recent biographies, which suggests that Chiang Kai-shek envisaged, and began to organize, the withdrawal as early as the autumn of 1946.[40]

It is probably because it was anticipated that this retreat was an undeniable success. However, its accomplishment presented many logistical difficulties. Whilst trying to pretend that the withdrawal to Taiwan was not really likely, Chiang had prepared it carefully. Over 2 million people were transported (including 500,000 soldiers). Foreign exchange and precious metal reserves were moved to the island – not to mention the nearly 6,000 crates containing the most precious objects from the former imperial collections that were shipped to Taiwan in December 1948 and January 1949.

The aim here is not to write the history of Taiwan after 1949, but to highlight the new data on what lay behind the maintenance of the regime on the island and its impressive development in the decades that followed. It is important to consider first of all how much Taiwan seemed, at the end of 1949, to be under the threat of a forthcoming invasion. The United States, very pessimistic about the Chiang Kai-shek regime's chances of survival, decided not to include the island in its defence perimeter. They would only do so after the outbreak of the Korean War. The temptation for Guomindang cadres to flee en masse to more secure climes (such as Hong Kong or the United States) was therefore great. In fact, in this respect, the situation would prove optimal for the Guomindang. On one side, the high-ups, such as Chen Lifu, Kong Xiangxi and Song Ziwen, mostly chose to go into exile (although the former returned to Taiwan in 1966 to finish his life). These men were the heads of the main families and cliques whose perpetual rivalries had greatly contributed to weakening the government, especially after the Nanjing decade. Delayed, as we have already said, for far too long, a renewal and rejuvenation at the top of the Guomindang could finally take place with the arrival, in the 1950s, of new men with the profile of technocrats such as Yin Zhongrong, Li Guoting and Yan Jiagan. They would be the major architects of the regime's modernization and Taiwan's economic development in the following decades. On the other hand, a massive loss of mid-level managers did not happen. For example, 104 of the 180 members of the Executive Yuan moved to Taiwan. Since it is reasonable to assume that it was the most motivated and least corrupt who followed Chiang into exile, the latter had a pool of valuable administrators.

Besides this, conditions were rather different. The island of Taiwan was, relatively speaking, a land of plenty, as it had remained untouched by land battles and benefitted from the infrastructure built during the fifty years of Japanese colonization. The confiscation of land from Japanese companies and nationals was also a boon for the new authorities.

Governor since December 1948, Chen Cheng initiated two crucial measures. On the one hand, by creating a local currency, he managed to save the island from the dramatic hyperinflation that was hitting the mainland at that time. The rise in prices, which reached the very high but still bearable level of 300 per cent in 1949, was tamed in the following years (to less than 10 per cent in 1954). On the other hand, from 1949 onwards, a skilful agrarian reform created a class of small landowners who were obviously won over by the regime which had enabled them to attain this status.

On the advice of his son, Chiang Kai-shek was careful not to let secret societies such as the Green Gang establish themselves on the island.

Finally, there was obviously a change in scale: the administration of a country-continent is an entirely different challenge from that of an island smaller than Switzerland (and which had only about 6 million inhabitants in 1945). Such a habitat is not conducive to the development of local potentates (warlords). For the same reasons, the nightmare of communist subversion was unlikely. Potential guerrilla zones could indeed be fairly easily kept within bounds. Finally, following the outbreak of the Korean War, the United States did not skimp on its support. Let us consider: the aid lavished by the United States on the Guomindang between 1949 and 1953 was greater than that given to it during the civil war (1945–9), a period of comparable duration but during which the nationalist party administered the whole of China! Between 1951 and 1960, US aid amounted to 6 per cent of the island's gross domestic product (GDP).

As for the intelligentsia, the divorce from the Guomindang was consummated around 1948. Almost all the intellectual youth joined the communists. As for the older generation, who were much less enthusiastic about the CCP, they saw the Guomindang as having badly wasted their chance. Despite a few exceptions (such as Hu Shi, or the philosopher Fu Sinian), only a small proportion followed Chiang to Taiwan, and a few went into exile (such as the mathematician Chen Xingshen). It is remarkable that people whose reputation would have ensured an academic career in the United States or Europe, such as Qian Duansheng or Xiao Qian, remained in China. Their support should not be attributed to any naivety. Few held any illusions about the CCP's plans: in their private correspondence and diaries, the idea often emerges that their generation would be sacrificed, but that this sacrifice would be fruitful in preparing for the future.[41] They nevertheless wanted to believe in the construction of a new China and to contribute to the national recovery. The situation was similar for entrepreneurs, very few of whom chose to follow the Guomindang to Taiwan.

The year 1949 marked the end of the mainland rule of the Guomindang, whose experiment in government unquestionably dominated the republican period. In addition to the verdict of defeat at the end of the civil war, the Guomindang's collapse can be explained more broadly, as we have pointed out, by the war of 1937–45 and by circumstances that generously served the interests of its adversary. But noting that Chiang Kai-shek and the Guomindang navigated the civil war badly should not exempt us from examining the political project carried out by the party for two decades.

From this point of view, it is clear that the nationalist party had, on the whole, applied the programme set out by its founder, Sun Yat-sen, with remarkable fidelity and a certain degree of success. The struggle against imperialism and the warlords, which remained two of its guiding principles, led to the abolition of unequal treaties and the disappearance of the warlords from the political arena. Even if the results did not meet expectations, progress was made in the construction of the state, in the modernization of the economy, coupled, especially from the 1940s onwards, with the advent of the powerful public sector that Sun had called for in his wishes.[42]

Chiang Kai-shek's main departures from the political line laid down by Sun were the assertion of personal power, the abandonment of the strategy of mass mobilization and, above all, the progressive militarization of the regime and society.[43]

SIX

Overview of the Chinese Economy

Making China 'rich and powerful' was a goal shared by all parts of the elite in the republican period. It is not a new idea that prosperity is one of the foundations of power for a country. It goes back at least to the *Guanzi* 管子, a collection of texts dating from the fifth to the first centuries BC, which became the authoritative reference for economic thought in the late Han period. Since the end of the nineteenth century, however, there has been an increasing tendency to equate prosperity with industrial development. In various writings, Sun Yat-sen clearly states that the latter is one of the conditions for China's political emancipation. Sun also believed that the state should play a leading role in the industrialization process. Once they were in power, the Guomindang therefore intended to take action to catch up industrially with the West as quickly as possible. This did not exclude the existence of divergent interpretations of Sun's credo, notably concerning the priority to be given to the respective development of light and heavy industry. Similarly, while everyone agreed that military power could only be conceived as associated with an evolved industrial base, the allocation of fiscal resources between the army and industry was a matter of debate.

Given its centrality to the concerns of the political elites of the Republic, it is not surprising that the question of industrialization – its pace and scale – has dominated works on China's economic history. Two questions in particular structured the scientific debate in the 1970s and 1980s – were Western competition and investment factors of emulation or, on the contrary, a hindrance to the development of Chinese industrial capitalism? Most historians now conclude that the positive effects of the Western presence prevailed. The second question, whether the Guomindang was a predatory state or a catalyst for modernization, has not been definitively answered.

Somewhat later, in the 1990s, a range of issues emerged that were unrelated to the interconnection between political and economic spheres. Much has been written about China's economic growth during the period. Historians are on shaky ground here, as the data remains incomplete, despite the appearance of the first statistical studies around this time. They are forced to use a great deal of cunning and imagination to construct arguments whose sophistication is inversely proportional to the amount of reliable data they can use. The main historian to have taken up this question is Thomas Rawski. In a remarkable book, Rawski painted a picture of a rapidly expanding Chinese industrial sector during the first two decades of the republican period. This view was radically new at the time but is now the subject of a fairly broad consensus. Much more controversial, however, are his estimates of growth in the agricultural sector. Also very optimistic (with a rate of 1.5 per cent growth per annum between 1914 and 1936 according to Rawski), they led him to conclude that the Republic was a period of vigorous economic growth because of the very dominant contribution of this sector to Chinese gross domestic product.

In the last few years, partly under the influence of China's spectacular economic performance in recent decades and partly due to interest in the theme of modernization, the dominant topic has been the emergence of a Chinese-style model of capitalism, beginning in the 1910s. The focus is on enterprises, which are the subject of several monographs. The American historian Sherman Cochran, author of some of the most remarkable of these, has done more than any other to show the many facets of a capitalism that was both original and successful. In parallel, there has been a fundamental trend towards a shift in research from the productive hierarchy to the consumer sphere. The increase in monographic studies has, however, been accompanied by a certain lack of interest in the overall picture. For example, the excellent work of T. Rawski and A. Feuerwerker dates back some forty years.[1] They are yet to be supplanted. Richard Von Glahn's recent masterful synthesis, *The Economic History of China*, stops at the dawn of the twentieth century.

The synthesis attempted in this chapter is therefore necessary. The presentation of China's insertion in the international economic scene will be followed by a portrait of each sector of activity (primary, secondary, tertiary). Although seemingly academic, this approach has the important advantage that it does not immediately focus on the problems of industrialization or modernization.

China in an international context

The economy of young republican China received a (quite involuntary) gift from Europe in 1914 – a long self-destructive orgy for the countries involved, the First World War opened up tremendous economic opportunities for the rest of the world. While it is true that in some countries, such as Argentina, the war may have had mixed economic effects, China is one of the non-belligerents that prospered during these years, along with the United States and Spain.

The primary sector benefitted from the huge demand for raw materials generated by the conflict, and from the context of generally rising prices. The case of tungsten, essential for the arms industry, was probably the most spectacular: the Dayu region, located on the borders of Guangdong and Jiangxi, which contains the largest deposit in the world, experienced a spectacular economic boom due to the enormous demand for this metal.[2]

Above all, Asian countries were freed from competition from European manufacturing industries for four years. Not only did the latter convert to feeding the war economy, but the significant increase in sea freight costs (because of submarine warfare) acted as a customs barrier that protected Asian markets. Of course, China had to reckon with the United States and Japan, which were doing their utmost to supplant European producers. The fact remains that the slackening of European competition was a boon to Chinese industry – the margins were enormous. They had a dramatic impact on the growth of businesses launched at that time by courageous businessmen. This was the case of the Shenxin 申新 group, founded in Shanghai in 1915, which would become the country's largest cotton yarn company in under twenty years. The textile sector was not the only one to benefit from these boom years; a host of light industries (especially those producing consumer goods) followed suit: milling, paper and rubber, amongst others.[3]

The international context became less idyllic in the post-war period, marked in particular by the gradual return of Europeans to Asian markets. However, the economic situation in the 1920s remained generally favourable. America, launched at full speed on the road to Fordism and the consumer society, was the engine of world growth. The 1929 crash did not have an immediate impact in China because of a sharp fall in silver prices in the early years of the crisis (silver lost more than half its value on world markets between 1928 and 1931). As China's currency was based on the silver standard, this decline had an effect equivalent to a devaluation. It made exports more competitive and made imports more expensive. China still suffered a delayed backlash. However, because of its economic backwardness, like the rest of Asia excluding Japan, it was less affected than the more industrialized countries. The impact of the crisis was felt in very different ways depending on the level of economic development and openness of the regions. While it affected the Lower Yangtze River valley quite severely, its impact was much less in Sichuan. It scarcely affected remote provinces such as Yunnan and Guizhou.[4]

Despite the vagaries of the international situation, the period 1911–37 was marked by weak but continuous growth in foreign trade, which can be explained in part by the downward trend in freight costs. Trade contracted only temporarily under the effect of the Great Depression, at the beginning of the 1930s. It passed through a relatively small number of ports, led by Shanghai and Hong Kong. The second half of the nineteenth century had seen the overwhelming domination of certain products in imports (opium, and then cotton) and exports (tea and silk accounted for more than 90% in the 1870s).[5] Throughout the republican period, a trend towards diversification took place.

International trade represented a part of GDP that is difficult to estimate but was probably around 10% and generally on the rise. From this point of view, China ranked behind most industrialized nations, which is not surprising since the degree of openness of a country is always closely correlated with its degree of economic development. More remarkable is the fact that it was also placed behind countries such as India, Canada, Australia and Argentina. This had nothing to do with an atavistic tendency to isolationism, but is a common effect of size: very large countries always participate proportionally less in international trade. For example, the exports of another country of a continental dimension, the United States, represented only 3.6% of its GDP in the 1920s; at the same time, those of the Netherlands exceeded 17%.[6]

In total, although one in five of the world's population was Chinese, China contributed only about 1% to world trade.

Since the mid nineteenth century, the UK had been China's main trading partner. Japan, which had been a close second since the beginning of the twentieth century, benefitted not only from its geographical position but from the products of its manufacturing sector being well adapted to the Chinese market. They struggled to gain a foothold in Western markets, where they were seen as lacking in quality. In China, on the contrary, the country's industrial backwardness meant competition from local products was less threatening. On the other hand, as the purchasing power of Chinese consumers was lesser, the low price of Japanese products became a decisive advantage. Building on its spectacular progress during the First World War, Japan emerged in the mid-1920s as China's main economic partner. From 1945 to 1949, it was the turn of the United States to occupy this position.

Although the main economic partners changed, the trade deficit remained a constant; only the exceptionally favourable context of the 1914–18 war made it possible to almost reach a balance. By making the mobilization of so-called national products one of its central themes, Chinese nationalism reflected the reality of the trade deficit.[7] The constant refrain about the impoverishment, or even the risk of annihilation, of the country as a result of the invasion of foreign goods clashed with the actual figures, however. The balance of payments was much healthier than the trade balance. The trade deficit was in fact offset by two factors – inward investment from the most industrialized economies (mainly the UK, Japan and the US) and capital flow from overseas Chinese communities. These were, of course, the money orders that emigrants (in South East Asia, North America, South America/the Caribbean, in descending order of importance) sent to their families. Chinese launderers in major US cities supported entire regions in the far south of the country. The Chinese overseas were also investors. However, notwithstanding a Chinese historiography that wants to see them as patriots devoted body and soul to the development of their country of origin, their importance should not be exaggerated. Firstly, overseas Chinese invested infinitely more in the South East Asian countries where they had their homes and businesses than in China itself. Moreover, their investments in China were almost exclusively limited to the two provinces from which they mainly originated – Guangdong and Fujian. Furthermore, investments were limited to specific sectors – first and foremost, property. In the Kaiping region of western Guangdong, more than a thousand *diaolou* 碉樓 still evidence this effort today. *Diaolou* are multi-storey towers with a residential and defensive purpose. Mostly built from reinforced concrete, they blend elements of Western and Chinese architecture. The vast majority of them were built in the period between 1920 and 1930 with money sent by emigrants.

In addition to real estate, overseas Chinese investments were, albeit to a much lesser extent, in services, particularly in the transport sector. In the end, very few were led to invest where the need for capital and know-how was most acute – that is, in the industrial sector.

The financial and monetary system

Research on the financial and monetary sectors is often neglected by historians of the Chinese economy. This is wrong, as these are crucial elements of economic development.

The shortcomings of the financial system

It would be even less legitimate to neglect the influence of the Chinese financial system, given that it was clearly affected overall by a relative fragility.

The first cog in this system, underpinning it all, was the pawnshop (*diandang* 典當). Progressive or communist literature depicts these establishments as the haunts of usurers, typically repulsive figures of pre-1949 society, who unscrupulously took advantage of the unforeseen problems of families and of the difficulties of the peasants in a lean season or after a poor harvest. However, pawnbrokers were quite effective in lending small amounts of money to households in the short term. The latter could also resort to various forms of tontines[8] and loans between individuals. In the early republican period, apart from the pawnshops, the banking system consisted of three protagonists: the *qianzhuang* 錢莊 (traditional banks), the *piaohao* 票號 (also known as Shanxi banks) and the large Western banks such as HSBC (Hong Kong and Shanghai Banking Corporation).

The latter were important players, whose two main roles were to lend to the government and to finance international trade. *Qianzhuang* had an essentially local role. They mainly provided short-term loans and liquidity facilities to craftsmen, traders and small industrialists. As for the *piaohao*, whose network covered the whole country, their main activities were money transfers and bills of exchange. Having become more and more closely associated with the imperial regime during the second half of the nineteenth century, the revolution represented a formidable shock for them, which the blindness and immobility of their leaders soon turned into a mortal blow. The decline of the *qianzhuang*, on the other hand, came later. In the 1920s, they lived in symbiosis with the modern banks, whose growth benefitted them. But this practical coexistence only lasted for a short time. They experienced the fate of the clay pot versus the iron pot and were destined to decline in the decades that followed.[9]

The traditional banking system was not without its virtues. It played its role well in financing medium-sized businesses, such as silk mills.[10] However, *piaohao* and *qianzhuang* did not have the financial stamina to back large-scale ventures such as railways, mining and heavy industry.[11] The latter required larger and longer-term investments. Could the modern Chinese banks that emerged at the turn of the century provide for this? The 1920s saw a significant increase in their capitalization, which was accompanied by a trend towards concentration. Their progress accelerated during the Nanjing decade. In particular, they expanded their branch network in the interior to take advantage of higher interest rates. In the present state of research, it can no longer be said that these banks totally failed in their mission to drain savings and direct them towards investment. In particular, they showed themselves capable of attracting the savings of a significant part of the urban population. And while it is true that these banks probably did not finance enough companies in the production sector, they were not entirely to blame. To cover its borrowings, the state appropriated too large a proportion of the capital at their disposal.

Financial markets cannot provide an answer to the shortcomings of banks. Although the stock exchange was inaugurated in Shanghai in July 1920, and the status of the limited liability company was defined by the laws of 1914 and 1929, the role of these two essential players in the development of European capitalism was not very important here. The joint-stock company model was still very poorly accepted by Chinese entrepreneurs.

All in all, the Chinese financial sector did not allow the Chinese economy to overcome one of its structural weaknesses: a lack of capital.

In previous centuries, this lack had been reflected in higher interest rates compared not only to Western Europe, but also to Japan and India.[12] The trade-off between scarce (and therefore expensive) capital and overabundant labour tends to be in favour of the latter. This is not necessarily crippling for all sectors, as we will see with the consumer goods industries. Nevertheless, Sun Yat-sen rightly underlined the major constraint that the scarcity of capital placed on China's economic development. In one of his best-known texts, the *National Reconstruction Plan* (*Jianguo fanglüe* 建國方略), he advocated overcoming it by using foreign capital. The lesson was recalled by Deng Xiaoping, who, half a century later, successfully applied this recipe. From 1978 onwards, China's development was based on massive foreign investment.

Progress and crisis in the monetary system

The monetary system situation was paradoxical under the Republic. We have seen that the inflationary spiral of 1940–9 was one of the main causes leading to the victory of the CCP.

There is no need to revisit the surge in prices during these years, except to emphasize that it should not be concluded that inflation played a uniformly negative, or even destructive, role throughout the republican period. In fact, the opposite is true. China experienced a long period of moderate inflation from the 1890s until 1933. This phenomenon was mainly explained under the Republic by the increase in the quantity of money in circulation, itself the consequence of the development of modern banks that issued paper money. In terms of inflation, the climate was therefore very favourable for business development.

In addition, one should not forget two notable advances in the Chinese monetary system in the mid-1930s: the abandonment of the silver standard in favour of paper money, and monetary unification. This was accomplished in the 1930s under the Guomindang. It was a very positive move as the multiplicity of regional currencies issued by the various warlords (and communists), especially since the 1920s, had a negative effect. This multiplicity complicated commercial operations and was an obstacle to a national capital market. Another drawback was that these currencies tended to fluctuate wildly in relation to each other, in line with the ups and downs of local politics. There was also a decline, to a somewhat lesser extent, in the flow of currency from neighbouring countries. Throughout very large parts of China, they represented a significant portion of the currency in circulation, such as the Indochinese piaster in Yunnan province, or the Hong Kong dollar in the Pearl River Delta region.

The primary sector

While the fragility of the financial sector was an important element in the transformation dynamics of the Chinese economy during this period, a prominent position should be given to what had always been its bedrock, unchanged since antiquity: agriculture.

The very slow evolution of the agricultural sector

If, almost everywhere, Chinese agriculture remained overwhelmingly crop-based, with livestock occupying a marginal place, the diversity of situations defies generalization. In simple terms, we can contrast north and south China. The northern countryside had been modified by man to an extreme extent and turned over to dry farming, favouring the cultivation of wheat. South of the Yangtze River, farmers benefitted from a much more favourable climate and hydrography, and irrigation was developed there on a large scale. The significantly longer growing season allowed several harvests per year. Rice was the dominant cereal.

Under the Republic, agricultural production contributed more than two-thirds of GDP and, more importantly, mobilized almost 80 per cent of the labour force.[13] The limited but real increase in production was mainly due to the increase in cultivated area. This was no longer at the expense of forests, as had been largely the case, with disastrous ecological consequences, during the previous two centuries. In the most densely populated provinces, forest cover could now be described as residual: 5–10 per cent of the area of Guangdong and Guangxi in the 1930s, even less in much of northern China. The main driving force behind the expansion of cultivated areas was the rapid development of agriculture on the vast plains of Manchuria.

A modest growth in yields was feasible. This was thanks to the intensification of work (for example, more careful weeding) and to the spread of more efficient techniques. Like their ancestors, the farmers of the republican era continued to perfect their crop rotation and to learn how to make the most of the different soils at their disposal. The use of soybean cattle cake (already common in the Lower Yangtze region in the eighteenth century) was thus slowly becoming more widespread. Higher-yield American cotton varieties were spreading.[14] Overall, however, technical improvements were minimal. This was clearly not a prelude to the green revolution with its trinity of step changes (high-yield varieties, chemical fertilizers, and pesticides). The irrigated area continued to expand (in the Wei valley, for example), even if the general trend was interrupted by occasional setbacks, whereby irrigation infrastructures were damaged during episodes of political unrest. Finally, the practice of double-cropping rice, which allowed for a considerable increase in yields, continued its slow spread northwards from its original centre in Guangdong province. It was during this period that it took on increasing importance in Hunan.

These advances were much more the final fruits of a long-term movement that began in the Ming period and followed, among other things, the arrival of plants from America (maize, peanuts, potatoes and sweet potatoes), which considerably broadened the range of plants to be cultivated.[15]

Two other long-term phenomena which continued to unfold were the spread of regional specialization and the development of cash crops. They were even amplified thanks to the opening up brought about by the extension of the transport network and the accelerated monetization of the economy in rural areas. The transportation of cereals was particularly strong, and it should be noted that it was not limited to flows between surplus and deficit areas. There were entire regions, in Henan or Guangdong for example, that were dedicated to growing high-quality rice varieties to supply the markets in the big cities and even overseas. For their own consumption, the local community fell back on mediocre rice from other provinces.

The most telling example of the link between progress in transport and progress in commercial agriculture was in Manchuria. Here, the development of the railways led to a rapid expansion of soybean cultivation, largely for export. In 1930, Manchuria produced 60 per cent of soybeans traded globally. Other cash crops, such as cotton, peanuts and tobacco, were booming. Even though the breeding of silkworms[16] suffered from Japanese competition (both due to its superior quality and because it also followed the evolution of European demand better), it continued to progress until the beginning of the 1930s. It suffered a serious setback when the 1929 crisis led to a sharp drop in foreign demand and a dizzying fall in prices. The invention of rayon, which became widely available from the mid-1920s, did not help matters (nylon only entered the picture in 1939).[17] Internationally, very strong competitors in the tea (India, Ceylon) and sugar cane (Java) markets also emerged. However, the most notable decline in a cash crop during the republican period was in poppies. It fell far short of the levels reached at its peak in the late nineteenth century. In this case, it was neither the general economic context nor competition from another country that was behind the fall, but the change in perceptions about opium and, hence, the decline in consumption.[18]

While there is no doubt about the quantitative rise of cash crops in China, the problem of quality often arose. For example, cotton cultivation in Jiangsu province expanded enormously in the 1920s to supply the textile sector in Shanghai. At the same time, however, the quality of fibre showed no marked improvement.

Finally, the expansion of cash crops was also made problematic by the 1937–45 war, which disrupted industrial production and considerably impeded the flow of raw materials. Reliable statistics are lacking for the war years, but it can be seen, for example, that for cotton, one of the main cash crops, production levels in 1946–8 pale in comparison to those of the mid-1930s.

In general, there has been an over-dramatization of the negative socio-economic effects of the enthusiastic conversion of certain regions to one or more cash crops (see Chapter 8). Without denying that this has the disadvantage of increasing dependence, subject to price fluctuations or the emergence of new competitors, it must be stressed that this diagnosis owes much to the ideological positioning of certain historians on the one hand, and to the common effect of sources on the other. In an excellent study, Robert Eng provides convincing evidence that, despite the vagaries of the global economy, farmers who switched to sericulture were, on the whole, better off.[19] In general, cash crops require more work but give better yields. Thus, the case of Shandong province shows how beneficial the adoption of tobacco cultivation was, by providing work for the rural labour force during the off-season. However, while the benefits to peasants of cash crops were real, they were not very obvious from the sources and it takes patient and rigorous work by historians to bring them to light. On the other hand, the misfortunes that may result with cash crops (famines, massive indebtedness and revolts) are particularly clear.

Finally, in the case of setbacks, especially when the decline in price proves to be long-lasting, there is always the alternative of reverting to food crops (or trying another cash crop). This was the case for sericulture in the Wuxi region, where peasants cut down mulberry trees to make way for rice fields. Although the former occupied 30 per cent of the land in 1927, this figure fell to less than 7 per cent by 1932.

Mining: the triumph of coal and emergence of oil

While there is no doubt that agriculture was a very important part of the primary sector, this does not justify ignoring mining, as often happens. This was an activity that expanded rapidly in the first part of the twentieth century, particularly as a result of the providential increase in international demand during the years 1914–18. The republican period was marked by the beginning of an ascendancy that continues to this day: that of coal. This does not mean that coal was not used before, or that the role played by wood was no longer significant. Wood remained essential not only for rural household consumption (heating and cooking), but also for certain activities such as small-scale metallurgy and porcelain production (the famous Jingdezhen factories only turned to coal after 1949). Nevertheless, for modern transport (rail and steam navigation) as well as for industry, the use of coal was necessary. The importance of coal was also increased because electricity was produced solely from coal. And there was a big increase in electricity production. Its introduction was making rapid progress not only in the largest cities, but also in small towns, where it often came with the installation of street lighting. While only 100,000 tonnes of coal were used to produce electricity in 1912, almost 3 million tonnes were needed in 1936.

This resource is present in great abundance in China's subsoil; it was mainly its transport after extraction that was more problematic.

17 Coal transport in Shanghai circa 1930.

The deposits were principally located in the north, where transport by water was often impossible. Small mines with rudimentary mining methods (Shanxi) could meet a very local demand that was perhaps not too exacting about quality. However, where rail or water were used to transport mined coal to relatively distant markets, more sophisticated technology and investment were set up to exploit the deposits. The two main coalfields were Kailuan (Hebei) and Fushun (Liaoning). They employed over 40,000 miners each.[20] Production growth was spectacular (16 million tonnes in 1926, 58 million in 1942). At the beginning of the 1930s, this sector of activity ranked third in terms of added value, behind only cotton mill production and the tobacco industry.

Contrary to the trend in more developed countries at the time, coal did not suffer from competition from oil and remained virtually the sole source of energy for the modern sector of the economy throughout the period. Although in absolute terms its importance was marginal, oil was an indispensable strategic product for armies. It was almost exclusively imported. The advance of Japanese troops in 1937–8 posed a serious problem as it cut off import channels. The government reacted by developing oilfields in the Gobi Desert in Yumen (Gansu province).

Despite enormous difficulties, refining facilities were built, allowing the crude to be processed on site. The finished products were then transported to Chongqing; the many difficulties on the way were overcome with ingenuity and determination, allowing China to become self-sufficient in hydrocarbons.[21]

The secondary sector

Just as the primary sector was not simply about agriculture, the secondary sector was not limited to industry, even though sources tell us mostly about the latter. The numbers of workers in modern factories, the focus of so much attention from researchers, remained extremely small compared to those in cottage industries. The historian Wang Di pertinently observes that, in the 1910s, the number of workers employed in modern factories throughout China (which he generously estimates at around 1.5 million) was of an order of magnitude comparable to the number of craft workers *in a single province* (2.1 million in Sichuan in 1912).[22]

Industry and the rise of Chinese capitalism

The manufacturing sector (that is, using machines) represented only 2.1% of GDP in 1933. It was a dynamic sector, with an average annual growth rate of 8.1% between 1912 and 1936, a rate that put China on a par with Japan and far ahead of the United States. Light industry and consumer goods dominated the sector. Indeed, during the republican period, Chinese entrepreneurs exerted themselves and successfully competed with imports and foreign companies established in China. This was in fields that did not require massive investment and were based on fairly simple techniques – such as textiles, cigarettes, light chemicals and food processing. Their products were cheaper and less sophisticated, but also of lower quality. On the other hand, the heavy industry sector, and even more so the goods production sector, remained insufficiently developed. The lack of capital and difficulty in raising it were major obstacles to development. In 1933, China's production represented a significant share of Japan's for cotton yarn (79%) and garments (63%), much lower for cement (19%) and frankly derisory for sulphuric acid (3%) and steel (1%).[23]

The share of foreign companies in the industrial sector was significant but not dominant. During the 1930s, 30% of employment and 20% of production came from these companies. However, it should be noted that they represented 63% of the industrial sector's capitalization.

Another characteristic of the industrial sector was its geographical concentration, with two dominant regions. Industry in Manchuria, accounting for 14% of industrial production, involved transformation of agricultural surpluses, and its product could be exported due to an efficient transport network. But Shanghai in particular furnished the lion's share (40%). Its industrial fabric was very diverse, although, like that of the country as a whole, light industry and consumer goods predominated. Primarily, Shanghai was a very important textile centre. Mechanical industries, printing, light chemical and food processing were also well developed. On the other hand, heavy industries still remained at a fairly low level (12% of Shanghai's industrial production at the end of the Republic). Shanghai already had an industrial history, since it was here that Westerners had invested heavily in building factories after the Treaty of Shimonoseki (1895) granted them authorization. Under the Republic, the stability and security of the concessions (especially the International Concession) continued to add to the city's attractiveness for both Chinese and foreign investors, although factories were also built in the northern Chinese quarters near the railway station.[24] In Shanghai, industrialists had an abundance of available labour, and the transport network allowed raw materials and semi-finished goods to flow in. The level and comprehensiveness of the services available to them were unparalleled. The Shanghai Stock Exchange was the country's leading financial centre and all major banks had their headquarters there. Marine insurance companies had earlier formed the embryo of a sector that rapidly developed and expanded to include all insurance activities, from the second half of the nineteenth century onwards. Finally, the city is located in the heart of the Lower Yangtze River valley, the most prosperous and populous region in China, which offers considerable market opportunities.

Apart from Shanghai and Manchuria, China had other, secondary, industrial centres, such as Tianjin, Qingdao and Wuhan. However, the price of land in Shanghai and wages there were relatively high, so it tended to spin off some of its low-value-added industries to nearby cities such as Wuxi, which soon earned the nickname 'little Shanghai' as well as becoming the country's fifth-largest industrial city. This phenomenon explains why, taking Shanghai together with the province of Jiangsu, where it is located, the share amounted to more than 48 per cent.[25] But, apart from this phenomenon of a decentralization around Shanghai, there are no significant indications of a diversification of the industrial geography of republican China before the inward retreat following the Sino-Japanese War.

During the republican period, a capitalism with distinctive characteristics emerged and quickly demonstrated its efficiency. The organization of companies was based on a system of values and practices that the American historian Yeh Wen-hsin has called 'enlightened paternalism'.[26] In fact, this capitalism was fundamentally family-based. The sons of the business leaders were involved in the business at an early age, as it was they who would be called upon to take over.[27] The main role of daughters was to extend and consolidate the family group's network of alliances through advantageous marriages.[28] The prestige of education had not disappeared and it was still a crucial investment and, as such, very carefully weighed. But it was no longer a matter of acquiring bookish knowledge in order to compete for a mandarin career. The children were educated with a view to taking over and developing the family business. The favoured path now went via the most prestigious Western universities or, failing that, through institutions founded in China by Westerners.

Chinese companies paid the price for favouring family ties, and many businesses failed when the second generation of managers was not as able as the founder, even if there was no hesitation in looking to the wider family.[29] There were strategies to get around this. The first was to have many offspring, which made it more likely that someone with sufficiently broad shoulders to take over the business would emerge. Liu Hongsheng, one of the main entrepreneurs of the period (matches, cement and coal), had thirteen children.

Family ties not only were of great importance in the organization of the company, but also constituted an ideal that would shape the relationship between employees and their superiors. The company should be seen as a family (*yi hang wei jia* 以行為家), and therefore the benevolent authority of superiors was based less on the obedience inherent in a hierarchical organization than on the asserted existence of a common destiny and interest for all. This premise is the basis for a powerful paternalism. From the 1920s, employees of some companies were housed with their wives and children in complexes built by their employers. The latter took responsibility for their leisure time, medical care and, if necessary, the education of their children. This practice took on a new dimension during the Sino-Japanese War, when the need to retain the most qualified employees became a vital issue for companies in the free zone. It became increasingly widespread during the civil war, as companies set up logistics to pay their employees at least partly in food in order to protect them from the effects of inflation. All these practices prefigured the work unit of the communist era, the *danwei* 單位, a term that was actually coined during the Republic.

Investment was the Achilles heel of Chinese companies. They tended to focus on the short term (which is also partly explained by the troubled political context) by paying high dividends, to the detriment of investment. This tendency exacerbated the effects of their chronic undercapitalization. One consequence was the insufficient renewal of the apparatus for production.[30]

However, it would be a mistake to judge economic performance by comparing it with a European or North American model. This is particularly true of the substitution of capital for labour, a major trend in Western industrial development.

In China, the contrast between capital that is scarce and diversified, and therefore difficult to siphon off and mobilize, and an overabundant, very cheap (and generally docile) labour force, is striking. Such a state of affairs imposes trade-offs which, although different, are nonetheless rational and can produce excellent results. In the match industry, for example, the non-adoption of Western technology was not necessarily the result of backwardness or a rejection of progress, but instead a rational choice. Under these circumstances, the pursuit of productivity was not necessarily a priority. There is evidence that the profitability of Shanxi coal mines based on traditional labour-intensive mining methods outperformed that of mines operating with more modern techniques.

Entrepreneurs were quite open to technology transfers if they were relevant. In various sectors, China was catching up with the technical level of Western manufacturers. There were many factories that resembled their counterparts in Manchester, Ivry-sur-Seine or Yokohama. A recent study puts forward an example of technological upgrading in the case of several Shanghai entrepreneurs, whose primary activity was to repair imported presses and manufacture spare parts. They ventured to make imitations, and their workshops turned into factories that marketed their own machines. More generally, the increase in the space of a few years in capital goods and the machine tools sector is clear. It was so under-developed at the beginning of the republican period that it was hardly able to take advantage of the favourable context of the First World War. But by the end of the 1930s, it was able to compete seriously with imports: the low prices of Chinese-made machines compensated for a technical level that was generally still somewhat inferior.

In connection with the efforts of some Chinese captains of industry to appropriate the latest and best technologies, it is worth mentioning one of the unseen motivations driving the economic expansion of the time: patriotism. The caustic soda manufacturer Fan Xudong, who from 1914 onwards created an industrial complex in the Tianjin region capable of competing with the Japanese and European giants of the sector, is remarkable in this respect.[31] As Xiaohong Xiao-Planes has shown, Fan's most remarkable trait was not his technical skill acquired during his studies in Japan, nor his constant attention to learning about the best existing methods, nor his perseverance in the face of the very many difficulties he had to confront. His most remarkable trait was his readiness to reinvest, to take on all the risks (to the detriment, or even disregard, of his personal enrichment) and raise the techno-logical level of his group to that of its competitors. In 1937, when the Sino-Japanese War broke out, Fan responded without hesitation to the government's call to move his facilities to the interior. In this respect, Fan Xudong was not alone. This is just one example of these industrial pioneers, men driven by the idea that emerged at the end of the previous century that winning national independence would also involve a trade war that China would only win if it industrialized.[32] They had no hesitation in devoting their entire lives to this idea. Given pride of place in Chinese historiography, the term 'patriotic entrepreneur' (*aiguo shiyejia* 愛國實業家), in the end, does not appear such a cliché.

Chinese entrepreneurs were equally successful commercially, deploying very effective and aggressive strategies. Sherman Cochran's numerous studies of them show that they opted for an intensive use of advertising, especially in the form of posters.[33] One of the consequences was that advertising came to have a substantial role in the daily life of the Chinese, especially from the 1930s onwards. It was everywhere, on city walls, on the radio and in the press (it was common for half the columns in a daily newspaper to be devoted to advertising).

Finally, Chinese capitalism at that period was resolutely trans-national. Asian markets were open to them thanks to the presence of a diaspora unrelenting in its search for conquest of local and regional commercial networks. Family or regional solidarity made it possible to attract capital, including from overseas. There was no hesitation in taking pragmatic advantage of the existence of foreign concessions to secure the family fortune. Thus, the Liu industrial dynasty developed its activities in the international concession of Shanghai, as well as in Hong Kong.[34]

Maintaining cottage industries

Due to the overabundance of labour, the use of economic activities to supplement agricultural production was the rule rather than the exception in rural China. In the Hubei plains, for example, fishing provided an important supplementary income.[35] But the most widespread supplements were derived from cottage industries.

It is now well established that family handicrafts did not suffer a general decline due to competition from imports and industries in the coastal cities. However, distinctions must be made. In the textile sector, for example, spinning was in decline while weaving held up rather well. This example shows that the impact of industrial development varied greatly depending on the advantage provided by mechanized production techniques. This was considerable in the case of spinning since the productivity of mechanized spinning spindles was more than forty-four times higher than that of traditional spinning wheels. The orders of magnitude were completely different for weaving: industrial looms were only about four times as productive as hand looms. The use of hand looms in peasant households held up fairly well. They were significantly improved by the addition of metal shuttles, and their production increased in absolute value until the end of the 1920s. In fact, the use of industrially produced yarns in the coastal towns even overcame a bottleneck in the traditional textile sector: to produce enough to feed a loom for one hour, it took three to four hours of work on a spinning wheel.

Generally, other than textiles, the craft industry remained a very strong economic sector in the field of consumer goods. Bamboo-based products covered an extremely wide spectrum of everyday objects (chopsticks, furniture, tools, toys, umbrellas and fans, etc.) which would only ultimately decline decades later, under the influence of the advent of plastics. The same applied to objects made from straw (hats, mats, soles and baskets). The importance of recovery and recycling should also be stressed. As early as the 1930s, the sociologist Fei Xiaotong showed the extent to which any form of waste was banned in the Chinese countryside. For example, even completely worn-out clothes were then reused to make shoe soles.[36] More recent studies have shown that many everyday objects had multiple lives. The size of the recycling sector is also explained by the very low cost of labour, which enabled an activity such as the collection and recycling of cuttlebone, for example, to provide a living for those engaged in it.[37] However, the contribution to national wealth of this sector of the economy has been considerably underestimated, or even ignored, because it is poorly taken into account by modern statistical methods, which more or less identify consumption with destruction.

A recent monograph about paper made from bamboo fibres by a multitude of craft workshops in the Jiajiang region of eastern Sichuan province shows that this sector was doing very well under the Republic. It remained the most appropriate material for painters and calligraphers, as well as for other uses such as packaging or making paper money for the dead. And thanks to the adoption of some technical innovations borrowed from the West, such as the use of alum and chlorine, it became capable of supplying paper for modern printing. We may generalize from this example: instead of a binary alternative between traditional and Western techniques, there was much more often a combination of both.

18 The success of traditional crafts – a pottery workshop near Suzhou in 1932.

19 A tinker offering his services on the street, north China, circa 1918.

We have just covered the partial introduction of European techniques (addition of metal shuttles) or imported materials (industrial yarns) for the handlooms of peasant households. Tailors are another example: they adopted sewing machines on a large scale.[38] Thus, this trade, whose organization remained apparently very traditional, and which did not belong to the so-called modern sector, nevertheless underwent a notable improvement.

The service sectors

Undoubtedly, these sectors are a major omission from traditional historiography. The close attention paid to agriculture may seem perfectly legitimate since it remained the foundation of the Chinese economy. At the beginning of the chapter, it was explained why historians have long made industry, a key issue in China's quest for power, the focus of their work. This does not, however, justify overlooking this important fact:

in republican China, the service sectors were notably more developed than the industrial sector. According to data compiled by Ma Debin, the services share contributed a quarter of China's GDP in the early 1930s, compared to industry's share of only 10%. In the most advanced region, the Lower Yangtze Valley, the figures were even more impressive, at 37% and 16% respectively.[39]

Transport

The transport sector expanded considerably under the Republic. There was an important development of the railways, already mentioned in Chapter 3 (see Map 6). From 60,000 in the mid-1910s, its workforce reached 130,000 in the early 1930s. The completion of the last section of the Beijing–Hankou–Guangzhou link in 1936 finally gave the country the major north–south radial route it had lacked until then. But with a network of 20,000 kilometres, China still lagged behind India, for example. India, which is half the size and was significantly less populated, had a network that was three times as extensive at the same period.[40] Indicators such as the number of passengers per kilometre or tonnes of goods per kilometre were incomparably higher for India. These factors put the importance of rail in the transport sector – and, more broadly, in the Chinese economy – into perspective.

In fact, the modernization of transport was far from confined to the development of rail. The road network, which reached 75,000 kilometres in 1935, was covered by regular bus services from the 1930s. Steamboat navigation continued to develop. The first scheduled airlines date back to the early 1930s. Fifteen years later, Shantou, a medium-sized city, was connected to Hong Kong, Xiamen and Shanghai.

In this context of a general boom in the transport sector, old modes of transport were combined with new ones: there was not only competition but also, in many cases, complementarity. Thus, the speed of the railways gave them a decisive advantage in direct competition with water transport for the movement of passengers and perishable goods. However, for bulk commodities such as coal, the waterways remained competitive. In addition, the network of waterways was incomparably denser (especially in the most populated and developed parts of the country: the Lower Yangtze valley and Guangdong). Remarkably well organized, more economical and very flexible, it was not, therefore, a second-best option to rail, which it complemented. Moreover, the bargemen, although inclined to use force to make their demands heard, did not engage in violent collective action against the competition they faced from steamboats. The reason for this was simple: modern boats did not have access to almost half of the navigable rivers because of their excessive draught. Only sailing ships and conventional boats were able to navigate them. So, far from being supplanted by the advent of modern means of transport, sailing boats benefitted from them because the former caused an enormous increase in the flow of goods: their characteristics were quite simply complementary.

While much emphasis is placed on the considerable progress made in the development of inter-regional links, there were also considerable improvements in transport within the major conurbations. The demolition of the ramparts that surrounded most cities made it possible to build in their place vast boulevards that facilitated traffic flow. Cars remained rare, but the rickshaw, an innovation introduced in the 1880s, became widespread in the 1910s, aided by technical improvements such as tyres that made it safer, more comfortable and less strenuous to pull. Particularly suited to Chinese cities, it enjoyed a golden age throughout the Republic. There were about 45,000 of these vehicles in Beijing in 1930. There were 55,000 at the same time in Shanghai.[41] However, it began to be challenged by the bus in the 1930s. In 1945, the density of Shanghai's public transport network (trams, trolleybuses and buses) was comparable to that of a large European city.

Traditional services

Wang Di makes a very accurate observation in his excellent book on Chengdu teahouses – the employees of these shops were much more representative of the service sector in republican China than those in the more modern service sector.[42] However, it is a fact that, in the tertiary sector, the attention of researchers has been focused almost exclusively on the growth of activities that were previously foreign to China: insurance companies, banks, the press, the tourism sector and even dance halls. The example of distribution speaks for itself: the development

20 Freight transport by river in the Lower Yangtze valley in 1932.

of department stores was undoubtedly the main innovation of the period. It was very much linked to foreigners and overseas Cantonese, who imported its principles (a full offer of goods, non-negotiable prices, monumental proportions and comfort of the shops plus massive advertising) while making some marginal adaptations. Shanghai's two most famous department stores, Sincere and Wing On, set the tone for the entire period and were built in the late 1910s. They have been the subject of numerous in-depth studies. On the other hand, historians have remained almost silent about the world of the small shop and traditional retail trade, a labour-intensive sector which employed incomparably more people.

More generally, the centre of gravity of the service sector under the Republic was indisputably placed in the profusion of small tertiary occupations. For want of a better word, and given their great variety, we must resign ourselves to classifying them under the necessarily vague label of 'traditional'. Not only did their actors not participate in the dominant narratives of revolution and modernization, but these trades were located in a blind spot in traditional sources. One of the rare examples to the contrary is the report of an English consul who observed, at the beginning of the twentieth century, the presence in the city of Changsha in Hunan of 'pipe carriers' who offered passers-by a few puffs of tobacco for a derisory price.

However, the situation has changed in the last fifteen years or so, thanks to the use of images, a type of source richly represented in the republican period, with media such as photography or ink drawings (a genre in which Feng Zikai was a master). The historian Feng Yi, for example, has examined the incredible variety of services offered by Beijing peddlers by drawing on rich photographic collections.[43] Her study highlights a veritable army, one might say, whose foot soldiers crisscrossed the city providing a host of services at an extremely affordable cost. There were very many street vendors or owners of small stalls. With extremely low margins, they offered fresh produce (fruit and vegetables) as well as various refreshments, sweets and snacks throughout the year. Urban workers and schoolchildren liked the stalls where they could have breakfast on the go in the street. By the middle of the day, they would pack up, as the supply varied constantly between different times of the day. All kinds of items needed in daily life were on sale to housewives, as long as they were not too bulky.

Other vendors offered a host of services ranging from the essential – water carriers, chamber pot emptiers, repairers of objects (china, furniture and shoes) – to the ancillary – barbers, hairdressers and masseurs, not to mention fortune tellers. The streets were also almost permanently enlivened by acrobats, musicians and animal trainers who provided passers-by with much-appreciated moments of relaxation.[44] The availability of traditional leisure activities was not confined to the streets. The choice of recreational establishments was extremely wide: bathhouses, opera houses, opium houses, brothels and gambling houses were just the main ones. It could easily be imagined that such services were mainly found in cities. However, there is evidence to suggest that these were also the occupations of many workers in the countryside. In Guangdong, even a modest village of 750 inhabitants had two opium houses, a small teahouse and a *fantan* 番攤 house (gambling den) in the 1930s. Similarly, the multiplication on a vast scale of eating places (restaurants, wine merchants and teahouses) – a phenomenon that is older than you might think, since it dates back to the eighteenth century – took place in towns and villages as well as major cities.

21 A fortune teller in Hangzhou in 1919.

The effects of the 1937–1945 war and the civil war

Relocation and state control of the economy

If there is an important limitation to the economic history literature that focuses on the republican period, it is certainly that the reality it describes is that of the first half of the 1930s. This period of relative stability represents a golden age for statistical publications, during which data was fairly plentiful and reasonably reliable. After 1937, the upheavals caused by the war against Japan and the civil war make it very difficult to assess the evolution of the economic situation. And although it is clear that the war changed everything, studies shedding any light on the years of the Sino-Japanese War and the civil war remain scarce.

Nevertheless, it seems that the 1937–45 war had a double impact. The first was geographical. The advance of the Japanese troops led to the decision to redeploy part of the industrial infrastructure to the safety of the interior. No fewer than 639 companies and 60,900 tonnes of equipment were transferred to west China in 1937–40, mainly in the sectors considered most strategic: steel, chemicals and mechanics. Located principally in the province of Sichuan, these factories developed rapidly, taking advantage of the huge orders from the state. However, this spectacular relocation had little long-term effect, with the vast majority of installations returning to the former occupied regions in the immediate post-war period.

The impact was much more profound and lasting in the area of state involvement. The early 1930s saw the emergence of a new economic model, in which the role of the state became increasingly significant, with the three strands (found, for example, in Nazi Germany) of planning, centralized management of raw material resources and the development of industries directly controlled by the state.[45] Nevertheless, the size of the public sector in industrial production was still small at the beginning of the Sino-Japanese War and limited mainly to heavy industry and mining. However, as the war continued, the share of the state-owned sector in the economy increased. Recent work has also shown that this phenomenon was accompanied by a reorganization of the administrative management of state-owned enterprises. In order to retain employees, the management tended to increasingly manage their entire personal and family life by giving them access to housing, food, childcare and medical care. These were the beginnings of the work unit model (the *danwei*), which would have a bright future after 1949.

Far from ending the trend towards state control, the end of the war accentuated it in so far as Japanese property, as well as businesses whose owners had been convicted of collaboration, were confiscated. After 1946, the country fell back into war and – the same causes producing the same effects – the role of the state sector continued to expand rapidly. From then on, the consumer goods industry was also affected: the state's share increased from 6.1 per cent in 1945 to 33.6 per cent two years later.

The origins of communist China's planned economy?

Obviously, post-1949 China was a continuation of the republican period because it inherited its infrastructure, its production apparatus, its labour force and its entrepreneurship, with the exception, in the latter case, of the few clear-sighted businessmen who took their business elsewhere, in particular to Hong Kong. However, recent research has shown that the policy of forced nationalization and industrialization of the 1950s owes much to the republican period.

The general strategy of sacrificing the countryside to the development of heavy industry was indeed in line with the Soviet model.[46] However, in terms of its implementation, the idea that the CCP simply duplicated the USSR model has had its day. The *danwei* was just mentioned. The administrative foundations of economic planning in the 1950s were those laid down by the Guomindang in the last decade of the republican period. This is not very surprising when one considers that many of the senior officials who steered the Guomindang's economic policy remained on the mainland. As for the first five-year plan of the communist era (1953–7), it is largely based on the outline of the five-year reconstruction plan that the Guomindang had drawn up in 1945.[47] In terms of the economy, as in so many other areas, there are strong continuities in relation to the 1949 milestone.

SEVEN

Building the State

Historians today are less severe than some thirty years ago in their assessment, and agree that state-building under the Republic was partially successful. In this matter, the main credit long accorded to the period was the increasing establishment of nationalist feeling. Numerous studies have highlighted the very significant progress of nationalism in broad sections of the population, along with the transition from an essentially anti-Manchu proto-nationalism to a nationalism of unity, increasingly focused on resistance to Japan. There is no denying the importance of nationalism's progress, even if some recent studies tend to put its extent into perspective. However, it represents only one facet of a wider and, above all, more significant phenomenon: the invention and dissemination of a new post-imperial political culture. This was based on the fundamental idea that popular consent was the basis for the legitimacy of power. One of the consequences of this was a total rethinking of the political liturgy.

From an institutional point of view, and in terms of extending the state's reach, if the central governments that preceded the Guomindang (Yuan Shikai, Beiyang) are to be credited with some significant achievements, it is the action of the Guomindang from 1928 onwards that attracts particular attention. Firstly, it was the most coherent, since it implemented the plans drawn up by Sun Yat-sen, who went from being the tutelary figure of the party to the status of 'Father of the Nation'. The Guomindang undoubtedly had difficulties in successfully transforming themselves into a governing party: the lack of a clear strategic line, rivalries between the machinery of state, of party and of the army, and a certain factionalism were serious impediments. However, the state was exercising a new hold over many sectors of society during this period, although the countryside remained largely beyond its reach. And finally, as numerous studies have shown, this enlargement of the state's scope heralded and prepared for what was to come in communist China after 1949.

However, a prejudice persists behind the thinking about the state's role under the Republic: the political disunity of the country and the weakness of central power would have constituted almost insurmountable obstacles to the construction of the state. Of course, it is now recognized that central governments were not the only actors in this field. Justice has been done (albeit too little) to the achievements of some warlords. But should we not go further and remind ourselves that centralization and state-building are two concepts that do not necessarily overlap? The idea of state-building with a certain amount of political fragmentation deserves to be seriously explored, particularly because many local autocrats also shared the ideal of a strong state that is active in economic development.

Political culture

Inventing a political culture

Revolutionaries of all times and from all walks of life are always careful to flag up the break they make with the pre-existing political order. In 1911–12, the emblematic symbol of the advent of a new order in China was cutting off the queue. Imposed as proof of the Han population's rallying to the Qing dynasty in the seventeenth century, the wearing of the queue became customary over the following two centuries, as the population ceased to associate it with any form of subjection. It was only at the turn of the twentieth century that this idea resurfaced under the influence of revolutionary circles. The matter was, however, contested; some people even saw hostility to the queue as a consequence of slavish imitation of Western customs. Nevertheless, the refusal to wear a queue became a sign of support for the new regime during the months of the revolution. At a time when the country was in the grip of revolutionary uprisings, an edict made the wearing of the queue a criterion of loyalty to the imperial regime. The execution of some of those who ventured to cut it and had the misfortune to fall into the hands of authorities loyal to the Qing (in Fengtian, Zhang Zuolin executed any man who cut their queue) completed the emotional and symbolic charge conferred on it. And the general disappearance of queues in the months following the emperor's abdication was the most visible sign of regime change across the country.

22 The cutting of queues (1912).

Another element in the orchestration of the political rupture was the choice to proclaim the Republic on 1 January 1912. Sun Yat-sen, who had just arrived from Shanghai where he had been elected president a few days earlier, rushed things so that the ceremony would take place that very evening. It did not matter to him that it took place almost in secret: the main thing was to succeed in proclaiming the Republic on a significant date in the Gregorian calendar, which replaced the traditional lunisolar calendar.[1] This was certainly an important element of imperial symbolism. Establishing the calendar was one of the traditional attributions of the emperor, who thus manifested his position as Son of Heaven. As with cutting the queue, the choice of the Gregorian calendar reflected both a desire to break with the past and a desire to be part of Western-inspired modernity. It should be noted that it was not dictated by any practical necessity. The lunisolar calendar had undeniable advantages (for example, for coastal populations, the ability to predict the movement of the tides from a few very simple calculations). The authorities did not merely impose the Gregorian calendar: year 1 of the new calendar was 1912, and it included a succession of politically significant holidays, the most important of which was the national holiday on 10 October, the anniversary of the Wuchang uprising. In daily life, however, the lunisolar calendar was still widely favoured by the population, and it still exists to this day in secondary use.

The year 1911 instituted an even deeper break, with the introduction of a new form of legitimacy based no longer on the heavenly mandate, but on the assent of the people. This upheaval would be reflected in radically different political rites. Apart from the fact that these were stripped of all religious and cosmological dimensions, their main characteristic was their eminently *public* nature. The imperial political rites, centred on the person of the emperor, remained confined behind the walls of the Forbidden City, which concealed them from the eyes of ordinary people. With the Republic, not only was the population no longer kept on the sidelines, but it *had* to be part of the new rites, which could now be described as civic. The subject had become a citizen. Adherence to the new regime was demonstrated in practices such as saluting the flag. This, like the national anthem, was one of the symbols that must be respected by all citizens. Essential to the new nation, these attributes also situated the country on an equal level with other nations (or supposedly so), which translates into another rupture: the abandonment of the idea of China's centrality and pre-eminence.

From 1915 onwards, Yuan Shikai's attempt at imperial restoration put the assimilation of this new political culture to the test. And Yuan's crushing failure signalled the general refusal to return to the imperial form of power.

All this does not mean that the Republic's new political culture instantly took shape without some trial and error. The early days were particularly faltering when it came to its official architecture. During the late 1910s, the Graveyard of the 72 Martyrs (*Huanghuagang qishier lieshi lingyuan* 黃花崗七十二烈士陵園) was built in Guangdong. This clumsy and inelegant piling up of republican symbols heavily borrowed from American political culture (still visible today) would not be repeated. Official architecture really found its style during the Nanjing decade. Western architectural influence, especially in the fine arts, was certainly strong. Nevertheless, it was combined, especially at roof level, with certain features inspired by former official monuments. The ministry buildings in the new capital, Nanjing, were examples of

23 A new pedagogy in the service of the nation. From the very first lessons, this first-year primary school textbook presents the national flag (right-hand page).

this synthesis. They were pierced with many windows, thus expressing a desire for openness and the new attention that the rulers paid to the people. This had its limits nonetheless – as in the imperial period, they remained surrounded by an outer wall.[2]

In keeping with the eminently public nature of the new political ceremonial, verbal communication gained in importance. The era of the revolution was one of political speeches and oratory. The break was total and called into question the overwhelming preponderance of the written word that characterized imperial political culture. This change in practice would largely survive the first years of the Republic. Much of Sun Yat-sen's thinking was developed through the countless speeches he made throughout his political career. The political meetings of the various campaigns orchestrated by the Guomindang were, above all, a succession of lengthy speeches (whose influence was much increased through radio broadcasts). The same was true for the CCP, which would make the voice of the oppressed one of the cornerstones of its tactics to subvert traditional elites.

Citizen participation was also achieved through elections. In fact, their place in the new political order has been somewhat neglected by historians, for two reasons. On the one hand, political power at all levels came only very exceptionally through the ballot box, throughout the period. On the other hand, the elections were undoubtedly subject to massive manipulation and fraud, which has led to an underestimation of their significance.[3] Nevertheless, there was a certain 'acclimatization' to this practice within the political culture. Mention has been made of the parliamentary elections of the winter of 1912–13, which roused the country. The act of voting established itself as the basis of democratic legitimacy. Certainly, the members of this parliament, the only one of the period to be democratically elected across the whole country, would, in the ten years that followed, be repeatedly intimidated, bought and shuffled between the different aspirants to power. Paradoxically, such treatment was indicative of a significant fact. That so much effort (and money) was spent on suborning its members was because this parliament was seen by all as an important part of the political game. In the early 1920s, the issue of elections became central again. The federal movement that was sweeping the country was accompanied by intense debates about the voting system that should be adopted. Local elections were held in a number of provinces, such as in Guangdong under the leadership of Chen Jiongming (late 1921) to appoint county leaders.[4] The issue of elections remained important in the debate on institutions throughout the period of Guomindang rule, not least because, in principle, it was felt that local elections should be held with the aim of educating people in the exercise of their suffrage. Elections were held in 1936–7 to elect part of the Constituent Assembly, which could not meet due to the war. New general elections were organized by the Guomindang between November 1947 and January 1948. They were held on the basis of universal suffrage, but with a system of official candidatures reminiscent of the Second Empire in France.

Continuities with the New Policies period

However radical the rupture of 1911 may have been, the historian should not be misled by the revolutionary mythology of the clean slate. In fact, some of the radical reforms described above actually originated under the Qing: for example, elections, the first of which were held during the empire; and the Gregorian calendar, which had begun to be adopted in certain sectors of the Qing administration, such as the postal service, customs, railways and education. Irrespective of the revolution of 1911, there were strong elements of continuity with reforms that had emerged since the launch of the New Policies. As in the case of the abandonment of the Six Ministries system dating back to the Tang (Justice, Rites, Public Works, War, Civil Appointments and Finance) in favour of an organization inspired by Western ministerial cabinets, none of the major reforms of the New Policies, it is worth noting, was challenged by the revolutionaries. The revolutionaries were in almost all cases the continuators of the New Policies reforms. Probably the best example was the overhaul of Chinese law and the judicial system. The Provisional Criminal Code adopted in 1912 (*zanxing xin xinglü* 暫行新刑律) was replaced by a new code in March 1928 (*zhonghua minguo xingfa* 中華民國刑法), which was further amended in 1935. A Civil Code was promulgated in stages between May 1929 and February 1931. However, this very considerable work had its direct origins in the gigantic effort undertaken during the New Policies period by Wu Tingfang and Shen Jiaben and continued under the regime of Yuan Shikai (who was Shen Jiaben's patron).[5] Even the Beiyang governments, which have been shown to be weak in many respects, kept the momentum going under figures like Zhang Yaozeng. Three times Minister of Justice between 1916 and 1924, he worked tirelessly with other eminent jurists to reform the judicial system. This transformation of the law stems from the adoption of fundamentally new principles, in particular that of equality between all individuals, regardless of their gender or ethnicity. This was reflected in the areas of marriage (arranged marriages were prohibited and the right to divorce affirmed) and inheritance (heirs received an equal share). Other major areas of law reform were sentencing, the abolition of torture, and the separation of executive and judicial powers (which had previously been combined, notably under county magistrates). The concern to make justice more accessible was reflected in efforts to increase the number of courts, the objective (never achieved) being to have one in every county. Finally, there was also a wish to match the texts better with their application in reality. This was a grievance of Westerners who pointed out with sarcastic verve the extent to which virtuous prohibitions, such as that on gambling, remained utterly ineffectual. It should be noted that the aim of providing China with a law, and in particular a Criminal Code, corresponding to the idea that Western countries had of it, remained the same as at the end of the empire. This was to remove from the West one of their main arguments for opposing the end of extraterritoriality.

Finally, as Xiaohong Xiao-Planes has clearly shown, the constitutional question, which troubled political debate during the New Policies period, not only remained bitterly debated throughout the Republic, but was still at the heart of building the state.[6]

Such continuities with the New Policies period can be explained to some extent by the fact that the people were the same: the Republic, especially under the Beiyang governments, largely recycled staff from the imperial administration. The emblematic case of Xu Shichang, former governor general of Manchuria under the Qing, several times minister, who became president of the Republic in September 1918, comes to mind. But the capillary action between the stratum of Qing-era officials and the political staff of the new regime was a much more widespread phenomenon than just this. Of the 94 men who held ministerial posts between 1920 and 1928, 54 per cent came from the Qing bureaucracy.[7] The same was true of their underlings.[8] Many of them were young people trained abroad to whom the ranks of the administration had been opened during the New Policies. Others, often older, such as Liang Shiyi, one of the key public finance men of the central government in the first decade of the Republic, were perfect products of the mandarin examination system and Qing senior bureaucracy. The warlords were not the last to engage the services of competent administrators who had begun their careers under the Qing. Wang Yongjiang, Zhang Zuolin's big financier, worked wonders to provide his master with the funds for his political and military ambitions.

The fact that men who came directly from the Qing dynasty mandarinate continued their careers under the Republic is certainly not unrelated to certain forms of perpetuation of an older political culture, which merit attention.

Continuity with an older political order

In an amusing twist, the very term that designated the political project of the revolutionaries, that of *geming* 革命 (revolution), is drawn from the political vocabulary of the imperial era, by way of Japanese, being reinvested with a new meaning (the original meaning was the revocation of the heavenly mandate). This example might seem anecdotal, but, beyond the vocabulary, the perpetuation of numerous practices, ideas and concepts stemming directly from the imperial political system could be observed during the republican period.

In the mid-1920s, Chiang Kai-shek, then a young director of the Huangpu Military Academy, practised calligraphy on old newspapers in the privacy of the home he shared with his wife. This had nothing to do with relaxation, but with political calculation on the part of an ambitious man on the rise. Chiang took it for granted that it was essential for a leading statesman to have at least acceptable calligraphy. During the republican period, official buildings continued to be adorned with calligraphies in the hand of the leaders. Official publications that appeared in numbers opened with photographs of leaders and senior officials, but they were always accompanied by a few sentences they had calligraphed.

The promotion of the spoken word mentioned above had its limits. The prestige of writing and calligraphy remained very high. Chiang (like Mao) would rise to the highest office while remaining a poor orator.

The imperial culture's political legacy was rarely taken up so assertively as with the establishment of a Qing history office (*Qingshi guan* 清史館) in March 1914.[9] In the traditional dynastic system, it was the responsibility of each new dynasty to write the history of its predecessor. The *Draft History of the Qing* (*Qingshigao* 清史稿) was published as early as 1928. However, it went no further. No official Qing history ever joined the collection of the twenty-four official dynastic histories.

The administrative structure, unaffected by the New Policies, was another example of the resilience of existing state structures: at province level, things remained unchanged. Similarly, the division of the 1,400 districts, the most local level of administration in the imperial period, remained intact. The new administrative levels that appeared were located *below* that of the county. The Republic reversed an innovation introduced by the Qing: the general governorates, which combined two

(Shaanxi/Gansu or Hunan/Hubei, for example) or even three provinces (Jiangsu/Anhui/Jiangxi). The only significant change, in the end, was the disappearance of the two intermediary levels that were interposed in imperial China between province and county: the 70 circuits (*dao* 道) and 210 prefectures (*fu* 府) that the country had under the Qing rapidly disappeared. But the system developed during the Nanjing decade, in which the districts reported their budgets to the provincial governments, which the latter passed on (adding their own budgets) to Nanjing, enshrined the continued primacy of the three main tiers of the old administrative structure.

One of the customary activities of local governments was the publication of local monographs, the famous *difangzhi* 地方志, which reviewed the geographical, demographic, social and historical data of an administrative entity (usually a county or a prefecture). In She county (Anhui), where a local monograph was published in 1937, the previous edition was more than 100 years old.[10] More generally, with around 1,600 volumes, there had never been such regularly produced local monographs before than there were under the Republic.[11] In Hebei province, for example, in the 1920s and 1930s, almost every county published an updated edition.

In terms of culture and political ideas, it is not possible to make an exhaustive inventory of the old elements that continued to exist. Let us just consider a few of the most significant examples. Thus, special attention must be paid to the nomadism of the capital during the republican period. No other major country in the world offers an example of this, except Siam, and that to a much lesser degree. This is a direct legacy of traditional Chinese political culture, in which the location of the capital was considered an open question (a concept eminently foreign to a French or English person). For the person in power, the choice of location could be put at the service of a strategy and a general political orientation. The choice of Beijing in 1912 and Nanjing in 1927 are both of this order. Less well known is that, in the early 1940s, there were post-war plans that did not call for a return to Nanjing, but for a further change with the adoption of Xi'an as the capital.[12]

A proverb that states that good officials are the wealth of the country (*shi nai guo zhi bao* 士乃國之寶) captures another profound feature of Chinese political culture, which tends to place more importance on the

quality of the men who serve the state than on the structure of the institutions: 'finding the men' rather than 'finding the methods'.[13] Remarkably,
this idea survived the abolition of the imperial examinations in 1905 (a
system whose purpose was precisely to select an elite of individuals with
great care) and the advent of the Republic. Cao Kun stated bluntly in his
inaugural speech in the autumn of 1923: 'The key to good government
is to employ talented men.' But, above all, we find the same idea in Sun
Yat-sen. The latter made the power of examination (which consists of
organizing and centralizing the recruitment of civil servants) one of the
five powers, together with the executive, legislative, judicial and super-
visory powers. Much less iconoclastic than one might think, especially
in this area, Sun was even doubly heir to the imperial tradition, since the
power of control as he defined it consisted in reviving, in a very slightly
different form, the Censorate (*duchayuan* 都察院) of the imperial era.[14]

The Guomindang and the party-state model post-1928

After the military reunification of the Northern Expedition and the
founding of the Nanjing regime, the Guomindang began to reshape
the central Chinese state according to the principles laid down by Sun
Yat-sen. Although this undertaking has been assessed very differently by
historians, it was undoubtedly the most coherent and successful attempt
to reform the state during the period.

Sun Yat-sen, a guiding light

If Sun Yat-sen had become a totem of the Republic since his death in
March 1925, the Nanjing regime established, without exaggeration, what
could be called a state cult. The day of his birth and the day of his death
were public holidays. His face was everywhere, on banknotes, stamps,
and in Tiananmen Square, where Mao's face stands today. In his honour,
Xiangshan, the county where he was born, was renamed Zhongshan
(one of Sun's most common appellations and his *hao* 號– literary name).
His role in the revolution was exalted in speeches and in the pages of
textbooks, which endowed him with all the virtues. His remains were
placed, in a lavish ceremony, in a monumental tomb built in Nanjing
by the architect Lü Yanzhi. When they decided to adopt a new national

anthem in 1927, the lyrics were taken entirely from speeches made by the great man. Any public or official meeting had to be preceded by a short ceremony to honour the memory of the man whom it became compulsory in March 1940 to refer to solely as 'Father of the Nation' (*guofu* 國父): the audience bowed to his portrait, before observing a minute's silence. Then a short text, the Last Will (*yizhu* 遺囑), which Sun is supposed to have written on his deathbed, but which he most likely only approved, was read out (see Appendix 1). *Yizhu* is translated as Last Will for want of a better term, but the nuance of exhortation implied by the term *zhu* is somehow lost. The will became a sacred text, and by virtue of its brevity (only 146 characters), it appeared absolutely everywhere. It was featured on the front pages of both official publications and the most frivolous newspapers. The central theme of the necessary 'awakening' of the people and the priority aim of abolishing unequal treaties can be found in this short text. This text by Sun mentions the unfinished nature of the revolution to which he dedicated his life.

This promotion of Sun's personage took place mainly because it served a very specific purpose for the new Guomindang strongman, Chiang Kai-shek. The latter, indeed, was far from having as glorious a revolutionary past as his main rivals in the Guomindang, Hu Hanmin and Wang Jingwei. In order to establish his legitimacy, Chiang therefore resorted to a strategy of personality cult 'by proxy'. On the one hand, it was a question of developing the cult of Sun on a large scale and, on the other, of creating opportunities to assert that he, Chiang, was his sole political heir. Thus, under the pretext of exalting the 'Father of the Chinese Nation', the transfer of Sun's remains on 1 June 1929 to the mausoleum built for him in Nanjing served, above all, as a way for Chiang to pose as his worthy heir. He was the one who ostensibly conducted the mourning, marginalizing the relatives of the deceased. Chiang also took care to set up his offices in the building used by Sun Yat-sen during the few months he had spent as president of the Republic in early 1912. As for his official residence in Nanjing, the Lingyuan Villa (*Lingyuan bieshu* 陵園別墅), it was located right next to Sun's mausoleum.

At first, therefore, Chiang's rise to personal power during the Northern Expedition and the Nanjing decade (1928–37) was not accompanied by a real cult of his personality, but this was skilfully compensated for by the all-out promotion of his chosen political ancestor.[15] From the 1937–45 war onwards, however, Chiang's cult of personality became more explicit.

Sun's main writings were the soundtrack to the party's intellectual life. His thinking was taught throughout the educational system, from primary school onwards: neither athletes in the National Martial Arts Academy nor even opium addicts in their rehab clinics could escape it.[16]

The 1st Guomindang Congress (1924) established the Three Principles of the People as the official party ideology. The Three Principles (*sanmin zhuyi* 三民主義) revolved, as its name suggests, around three points: nationalism (*minzu zhuyi* 民族主義), democracy (*minquan zhuyi* 民權主義) and the people's welfare (*minsheng zhuyi* 民生主義). Although Sun Yat-sen tried to give it a more precise outline in a famous series of lectures given in Guangzhou between March and August 1924, it was not a very clearly defined doctrine. It even underwent considerable changes during Sun's career, one of the most notable being the transformation of the concept of nationalism. In the early 1920s, nationalism became synonymous with anti-imperialism (directed not only against the Western powers, but also their so-called henchmen, the warlords). If Sun was dependent on Russian aid and undoubtedly influenced by his Soviet advisors in his base in Guangzhou, there was no doubt in his mind that the Comintern should be at the service of the Chinese revolution and not vice versa. From among the ideological arsenal brought by the Comintern, Sun and the nationalists appropriated one notion above all, the only one that made sense to them and which they were to use and abuse from then on: imperialism. This theme became increasingly important in Sun's speeches from 1923–4. From this period onwards, the notion of 'unequal treaties' was used repeatedly to describe the treaties signed at the end of the two Opium Wars, which were themselves interpreted as premeditated aggression. It is a clever approach to denounce as exceptionally iniquitous something that is nevertheless quite common: unfavourable treaties concluded after a military defeat. The trilogy of imperialism, unequal treaties and warlords was blamed for all the country's difficulties at the time of the Northern Expedition and into the 1930s.

As far as democracy was concerned, while Sun was an advocate of government of the people, by the people and for the people (in Lincoln's phrase), he believed that China was not ready for a Western-style parliamentary democracy. He therefore posited the need to go through two transitional stages before arriving at constitutional government (*xianzheng* 憲政). They were a phase of military government (*junzheng* 軍政), which should last only as long as it took to gain power, and then political tutelage by the party (*dangzheng* 黨政). During the latter period, the people had to be educated under the one-party system before they could elect their representatives to draft a constitution.

Western observers at the time readily referred to him as a 'red'. Yet Sun remained totally impervious to that concept much more central to Marxist thought than imperialism: class struggle, which he equated with a pathological state of society resulting from the concentration of capital in too few hands. In a lecture he gave on 30 December 1923, he compared Chinese society to a beehive where tasks are shared peaceably and each individual contributes willingly to the common good. By no means hostile to capitalism and even less so to the market economy, Sun was a social reformist, only vaguely advocating reduction in inequalities. It was therefore necessary to insist on the moderation of positions in favour of the welfare of the people, a principle which it is wrong to translate, as is still sometimes done, as 'socialism'.

After Sun's death, the interpretation of his thought became a crucial issue in the struggles within the Guomindang. The interpretation of his texts by those on the right wing of the Guomindang (such as Dai Jitao) attempted to reduce the Three Principles to a form of conservatism by emphasizing a certain continuity with the Confucian heritage, a task made easier by the more or less explicit allusions to Confucius scattered throughout Sun's speeches. Conversely, the Guomindang left wing insisted on the revolutionary overtones of Sun's works.

Institutional structure

The 1928 Organic Law was a direct application of the theses developed by Sun. Power was divided between the five yuan, or branches of government: the Executive (*xingzhengyuan* 行政院), the Judicial (*sifayuan* 司法院), the Legislative (*lifayuan* 立法院), the Control (*jianchayuan* 監察院) and the Examination yuan (*kaoshiyuan* 考試院). The ministries were placed under the authority of the different yuan according to an allocation pattern that was unstable. In reality, the importance of the yuan was extremely uneven: the Executive Yuan covered the bulk of the ministries and was notoriously predominant.[17]

The President of the Executive Yuan was, in effect, more or less the same as a prime minister. It was, for example, the position held by Wang Jingwei between 1932 and 1935, the three years during which, allied with Chiang Kai-shek, he strongly influenced matters of state.[18] Other yuan presidents were much less powerful. Thus, when Sun Ke, Sun Yat-sen's son, was offered the post of president of the Legislative Yuan in March 1932, he bridled at what he perceived to be a relegation to a quasi-honorary position, heralding political marginalization.[19]

Other than the structure of the five yuan, one of the main characteristics of the Guomindang state was the coexistence of two parallel organizations, with the party organization superimposed on the state organization.

In the Guomindang, as in any centralized democratic party, power was supposed to emanate from national congresses (*quanguo daibiao dahui* 全國代表大會) convened at regular intervals. The national congress designated the members of the Central Executive Committee (*zhongyang zhixing weiyuanhui* 中央執行委員會) where the nerve centre of power lay. However, this arrangement should not be given too much importance, as it gives the doubly false impression of a collegiality of power and an internal democratic life of the party. Open debate within the party was reduced to a trickle during the 1920s, as shown, among other things, by the increasingly spaced out and irregular convening of national congresses. No less than ten years passed between the 5th (1935) and the 6th (1945). There was also an increase in the number of members of the Central Executive Committee and even of the Standing Committee (less than a dozen members until 1935, up to fifty-five in 1947). This inflation in numbers had the effect of making them lose all coherence and real influence. We have seen how the Sino-Japanese War favoured Chiang Kai-shek's personal power. From an institutional point of view, this resulted in a highly symbolic measure: the Extraordinary National Congress (*linshi quanguo daibiao dahui* 臨時全國代表大會) in the spring of 1938 ratified his predominance by elevating him to the rank of *zongcai* 總裁, a title that evokes the one conferred on Sun in 1924 (*zongli* 總理).

From a quantitative point of view, the Guomindang took on a new dimension in the second half of the 1920s. In 1929, it had 266,000 militants, 96 per cent of whom had joined less than five years before. The selection and training of these new members was much neglected. Opportunism reigned. For example, in areas where Northern Expedition troops arrived, local government personnel sought to ensure that they retained their position by joining them. During the 1930s, the Guomindang became a mass party – in 1937, there were 1.6 million members.[20] In the following years, membership formalities were gradually reduced to their simplest form. Add to this the practice of collective membership (through the company or the administration), and the number of party members exploded to the point where it becomes impossible to accurately estimate them.

However, the party's hold on the country was very uneven. Guomindang members were recruited from a limited number of social groups. Students and teachers were the first to join its ranks in the early 1920s. In the mid-1920s, civil servants and military personnel joined en masse. Yet the fact remains that the party never managed to penetrate society in depth. Those most involved in mobilizing workers or peasants during the period of the first United Front were either communists or members of the left wing. By abruptly breaking with the CCP and cutting themselves off from their left wing, the Guomindang lost their foothold among these sections of the population. Despite the spectacular increase in the number of members, in the years 1930–40, peasants were still conspicuous by their absence. Even in the city, the Guomindang remained inaccessible to the working classes. From the geographical viewpoint, the differences between provinces could be very great. In 1929 in Sichuan, China's most populous province, there were seventy-seven members, as the local warlords spared no effort in curbing its implantation. The rise in Chiang Kai-shek's personal power was not a good thing for the Guomindang's establishment throughout the country. Since the local sections were generally not very much in favour of him, he never allocated significant means for their development.

While the impression prevails that the party was somewhat disconnected from society, there was a 'partyfication' (*danghua* 黨化), or takeover by the party, of the various components of the state. The process has been particularly well studied in the judicial sector.[21] It was expressed in two ways. Firstly, historical Guomindang figures with a very political profile and limited experience in the field of justice (such as Ju Zheng, placed at the head of the Judicial Yuan in January 1932) replaced seasoned jurists who had come from the Beiyang administration, such as Wang Chonghui, a doctor of law from Yale University, who had been a minister three times under Beiyang governments (1912, 1921, 1924). This 'partyfication', however, only took place at the highest level of the judiciary. At grassroots level, the party's penetration was much less significant. Secondly, at the level of rank-and-file judges, there was strong pressure on existing men to join the ranks of the Guomindang, while the training of new judges was given a much more political bent. The tendency to turn the judiciary into the compliant instrument of Guomindang policy was emerging. However, it met strong resistance at various levels of the hierarchy. One of the main bones of contention was the special jurisdiction applied to communists.

As with the example of the justice sector, the party failed to subvert the state. This was reflected in various indicators, such as the fact that the salaries of local officials were notoriously higher than those of party officials of equivalent level.[22] The tendency of Chiang Kai-shek, whose relatively weak support within the party has been indicated, to favour the state was no doubt a factor.

But Chiang relied even more on the army as an instrument of his power. The establishment of the Huangpu Military Academy in 1924 was a major turning point, in providing the Guomindang with a military force that was no longer an ally to be dealt with, but an integral part of it. The army's importance increased with the Northern Expedition. In the following years, in an increasingly threatening international climate, it continued to take up a huge share of the budget. At the same time, Chiang Kai-shek emancipated the army from the party. After the break with the CCP, he quickly nullified the power of the political commissars that had been set up within the military forces, on the Bolshevik model. Later, in the 1930s and 1940s, he enabled an increasingly significant number of military personnel to take up important civilian positions. Thus, the post of mayor of Shanghai was held by Qian Dajun in 1945–6, while He Yingqin became president of the Executive Yuan in 1949. All in all, the Northern Expedition, followed by the emergence and assertion of Chiang's power, contributed to giving the military an importance and autonomy in relation to the party and the state that Sun Yat-sen had had no intention of giving them, that they did not possess before 1926, and of which they would never allow themselves to be dispossessed again.

The DNA of the Guomindang state was thus strongly marked by the problematic coexistence of three organizations: the state, the party and the army.

Cliques and clique struggles

We have seen how Chiang Kai-shek took the liberty of resigning from all his official functions on various occasions (from August to December 1927, from December 1931 to January 1932, and from January 1949 to March 1950). This puzzling approach was never of any consequence because the essence of his power lay elsewhere, in a network of loyalties, which allowed him to continue to exercise actual power in secret. As this example shows, grasping the very substance of power relations within the Guomindang state involves not just describing institutions, but accounting for the interpersonal networks and cliques (*xi* 系 or *pai* 派) that competed within the ruling spheres of the state, party and army. The list of cliques could be much longer, but four stand out in particular.

The Huangpu clique (*Huangpu pai* 黃埔派) is probably the easiest to discern, as it was made up of the former cadets of the eponymous academy. The lucky ones who survived the battles of the Northern Expedition generally rose rapidly to important posts. These members continued to ostensibly greet Chiang with forms of respect, in order to emphasize the special bond between them and him. Particularly powerful in the army, it counted among its most important members Du Yuming, He Zhonghan and Hu Zongnan.

The CC clique was also closely associated with Chiang Kai-shek. It centred on the Chen brothers, Chen Guofu and Chen Lifu, two nephews of Chen Qimei. He was an important revolutionary figure, who until his death in May 1916 was Chiang's mentor in the Guomindang. This clique was particularly powerful within the party organization and had numerous and widespread offshoots. Strongly established in the Lower Yangtze valley (where its links with secret societies were well known), it also had a hand in the civilian component of the Guomindang secret service (*Zhongtong* 中統).

The Reorganization clique (*gaizupai* 改組派), on the other hand, included supporters of Wang Jingwei. Its mainspring was Chen Gongpo. Its name came from the 'Society of Comrades for the Reorganization of the Guomindang' (*Guomindang gaizu tongzhihui* 國民黨改組同志會), founded in 1929 with the intention of obstructing Chiang's personal power.[23]

The last of the major cliques was the Political Science Clique (*Zhengxue xi* 政學系). Poorly structured and lacking a real leader, it mostly brought together high-level technicians, often trained abroad and working in the ministries, such as Huang Fu, Zhang Qun, Wang Chonghui, Zhang Jia'ao and Weng Wenhao.

While historians have profoundly reassessed the Guomindang's record since the 1990s, there is still a consensus on the pathological nature of the multiplicity of cliques and their rivalries. Yet it is far from self-evident. Firstly, we should be aware that factional fighting in the imperial court and in the upper echelons of the administration was part of the normal political scene, even during the most brilliant periods of Chinese history. More broadly, the phenomenon is inseparable from any political system that has reached a certain degree of sophistication, whether it be the Comanche Empire or the court of Louis XIV. It has undeniable advantages: Chiang Kai-shek, like the emperors, shamelessly played on these rivalries to consolidate his power.

Another mistake is to see cliques as devices designed only to defend the interests of their members. This overlooks the fact that they are also intended to promote a political line. Margherita Zanasi's work has, for example, shown the coherence and sophistication of the Reorganization clique's political programme, formed around Wang Jingwei. The development of the economy is its prime focus, with recourse to state intervention. The model of fascist Italy aroused great interest, particularly in its drive for economic self-sufficiency and the promotion of corporatism as a remedy for the conflicts between capital and labour. Wang Jingwei endeavoured to implement this programme during his presidency of the Executive Yuan between 1932 and 1935, accepting his share of responsibility for the highly unpopular (but necessary, given the need to prioritize economic development) policy of compromise with Japan.

The CC clique project, sometimes summarized as 'Cultural Construction on a Chinese Basis' (*Zhongguo benwei de wenhua jianshe*

中國本位的文化建設), on the other hand, was to seek a dynamic and selective combination of elements of traditional Chinese culture and borrowings from Western modernity.[24] Again, this was not just empty words: Chen Lifu, one of the main leaders of the CC clique, was very active in the development of two sectors that were at the forefront of technology at the time – radio and the film industry.[25] He intended to enlist them in strengthening the state and promoting traditional Chinese values. In short, without totally denying its negative effects, the phenomenon of cliques was therefore more commonplace and, probably, more benign than one might think during the Nanjing decade. It was only after the Second World War that the influence of the cliques became critical, and even toxic. Once again, we must be careful not to project later negative tendencies on to the Nanjing decade.

The endless return of revolution

It is useful to return to the text of Sun Yat-sen's Last Will, and in particular his most often-quoted sentence which states that 'The Revolution is not yet achieved' (*xianzai geming shang wei chenggong* 現在革命尚未成功). Echoing this phrase, the need to regenerate the revolutionary spirit within the Guomindang became an obsession from 1928 onwards. Chiang's famous statement in his opening speech at the Guomindang Extraordinary Congress on 29 March 1938 – 'our party has become a kind of empty shell' (*women de dang chabuduo yi chengwei yi ge kong de quqiao* 我們的黨差不多已成為一個空的軀殼) – has often been underlined. Many historians, most notably Lloyd Eastman, have seen this as an admission, as well as convincing evidence, of the party's decay, and have pointed to its bureaucratic excesses: a proliferation of regulations and reports, and an appetite for statistical production that sometimes turned into a fetish.

It is important, however, to set aside dramatization and rhetorical indignation from a Chiang inclined to self-flagellation (including in his private writings). The radically critical tone adopted in this speech is also explained by the fact that it was pronounced as part of the launch of the Youth Corps of the Three Principles of the People (*Sanmin zhuyi qingniantuan* 三民主義青年團).

This Corps was the latest in a series of groups created by Chiang Kai-shek with the stated intention of re-instilling revolutionary momentum and overcoming factional struggles within the Guomindang. The main groups were founded in 1932, to exploit the sense of urgency caused by the Japanese aggression of 1931. In February 1932, the Society for the Vigorous Practice of the Three Principles of the People (*Sanmin zhuyi Lixingshe* 三民主義力行社) was formed. This was a secret, elitist organization, each member of which was closely linked to Chiang. The *Lixingshe* was soon supplemented by three other organizations: the Revolutionary Military Association (*Geming junren tongzhihui* 革命軍人同志會) and the Revolutionary Youth Association (*Geming qingnian tongzhihui* 革命青年同志會) were also secretive, albeit recruited significantly more widely. Only the Rebirth Society (*Fuxingshe* 復興社), established in July 1932, was a mass organization (500,000 members). Then in 1938, the Youth Corps of the Three Principles of the People was created. The initial project was again ambitious: a mass organization, driven by a revolutionary spirit and cultivating a bond of personal loyalty to Chiang Kai-shek, intended to compete with and eventually replace the Guomindang themselves. However, the ensuing confusion was such that, by 1939, the role of the Corps was restricted to the management, ideological training and mobilization of student youth. Its subordination to the Guomindang was reaffirmed.[26] In every case, these different organizations were quickly overtaken by the same evils they were supposed to remedy – careerism and corruption.

The question of fascism

Some of the groups mentioned were clearly inspired by fascist regimes (members of the *Lixingshe* were nicknamed 'Blue Shirts' – *lanyi* 藍衣), which has provoked debates about the possible fascist nature of the Nanjing regime. Chiang Kai-shek and his entourage were undeniably fascinated by Nazi Germany and, to a lesser degree, fascist Italy. But certain similarities with Germany or Italy should not be misread. The nationalist regime was more akin to contemporary Iberian models, such as Salazar's Portugal, Franco's Spain or Getúlio Vargas' *Estado Novo* in Brazil (although it goes without saying that the idea of considering these countries – all too modest pieces on the world chessboard – as models would never have crossed the mind of a Chinese political leader of the period). All three authoritarian regimes relied on the personal power of men who, while being fine manoeuvrers, were all, like Chiang Kai-shek, remarkably lacking in charisma. Their socially conservative character (with strong corporatist overtones) did not exclude modernizing ambitions on the economic front. Strictly speaking, therefore, Chiang's rule can be described as authoritarian but not fascist. While there is little doubt that Chiang Kai-shek may have taken a close interest in the fascist model and may have been tempted to copy some of its elements, this was not a systematic undertaking. The following elements of the fascist repertoire are missing: an all-powerful state, massive indoctrination of the population, and enrolment and management in mass movements. Fascism also goes hand in hand with ruthless censorship and a powerful police force capable of suppressing any breath of opposition, a tool that the Guomindang never possessed. While he did not completely ignore the cult of the leader, he took a much less pronounced route. Let us add another ingredient (common not just to fascism but to all totalitarian regimes) which was missing in nationalist China: the project of creating the 'New Man'. Its corollary, an obsessive fascination with youth, was equally absent.

The long debates around the question of the fascist nature of the Guomindang state have obscured a much more structural and profound problem. In fact, the party remained stranded midway between two irreconcilable models. The first was that of the Bolshevik party: a pyramidal organization with a strong concentration of power at the level of the central authorities, iron discipline, presence at all levels of society, a dense coverage of territory and total adherence of its members to the revolutionary spirit. The other model was, quite simply, Weberian bureaucracy. It was undoubtedly at work in the Guomindang state, but only at the level of certain administrations, such as the Salt Tax Administration and Maritime Customs, or ministries like Finance or Foreign Affairs. These remarkably efficient ministries were marked by the stability of their personnel. For example, in the Ministry of Health, Liu Ruiheng served as minister from 1929 to 1938.[27] These administrations and ministries were isolates. They were subject to their own rules of recruitment, promotion and remuneration. This was their strength, allowing them to attract and retain the most qualified and motivated people, and to avoid factional in-fighting. On the other hand, although they were the most effective component of the Guomindang state, their influence remained limited within a restricted political perimeter.[28]

In reality, during the Nanjing decade, the Guomindang's evolution moved towards a renunciation of revolutionary ideals and conversion to a managerial and bureaucratic model (which did not exclude efficiency). A telling example is the school for party cadres set up in Nanjing in the summer of 1927. The first classes were taught by Guomindang veterans. The training was brief and focused on ideology and political activism. But from 1929 onwards, the curriculum was extended and the teaching made more academic, even arriving at a certain critical distancing from the orthodoxy of the Three Principles. By the mid-1930s, the school had become a classic academic institution. From then on, it trained competent managerial bureaucrats who were anything but ardent revolutionaries.[29] In short, all the initiatives launched by Chiang Kai-shek and his entourage to resurrect the revolutionary momentum of the early days ran counter to the natural inclination of the Guomindang to become a party of government.

The extension of the state's scope, a fundamental trend

As already mentioned in the previous chapter, there was a consensus on the need for a strong state among the intelligentsia, which Edmund Fung saw as one of the main features of the intellectual climate of the period.[30] A strong state had to combine two characteristics: efficiency and a broad sphere of intervention. Expanding the sphere of intervention in Chinese society and its economy was a particularly crucial innovation in China, which contrasted with a centuries-long tradition of what Pierre-Étienne Will calls a 'frugal state'.

There are countless aspects of the extension of the state's scope, which makes it impossible to draw up an exhaustive list. Some of these are well known and have been dealt with in previous chapters – notably, its increasing involvement in production (Chapter 6). Many other fields were concerned, such as music and the arts, with the creation of academies and conservatories. In the field of martial arts, there was a desire to recover age-old knowledge, which had been dissipated in a myriad of variants and regional schools. Their promotion involved standardization, while seeking to bring them into line with more scientific criteria. This was accomplished within the framework of an Academy of National Martial Arts that was under the close control of the state, which placed the teaching of martial arts under the aegis of national recovery. Comparable action was taken in favour of traditional medicine. In addition, there was a massive effort to 'reform customs' throughout the Nanjing decade. Its most famous element was the New Life Movement (*xin shenghuo yundong* 新生活運動), launched in 1934, which promoted a lifestyle based on military discipline, valuing frugality and hygiene. However, the Guomindang's ambition to reshape lifestyles was apparent from 1928–30 in large municipalities such as Shanghai and Nanjing. The latter's mayor, Liu Jiwen, launched a campaign on 1 September 1928 against soothsayers and fortune tellers of all kinds, who had to cease their activity and find a new profession. The movement resumed after a pause from 1930 to 1933. From 1933 onwards, the focus was on the area of funerals. The operation was unevenly enforced in different regions. Jiangsu especially led the way from 1933 to 1937, under the governorship of Chen Guofu.[31]

Classically, in contemporary history, periods of prolonged war result in an extension of the state's sphere of action. China was no exception during the Sino-Japanese War. While the Guomindang asserted their ambition to establish universal conscription from 18 to 45 years of age as early as the promulgation of the 1933 Conscription Law (*bingyi fa* 兵役法), this was not actually implemented until the outbreak of war. The enlistment of 14 million young conscripts was carried out amidst the worst difficulties and under conditions that were often terrible for the people concerned. Nor was it a model of justice and equity. Nevertheless, the state demonstrated an unprecedented capacity to draw on the country's human capital. Although an achievement on a lesser scale, it can also be pointed out that it was during the war period that an embryonic welfare state began to develop.

We will discuss in detail only two particularly important sectors of state action – higher education and municipalities – as well as an issue which sheds more light on new modes of state action: economic planning.

In the field of higher education, China's development in the first quarter of the twentieth century was characterized by a plurality of actors (see Chapter 9). The old public universities founded by the Qing, such as Beijing University, were among the most famous and prestigious, but they were few in number. The vast majority of students were enrolled in private institutions, whether foreign (such as the Aurora Catholic University in Shanghai or Qinghua in Beijing) or purely Chinese (such as Fudan and Xiamen Universities). The state's pre-emption of the sector began in 1927. The model that the Guomindang endeavoured to impose was that of Zhongshan University (*Zhongshan daxue* 中山大學), founded in Guangzhou in 1924. Its president, Dai Jitao, and, even more, its vice president, Zhu Jiahua, were to be the two key figures bringing higher education into line in the following decade (Zhu Jiahua was Minister of Education from 1932). Autonomy was out of the question: both teaching and research were subordinated to the dictates of the state. Every university had a duty to contribute to local economic development. In terms of disciplines, priority was clearly given to science, technology and medicine, to the detriment of literary disciplines, which were considered less useful for the modernization and industrialization of the country and suspected of fuelling political dissent. As for political indoctrination, it was intense, and the spreading of the gospel of the Three Principles of the People resounded on every campus.

Starting with the prototype of Zhongshan University, the government imposed a constitution on large provincial universities (in Wuhan, Hangzhou and Chengdu, for example). In the case of the two main centres of higher education, Beijing and Shanghai, its control was not so complete, and pluralism was still the rule. The Guomindang's reach, however, extended to all universities. Each higher education institution had its own department of political studies. According to the legal framework for higher education, which was established between 1927 and 1929, each university must be approved by the authorities. Some institutions suspected of being lukewarm to the Sun Yatsenist doctrine were closed, such as the Southeast University in Nanjing (ideologically too close to Liang Qichao).[32] However, the case should not be overstated: freedom of research was still possible. The Guomindang did salutary work by putting an end to a laissez-faire attitude that had shown its limits by generating a proliferation of establishments that were in danger of closing their doors at any moment because they had no financial stability, and where the education provided was mediocre, to say the least. In Shanghai, where they were particularly prevalent, these diploma mills had the unflattering nickname of 'universities that work the streets' (*yeji daxue* 野雞大學).

State intervention also appeared in a new form – that of the municipality. This often existed in embryonic form at the beginning of the twentieth century, as in Chinese Shanghai, where a General Office for City Works was set up in 1905. In the 1920s, all the major Chinese cities set up a municipal administration. Although they were generally based on a Western model, Chinese municipalities of the republican period differed in some respects. The prominent role assigned to the police was certainly the most notable of these.[33] Like the Japanese police, from which it had largely taken inspiration since the beginning of the century, the Chinese police force had undertaken an extremely wide range of activities beyond maintaining order: firefighting, prison management, collection of statistics and even charitable work, since it was not uncommon for police forces to run orphanages and soup kitchens. Another significant fact about its central role was that the administrative districts of Chinese cities at the time were based on the police districts.

In Chapter 6, we described the demolition of the city walls that surrounded most cities for the sake of ease of movement and promotion of trade. This was the major project for the municipalities in the 1920s.

Although Tianjin lost its walls in 1901, it was a retaliatory measure taken by the foreign troops who occupied the city following the Boxer Rebellion. The movement was really launched in Shanghai, which tore down its walls in 1912. Guangzhou's more imposing walls were torn down between 1918 and 1921, making way for a ring road. However, action was far from universal. Some voices were raised to denounce the enormous cost of these operations or even the damage caused to the city's geomancy. This explains why, especially in the north, some cities kept their walls, such as Xi'an (which still has them today) or Beijing (where they were pulled down in the 1950s). Many cities opted for a less expensive middle ground: keeping the walls but building new gates, as in Suzhou in the late 1920s.[34] Besides the walls that surrounded cities, other ramparts also isolated the districts previously given over to the Banners, inside the cities where they were garrisoned. These were almost systematically demolished to make way for wide avenues. In the early 1910s, the confiscation of the land occupied by the former Manchu garrisons provided a reserve of real estate that allowed for extensive urban development projects. In Hangzhou, a somewhat extreme example, the Banner county was razed to the ground, allowing for the creation of parks and official buildings.[35] In Beijing, the imperial gardens and altars, such as the Temple of Heaven, were opened to the public. Everywhere, backing up the insistent public health slogans, the construction of public gardens, sports facilities (stadiums and swimming pools) and advances in water supply created a living environment conducive to a population that the authorities dreamt of making vigorous, healthy and hardy. It should be noted that these urban transformations did not affect only the large coastal cities. Even some remote towns of little importance underwent major embellishments that surprised visitors.

Some actions taken by municipalities were less spectacular, but they eloquently translated the increasingly pronounced intrusion of public authority into people's daily lives. In the 1930s, the Beijing authorities introduced street-name signs for every street. This undertaking is representative of the ambiguity of their policies. On the one hand, it was justified by seemingly unquestionable practical needs: too many alleys bore the same name throughout the city, which led to much confusion. But this undertaking also reflected a desire to reshape the inhabitants' living environment, with the systematic replacement of names deemed 'vulgar' (*su* 俗) with 'cultured' (*wenya* 文雅) names. The most typical example is the character *ku* 裤 (trousers), often given by local people in reference to the shape of the street. Deemed too coarse, it was replaced by its homonym *ku* 库, meaning warehouse.[36]

State action in the economic sphere has already been discussed, but we must return to the use of planning. During the Nanjing decade, no less than three bodies coexisted to coordinate economic development. The first to emerge was the National Reconstruction Commission (*jianshe weiyuanhui* 建設委員會), founded in 1928, which was responsible for waterworks and electrical equipment. In 1931, the National Economic Commission (*quanguo jingji weiyuanhui* 全 國 經 濟 委 員 會) was established. Supported by the Shanghai business community and the economic elites of Jiangnan, it was primarily oriented towards supporting the industrial sector (especially the cotton industry – the basis of the national modern sector – and its supply of raw materials). To coordinate and modernize the production of raw cotton and the manufacture of yarns and fabrics, the National Economic Commission established, among other things, a Cotton Control Commission (see pages 78 and 233), financed with the help of American funds. It worked to establish new credit and marketing networks in the countryside and to improve the quality of the fibre produced. Eventually, from 1935 onwards, the National Economic Commission was eclipsed by the Resources Commission (*ziyuan weiyuanhui* 資源委員會), which gave priority to the development of the public sector and the establishment of heavy industries and arsenals in the interior provinces. The technocrat Weng Wenhao was the main facilitator.

The emergence of ad hoc organizations to orchestrate economic planning illustrates that the will of the state was reflected in the emergence of new forms of administrative structures. These were very specialized and characterized by the high standard of their executives, and might be described as technocratic. However, unlike the ministries such as Finance or Foreign Affairs to which we have alluded, they were contaminated by political intrigues and factionalism. The simultaneous existence of three bodies, whose remits largely overlapped, was the manifestation of powerful rivalries and divisions within the Guomindang. They were in fact the agents of struggles between powerful leaders, and representative of their respective influences. The National Reconstruction Commission was conceived by Hu Hanmin, whose influence in the government was at its greatest between 1928 and 1931, as a conduit for implementing the economic policy he advocated. Moreover, the chairman was his protégé Zhang Renjie. The National Economic Commission, however, was in the hands of Wang Jingwei and his allies (in particular Song Ziwen) and its action answered the concerns of the business community in the Shanghai area. The pre-eminence ultimately acquired by the Resources Committee reflected the new hegemony exercised by Chiang Kai-shek following the removal of Wang Jingwei, whose efforts to keep economic policy out of Chiang's hands had until then been generally successful.

The question of the relationship between the state and local elites

The low-profile presence of the state in imperial Chinese society was compensated for by local elites who assumed a significant number of public service tasks. The tendency to extend the scope of state intervention that emerged under the Republic could only lead to changes in the relationship between the state and local elites. It is pertinent to distinguish between the situations in urban and rural areas.

In the decade before the 1911 Revolution, urban elites had developed powerful collective organizations such as chambers of commerce, philanthropic institutions, militias and firefighting groups. Now, the municipalities, which we have already discussed, largely took over these activities of the elites, who therefore had to deal with an ever more present state. In some areas, such as charities, the state was generally satisfied to merely impose inspections. But in others, considered more vital, it completely replaced the local elites without demur. This was particularly true for law enforcement. In Shanghai, for example, the militias run by local elites were replaced by police forces as early as 1913–14. The Nanjing decade saw a new turning point, with the police now structured on a national level and powerfully centralized. Its elite cadres were trained at the Central Police Academy, whose director was none other than Chiang Kai-shek himself. The state was also less tolerant of politically motivated movements. In the 1910s, the merchant elites of the major trading centres had organized a very large movement for the protection of national products, with extensive information campaigns and boycotts of foreign products. Although manifestly bombarded with petitions and open letters, the Beiyang state remained aloof from the movement.[37] From the second half of the 1920s onwards, however, the climate changed. Under the new Guomindang regime, the authorities took an active part in the movement, setting up an official certification system in 1928 to identify national products and organizing exhibitions to promote them. More generally, the Guomindang sought to advance their influence in various ways in organizations run by urban elites. A famous case such as the arrest in April 1927 of the president of the powerful Shanghai Chamber of Commerce, Fu Xiao'an, who was soon replaced by the more docile Feng Shaoshan, might give the impression that the Guomindang were putting their own men in place. However, this was not generally the case. The prevailing impression is one of collaboration with activists. The Guomindang were usually content to weigh in on factional struggles, without seeking to take over entirely. Nonetheless, the nationalist government's tolerance was limited when the interests and objectives of the associations threatened to diverge too clearly from its own. Thus, for example, the fate of the National Anti-Opium Association was sealed when it had the audacity to oppose their opium policy. It was forced to close down in the mid-1930s.

The issue of state involvement at the rural level is subject to much more debate. Historians who have dealt with this question have reached highly differing conclusions based on different local studies.[38] What is not in doubt is the existence, since the New Policies of the 1900s, of an unprecedented project and one that was never denied throughout the period – to bring the state's influence to bear much more directly and deeply on life at a local level. The problem was that, in response to these repeated efforts, local elites almost always managed to make themselves indispensable. They fought tooth and nail to maintain traditional forms of collective organization, such as lineages, village schools and temple associations, or more recent ones (crop monitoring groups, for example), of which they held the reins. Similarly, secret societies such as the Red Spears (*hongqianghui* 紅槍會), which flourished under the Republic, were powerful conduits of elite rule, providing the cadres. Rural elites excelled at hijacking the state's various attempts to increase its hold at a local level, in terms of *baojia* 保甲 (a system of neighbourhood groupings based on the principle of mutual surveillance and accountability), taxation and self-defence militias.

The Guomindang chose early on not to confront the rural elites head on. They took a particularly important tactical turn at the end of the 1920s, when they abandoned attempts to mobilize peasants in line with the communist model, and any plans to reshape the social and economic balance of the countryside in favour of the poorer population. They decided to choose an alliance with the local elites, an arranged marriage that was often subject to great instability, but which they never renounced. The fact that land rent was the basis of the power of the rural elites explains why, although the Guomindang adopted the principle of a 25 per cent reduction in tenancy rents in October 1927, they never seriously undertook to implement it, with one exception: in Zhejiang, the local authorities struggled, up to April 1929, to enforce a ceiling set at 37.5 per cent of the value of the harvest.[39]

The effort required to increase the state's influence in the countryside was too great in the context of the republican period. It remained out of reach, except for very limited episodes in space and time (such as in Jiangxi where there was reason to eradicate communist influence). Should this political choice be chalked up as one of the major causes of the Guomindang's final defeat? Not necessarily. The mobilization of peasants (and workers) was not an obligatory step, but a tactical option among others. The fundamentally predatory and reactionary nature of local elites is an assertion of principle in communist historiography rather than the conclusion of rigorous studies. The choice of relying on them in order to hold the countryside in check, and locking down the working class by controlling the trade union organizations, while at the same time pushing for a top-down modernization of a technocratic state apparatus, was a perfectly sensible tactic which might have paid off had it not been for the mistakes made elsewhere, especially after 1945.

A plurality of state-building trajectories

Central governments did not have a monopoly on state building under the Republic. This fact has been slow to emerge because of the variety of local situations, which makes it difficult to paint an overall picture. But if we take three examples of areas where state building made significant progress during the period, the contribution of forces considered centrifugal is striking. Thus, in the case of primary education, a great many warlords can be credited with effective action: from Chen Quzhen, a local satrap of no great stature, master of western Hunan in the fifteen years preceding the Japanese invasion,[40] to the three powerful Muslim warlords of the north-west – Ma Fuxiang, Ma Qi and Ma Bufang[41] – not forgetting Zhang Xueliang in the three north-eastern provinces between 1927 and 1931. If we consider the transport sector, a quarter of the railway mileage built during the period 1928–37 (excluding Manchuria) was due to the efforts of Yan Xishan alone, in his province of Shanxi.[42] Sichuan and Guangxi, two provinces constantly under the rule of warlords, were nevertheless part of the process of rapid improvement of road transport.[43]

Studies have shown that the penetration of the state in the countryside, especially from a fiscal point of view, was a task carried out with significant results by various northern warlords. More recently, David Serfass has shown that the occupied zone during the war is largely absent from state-building studies. He has highlighted the major successes achieved by Wang Jingwei's collaborationist government in the countryside of the Lower Yangtze valley during the so-called Rural Pacification movement (*qingxiang* 清鄉), which was launched on 1 July 1941 and was directly inspired by Chiang Kai-shek's pre-war campaigns against the communists: extension of the local administration and supervision of the population, in particular by taking over the *baojia* system of surveillance and mutual responsibility.[44]

Recent studies have shown that, during the Nanjing decade, in terms of economic voluntarism – or voluntary action as it is also known – the action of the authorities in the zones outside the orbit of the central power was just as effective as that of those better-known ones under the Guomindang. In fact, among warlords of some stature, economic voluntarism was the rule rather than the exception. In Yunnan, one of China's most backward provinces, Miao Jiaming, an American-trained engineer backed by the warlord Long Yun, was a tireless promoter of industrialization. Moreover, Miao's methods were in line with those implemented by Nanjing: a driving role for the state through planning and ad hoc administrative bodies (creation of the Yunnan Economic Commission – *Yunnan quansheng jingji weiyuanhui* 雲南全省經濟委員會 – in 1934), substitution of imported manufactured goods, and a concern for acquiring mastery of the latest techniques. The main achievements were in tin metallurgy and textiles.

The attraction of economic planning was just as strong outside the Nanjing-controlled zone, as shown, for example, by the launch of a ten-year plan by Yan Xishan in Shanxi in 1932, and that of Chen Jitang's three-year plan in Guangdong. The latter surrounded himself with a veritable brains trust made up of very high-level advisors and technicians, whom he made sure of attracting by offering them more than comfortable salaries.[45] The very real friction of contradictory ambitions between the central power and these rivals should not make us lose sight of the fact that they shared the same diagnosis of the state of the country, the same conviction about the goals to be achieved (in particular, industrialization and strengthening of the state) and the means to achieve them. What is more, political rivalries were carried over to the sphere of state building. In the case of Guangxi province, where all kinds of reforms were implemented (education, roads, armed forces, industry and even a reorganization of the administrative structure of the districts), the desire to compete with Nanjing in the field of state building in order to challenge Chiang Kai-shek on the legacy of Sun Yat-sen was openly stated.

Public statistics, more than any other area, offer a better illustration of true emulation during the Nanjing decade between the central government and those who challenged its authority in the provinces. The first half of the 1930s, in particular, represents a brief golden age of statistical publications. This concerned central government publications such as the 1936 *Statistical Abstract of the Republic of China* (*Zhonghua minguo tongji tiyao* 中華民國統計提要), well known to historians, as well as those of many zones controlled by warlords. In Hunan, under the rule of He Jian, a remarkable statistical yearbook of almost a thousand pages was published in 1934. Even poor and remote provinces such as Guangxi were not left behind: the militarists who administered it (the new Guangxi clique) were credited with the publication of two huge statistical yearbooks of high quality in 1933 and 1935. The case of the municipality of Guangzhou is interesting: the publication of the finest statistical yearbook of the entire republican period occurred not when this city was administered by the Guomindang (1920–31), but after it came under the control of the warlord Chen Jitang (in 1935). These statistical yearbooks, notwithstanding their informative value, were also, for the warlords, appeals to public opinion in favour of the results of their voluntarist and modernizing action, with photographs, figures and graphs in support.[46]

It is therefore no exaggeration to say that the state-building experiment was shared between warlords and the central power. Objectives, methods and results are entirely comparable.

To describe the founding of the People's Republic of China, communist historiography still often uses the term *jianguo* 建國 (state/country building). The choice of this word is intended to signify, at least implicitly, that the Communist Party was building a new China on a clean slate from 1949 onwards. Yet, clearly, especially given the context, the record of the republican period in general, and the Guomindang in particular, is entirely honourable in terms of state building. The general belief that a strong state was a necessity for China's recovery is one of the reasons why, despite the country's political division, the work done in sectors such as education and transport was remarkable. Moreover, a number of dynamics were set in motion (supervision of the population, state control of the economy and, in general, an extension of the state's scope) which the CCP would continue with after 1949.

EIGHT

Changes in Society

In the last thirty years, no field of research on republican China has undergone such considerable renewal as social history. It has come a long way. Until the 1970s, it was content to play second fiddle, acting as a mere auxiliary science to political history. Indeed, both Chinese and Western researchers focused all their attention on the peasants and workers in an effort to shed light on the genesis of the revolutionary process leading to the communist victory. In the case of workers, for instance, research on trade unionism and social movements (*yundong* 運動), with their attendant strikes and boycotts, has taken up the lion's share.

Given the political context of the three decades after 1949, the unabashed glorification of the communist epic was, of course, a requirement in articles and books published in China. Western studies differed from research produced in China not in terms of their objects of study, but in the fact that they touched on the contradictions, disjunctions and limits of mass movements, as well as the fault lines that the very term 'movement' tends to obscure. Moreover, if their main preoccupation has remained fundamentally political, in the 1980s the best Western works began to reveal certain features of the working-class world in its strictly social nature: rifts governed by geographical origins, strong ties that continued to connect the working class to the rural sphere, and the importance of secret societies. For their part, studies of the peasantry gave full importance to lineage organizations.

A page has been turned, therefore. Thanks to the historians of the 1980s, we no longer portray peasants and workers as actors in the revolutionary movement, standing up and fighting to overthrow the established social order. Since then, they have been laid out on a dissection table, where the scalpel of research operates freed from the precepts of political history.

From the 1980s and, especially, the 1990s onwards, researchers have also turned their attention to many social categories outside the revolutionary

215

movement, such as employees and entrepreneurs. Marginal elements such as prostitutes, secret societies and beggars were also introduced for consideration. Gender studies have not ignored China and have described the changes in the status of women. Studies taking a transversal approach, focusing on the history of death or everyday objects, for example, have shed fresh light on Chinese society over time. Even more recently, there has been a development of a microhistory attentive to places such as streets, opium houses or teahouses, thus giving access to a more intimate understanding of socializing and ways of life. This trend marks a reversal of perspective in social history. It is increasingly concerned with showing not how different social groups oppose each other, but rather how, through interactions and negotiations, they form society.

We are therefore living in happy times for social history, whose horizons have been broadened. It is no longer a question of limiting ourselves to the revolutionary avant-gardes, but rather of apprehending Chinese society as a whole through a wide variety of perspectives and without neglecting any of its components or dynamics. However, a lot of work remains to be done. Social history is currently at the pioneering forefront of research on republican China.

The population

Demographic data

Despite the unstable political context, it is certain that the population increased during the period 1912–37. The years of the Sino-Japanese War most likely saw a slight decline, soon to be followed by a catch-up after 1945. The Chinese population increased significantly during the period as a whole. From around 410 million at the time of the 1911 Revolution, it exceeded 540 million in 1949.[1] China remained the most populous country in the world, the only one to exceed half a billion people: at that time, the Indian Empire, the only comparable demographic block, numbered around 390 million people. The increase from 410 to 540 million in 38 years represents an average annual population growth rate of 0.75%. Although strong, this is not exceptionally high, especially in a regional context. Indeed, the population of many South East Asian territories doubled (roughly) during the same period: for example, Burma's population increased from 8.5 million in 1891 to 19 million in 1954 (an annual growth rate of 1.3%). Indochina experienced an even greater increase: it had 16 million inhabitants in 1906 and 31 million in 1954 (1.4% annual growth).

The basic indicators are perfectly characteristic of a country that had not begun its demographic transition. Although it cannot be reliably estimated, it is certain that infant mortality remained at extremely high levels.[2] Life expectancy at birth was around 34 years. The mortality rate was between 25 and 35 per thousand, the birth rate between 35 and 40 per thousand. However, even if the scarcity and lack of precision of statistical data should lead to caution, the demographer Hou Yangfang estimates that the mortality rate was on the decline, thanks in particular to the first advances in hygiene (the teaching of which was made compulsory in schools in 1928), as well as a relatively effective battle against the consequences of natural disasters.[3]

The primary causes of mortality were infectious diseases, such as tuberculosis. Plague and cholera epidemics were still common, while malaria continued to take its toll in the south of the country. It was the large cities that led the way. The authorities' information and prevention campaigns, and the progress of the influence of Western medicine, which was much better equipped to combat these diseases than traditional pharmacopoeia, led to a significant drop in mortality rates.[4] During the Nanjing decade, in Shanghai, the most convincing achievements of the municipality in the Chinese part of the city were in the field of hygiene and public health. Directed between 1926 and 1937 by the remarkable Hu Hongji and Li Ting'an, the hygiene bureau developed health inspections in schools, and launched major vaccination and information campaigns, without neglecting to significantly improve rubbish collection.[5] Such progress was far from being duplicated in the remote countryside, where the provision of healthcare was often reduced to its simplest form. Around the same time, peasants in the Shaanxi, Gansu and Ningxia regions had only two options when they were ill: sweating under blankets after a hot soup or smoking a few pipes of opium.[6] In addition, the peasants had to suffer the effects of another scourge: intestinal parasites, which the universal use of human excrement as fertilizer spread on a very large scale. The human toll in the countryside was heavy.

Given the very marginal share of the population that was urban (around 6 per cent), population growth was mainly reflected in the rural population. Northern China was already a notoriously crowded region: in a province like Henan, the population density in many rural districts was well over 200 inhabitants per sq.km. With such high densities and given the state of technology at the time, the land was barely sufficient to feed the population, making them vulnerable to even minor climatic events (abundant in this region). One observer at the time (the economist Richard Tawney) likened the situation in the north of the country to that of a man standing in a body of water whose level is always up to his chin, so that the slightest ripple can be enough to drown him. The image was soon widely used. Indeed, the three major famines of the republican period hit the north of the country: that of 1920 (Zhili, Shanxi, Henan and Shandong) which caused between 500,000 and 1 million deaths; the little-known famine which ravaged Gansu, Henan and Shaanxi at the time of the confrontations between the Guomindang and the great warlords of the region in 1928–30 (perhaps 10 million deaths);[7] and finally that of Henan, which we have already mentioned, at the height of the war against Japan (1.5 to 2 million).

The acute state of overpopulation in rural north China was not the general rule throughout the country. The great revolts of the third quarter of the nineteenth century (Taiping, Nian, etc.) were not so very distant. The population voids they created in some parts of China were not yet filled under the Republic: in 1933, four of the provinces most devastated by the Taiping revolt (Hubei, Anhui, Jiangxi and Zhejiang) had still not recovered their 1850 settlement levels. The same is true for Shaanxi, Gansu and Shanxi provinces, bled dry in the 1850s and 1860s by the Muslim uprisings and their repression.

Migrations

Large population movements eased population pressure. Four main ones are distinguishable (see Map 10).

The first was the influx of migrants from central Chinese provinces such as Hunan, who continued the repopulation of areas affected by the revolts of the mid nineteenth century, notably the Lower Yangtze

River valley. The main outlet for the population surplus in rural north China was Manchuria. Officially opened to Han emigration in 1904 (to consolidate control over this region that was whetting Russian appetites), the three provinces involved (Heilongjiang, Jilin and Liaoning) received a net influx of nearly 9 million migrants between 1891 and 1942. The majority came from Shandong and, to a lesser extent, from Zhili/Hebei. Advances in transport by sea (steam navigation) and by rail helped to swell these population movements.

The rural exodus was a more diffuse phenomenon. It is true that some large cities experienced strong demographic growth. However, in relation to the immense reserve of population in the countryside, the rural exodus remained on a relatively small scale. As mentioned, the country's urbanization rate was around 6 per cent at the beginning of the twentieth century. It is reasonable to assume that it increased slightly during the republican period.[8]

Shanghai stands out as both the most populous city and (along with Nanjing) the fastest growing. The population grew from 1.3 million in 1910 to 5.5 million in 1949 due to its extraordinary economic dynamism. The cities that experienced the most spectacular growth were confronted with a serious housing shortage and the emergence of gigantic makeshift housing areas. Even though Shanghai was the only Chinese megalopolis (placing it amongst the ten largest cities in the world), a few other cities exceeded the million-population mark under the Republic: Beijing, Tianjin, Guangzhou and Nanjing, to which should be added the Wuhan agglomeration with its three components Hankou, Wuchang and Hanyang.

Overseas emigration was the last major migratory movement of the republican period. Its particularity was that it concerned almost exclusively the two southern provinces of Guangdong and Fujian. It is very difficult to quantify the numbers in overseas Chinese communities precisely, not only because they were highly mobile, but also because assimilation and ethnic integration blurred their outlines.[9] However, it may be estimated that they numbered around 10 million by the middle of the twentieth century. After the second half of the nineteenth century, which was marked by all-out growth, the period 1900–50 saw more differentiated geographical situations. Schematically, two cases stand out.

Chinese communities in countries with a predominantly European population (principally the United States, Canada, Peru, Cuba and Australia) faced increasingly hostile attitudes.[10] This hostility was reflected in the adoption of laws designed to discourage Chinese immigration by various means (language tests, prohibitive entry fees and restriction to certain very limited categories of migrants). The numbers in the Chinese communities tended to stagnate. In Canada and Australia, two countries where they were commonly referred to in the press as 'Chinks', they even declined significantly. In all these countries, the migrants, overwhelmingly from Guangdong, were almost all young men whose objective, after accumulating sufficient capital, was to return to live with their families back in China.

In the countries just mentioned, the Chinese numbered in the thousands – at most, in the tens of thousands. The orders of magnitude were quite different in South East Asia, by far the main area of Chinese emigration. There, the figures reached the hundreds of thousands, or even several million (1.2 million in Indonesia in 1930, perhaps 2 million in Thailand in 1950). These countries remained essentially welcoming to Chinese migrants. The growth of Chinese communities continued, despite a marked slowdown in inflows during the 1930s (due to the Depression) and the 1940s (due to the war). This growth resulted not only from positive migration flows, but also from a demographic surplus. The latter reflected a structural change: whereas adult men had represented the overwhelming majority of migrants, the proportion of women and children was increasing significantly. In 1910 there were still very few Chinese women in Bangkok; by 1937, there were 189,000. As a result, it became possible for overseas communities to renew and even grow without a new influx of migrants from China.[11]

Social groups

The republican period was too short for the tectonics of the great social aggregates to undergo fundamental changes. Chinese society was naturally still founded on the same bedrock of the peasantry. In addition to a certain recomposition of the elites, the main transformations took place in the cities, with the emergence of an industrial working class and a middle class of wage earners.

The proletariat

The proletariat or working classes comprised a very small proportion of the Chinese population. The figure of 1 million in the mid-1930s is the highest of the available estimates, between which it is difficult to decide. Reference has already been made to the overwhelming preponderance of traditional manual occupations (see Chapter 6), the importance of which has been consistently underestimated because most are still waiting for historians to study them. The same was true of all the trades associated with a thriving salvage and recycling economy, which provided a livelihood for scores of odd-job men.[12] Even in Shanghai, the country's main industrial centre, the multitude of more traditional manual occupations dwarfed the numbers of labourers associated with modern industry.

Moreover, the latter continued to be bound by strong links to the rural sector from which its members were drawn. Returning regularly to the village was customary in both large and small industrial centres, to the extent that this was a significant charge on workers' budgets. This item of expenditure sometimes came as high as fourth (after food, clothing and housing) in the workers' family budget. Industry had no choice but to adapt to this state of affairs: for example, the rice mills in Hankou closed during the transplanting season because, no matter what they did, their workers abandoned them to help in the fields. Harbin's oil mills acted likewise in July–August at harvest time.[13]

A strong division of labour according to geographical origin was another characteristic of the Chinese working environment. In one tobacco factory in Shanghai, for example, the preparation of the leaves, which was a very arduous task because it was carried out in humid and unhealthy conditions, was done by workers from northern Jiangsu province. The less arduous and better-paid packaging was carried out by women from the Yangtze valley.[14]

The feminization of the proletariat became very pronounced in the 1920s; the workers were increasingly female. This trend resulted from an employers' strategy to lower wages (since the women were paid less than men for the same work). It was also a question of counteracting the rise of protest movements, as women were considered more docile.[15] Despite the existence of a slightly better-off working-class 'aristocracy' in

24 Young children working in a Shanghai spinning mill, 1920.

highly skilled trades (metalworkers, mechanics and printers), working conditions and daily life were particularly harsh.[16] It is true that the 1929 Labour Act limited the length of the day to ten hours, prohibited the employment of children under the age of 14, and imposed a weekly rest day. But it was not enforced any more than a similar law enacted in 1923.[17] Workplace accidents were commonplace, and republican China held the sad record of having the worst mining disaster in history. More than 1,500 workers perished in Benxihu (Liaoning) on 26 April 1942.

The urban middle classes

The emergence of a new middle class in the big cities was already noticeable from the start of the twentieth century, becoming more pronounced from the 1920s onwards. It included junior employees in industry, banks, transport and department stores, junior civil servants and schoolteachers. This new social stratum has attracted a great deal of attention from historians, for two main reasons: on the one hand, it personified, par excellence, the impetus of urban modernization;

on the other hand, it remained one of the Guomindang's main social bases until the 1940s. After 1945, its economic difficulties redoubled its frustrations, and it tended more and more towards the CCP.[18] Another of its characteristics was that its ranks included a significant proportion of women: the schoolteacher, the department-store saleswoman, the nurse or the typist thus become true social 'paradigms', which literature and the cinema willingly portrayed. In a single year, 1930, Mao Dun published a novel, *The Rainbow* (*Hong* 虹), and a short story, *The First Half Day's Work*, whose heroines are a schoolteacher and a typist, respectively. Wage-earning, feminization and the possession of at least a veneer of modern education were the three features that distinguished this new middle class and elevated it (in the eyes of its members, at least) above the common man, and in particular the world of small shopkeepers, whose standard of living was, however, quite similar to theirs. The difference between them should not be exaggerated. Similarly, the feminization also affected certain professions in traditional trades, such as catering.

However, the bulk of the urban tertiary sector, even in the most modern cities, was still made up of craftsmen and the staff of traditional shops and services. Domestic servants, employees of teahouses, restaurants, hotels, hairdressing salons and pawnshops, and hawkers were the most representative figures. To this must be added the marriage brokers, fortune tellers and other geomancers. The inventory of the service sector would be incomplete without including priests and other religious orders. There were at least 500,000 Buddhist monks, perhaps double that number, while Taoist priests numbered over 200,000. Taking into account Confucians, Christians and Muslims, who were admittedly much less numerous, the number of people conducting religious activities is therefore very likely to have exceeded 1 million. It is also worth mentioning semi- or totally illegal activities such as begging (20,000 beggars in Shanghai in the early 1930s) and prostitution.

The recomposition of elites

The most significant changes in Chinese society can probably be observed at the elite level. There were three cornerstones that sustained the positions of the traditional elites: land ownership, control of trade channels and imperial examinations. The abolition of the examination system in 1905 in favour of a Western-inspired education system was a crucial breach. For more than a thousand years, examinations, the key access to sparse and prestigious positions in the administration, had been by far the most valued route to upward mobility. Not only were the strategies for gaining access to the elite for millions of families rendered obsolete in 1905, but the symbolic capital acquired through success in examinations (and the local prestige that went with it) suffered a dramatic downturn overnight. The disappearance of examinations increased the erosion of rural elites in particular. The insecurity of the third quarter of the nineteenth century, which was marked by major revolts, had led them to seek refuge within the city walls. Many had never left. The days when traditional educational methods, which relied heavily on the memorization of the Classics, had made it possible to make do with the services of a tutor, were now over. The demands of the new education (with subjects such as Western science and foreign languages) meant that they had to live in the city, where the modern-style schools were located. The rural elites were thus further inclined, when they had the means, to abandon the countryside. The late Qing period saw the start of another fundamental movement that Marianne Bastid describes very well in her benchmark study: the promotion of the military element within Chinese society.[19] While careers in the military had previously been held in low esteem, the more privileged classes began to revise this judgement at the turn of the twentieth century and to consider it as a path offering prospects for their offspring. It is noteworthy that Yuan Shikai had his eldest son given a very thorough military education by French and German experts. A further explanation for this new interest in the profession of army officer was burgeoning nationalism. The military academy founded in Huangpu near Guangzhou by the Guomindang attracted many young people whose primary motivation was to contribute to the recovery of the country. Others, such as those warlords who started from nothing, or very little, and took advantage of the political disorder to become masters of certain parts of the country, were less idealistic. Although they were relatively few in number, in the wake of their own social advancement they attracted legions of young people from all over the country to join their armies, where they managed to earn their stripes.

Marie-Claire Bergère has described an equally important phenomenon: the emergence of an industrial, banking and commercial bourgeoisie.

She has shown how in the first decades of the twentieth century they managed to impose their organizations (professional associations and chambers of commerce, for example) and their values of pragmatism, modernism and nationalism. Nevertheless, she underlines the limits of their assertiveness, particularly in the area of autonomy from the state. Shanghai's large industrial and banking bourgeoisie tends to be the focus of attention, but it was by no means the only one to emerge: other urban centres, especially among the coastal cities, were also affected.[20]

Apart from the military and business, there were other paths that could lead to the elites. A revolutionary career also gave men of very modest extraction the opportunity to play leading roles. The cases of Chiang Kai-shek and Mao Zedong are only the most famous; others managed to break free of their background by joining the Guomindang and CCP at much lower levels.

The modernization of urban societies led to the emergence of new prestigious professions, such as those of lawyers, engineers and Western-style doctors. The emergence of new cultural elites also followed the advent of previously unknown media. However insignificant they may have been from a quantitative point of view, they were important because of their raised profile in common representations. The written word remained the main road to building a reputation. The development and professionalization of the press and publishing industry, as well as the progress of education (and therefore of the readership), enabled writers to gain wider recognition. Moreover, for the first time, it had become possible to make a living from writing.

With far wider dissemination of the image (pictorials, posters and the cinema), the form of notoriety itself evolved radically. The Republic saw the emergence of the first stars, closely linked to the advent of an increasingly visual urban culture. The important place of women among them deserves to be highlighted, with film actresses at the forefront. The suicide of one of them, Ruan Lingyu, following a romantic episode, had a national impact. A crowd of 100,000 people attended her funeral. Performers of more traditional art forms (Mei Lanfang for the Beijing opera), and sportsmen and sportswomen such as the champion swimmer Yang Xiuqiong, also rose to fame. Certain celebrities may have had a considerable number of devotees – limited, however, to a smaller area by geographical or linguistic contingencies. This applied to the great Cantonese opera singers, who were adored in Guangdong and in overseas Chinese communities where they toured.

The Sino-Japanese War completed the elite's dislocation. In the occupied zones, the inevitable compromises with the occupiers contributed to the discrediting of both traditional and more recent elites. The decline affected not just those who actively collaborated with the enemy. In the immediate post-war period, as we have seen, the Guomindang, by setting the conversion rate of the currency issued by the collaboration governments very low, left many wealthy families in the former occupied zones out of pocket.

Highly resilient intermediary bodies

For want of a better term, we call the multitude of unofficial forms of organization that help to structure society 'intermediary bodies'. Compared to the changes generating deep-seated alterations amongst the elites, those that affected the intermediate bodies were very limited. Urban labour continued to be mainly organized around guilds. These were modelled on the family structure: master–worker–apprentice relationships were expected to be of the same nature as those which linked the different generations cooperatively. Guilds were self-help and regulatory bodies that defined and enforced their own rules. A guild not only protected its members, but also arbitrated conflicts that might arise within it. Finally, there was a religious dimension, as each guild placed itself under the patronage of a deity. Significantly, even the life of the labourers spawned by industrialization was structured by a mixture of organizational modes inspired by Western trade unionism and practices inherited from the guild tradition. New trades, which resulted from the introduction of Western techniques, retained a strong imprint of tradition in their organization: for example, mechanics frequently organized themselves into associations dedicated to Guan Yu (the god of war in the traditional Chinese pantheon).[21] If unions were set up, they remained very much part of a corporatist logic, often combining the functions traditionally assigned to guilds (mutual aid, settlement of internal disputes, protection of members vis-à-vis the authorities) with struggles that were encompassing broader ideological views and part of wider political issues.

In Shanghai, the April 1927 coup and massacre broke the back of communist-oriented trade unionism. In the years that followed, the Guomindang filled the vacuum it had brutally created. Despite the efforts of the communists to regain influence, the Guomindang managed, in various sectors (such as the postal service), to set up moderate unions with a corporatist slant in which the Green Gang often had a say, but which they kept under their control. After 1931, the Guomindang's attitude tended even more strongly towards the maintenance of order and the preservation of social consensus. In Shanghai, the seven powerful unions formed in the autumn of 1927 had to fold. At the same time, the amount of autonomy left to workers within the surviving unions was drastically reduced. As Alain Roux writes, 'control had turned into suppression'.[22]

Societies based on regional solidarity (*huiguan* 會館, *tongxianghui* 同鄉會) were another important type of urban organization. They also played a very important social role, for example by organizing the repatriation of members' bodies to their region of origin, for burial.

Intermediate bodies in Chinese society were not exclusively urban. Peasant unions organized by the CCP or the left wing of the Guomindang have received disproportionate attention. Their importance is indeed anecdotal compared to pre-existing forms of organization in rural China, which followed a vertical logic, the complete opposite of the class struggle. The main ones among them were the redemptive societies, secret societies and lineages. The redemptive societies were one of the products of the religious revival that took place during the Republic (see Chapter 9). The lineages, on the other hand, were organizations pretty comparable to the *gentes* of pre-imperial Rome. Theoretically, they grouped together all the individuals descending in patrilineal line from a common ancestor (who may have been largely mythical) and therefore bearing the same name. Lineages were a particularly important social reality in south China. Apart from their primary purpose, the maintenance of the ancestor's temple and graves, they had a variety of functions ranging from mutual aid to the running of schools, not to mention the administration of a common property (lands) which could be quite considerable. Secret societies, like the European mafias, combined illicit activities with more or less constraining supervision of the population. The three main ones were the Green Gang (*Qingbang* 青幫) in the lower Yangtze; the Elder

Brothers Society (*Gelaohui* 哥老會) in the upper Yangtze, especially in Sichuan; and the complex nebula of the Triads (*Tiandihui* 天地會) in southern China and overseas.

While warlords, Japanese occupation troops and collaborating governments were quite comfortable with the existence and important social role of all these organizations, the CCP and Guomindang were not. The latter, in particular, took a hard line against them, denouncing their fundamentally conservative influence. But, in reality, keen to make a bond of obedience and loyalty between each citizen and the nation and party a priority issue, the Guomindang were, above all, jealous of the intermediate bodies' powers of organization and mobilization. Indeed, it cannot be denied that these were potentially subversive forces, capable of giving substance to popular discontent. The great revolt in eastern Guizhou between August 1942 and 1943 is an excellent example. It concerned ethnic Miao populations who were exasperated by the burden of conscription and taxes, as well as by the increasing number of infringements of the autonomy they previously enjoyed de facto. This uprising was coordinated partly by the Society of Goodness (*Tongshanshe* 同善社), which had been banned since 1927, and which provided its leaders – as well as by a secret society, the Red Gang.[23]

All of these forms of organization continued to thrive virtually independent of state control, despite the efforts of the state. The case of the Shanghai *tongxianghui* (an association of people from the same place of birth) shows that even in this city, which was tightly controlled by the Guomindang, its attempts had only very limited results. Keith Schoppa, in his fine study of the elites of Zhejiang, finds that the lineages of this province lost neither coherence nor influence during the first part of the twentieth century, showing instead a remarkable ability to adapt.[24] It seems that these conclusions can be applied generally to all lineages in southern China. In western Yunnan, for example, where they were relatively recent, their activities tended to develop on an increasingly large scale. In this instance, it was the local society's response to the need for collective organization brought about by the development of trade with Burma. In western Fujian, the amount of land owned by lineages tended to increase, not least because in troubled times it was easier for a community than for an individual to collect ground rents.[25] This was representative of a much more general state of affairs in the countryside:

in a situation where the state, although willing, was unable to ensure order and security, everyone felt the need to join collective forms of organization capable of guaranteeing protection and putting a certain amount of coercive power at the service of commonly accepted standards. Other changes that occurred in the lineages under the Republic were an effect of the loosening of the links between town and country. The inter-lineage temples (*hezuci* 合族祠), veritable consulates providing help and advice to members of lineages coming to the provincial capital on business, were in serious decline.[26] More generally, the members of the lineages settled in cities tended to emancipate themselves under the influence of a certain individualism associated with the new ideas, and leaned towards forms of organization more centred on the nuclear family. As for the cultural practices associated with the activity of the lineages, closely linked to popular forms of religiousness – these were increasingly seen as archaic and superstitious remnants. All these changes made them feel that the financial solidarity imposed on them was a burden, even more unbearable because the growing gap between town and country in terms of lifestyles tended to loosen the human ties that, ultimately, gave the lineages meaning.

Living standards and lifestyles

The issue of the impoverishment of Chinese peasants

Sociologists in the republican era took up the question of the population's standard of living with enthusiasm. Many surveys were conducted from the 1920s onwards. Under the influence of the Chicago School, a large proportion of them focused on categories of the urban population (for example, rickshaw pullers were one of the most studied subjects). However, in the context of growing interest in the countryside among the intelligentsia and academic world in the 1930s, the focus was increasingly on the mass of the peasant population. (In 1929, 6.5 per cent of the sociological surveys conducted focused on the countryside; this figure had risen to 38 per cent by 1935.)[27] In no way free from ideological bias, these studies notably took up the Marxist-inspired thesis that competition from manufactured goods (whether imported or produced in factories in open ports) represented deadly competition for rural crafts, which were doomed to decline. According to this thesis, farmers, deprived of this additional income, would be increasingly impoverished. Forced to go into debt to the elites, they would eventually be obliged to sell their land.

Post-1949 communist historiography took its inspiration from these studies and has drawn heavily on them. It paints a particularly bleak picture of the situation of peasants under the Republic. To sum up, it took the view that three main factors were at work, worsening their plight: competition from imports and the products of urban industry ruined the craft industry; plus there was increasingly voracious taxation; and, finally, they considered that landowners (*dizhu* 地主) shamelessly increased the amount of rent. In addition to a general impoverishment, the result was allegedly an increasing concentration of land in the hands of landowners.

This diagnosis does not stand up to objective examination. There is no serious empirical evidence to support the thesis of a generalized impoverishment of peasants, nor of a trend towards concentration of land in the hands of landowners.[28] On the contrary, it should be noted that the elites were increasingly reluctant to invest in land, which can be explained by the relatively low returns. The decline in the value of agricultural land in the 1920s and 1930s is a clear indication of this investment's feeble appeal.[29] Moreover, the universal practice of equal sharing among male heirs was particularly effective in preventing the concentration of land in the hands of a minority. With each generation, the most sizeable properties were unfailingly divided up.

It does seem true that the burden of taxes was tending to increase. However, they did not, with limited exceptions in time and place, reach particularly high levels. Moreover, if there was an increase, it was largely cushioned by inflation and, above all, by the underlying trend of rising agricultural commodity prices during the period.

Two important studies suggest that the thesis of impoverishment caused by an increase in rent and tax pressure should be rejected. In the most comprehensive regional study available, Kathryn Bernhardt has shown that, in real terms, land rents in the Lower Yangtze valley were much lower in 1937 than a century earlier. She also shows that the weight of taxation remained low.[30] Lucien Bianco has also drawn attention in another approach to the fact that the increase in rent or taxes was not such a critical issue for the peasants. By studying the statistics of peasant revolts and violence throughout the country, he points out that they were directed much less against the state and landowners than against other communities (clans or villages). Rivalries arose over the appropriation of local resources, starting with water. We should not assume that tenants were totally defenceless: a very significant proportion of them, and one that increased overall, held farming rights for an unlimited duration (which made them, de facto, co-owners of the land they cultivated).[31] In addition, various customs gave them the possibility, in certain circumstances (drought or other natural calamity), to defer the payment of the land rent or to significantly reduce the amount. It was also common for the tenant to pay rent only for the main crop, and to keep the full benefit of the harvest of secondary crops for himself.

While there is no evidence to support the theory of an upward trend in land rents under the Republic, this does not mean that the relationship between landowners and tenants remained unchanged.[32] Land rent was paid in three different ways: either as a tenancy with a pre-determined fee that could be paid in cash, or in kind, or as sharecropping (that is, as a percentage of the harvest). In the first half of the twentieth century, sharecropping declined, reflecting an increased monetization of the rural economy. More generally, Lucien Bianco notes various manifestations of 'a growing depersonalisation of the bilateral relationship between farmer and landowner'. This was aided by the progression of the written contract to the detriment of the oral agreement, the payment of a deposit, and the increasing absenteeism of landowners who resorted to using stewards to assert their rights.[33]

It also seems important to identify the full implications of the three phenomena considered to be responsible for the impoverishment of the peasantry.

Thus, the impact of competition from imported goods and the products of urban industry had (as has already been said) an important impact on rural crafts, but it cannot, in all intellectual honesty, be separated from its flipside: peasant access to more distant outlets for their products (see Chapter 6). In addition, the countryside benefitted from industrialization in another way. For the new industrial proletariat of the cities came precisely from the most landless rural strata. The only goal of these uprooted people was to earn enough money to return home to buy some land. Although they did not always manage this, the financial aid they sent contributed significantly to improving the lot of their relatives in the villages. Similarly, what the villagers lost on the one hand through increased taxation, they at least partially gained on the other: they derived some benefit from the extension of the state's scope of action, as, for example, when the authorities financed schools.

Neither the consequences of industrialization, nor taxation or the weight of rents seem to have had any significant effect on the impoverishment of the peasant masses. Although largely ignored by researchers, there is one factor that weighed more heavily than any other on rural living standards: demographic pressure. We have mentioned that it was particularly pronounced in northern China. It should be emphasized that, apart from the famine episodes which were its most tragic expression, more insidiously it affected the standard of living of the peasants, who were forced – several surveys carried out in different regions show this – to reduce their consumption of grain cereals, such as wheat, and substitute them with maize or even sweet potatoes.

Finally, the period 1912–49 should not be seen as all of one piece: the fact that the vast majority of surveys providing data on the situation in the countryside – such as that of the great sociologist Fei Xiaotong – were carried out in the 1930s is anything but trivial. Indeed, this is precisely when they were feeling the brunt of the economic crisis. The bleak picture these surveys paint of the Chinese countryside may be considered relevant for the 1930s or even the 1940s, but this was by no means the case for the previous two decades.

It is therefore likely that the situation of the peasantry did not improve under the Republic, but that it did not get much worse either.

Did the Guomindang lose interest in the countryside?

Another common idea in the historiography of the Chinese countryside is that the Guomindang were largely uninterested in it, unlike their rival the CCP, and that this was one of the main reasons for the latter's victory. Things were not that simple.

In the mid-1920s, the political mobilization of peasants was achieved through the formation of unions. However, this was not only brought about by communist activists. Elements of the Guomindang left wing were also involved. But if, within the Guomindang, the mobilization of the masses was no longer an option after the break-up of the first United Front and the serious shift to the right that followed, the path of prudent reformism driven from above remained completely open. Improvement of the peasants' lot was part of the Guomindang's ideological platform: Sun Yat-sen's writings made it an objective, and the 1924 Congress pronounced itself in favour of a 25 per cent reduction in rent. At the start of the Nanjing decade, the famous 1930 Agrarian Law set a ceiling on land rent: 37.5 per cent of the harvest. This measure was likely to improve the material situation of tens of millions of farmers. The problem was that it would remain a dead letter because of the lack of political will to implement it.[34] In fact, the Guomindang's interest in the countryside was reflected in the implementation of actions aiming to solve problems of an essentially *technical*, rather than social or political, nature. Efforts were made to improve cotton cultivation: they represented an important part of the activities of the Cotton Control Commission (*mianye tongzhi weiyuanhui* 棉業統制委員會) established in 1933. However, campaigns of this magnitude were not representative of the actions carried out in the sphere of agriculture. Apart from an effort in the lower Yangtze region after the 1931 floods, major water development programmes belonged to the past. There were no significant steps taken towards rural electrification. Other projects were carried out on a more local scale, such as those in Zhejiang and Jiangsu provinces in the years 1927–37 for sericulture, which included the development of technical education, the improvement of eggs, and the setting up of experimental farms and networks of cooperatives.[35] Similarly, pilot projects were carried out to select rice and wheat species using modern processes. However, the overall impression is that there was a contrast between the intellectual interest in the countryside and the very limited concrete actions that were carried out.

Endemic insecurity in the countryside

Despite the criticisms we have made of the thesis of dramatic impoverishment of the peasants, a relatively dark palette is needed to paint the condition of the vast majority of Chinese peasants. Their lives were not a bed of roses, any more than they had been pre-1912 or would be post-1949. Violence was especially commonplace. Along with the troops living off the country, brigandry was one of the darkest aspects of the period for the peasants. The proliferation of bandits stemmed, as usual in Chinese history, from the disintegration of central power. By the end of 1911, outside the major urban centres, the presence of elites who were both close to revolutionary circles and sufficiently organized to take over from the Qing administration was the rule rather than the exception. Numerous groups of bandits and secret societies were quick to seize the opportunity. After declaring themselves in favour of the revolution, they looted and held to ransom areas where there was no organized force to oppose them. So that, for their inhabitants, the only concrete manifestation of a revolution they did not understand was the chaos into which their familiar environment suddenly fell.

Some historians estimate the number of brigands at 25 million. It is difficult to hazard an estimate as this was a hard-to-define, ever-changing phenomenon. In terms of recruitment, the brigands originated from the peasantry, and the line between bandits and peasants was often extremely thin. This is shown by the case of the famous Red Beards (*honghuzi* 紅胡子) of Manchuria. These mounted bandits were most active in the summer, when sorghum, which was planted in abundance in this region, reached maturity. This plant, which reaches several metres in height and can therefore hide a group of men on horseback, was their best ally. As there was little to do in the fields in the summer, the poorest and boldest formed bands that journeyed a respectable distance away from their homes to loot villages and rob travellers. It might be called seasonal banditry, because in September they returned to their homes. Once their weapons were hidden, they returned to their ordinary peasant lives, busily bringing in the sorghum crop and preparing to sow winter wheat.[36]

As for the porosity between bandits and soldiers, it was even plainer. As so often elsewhere in the world, dismissed soldiers kept their weapons and used them to live off the land. Conversely, when a warlord raised troops or a notable organized a militia, the first men attracted by the prospect of regular pay were often the bandits. Finally, it should be noted that outlaws also operated at sea; the coastal populations of Fujian and Zhejiang were subject to the predations of a particularly flourishing piracy.

'Problems' in Chinese society

In *City of Cats* (*Maocheng ji* 貓城記), written in 1932–3, the novelist Lao She portrays a man who sets out to explore the planet Mars and arrives in a country of cats. This *roman-à-clef* reads above all as a satire of China in the 1930s. Society in the country of cats is plagued by terrible flaws: the slave status of women, polygamy, prostitution, opium, the extreme dirtiness of the cities, armies that are nothing more than a collection of cowards and looters, an old-fashioned education, a bureaucracy that functions in a vacuum and, finally, an excessive complacency with regard to a long and glorious history. The grimness of the picture is as striking as its pessimistic conclusion: at the end of the book, a war breaks out against foreigners and the cat people are exterminated.

While far from a masterpiece, *City of Cats* shows how the feverish search for the social causes of weakness in China, sometimes referred to as the 'sick man of Asia', was not confined to the May Fourth 1919 Movement (the book was published some fifteen years later). It is true that there has never been a lack of lamentations about the mores of the time at any stage of Chinese history. But, strikingly, morals were no longer denounced in the name of morality or because they departed from those of a bygone golden age. What was at stake was the weakening of the country that they induced, the consequences of which were seen as potentially dramatic in the context of a merciless struggle between the nations of the world. Many social practices were now considered to be plagues. It is true that some of them were already the subject of moral condemnation, whether since long before, as in the case of gambling, or much more recently, as for opium. In other cases, however, practices that were considered neutral or even positive until the end of the nineteenth century took on a new aspect. The invention of 'problems' occupied many thinkers at the beginning of the century. In a monotonously alarmist rhetoric, each of them was in turn accused of being the primary cause of China's weakness. The list was almost endless. In addition to the gambling and opium already mentioned, there was foot binding, prostitution, superstition and homosexuality. But as we shall see, beyond the rhetoric, these practices received very unequal attention in practice.

The nationalist state was the only one tackling some of these 'scourges' on a countrywide level (other actors did likewise, but at more local levels). Some significant results were recorded. The practice of foot binding virtually disappeared within a generation. Similarly – contrary to a legend stemming directly from the historiography of the People's Republic of China, which has been anxious to blacken society before the radiant dawn of the 'Liberation' of 1949 at all costs – there was a clear marginalization of opium consumption during the republican period.[37] Other practices continued, possibly with better supervision by the authorities (often for the sole purpose of raising tax revenues). Indeed, some of the campaigns against them were localized and short-lived attempts, such as the one targeting gambling in Guangdong in 1936–7. Similarly, apart from an attempt to prohibit it in the provinces of Anhui, Zhejiang and Jiangsu in 1928, prostitution continued to flourish.

New leisure activities

The working classes and urban elites of the period experienced what Robert Ardrey has identified as a major turning point in modern societies where, according to him, 'the hungry psyche was replacing the hungry belly'.[38] The range of leisure activities on offer in the major cities was expanding considerably and leisure consumption patterns were also changing rapidly. Travelling theatre groups, acrobats and itinerant artists of all kinds still brightened up the towns and fairs of the rural world. Some traditional leisure venues continued to do very well. Chengdu's teahouses more than held their own – they were thriving. At the same time, other leisure venues were languishing or even threatened with disappearance. Demand for opium dens was falling, less in the interior of the country than in the coastal cities. Traditional luxury brothels were losing their clientele, who now felt the complicated rules governing them were too restrictive. Prostitutes moved elsewhere – for example, to dance halls. Together with cinemas, these figured among the new leisure facilities. The practice of sport was growing, particularly under the influence of educational institutions that provided Western-style education.

A more radical change than the diversification and renewal of leisure practices was that the idea of a fundamental distinction between work and leisure time was gaining ground. Tourism was developing for wealthy city dwellers. Short leisure trips became possible due to the extension of the railway network and the time off people enjoyed every week. To meet this new demand, services were developing – travel agencies, hotels and restaurants specifically for leisure travel. Masses of ad hoc publications, maps and tourist guides were becoming increasingly popular. A specialist journal, *Travel Magazine* (*Lüxing zazhi* 旅行雜誌), was established in 1927, aiming to encourage and facilitate tourism in China and beyond. It had over 10,000 subscribers in 1934. The 1920s saw Hangzhou and Suzhou reinvented as tourist destinations, because the railway had brought them within a few hours' reach of Shanghai by the end of the 1900s (when previously it had taken three days by boat).

Can we call it Westernization?

As is the case for sport, the progress of certain practices of Western origin has received much attention. And Shanghai appears par excellence as the place where Western-inspired lifestyles were entering the picture. With its port, its twenty-six diplomatic presences and its two enormous foreign concessions, it was the city most open to the outside world, the first in the nineteenth century to be equipped with running water, gas and electricity. The concessions obviously played a crucial role as a place of cohabitation with foreigners, and of discovery for their Chinese residents of new ways of life and administration. Their modern facilities and urban planning gave rise to feelings of frustration, but also to emulation. The visual impact of the architectural verticality of the Shanghai Bund clearly shows that the city had been involved since the 1920s in an international movement of emulation in the field of luxury and architecture, and that it could claim to compete with the other great metropolises in Asia, and even worldwide. Its large shops, equipped with electric lifts, where imported products abounded, combined new modes of distribution and consumption. But other cities were not necessarily outdone – modern facilities and department stores could be found elsewhere than in Shanghai. Water supply was progressing everywhere, and the proportion of homes having telephones in a medium-sized city such as Jinan was around 5 per cent by 1922.[39] Characteristic of the industrial age, the measurement of time in minutes progressed in all cities. In Nantong, for example, this was reflected in the presence of clocks on public buildings, which symbolically marked the public space and confirmed the decline of the traditional method of measurement, which was much less precise.[40]

25 The Shanghai Bund in 1932.

There was no shortage of consumer practices imported from the West spreading throughout the country. One product has attracted more research than any other: the cigarette. A Western invention, its diffusion remained anecdotal at the end of the nineteenth century. But in 1900, the existence of the walled library in the Dunhuang caves, one of the greatest archaeological discoveries in history, was revealed to an observant monk through the coils of smoke from his cigarette.[41] The fact that this man living in a remote area of an inland province (Gansu) was aware of this new consumable was already an indication of its spread. In 1900, 300 million cigarettes were sold, 7.5 billion in 1910, and 90 billion in the late 1920s. Cigarettes were becoming widely available (at the expense of various types of pipes), in even the most remote rural areas.[42] However, the geography of the cigarette's spread is complex: while it won the favour of almost all social categories in Shanghai, it turned out that traditional methods of tobacco consumption (notably water pipes) continued to hold up quite well in Beijing and in the countryside, such as in Shandong.[43]

Moreover, dissemination of new consumer products did not necessarily signify direct adoption. Novel items were largely reappropriated:

reinvented in a different social and cultural context by the people of China. The recent development of the history of things has shown the selective nature of the process of adoption of European innovations, coupled with a marked tendency to subvert their modes of use. The most telling example is probably the Thermos flask. Used almost exclusively in a medical context in much of Europe, it quickly became an object in family use in the 1920s and 1930s in urban and even rural China (which it still is today). The two most common beverages in China are tea and, above all, boiled water, which is more convenient and cheaper to buy from teahouses or street vendors than to heat at home. The Thermos flask is very useful for keeping a liquid at the right temperature for a long time.[44]

The extent of the changes in lifestyles must be put into perspective. When it comes to setting in motion elements as deeply rooted in culture as food or attitudes towards death, one gets the feeling that permanency largely prevails. Many fads do not go beyond a simple effect of fashion. Thus, the vogue for Western-cuisine restaurants in Shanghai in the late Qing period proved to be short-lived. They were ousted under the Republic when the curiosity of city dwellers turned to the cuisines of other provinces, with Cantonese cuisine quickly becoming the most popular. The eating habits of the rural Chinese, on the other hand, remained generally free of any Western influence. Other innovations remained confined to very thin strata of urban society. This was the case for the consumption of cow's milk. It gained a place among the urban elite in powder form, but also fresh, thanks to the establishment of an ad hoc distribution network promoted by abundant advertising that made it an attribute of Western modernity. But it remained an expensive product that did not spread beyond the urban elites.[45] In the realm of funerary practices, only a very small urban elite adopted ones that broke with ancestral customs.[46] Similarly, although the nuclear family was beginning to emerge as an alternative model to the traditional ideal of four generations under the same roof (*sishi tongtang* 四世同堂), it was hardly ever put into practice.

A close look at the living conditions of the urban working classes shows that the extent of acculturation taking place in the big cities should therefore not be exaggerated. Even in Shanghai, life in the slums of Fangualong and Zhaojiabang was pretty similar to that in the

Jiangnan villages from which the recent migrants who populated them came. Moreover, even if life there was known to be better, the pace and way of life of the middle classes living in Shanghai's housing estates (the famous *lilong* 里弄) did not differ significantly from those in Chinese villages. Running water and electricity remained unknown in the daily lives of the majority of Shanghai's inhabitants.[47]

The idea of a fundamental difference between urban and rural consumers must be challenged: the latter were not left behind when it came to adopting certain innovations when appropriate. The changes in material living thus affected the countryside, where consumption patterns from the large cities of eastern China were spreading. The widespread adoption of kerosene – or paraffin, as it is also known – is an excellent example. Compared to the vegetable oils and candles used up until then, it considerably improved lighting at a modest extra cost. It became a commonplace part of everyday life in the countryside, used by more than one in two families according to a 1935 survey. Throughout the country, in small market towns, the oil merchant was often one of the only permanent shops, along with the teahouse, restaurant and small tavern.[48] Archaeological excavations in a rural area in the north-east of the country show that clothing was undergoing a profound transformation. In particular, this was reflected in the change in buttons from spherical to the flat, round buttons seen in Europe.

The generalization of primary education and its reform were the main factors explaining the spread of new attitudes and ways of thinking in the countryside. The horizons of young peasant farmers were broadening. Neither Christian denominational education nor that provided by the lineages' schools could withstand the profound rethinking of pedagogy that swept through primary education after the New Policies. Although the influence of the school on young peasants has been mentioned many times, Hua Linshan and Isabelle Thireau have the merit of highlighting the variety and importance of the post-curricular in this influence. Years after they left school, they were still exposed to the flow of new ideas: 'The press, but also the books in the Taicheng bookshops or in the travelling libraries that roamed the countryside and visited the towns on market days, enabled these young, educated peasants to be informed, albeit incompletely, about the ideas and debates concerning the "new culture".'[49]

26 Street library adjacent to a small restaurant, 1941. Note the chalk inscription on the left-hand wooden panel, 'Down with Japan' (*dadao Riben* 打倒日本).

However, there was still a long way to go: in terms of customs, changes were still slower than in the city. As we shall see, in terms of the law, particularly in relation to marriage, some rather bold advances were being made. Yet the influence of the Guomindang state barely extended to village level, where it came up against powerful bodies capable of enforcing and perpetuating traditional norms of customs and family. However, there had been changes – as shown, for example, in the increasing tolerance of widow remarriage.

Women

The subject of women was not just the object of passionate debate during the May Fourth 1919 Movement (see Chapter 9). On the contrary, it is striking that it was central throughout the period. Interest was even shown in the more frivolous publications, where one of the favourite tropes was to denounce the most recent developments or to make fun of 'young fools' who had gone overboard with new ideas. However, recent studies have had the merit of showing that women were not only objects of debate and reformist policies, but also the actors, voicing their demands themselves. Some of them, educated in the new ideas in Japan during the 1900s, played an active role, sometimes bearing arms, during the revolutionary watershed of 1911–12.[50] These activists had a legitimate feeling of having been sacrificed, as the promises in the revolutionary programme that represented advances in the promotion of women's rights – such as access to the vote – were retracted when the Guomindang set out to win the parliamentary elections.

Thereafter, the Guomindang and the Communist Party were extremely circumspect in their approach to women's emancipation. Certainly, both accepted women into their ranks. But they constituted only a tiny minority and the responsibilities they were allowed to take on were very limited. The CCP's policy followed a fairly clear path: after adopting very liberal laws during the Jiangxi Soviet period, particularly in terms of freedom of marriage and divorce, it changed course in Yan'an, turning a blind eye to arranged marriages and increasing obstacles to the exercise of the right to divorce.[51] More generally, the cause of women's emancipation was clearly relegated to the sidelines. It was a tactical choice: to gain a foothold among the peasant masses, the Party could not run the risk of acting against too deeply rooted attitudes. Moreover, it should be noted that, from the very first attempts by activists such as Peng Pai to organize peasant unions in the early 1920s, one of the most common accusations made against them was that they intended to 'share women'. And in the following decades, this deft little argument would continue to occupy a prominent place in the repertoire of anti-communist propaganda.

The Beiyang and Guomindang governments can certainly be credited with progressive legislation. The Civil Code of 1929–31 enshrined the public nature of marriage (it was no longer a private contract between two families). Marriage was deemed to be a freely adopted commitment between two equal individuals, and polygamy was prohibited. The code was also very liberal with regard to divorce. The procedure by mutual consent was simplicity itself: no judgment, not even registration by an administration; a simple divorce agreement countersigned by two witnesses sufficed.[52] Despite this, the number of divorces remained extremely low. The norm was still marriage arranged by families, except in very limited urban strata. In Shanghai's working-class communities, for example, weddings did not differ from the norms established in the countryside.[53] Group wedding ceremonies were introduced in the mid-1930s in the interests of frugality and economy, but, like all the initiatives to remove marriage from the tight control of families, they were unsuccessful.[54]

The gap between progressive, even pioneering, legislation and the inertia of social practices can be seen in the case of the servitude of young girls: prohibited since 1910, it continued on a large scale. While such a status quo can be attributed to a lack of political will, the difficulty the legal system had in implementing particularly radical innovations, some of whose effects might have been potentially destructive, must also be taken into account. A case in point is the ban on polygamy: for Chinese judges to actually implement this measure would have been to deprive millions of women of a status that was admittedly inferior, but which nevertheless guaranteed them some protection.

Changes in the status of women were not only confined to the law. They were most definitely present in the reality of social practices – modest but not insignificant. The main advance, already mentioned, was the radical withdrawal of the practice that the revolutionaries and writers of May 1919 had made one of the symbols of the old society and of the oppression of women – foot binding. Access to education was increasing, but still lagged behind that of boys; wide under-representation of girls was the norm at all levels of education. Very few girls continued on to secondary education, let alone university. In the cities, certain professions opened up to women, such as that of lawyer, in 1927. The celebrated Zheng Yuxiu trained in Paris and was called to the Shanghai bar in 1929. Professions such as those of teachers, department store sales-women and nurses afforded women access to financial independence. From 1929 onwards, the police force also opened up to recruit women, even though the responsibilities of female police officers in the field remained much more limited than those of their male colleagues. Access to the professions we have just mentioned undoubtedly had a strong symbolic and exemplary value. But it involved a very limited number of women. It should not overshadow a more important phenomenon: the slow, often hard-won, feminization of some professions in the huge traditional service sector, such as catering or teahouses.

Furthermore, it is an illusion to believe that emancipation and the development of women's urban employment necessarily go hand in hand. Being a blue-collar worker, in particular, was anything but the road to emancipation. They were usually cooped up in dormitories with their fellow women, under the thumb of middlemen who recruited them from the countryside. Despite the distance, they did not really leave the orbit of their families, who expected to take advantage of their meagre salaries before ordering them to return to the countryside after a few years, to marry.

While we have chipped away at the image of the countryside as being totally closed to novelty by showing, for example, the rapid success of certain consumer goods, this receptiveness had its limits when it came to marriage, family organization and, in particular, the status of women. Life in the countryside still moved to the rhythm of the traditional patriarchy and the extended family.

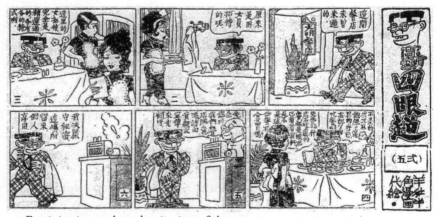

27 Feminization and modernization of the restaurant sector as seen in a Cantonese comic strip from 1934. It should be read from right to left. The influence of American comics is clear.

Translation of the text:
'Here is a restaurant where I have never eaten before...' 'And here they employ women as waitresses.'
'The waitresses are carefully selected, each with her own style.' 'You're not eating but just looking at us, sir. Do you dislike the food?'
'No, it's not that, I'm enjoying looking at you so much that I've forgotten to eat!'
'My dear Sir, are you satisfied with our establishment? If you could recommend it to your friends ...'
'On the contrary, I will be careful to keep it to myself. I want to be the only one to enjoy such a place!'

Given the brevity of the republican period, it is understandable that the changes in society appear to be relatively limited and as an extension, in many ways, of the late Qing period. It was amongst the elites that the most significant changes in composition occurred, and where, at the same time, the greatest permeability to new ways of life could be observed. It should not be too surprising therefore that the elites were the location of the most significant upheaval of the period – the May Fourth 1919 Movement – corresponding to a real crisis in Chinese culture, which will be the focus of our next chapter.

NINE

Cultural Renewal

In Chinese history, the period immediately preceding the founding of the empire is called the Warring States period (*Zhanguo* 戰國 481–221 BCE). The republican period has often been compared to it. They have in common that they were marked by a powerful intellectual vitality, made possible by two factors – the absence of both a strong central power, and, above all, the intellectual and institutional normative framework of empire. Since the imperial order only emerged in 221 BCE, it obviously did not cover the Warring States period. As for the Republic, it followed the collapse of empire with the revolution of 1911.

Thus, from the outset, the Republic could not escape a gigantic undertaking. The 'exit from empire', far from being reduced to a simple political moment, implied a radical intellectual reconstruction. The advance guard that tackled this challenge would prove exceptionally brilliant, so much so that their work continues to resonate to this day. One of the most remarkable aspects of the Republic was the questioning of some of the very foundations of Chinese culture as a result of the profound intellectual renewal. This regeneration was largely fuelled by ideas from the West. In a book published in 2008, one of the best specialists on republican China, Frank Dikötter, saw an opening up to the rest of the world as the dominant characteristic of the period.[1]

However, while they were undoubtedly of great importance, the debates that marked the period primarily involved an intellectual elite. They should not overshadow other changes that affected the mass of the population more directly and often receive far less attention, such as the democratization of primary education (with considerable progress at secondary level) and the religious revival. We will also give prominence to another aspect of the intellectual life of the period that is too little known: the considerable extension of the influence of Chinese culture abroad through the diaspora.

The dissemination of ideas

The extraordinary intellectual ferment that characterized the republican period cannot be understood independently of a number of changes that favoured the circulation of ideas and contributed to the kindling of intellectual debate.

The development of primary and secondary education

The development of education is rarely highlighted as one of the defining features of the republican period. However, from a quantitative point of view, there is a rapid and impressive advance at all levels of the education system. Primary education had 2.8 million pupils in 1912, 11 million in the early 1930s and 17 million in 1945. Secondary school enrolment, which was around 100,000 at the beginning of the republican period, rose to over 500,000 in the early 1930s and reached 1.4 million in 1945.

With the number of pupils increasing by a factor of 6 within a generation, primary education was becoming mass education. This was of great significance. A relative consensus among historians estimates the proportion of people able to read a simple text at around 30 per cent of the population at the beginning of the republican period.[2] This rate increased among young people, a much higher proportion of whom were in school.

Modern primary education, introduced during the New Policies, spread widely. However, the traditional schools (the *sishu* 私塾), for a long time the only ones providing primary education (apart from tutors for the wealthiest families), were far from disappearing. Their number was estimated at 100,000 in the mid-1930s, a good third of the total number of primary schools in the country. They continued to follow a fairly flexible timetable, in a single class.[3] Students learnt their first characters from the three pillars of its pedagogy: the *Three-Character Classic* (*Sanzi jing* 三字經), the *Thousand-Character Classic* (*Qianzi jing* 千字經) and the *Family Name Classic* (*Baijia xing* 百家姓). After that, the teaching was based on rote learning of the Classics from the Confucian canon.

Modern primary education was not different merely because of the inclusion of Western knowledge. New teaching methods were being used. They were based in particular on ability groups, a rigorous

28 A public writer on a street in Chengdu (Sichuan), 1941.

definition of the curriculum, and a distribution of the volume of hours between different subjects. The notion of groups, made up of pupils of the same age and progressing at the same pace, which was at the heart of its organization, had the effect of necessitating strict attendance. The content of some lessons disconcerted parents. This was, as one can easily imagine, the case for the lessons on Western sciences. However, without question, the greatest lack of understanding surrounded physical education. What kind of school is it where children are taught to do things that the average coolie can do? As Thomas Curran points out, with some welcome humour, modern primary schools were simply unsuited to the mental and material world of peasants' sons and daughters. They were too expensive, too restrictive, too discordant with the value system of rural society. In general, therefore, modern schools developed mainly in the cities.[4] However, the sharpness of the boundary between *sishu* and modern schools should not be exaggerated. The reality was one of reciprocal influences.[5] The *sishu* did imitate some of the practices of the new schools, and many elements of traditional education found their way into the latter. For example, in the late 1930s, some modern schools also used the *Three-Character Classic* or the *Thousand-Character Classic*.

Despite its undeniable expansion, secondary education remained accessible to just a small minority of children. Only the larger cities had secondary schools. And of the young people who attended them, a very small proportion went on to higher education – less than 10 per cent in Jiangsu in the 1920s.[6]

The diversity of actors in the education sector should be pointed out. While the central authorities enacted laws, they left the management and financing of primary education to the local administration and elites. Secondary education was mainly administered and funded at provincial level. The central state only set the programmes, without any financial involvement. At the beginning of the 1930s, the central government only funded 3 per cent of secondary education, with the provinces providing 63 per cent and the districts the rest. As during the imperial period, local elites and lineages continued to play a crucial role, especially in primary education. Large-scale achievements can be attributed to some important industrialists and businessmen, such as Zhang Jian in Nantong.[7] For the provinces of Guangdong and Fujian, the role of overseas Chinese should be pointed out. The case of Chen Jiageng, an emigrant who made his fortune in Singapore in the rubber and canning industries and provided funds to open schools in his home region (Jimei, in Fujian), is particularly illustrative.[8] He is best known for founding Xiamen University in 1921. The university developed rapidly and was able to attract some of the most important intellectual figures of the time, such as the great historian Gu Jiegang, the essayist Lin Yutang and the critic and novelist Qian Zhongshu. It remains one of the best in the country to this day.

Already active for more than half a century, Christian missionaries of different denominations continued their efforts, from primary school to university. Significant at the end of the Qing era, their teaching provision registered two decades of strong growth in the 1910s and 1920s. It concerned all levels of education, from the small rural primary school to the prestigious Aurora University in Shanghai. Muslim denominational education was also developing quite significantly.[9]

Higher education

The number of undergraduate students increased from about 1,000 at the beginning of the republican period to 34,000 in the early 1930s. However, while higher education remained limited in terms of numbers, its quality improved at a very steady rate. Chinese academics were meeting international academic standards with admirable speed. In the field of science, a florescence occurred between the 1920s and 1930s, a decade in which Chinese scientists were fully involved in international scientific debate (they often used English as their working language). In the field of the humanities, a blending with classical scholarship bore remarkable fruit. In addition, Western academic disciplines were a recent import and did not shape the structure of academia as habitually as in the West. Disciplinary boundaries had not had time, as in Europe, to become so institutionalized as to become trammels. To see a chair of history occupied by a trained economist or sociologist (as Fu Yiling did at Xiamen University) was common. On the other hand, academics showed little appetite for developing scholarship that was detached from the present and the issues of the society around them. Not surprisingly, the Republic was the golden age for ethnological and folkloric studies, launched in the 1920s at Beijing University by Gu Jiegang.

The very high mobility of academics should also be underlined. This depended on the political context. There were alternating periods in which the very best minds were clustered together and others in which they were scattered between different urban centres. One such concentration occurred in the mid-1910s at Beijing University (Beida), under the intellectual leadership of Cai Yuanpei. He was appointed rector in 1917 and worked in a non-partisan way to attract the brightest and most advanced individuals. A decade of incredibly fertile intellectual freedom came to an end in Beijing in 1926. Zhang Zuolin, who had taken control of the capital, imposed a climate of terror. Arrests increased. Beijing University, financially strangled and dictatorially remodelled by Zhang, closed its doors.[10] Its leading lights fled to other horizons (Xiamen, Guangzhou and especially Shanghai), followed by many of their students.[11] While Shanghai dominated the landscape in the years that followed, other centres also attracted attention. On the other hand, the prevailing norm was a high degree of mobility between them, depending on local politics, personal and intellectual affinities and enmities. The vicissitudes of the Sino-Japanese War led to a new cluster in Kunming, with the founding of Lianda University, to which we referred in Chapter 4. To name just a few of the most prominent academics, the philosopher Feng Youlan, the historian Qian Mu and the sociologist Fei Xiaotong were all teaching there at the same time.

The media

After the mass expansion of primary education, the second factor promoting the circulation of ideas was the development of the media. Where books and magazines were concerned, the fierce rivalry between powerful publishing houses, almost all based in Shanghai, ensured low prices and wide distribution. The proliferation of journals is particularly noteworthy. In addition, a great effort was made to create public libraries (even in modest villages) to give a poorer readership access to books, magazines and newspapers.

Indeed, the Republic was also marked by the very rapid development of its press. An economic model for the daily press emerged – the major Chinese newspapers were equipped with the most advanced rotary presses, which allowed them to achieve considerable print runs, while abundant advertising lowered the price of newspapers to the point where they were entirely affordable for the average person.[12] In Guangzhou in the 1930s, a newspaper cost half as much as a bus ticket. A bricklayer, for example, would use less than 3 per cent of his daily income if he wanted to buy a newspaper.[13] Newspapers adapted to the widest possible demand by giving considerable space to minor news items and serializations. Some newspapers, such as the *Dagongbao* 大公報 (*The Impartial*) published in Tianjin or the *Shenbao* 申報 (*Shanghai News*), were very good and represented what were then called the 'quality newspapers' (*dabao* 大報). A more accessible press such as the *Yuehuabao* 越華報 (*The Meridional*) in Guangzhou targeted a popular readership.

The relative freedom of the press made it possible to express some political opposition. Thus, during the period of Guomindang rule, while the existence of an opposition was not reflected in political institutions, its voice could nevertheless be heard through public opinion. Some historians have tended to paint an overly bleak picture of press freedom under the Republic.[14] True, corruption, intimidation and violence regarding publishers and journalists were commonplace. A number of them paid with their lives for upsetting the central government or the local warlord. But, in this sector as in many others, people could play on the country's political divisions. For example, in the mid-1910s, the Hong Kong Chinese-language press was very successful in Guangdong, because it enjoyed much greater freedom. Between 1930 and 1937, the governor of

Shandong, Han Fuju, permitted criticism of the policies of the Nanjing government to be voiced.[15] And even in the regions closely controlled by the Guomindang, the censorship put in place was not very effective until a law in December 1930 organized it a little more systematically. In theory, the press published within concessions and territories subject to foreign jurisdiction could escape Chinese government censorship entirely. On the other hand, it should not be forgotten that concession authorities also exerted pressure of their own (it was not advisable to publish articles that were too critical of them). Moreover, the concessions did not exist in complete isolation. Physical intimidation remained a possible means of coercion. The fact that the *Shenbao* newspaper was published in a concession did not prevent its editor, Shi Liangcai, from being shot by Guomindang killers on 14 November 1934. The press published in the concessions was additionally vulnerable through its distribution on Chinese territory. By hindering or preventing the latter, the financial asphyxiation of the newspaper could be rapidly accomplished. However, all in all, while the freedom of the press was not guaranteed, the degree of freedom it enjoyed was incomparably greater than that of the post-1949 state-controlled press.

It should be noted that, although magazines, the press and publishing houses allowed avant-garde ideas to be disseminated and a new literature to flourish, the vast majority of what was printed was in response to a demand for works of entertainment such as *wuxia* (martial arts novels featuring heroes who righted wrongs), scandalous novels and detective stories. The bestsellers of the time, such as Xu Zhenya's *The Spirit of the Jade Pear Tree* (*Yulihun* 玉梨魂), belonged to the so-called 'mandarin duck and butterfly' literature (*yuanyang hudie pai* 鸳鸯蝴蝶派). This genre emerged in Shanghai at the beginning of the twentieth century. It consisted of stories published in the form of serialized novels in the press, and whose scenarios were mainly based on stories of thwarted love.[16] Even if they were not totally unfamiliar with the changes of their time, all these genres continued to play out against the background of a morality and a fantasy world that were very traditional.

The new medium of cinema was rapidly developing. The first specialized magazines appeared as early as 1921. A cinema directory from the mid-1930s lists 239 cinemas (many of which had more than a thousand seats), a census that is probably incomplete.[17] The historiography has tended to highlight the most ambitious films in terms of form and background, particularly 'left-wing' films denouncing the social order that existed prior to the victory of the CCP, and produced by Chinese companies such as Lianhua. However, one should not ignore the fact that the audience favoured American productions, whose domination persisted (80 per cent of the films programmed in Shanghai at the end of the 1940s). Moreover, a large proportion of the films produced in China were in fact works of pure entertainment, such as kung-fu films.

Compared to the press, publishing and film, radio has been notably neglected by historians. Although the number of receivers was limited compared to Europe or the United States (there were, nevertheless, around 100,000 in Shanghai in 1937), collective listening in places where people socialized, such as opium houses or teahouses, swelled audience numbers. In Guangzhou, the first radio broadcast dated from May 1929. There were three stations in the city in the mid-1930s, and half a dozen in the late 1940s. Except for the municipal radio station, these were private companies whose programming was based mainly on the broadcasting of Cantonese opera (regularly interrupted by advertising). But this was not the only choice for the Cantonese listener, who could also receive radio from Hong Kong and French Indochina, as Radio Saigon broadcasted partly in Cantonese. The Manila transmitter, on the other hand, made it possible to listen to 'The Voice of America'.[18] In the wake of radio, the recording industry was also booming.

Passing influences

We have noted the positive role of concessions and leased territories, which, without being sanctuaries for freedom of expression, nevertheless offered opportunities that journalists and publishers knew how to exploit. These places, which, with the important exception of Tianjin, were located in southern China, played a crucial role in the spread of foreign influences. Cultural assimilation was disseminated through many channels. One of the most important was the enrolment of some of the young people at popular foreign-run educational institutions, such as Aurora University in Shanghai or Queen's College in Hong Kong. Cultural assimilation also took place through co-opting elites at the level of local administration and power. It could take other forms too (including among the mass of the population): through conversions to Christianity (15 per cent of the population of Hong Kong) or new recreational practices such as sport.

Shanghai's role in transmission has been highlighted in many works. It is often said that its newspapers had the largest circulation, that the vast majority of films were shot there, and so on. The cosmopolitanism of Shanghai, where daily newspapers were published in English, French, German, Yiddish, Russian and Japanese, did indeed fascinate contemporaries, a fascination that has been reflected amongst historians.[19] For example, recent research has shown the crucial role played by Russian émigrés in Shanghai (where the first National Conservatoire opened in 1927 at the instigation of Cai Yuanpei and Xiao Youmei) in the spread of European classical music.[20] Although it did not receive a similar official endorsement, jazz was popular with the elite and all the rage in Shanghai. Soon there were all-Chinese jazz ensembles (supported by Du Yuesheng, the godfather of one of the most powerful secret societies of the time, the Green Gang).[21]

But, without underestimating its role, there is reason to be more circumspect and to avoid making Shanghai the only gateway for foreign influences in China – the vanguard of modernity in a country condemned to a passive reflection of its influence. Shanghai did not have a monopoly of cosmopolitanism. Tianjin, with its many concessions, had an equivalent range of foreign-language newspapers. We will see that Beijing was the place where the most important intellectual event of the period, the May Fourth Movement 1919, took place. In Guangzhou, the most significant painting movement of the time – the Lingnan School (*Lingnan huapai* 嶺南畫派) – flourished, successfully attempting to assimilate some of the processes and themes of Western painting. Finally, although the major centre of the film industry was undoubtedly Shanghai, Hong Kong also managed to achieve success. It had been the bridgehead in the Asian market for Hollywood companies since the 1910s. In the early 1930s, Hong Kong made the transition to talking pictures more quickly, and, by 1935-7, production companies in the British colony were releasing about thirty films a year.[22]

While foreign influence was felt in China itself through the concessions and foreigners present there, many young Chinese enrolled in training outside their own country. This was not a new phenomenon, but, especially from the 1920s onwards, it reached completely unprecedented proportions. In total, no less than 40,000 Chinese students graduated from foreign universities during the republican period. The lack of interest in Japan, where at the beginning of the century the vast majority of Chinese students went to study abroad, was relative, and that country continued to attract approximately a quarter of the students. Altogether, the main European countries hosted about the same number. Nevertheless, it was American campuses that made by far the greatest contribution to the training of China's elite. Several factors should be taken into account. In the late 1900s, the United States reached an agreement with the Qing government to return the surplus of its share of the Boxer Indemnity as long as the money was used to organize the sending of students. This visionary choice would have far-reaching effects. It provided funding for scholarships and the organization of the Qinghua Preparatory College (the first avatar of the university of the same name), which was founded in Beijing in 1911. This institution, with very significant resources, prepared carefully selected students for entry to American universities. Important figures in the Republic's intellectual elite, such as the architect Liang Sicheng (one of Liang Qichao's sons), the playwright Hong Shen and the archaeologist Li Ji, passed through this scheme. But the American universities' power of attraction also stemmed from the number of foundations with abundant resources. The Rockefeller Foundation, for example, was particularly active in funding the university education of young Chinese geneticists.

Students were not alone in training abroad. Long study trips to the West were particularly popular with politicians of the period, who were keen to broaden their ideas. A typical example is, of course, Wang Jingwei, whose entire political career was punctuated by interludes that were translated into long trips to Europe (especially France). But this was no exception. Similarly, at the end of the 1920s, Gan Naiguang, a high-ranking Guomindang official in his thirties and in the midst of his political rise, decided to leave for several years to study in the United States.[23]

The experience of overseas Chinese who also encountered European knowledge, languages and ways of life should not be overlooked either.

Thanks to the close ties they maintained with their home regions, they were one of the most important channels for the penetration of foreign influences in China.

Among the intellectual and political elites, mastery of one or more foreign languages, already common in the early period, tended to become universal. English became the preferred language of communication between the Chinese and foreigners. Pidgin languages had had their day. They were now relegated to a more or less folkloric use for tourists.

Understandably, not everyone could attend university outside the country, or study at a foreign educational institution in China, or even achieve a sufficient level of fluency in a foreign language. This meant that most Chinese people came into contact with ideas from elsewhere through reading, and therefore translations. Not only did they increase in number from the 1910s onwards (a great number of journals devoted a large part of their editorial space to them), but their quality also improved considerably. Like those of Yan Fu, the translations from the turn of the twentieth century were copiously rewritten. At least Yan Fu could read English. This was not the case with the other great translator of the time, Lin Shu, who, being ignorant of European languages, had his works translated into spoken Chinese by collaborators and then rendered them in classical language himself. Another important source was translations from Japanese. In the 1920s and 1930s, translation from source languages became the norm. More faithful translations were made possible by the adoption of *baihua* (see below) and, above all, the gradual settling on a set of neologisms borrowed essentially from Japanese and intended to render purely Western concepts.

New interest in the non-Western world

The end of the imperial period had seen the Chinese intelligentsia develop an unquenchable thirst for knowledge about the major European countries and Japan, with the aim of understanding the sources of their power. Under the Republic, there was growing interest in other routes to modernization. The 1914–18 war, which pitted the European powers against each other in an atrocious slaughter, played a role in establishing that the European way was not necessarily a panacea. But we must also take into account a longer-term process, facilitated by the development of transport and communications, which, from the end of the nineteenth century, led to a broadening of China's view of the world.

The new interest in European countries not amongst the great powers was therefore remarkable. On the literary front, for example, a journal such as *Xiaoshuo yuebao* 小說月報 (*The Novel Monthly*) had a special issue on 'oppressed nations', which included literature from various Baltic and Balkan countries, among them Finland, Armenia, Georgia, Serbia and Czechoslovakia.[24] As for Switzerland, the organization of its armed forces was of great interest to the new Guangxi clique in the first half of the 1930s.[25] Russia's case was somewhat different. From the start of the October Revolution, China's intellectual elites were fascinated by the Soviet experience. This interest continued throughout the May Fourth 1919 Movement, to the extent that, between 1919 and 1927, the source language of more than a third of the works translated into Chinese was Russian.[26]

But, in reality, it can be said that, with the possible exception of South America and Africa, the Chinese horizon now extended globally. The experience of Mustapha Kemal's Turkey was all the more interesting because it was a young republic, built like China on the ruins of an empire. Hu Hanmin, for example, showed particular interest in the Turkish experience of modernizing and he visited Turkey on a trip in 1928. Plans for the construction of the capital in Nanjing were partly inspired by Ankara, the new capital of the Turkish state, but also by Delhi (which had become the capital in place of Calcutta in 1911), as eyes were also turned towards neighbouring India. Tagore had many admirers in China, even before he won the Nobel Prize in 1913. His audience soared with the flourishing of the new culture movement. He went on a lecture tour in 1924. The same was true of Gandhi, to whom one of the country's most important periodicals, the *Shenghuo zhoukan* 生活周刊 (*Life Weekly*), devoted several issues on his sixtieth birthday in 1929. More generally, Gandhism as a project of political activism based on non-violence and non-cooperation aroused great interest, particularly at the time of the May Fourth Movement 1919.[27]

While it was certainly not the result of pure curiosity (as can easily be seen from the examples we have developed, answers to China's difficulties were being sought first and foremost), its elites were remarkably open to the world. This was one of the origins of the most important intellectual movement of the period, that of May Fourth.

The May Fourth Movement 1919 and that of the new culture (xin wenhua yundong 新文化運動*)*

Chinese culture's Western crisis[28]

In terms of the history of ideas, the May Fourth Movement 1919 refers broadly, as we have pointed out (see Chapter 2), to a large-scale intellectual movement that ran from 1915 to the mid-1920s. Hopes raised among China's intellectual elites by the fall of the Manchus and the advent of constitutional and republican rule were dashed. This profound disillusionment led to the question of a radical cultural reconstruction, challenging the old dogma of the intrinsic superiority of Chinese culture. The movement started at Beijing University. The array of intellectuals gathered there by Cai Yuanpei was exceptionally brilliant. A whole generation, whose leading figures were Chen Duxiu, Hu Shi and Lu Xun, came to maturity. It was the first (and, unfortunately, the last) to have a truly dual culture. Its members had sound knowledge of the Classics acquired during their childhood and adolescence. They went abroad and, after long studies in the best Japanese and Western universities, acquired a remarkable mastery of a field – or sometimes several – of Western knowledge. Armed with this dual culture, they undertook a systematic critique of the very foundations of Chinese culture, in the name of science and progress. Although these luminaries were few in number, they had a large audience. Their students and all the educated youth of the big cities, who devoured the radical magazines that flourished at the time – among which *New Youth* (*Xin qingnian* 新青年) was the foremost – followed them with enthusiasm. Moreover, unlike the traditional scholar's criticism – a purely individual act taking the form of a complaint directed towards the emperor, the embodiment of the state – the May Fourth Movement took a collective form, and addressed itself to society in general. Its promoters expressed themselves through the press, demonstrations, public speeches and even evening classes.

These elites took every possible opportunity to point out that China's survival was their only concern. Of course, they assessed their country's weaknesses with lucidity. But they still evinced a surprisingly dark pessimism. The influence of Spencer's social Darwinism, popularized by Yan Fu in the late nineteenth century, partly explains this. Indeed, the theme of the survival of the fittest, applied to nations or races, suggested the short-term prospect of the total disappearance of the country and the extinction of the Chinese race.[29] The intellectuals of the May Fourth Movement therefore wanted to believe that their country was threatened with annihilation. Never mind the complete impossibility, objectively speaking, of more than 400 million Chinese people and their culture 'disappearing'. The important thing was that they transmitted this fear to some of the population, a fear that would remain as an obsessive backdrop to the whole period, parroted in tens of thousands of articles.

The term 'iconoclastic', generally applied to the May Fourth Movement, is particularly suited to describe the radical nature of its attacks on traditional values. The ideological content of May Fourth 1919 is often equated with an all-out attack on Confucianism and the emergence of new values: nationalism, promotion of the individual, youth, science and democracy. To this must be added a feeling which, beyond nationalism, is akin to a 'passion for unity' (to borrow Mona Ozouf's term).[30] The exaltation of individual freedom is in no way contradictory to such a feeling. Marianne Bastid has shown that this concern has its roots in the political thought of the last century of the Qing dynasty, which was increasingly inclined to consider the pillar of the state, the emperor, less as an intermediary with Heaven than as the guarantor of unity.[31] This passion for unity was expressed in many ways, for example by breaking the momentum of curiosity about local particularities (languages, customs) that had developed in the last decades of the empire. The affirmation of unity could also take a distinctly racial turn through the glorification of a community of blood leading to the unity of the race of descendants (Han) of the mythical Yellow Emperor. Early twentieth-century authors such as Yan Fu tended to equate the defence of the country with the defence of the race: unifying and protecting the race became the primary condition for its survival. A sometimes extreme distrust of the intermediary bodies in society was apparent, including with regard to the family. This is also how some forms of attack on it should be interpreted. Certain fanatical youths wrote to their parents to declare that they no longer considered themselves to be their sons: the continuance of a family bond (insofar as it is a given and not the consequence of a personal choice) was unbearable for them because 'we are all friends and equals'.[32] Such individualism is inseparable from nationalism. The individual tears himself away from the shackles of the extended family and the lineage only to better take his place among his equals in a whole that transcends the old divisions: that of the nation.

A reinvented language

The idea of language reform as a necessary step in the modernization process was not unique to China. Turkey, for example, experienced very similar debates at that time. Nor were they entirely new. From the end of the Qing dynasty onwards, some intellectuals began to question the influence of language (and, in particular, the use of Chinese characters) in explaining China's backwardness compared to the greater Western powers. In the years immediately following the revolution, the young republican institutions mobilized some of the brightest minds of the time (Lu Xun) to reflect on language reform, and in particular the need for some standardization.[33]

However, the May Fourth Movement is particularly notable for making the promotion of the vernacular language, *baihua* 白話, one of its main warhorses. In order to understand what was at stake in this crucial question, it is worth recalling that the diglossia[34] between the classical language (*wenyan* 文言), which was used in writing, and the spoken language was then extremely pronounced. *Baihua* can be defined as a close derivative of the spoken language. It is characterized above all by the use of terms composed of two characters (a procedure which, in spoken language, makes it possible to avoid the ambiguity created by the innumerable homonymous characters) and a relatively explicit syntactic construction. It contrasts with the extreme conciseness of classical language, often a source of ambiguity, showing a pronounced predilection for constructions based on symmetry and parallelism.[35]

In fact, literary texts written in *baihua* have existed since the Ming period. A certain trend towards the vernacularization of written expression began as early as the mid nineteenth century, at least. However, the May Fourth Movement innovated in a decisive way by making the substitution of *baihua* for *wenyan* the answer to a problem of a properly political nature. It was hoped that the establishment of *baihua* as a clearer language, closer to the spoken language and therefore likely to be understood by the mass of the population, would create the conditions for democratic debate by facilitating people's participation. *Wenyan* was accused of all evils, of being an obscure language, completely fixed (which was not true), and an instrument in the hands of a class of scholars clinging to outdated values. The problem was therefore also cultural. Irreparably linked to the old society, *wenyan* was unfit to render and propagate new ideas.

Hu Shi, Lu Xun and the other writers who published in the journals that sprang up around Beijing University (such as *Xinchao* 新潮) did a great deal of work in a few years to forge this new literary language.[36] In the 1920s and 1930s, it was to be given its patent of nobility by a host of major writers (such as Mao Dun, Lao She and Ba Jin) in novels that are among the great works of Chinese literature. Indeed, the May Fourth Movement also brought about another important change in the literary field by bringing to the forefront a genre that had previously been considered quite minor: fiction (whether in the form of novels or short stories).

However, even though the Ministry of Education decreed the adoption of *baihua* in primary schools in 1920, and this decision was followed by action, it would be wrong to believe that it was completely triumphant in the early 1920s. The struggle to impose it continued throughout the republican period. It must be said that a guilty overzealousness in introducing Western words and phrases transformed the *baihua* of some writers into what others have denounced as a veritable pidgin. One of the main battlegrounds was the quality press (*dabao*), which for a long time remained closed to *baihua*, not out of conformism, but for editorial reasons: the classical language, with its greater conciseness, saved space. *Baihua* remained a minority language in the press until the 1930s, and the same held true for the administration. In the literary field, the characteristics of *wenyan* make it wonderfully suitable for writing poetry, so the choice of many poets to continue using it was quite natural. Even radical political figures such as Mao Zedong and Liao Zhongkai wrote poetry in classical Chinese. Finally, the boundaries between *baihua* and classical language were in fact extremely porous. Many texts exist in an indefinable halfway house.

The work on language was not limited to the promotion of *baihua* or the context of the May Fourth Movement. Under the Republic, the use of punctuation, absent from the classical language, was gradually imposed. Similarly, for the first time, precise thought was being given to simplifying the writing of Chinese characters, with a view to making them easier to memorize and, beyond that, to promoting the development of elementary education. It took shape in a reform enacted in 1935, which involved the simplification of 324 characters, but that was withdrawn by the government the following year due to an outcry from the conservatives.[37]

The *wenti*

The intense interest of Chinese intellectuals in the 'plagues' that afflicted society (see Chapter 8) is only one component of a wider dynamic that was driven, with a characteristic sense of peril and deep crisis, by the May Fourth Movement, which saw intellectuals take up a large number of social, economic and political issues in a general search for the causes of the backwardness – or, rather, according to the metaphor that flourished in the writings of the time, the sleep – into which they liked to depict their country as being plunged. These subjects were the focus of the greatest attention and were discussed even more passionately because they were weighed in the scales against China's salvation. This was the period when the term *wenti* 問題 gained great popularity. The word can only be imperfectly rendered in English as: issue, topic, problem, question – this last translation being probably the least bad. In fact, *wenti* is more accurately 'a question which poses a problem'. Thus, a host of issues such as opium consumption, passion for gambling, the existence of a thriving prostitution industry, poverty, superstition, the status of women, and even the lack of aesthetic education, were all interpreted as debilitating factors for the country and, as such, passionately debated.[38]

Diatribes rained, especially against the family based on patriarchy, ancestor worship and filial piety (*xiao* 孝) – that is, the affectionate respect due to the older generations. The resulting unquestioning obedience justified, among other things, one of the pet hates of the May Fourth Movement: arranged marriages. In contrast to this model, unions based on the equality of the sexes, freedom of choice and mutual love were promoted. This new conception of love was extraordinarily unworldly and devoid of all eroticism. In the novels and short stories, it is noticeable that sexual desire always took the form of libidinous impulses, which only manifested themselves in old-fashioned conservative types and young degenerates who embodied the 'old society'.

Closely linked to the patriarchal family model, where they occupied a subordinate position, and of equal importance to the promoters of the May Fourth Movement was the issue of the status of women. However, if female 'slavery' was condemned in the name of equality and freedom, the question was put not just in these terms. The thinkers of the May Fourth Movement saw gender inequality and the status of women as one of the causes of the country's malaise. They argued that, since women's horizons were limited to a narrow family setting, they were incapable of giving the slightest attention to, let alone making an active contribution to, the salvation of the country. The traditional status of women amounted to an amputation of the social entity. We are therefore dealing with a feminism that can be described as integrative, in the sense that it aimed above all to make women fully fledged members of society and left very little room for reflection on the specificity of feminine identity.

The competition of 'isms'

The idea of the West's intrinsic superiority, seriously undermined by the horrors of the 1914–18 war, rapidly declined. Yet the May Fourth elites were still looking to Europe for a system of thought that could counter Confucianism. The May Fourth Movement inaugurated the competition of 'isms' that was to last throughout the period. The term 'ism' (*zhuyi* 主義) refers to general forms of apprehending the world and society, which produce a representation and interpretation subsumed under a general principle. Systems of political philosophy such as Marxism or liberalism, anarchism, and a certain form of belief in the ability of science to explain the world (scientism), all fall under this notion.

Interest in each of these isms can vary according to the period; scientism, for example, enjoyed particular favour around the May Fourth Movement 1919, but this soon faded. All these systems were reinterpreted in specific ways and adapted to the Chinese context: so, liberalism was strongly influenced by the pre-existing intellectual category of the gentleman (*junzi* 君子), while the link between political and economic liberalism would remain extremely tenuous in China. Although Chinese conservatives differed from their predecessors because they had read Babbitt and Bergson (*Creative Evolution* was published in 1907 and translated into Chinese as early as 1919), Liang Shuming argued that in their writings thinkers such as Bergson were simply rediscovering long-held truths in the Chinese intellectual tradition.

In terms of the evolution of ideas, Lloyd Eastman saw around the May Fourth Movement 1919 a period of enthusiasm for Western ideas, parliamentary democracy and liberalism, followed by disillusionment with the political chaos of the early years of the Republic, as the intelligentsia turned to increasingly authoritarian forms of government. The idea that individual freedoms must give way to the imperatives of safeguarding the country would thus be imposed. Such a vision, too synthetic not to be somewhat reductive, must be qualified. It should be emphasized that, before the CCP vitrified intellectual life by imposing the Maoist creed, all these systems of thought were in competition. Intellectuals moved from one to the other according to their intellectual journey. There were still advocates of forced Westernization in the 1930s, such as the sociologist Chen Xujing. Far from being radically opposed to one another, all these currents dialogued with and interpenetrated each other. There was much less of a penchant for authoritarianism at the expense of freedoms than the idea that a strong state was necessary to straighten out the country (which explains the very limited support for anarchism). Equally false is the idea that communism was the necessary end of a succession of disillusionments. Edmund Fung has clearly shown the resilience of a liberal intellectual tradition throughout the period. In the late 1940s, the rallying of intellectuals to the CCP was only exceptionally an enthusiastic conversion to Marxism and class struggle. Firstly, in the absence of an alternative, the CCP collected those disappointed by the Guomindang and, above all, it should never be forgotten that rallying took place along ideological lines that Mao insisted should be extremely moderate: that of the New Democracy (see Chapters 4 and 5).

Examples abound of intellectual trajectories that moved in the opposite direction, away from communism. Two cases in point are Zhou Fohai and Chen Gongbo, who both participated in the founding of the CCP and moved to the Guomindang and ended their political careers in the collaborating government of Wang Jingwei. It can be argued that these men's progressions are simply a reflection of their opportunism. Such suspicions cannot be levelled at Zhang Shenfu, who, at the beginning of the 1920s, was one of the most extreme elements in Marxist-leaning circles in Beijing. Charged by Chen Duxiu with developing communist cells in Europe among Chinese students, he recruited Zhou Enlai and Zhu De in particular. But soon after his return to China, he left the CCP (1925), and the rest of his intellectual career had nothing to do with Marxism.

Religious revivals

The intellectual rebuilding implied by the departure from the normative intellectual frameworks of the empire was also reflected in the religious sphere, which has recently been under the spotlight of an overabundant historiography.

Christian missionaries were very active in China where, more generally, Christianity benefitted from Western prestige. This was sometimes seen as one of the reasons for its advance. Overseas Chinese communities, where conversions were high, also played their part. In 1949, there were about 3 million Catholics and 1 million Protestants, in total less than 1 per cent of the population. In both cases, the number of believers was six times higher than in 1906. However, the place of Christians within the elites was out of all proportion to their small weight in the population. Of the 274 members of parliament elected between December 1912 and January 1913, there were 60 Christians (21.9 per cent). In revolutionary circles, and those close to the Guomindang in particular, Sun Yat-sen, baptised at the age of 18 (1884), was emulated: conversion to Christianity (basically Protestantism) was an act of faith in favour of modernity. Chiang Kai-shek converted following his marriage to Song Meiling. She and her brother Song Ziwen belonged to a family which had been Protestant for two generations. Other prominent political actors were Christians, such as Kong Xiangxi, or the great warlord Feng Yuxiang, also known as the 'Christian general', not to mention less prominent figures such as He Yingqin, Sun Ke or Zhang Qun. Further members of the elite were also affected, such as those in the world of diplomacy, including Lu Zhengxiang, who collected various ministerial portfolios under Yuan Shikai and ended his life in a Benedictine monastery in Belgium, or Wang Zhengting, several times Minister of Foreign Affairs from 1922 to 1931. The attraction of Christianity was much less pronounced in intellectual and academic circles.

The crucial fact, however, is not so much the progress of Christianity as such but the fact that it served as a *model*. The idea established itself that, to be legitimate, a cult must, like Christianity, have a well-defined canon and doctrine, and a hierarchical organization with a clergy capable of supervising the faithful and imposing the norms of practices. Otherwise, it fell under an infamous label that appeared at the turn of the century: superstitions (*mixin* 迷信). The three most important Chinese religions (Buddhism, Taoism and Islam) would therefore work to draw closer to this model. For example, a spiritual revival of Taoism took place, under the influence of laypeople in the major urban centres, where it incorporated elements of Western science, while skilfully emphasizing the purely Chinese character of Taoism.[39] Nor were religions oblivious to the progress of nationalism either. This is evidenced by the establishment in 1938 of the Chinese Islamic National Salvation Association (*Zhongguo huimin jiuguo xiehui* 中國回民救國協會) and similar ones for other faiths.

If the major religions escaped the opprobrium of being labelled as 'superstition', this was not the case for the myriad of local cults which not only were the very essence of popular religiosity, but also played a crucial role in structuring the life of both rural and urban communities. From the first decade of the twentieth century, local cults came under intense criticism. While they had previously enjoyed the support of the imperial authorities, the state now took action against them in the name of the fight against superstition.

During the period of the New Policies, it was merely a case of confiscating some temples to allocate them to other uses. Under the Republic, the authorities actively, if somewhat intermittently, fought against local cults. The latter did not disappear, however. A difference was compounded between the cities, where campaigns against superstition had a significant effect, and the rural world, where local cults were much more resistant. There, local elites often managed to ward off attacks on long-established cults whose integrative virtues they understood better than anyone else, as in Putian in Fujian province.[40] For example, local cults were very helpful in regulating perennial sources of conflict such as the sharing of water resources for irrigation.

The vacuum created by the retreat of local cults was filled, in particular, by newcomers on the scene of Chinese religiosity, which a historian, Prasenjit Duara, has called *redemptive societies*. These were organizations whose discourse was apocalyptic and millenarian. They refreshed the religious landscape by emphasizing a self-improvement ethic (both physical and spiritual). Deeply rooted in Chinese thought, the belief in the complementarity of the three doctrines was manifested in redemptive societies by a very marked syncretism.[41]

One of the main ones, the *Yiguandao* 一貫道 (Way of Unity Connecting All Things), which had millions – if not tens of millions – of followers, had the aim of achieving the unity of the three doctrines (Confucianism, Taoism, Buddhism) by adding Islam and Christianity. Particularly active and influential in north China, the redemptive societies were also characterized by their centralized hierarchical organization at national level, their modernized discourse, as well as their important charitable activities. They undertook many services needed by the population (funerals, in particular).

The flourishing of redemptive societies had a very strong echo in Asia, especially in Cochin-China. This was particularly true of Caodaism, a religious movement born in the 1920s whose founder, Ngo Van Chieu, was partly educated among overseas Chinese. Caodaism borrowed many elements from the matrix of redemptive societies, from the point of view both of doctrine (the crucial importance of the figure of the Jade Emperor), and of the objects of worship (mediumistic materials). Eloquent proof of the Chinese influence is the presence of Sun Yat-sen at a very high rank in the Caodaist pantheon (in excellent company, alongside Victor Hugo and Jesus Christ).[42]

China's cultural influence

The instances of religious diffusion should prompt a much broader examination of China's ability to exert cultural and intellectual influence outside its borders. Can we agree with an article published in *Shenbao* in 1934, which deplored the fact that China was only able to export two products of its civilization: Mei Lanfang (the great performer of Beijing opera, then at the height of his glory) and mah-jong?[43] This embittered observation is highly exaggerated. In fact, China's cultural influence covered an infinitely wider spectrum. Such a statement may seem surprising, even paradoxical, when it has been shown how eagerly its intellectual elites looked to the West for new ways of thinking and creating, and how enthusiastically some of them attacked traditional culture. This paradox, as we shall see, is not actually paradoxical at all.

The undiminished prestige of classical culture

Chinese classical culture had no shortage of admirers. Although very small, the European and American sinological community tended towards significant growth during the inter-war period. The fundamental work of translating classical Chinese texts continued, but this period saw an evolution: the gradual renunciation of relay languages. This meant that, for languages such as German or Italian, it was no longer sufficient to simply translate the French or English version. Translations were now made directly from Chinese.[44]

The main thing, however, was that the classical culture of China continued to reign in the territories under former Chinese influence. In 1910, a senior administrator in French Indochina could write in a report: 'The Annamites under our protectorate and direction are in fact influenced by China. More than ever, the literate class is intellectually dependent on it; it knows and thinks only through it, according to it and for a long time after it ... [Chinese] characters are the only vehicle of instruction for this class.'[45] Indeed, Vietnam, along with Korea, was one of the countries whose elites continued to be immersed in classical Chinese culture. Far from diminishing, the audience for classics such as *The Water Margin* (*Shuihu zhuan* 水滸傳), and even more so for *Romance of the Three Kingdoms* (*Sanguo yanyi* 三國演義), grew even larger as a result of numerous translations into different Asian vernaculars (five for Vietnamese alone between 1909 and 1937) and better dissemination thanks to modern printing techniques.[46]

China as a conduit for knowledge from the West

The role Japan had played for China as a conduit for Western knowledge at the turn of the twentieth century was now being played by China in relation to other Asian countries – primarily those that had long been under its cultural and intellectual sway. This role has been obscured, largely because the historiography of colonized countries such as Vietnam has tended to see the colonial administration as the sole agent of Western influences. Although Vietnam and Korea were removed from Chinese suzerainty by France and Japan, Chinese influence did not evaporate on the morning of colonization. That the local elites had been deeply influenced by China for generations was certainly a factor. But this receptivity can also be explained by the fact that, since the middle of the nineteenth century, overseas Chinese communities had undergone very significant development under the influence of migrant flows. These further increased the importance of culture of Chinese origin (by giving a critical mass to the population likely to read Chinese, making it possible, for example, to increase the number of newspapers published in this language).

A lot of activists engaged in the struggle against colonial rule used China as a rear base. The many Korean historians who were working to write a great national history, which was their way of resisting the Japanese colonizer, were doing so from their exile in China. One of the most notable of them, Pak Ŭn-sik, published his *Painful History of Korea* in China … and in Chinese. In the early 1930s, Korean filmmakers and actors went to Shanghai to escape censorship. During the period of the first Guomindang–CCP United Front, Guangdong was the breeding ground for Vietnamese revolutionaries. No less than 200 Vietnamese students passed through the Huangpu Academy between 1925 and early 1927. According to Christopher Goscha, they constituted nothing less than 'a sort of Who's Who of the Vietnamese Communist Party and its future army'.[47] In the 1920s and 1930s, communism spread in South East Asia via the overseas Chinese communities. Founded in April 1930, the Communist Party of Siam was dominated by Chinese elements, as was its successor, the Communist Party of Thailand. The general secretary of the Malayan Communist Party between 1938 and 1947, Lai Teck, was Chinese Vietnamese. More generally, apart from in the Philippines and Indonesia, the emerging communist parties were led by Chinese and, to a lesser extent, Vietnamese revolutionaries (the vast majority of whom were trained in China). Quite logically, written Chinese became the lingua franca of revolutionary networks throughout the region.

However, China not only afforded refuge, it also provided an entire intellectual arsenal, whether it was the products of its own reflection on the West and the threats it might represent, or the Chinese translations of the works of Rousseau, Montesquieu and Darwin, thanks to which these thinkers were beginning to be known in Vietnam.[48] The writings of Kang Youwei, and especially Liang Qichao, thus had a very large audience in Vietnam.[49] Lu Xun was translated into Burmese during his lifetime. In fact, it was the entire cultural renewal that China experienced from the end of the nineteenth century, and even more so after May Fourth 1919, that was exported. China therefore did not simply act as a mirror reflecting Western influences; it also transmitted its own view of the West.

Transmission of popular culture

The *Shenbao* article mentioned at the beginning of this section referred to a genre of High Culture, Beijing opera, with some irony, alongside a practice from a totally popular culture, mah-jong. In doing so, it pointed out an important fact: China's influence was far from being limited to the field of ideas and great literature. Texts for a more general audience were translated in large numbers. All the genres of popular literature we have mentioned were included in this. *Wuxia* (武俠) stories were abundantly translated in Vietnam and on the island of Java, where, in the 1930s, no less than half a dozen magazines specializing in this literature were in competition. In Thailand, the immense success of the Thai-language daily *Siam Rat* was based on the publication of these stories, adapted by a battalion of Sino-Thai translators.[50] The literature of the 'mandarin duck and butterfly' genre was also very successful in Vietnam. Altogether, the role of the Chinese in the translation and dissemination of these works was very important.[51] The responsibility of Chinese in the diaspora for the development of new forms of expression such as cinema is worth noting. It was Chinese entrepreneurs who introduced it to Indonesia, and, until 1942, three *peranakan*[52] companies produced most of the archipelago's films. Other ways of life penetrated deeply into indigenous societies: this was the case of the famous game of chance that fascinated southern China at the time, *fantan*, which became very popular in Indochina under the name of *baquan*, and even cricket fights, which were enthusiastically followed by the people of Java.[53]

The influence even extended to more distant reaches of Chinese emigration, such as South America and the United States, where Chinese cuisine began to attract a clientele far beyond the Chinese community in the 1930s. At that time, the 3-4,000 establishments run by Chinese accounted for 30 per cent of the restaurants in Lima. The Republic also stands out as the period (along with the late Qing) in which the borrowings from Chinese into the English language were most numerous. In France, under the impetus of the former diplomat Georges Soulié de Morant, the 1930s saw the spread of acupuncture. In particular, it was used in medical circles promoting homeopathy and met with some interest among the elite: Colette, Jean Cocteau, Antonin Artaud and Maurice Ravel, for example, all used it.[54]

Politically weak, China had undoubtedly been so since the mid nineteenth century. Its decline was not in doubt, and its status as the dominant power in the Far East was now only a memory. The elites of the republican period never ceased to notice this debility, to deplore it and to try to remedy it. Yet, however flawed it may have been politically, China's influence was reaching geographical areas where prior to 1850 it had had no actual presence (especially the Americas and Oceania). Some cultural transfers to the West had occurred, although the proportions should not be exaggerated. The situation in South East Asia was quite different. There, the prestige of Chinese culture was often high and the Chinese communities had long been present. The influx of migrants at the end of the nineteenth century increased their strength and influence.

Moreover, while many overseas communities seemed to be in the process of assimilation at the beginning of the twentieth century, they were to be the object, in the words of Denys Lombard, of a 're-sinisation', whose initiative came essentially from China itself.

Although uneven in different regional contexts, this process was indeed an important turning point in the history of these communities. One of its main vectors was the establishment of a network of schools where the content of teaching, largely in Mandarin, was strongly tinged with nationalism.[55] This contributed to the development of a sense of belonging to the Chinese nation among overseas Chinese, rather than exclusively to their region of origin. It should be remembered that the

1911 Revolution was largely organized and financed by overseas Chinese. It was greeted with enthusiasm in San Francisco, for instance.[56] In Hong Kong, on 6 November 1911, the (false) news of the entry of the revolutionaries into Beijing provoked a huge spontaneous demonstration, in which the crowd brandished portraits of Li Yuanhong and Sun Yat-sen. In general, the advent of the republican regime contributed powerfully to the strengthening of nationalist sentiments. The Guomindang took particular care to fan the patriotic flames overseas. They fought to bring the teaching in the schools of overseas communities under their control and to spread the orthodoxy of the Three Principles. During the Sino-Japanese War, Chinese communities were strongly encouraged to support the war effort through donations, or by taking out loans.[57] The idea that the diaspora constituted an intellectual, financial and human resource to be organized and mobilized in the service of China was definitively imposed.

One of the most attractive aspects of the republican period is the intellectual effervescence afforded by the weakness of power and nourished by an insatiable curiosity for ideas, ideologies and artistic modes of expression from elsewhere. Moreover, as we have shown, during this period China exerted a powerful cultural and intellectual influence over large parts of the world. In these fields, the rupture in 1949 was marked. The grip of the CCP led to a dramatic withdrawal of China into itself, which culminated in the Cultural Revolution and resulted in three almost blank decades in intellectual terms.

Conclusion and Epitaph

The year 1949 saw more the defeat of the Guomindang than the victory of the CCP. It was a defeat that resulted from a combination of circumstances that may be described as extraordinary. It should be remembered that the Nanjing decade did not see a degeneration of the Guomindang, but a process of institutionalization by which the Guomindang were transformed from a revolutionary party into a governing party that effectively pursued a policy of modernization and centralization. This policy began to bear fruit in the mid-1930s, with a very significant strengthening of its control over the country. The CCP, totally marginalized, was on the verge of being wiped out. The outbreak of the Sino-Japanese War in 1937 rescued it. Initially, this war forced the Guomindang (which, for lack of alternatives, could not manage without the Russian alliance) to reconstitute the United Front. In the long term, the Guomindang, which had taken refuge in Chongqing, was worn down by the Japanese army, an enemy powerful enough to take over the richest part of the country, but not strong enough to control the conquered areas, where the CCP was able to put its guerrilla know-how to good use and develop a string of bases. From 1940 onwards, the war also led to galloping inflation, which increased the disorganization of the country and the unpopularity of the Guomindang.

However, we should be wary of the biological metaphor that likens political constructs to living things that necessarily go through a period of growth, then a peak, a decline and death. When the war ended, the Guomindang were certainly weakened, but the conditions for its reboot remained present in 1945, from a political, economic and military point of view. If, against all odds, it squandered this opportunity, it is because it failed to renew itself, particularly in terms of its political staff. The profound reforms needed were not undertaken. It is only from this period that the accelerated rigidifying sclerosis of the Guomindang dates, which, aided by a succession of disastrous political and military decisions (for which Chiang Kai-shek bears a very heavy responsibility), would lead to its downfall.

The ellipsis is an obligatory feature in a synthesis such as the one the reader currently has in their hands. For example, I have dealt briefly with the role of the United States during the Sino-Japanese War, thus deliberately countering a historiography that treats this conflict through the prism of the relationship between Chiang Kai-shek and his volcanic chief of staff, General Stillwell.

But the main criticism of this book will certainly be that it deals too casually with the CCP's organization, ideological development and internal struggles, to which so many eminent historians have devoted books and even careers.[1] In particular, I have neglected to trace in detail the history of the CCP in its early years. I felt it important to measure the attention I paid it not by what it was going to become, but by what it was: a clique of intellectuals with very little grasp of the working-class world. In doing so, the aim was to refute a teleological approach, in which the treatment of the years 1929–30 in works synthesizing the republican period is perhaps the best example. These books, indeed, give pride of place to Mao Zedong's base-building enterprise in southern Jiangxi (a few thousand poorly fed and even more poorly armed men cornered in a province of little strategic importance itself). At the same time, in these works, a few lines are enough to describe the nonetheless determining operations taking place in North China during those two years.[2] Even the colossal clash between the armies of the combined forces of the warlords and the Guomindang in the Central Plains War (which resulted in 300,000 casualties) has the effect of mere background interference. They only bother to mention it because, in mobilizing the military forces of the Guomindang, it offered a precious respite to the Jiangxi Soviet.

In fact, there are two arguments for devoting more attention to the CCP, despite its mediocre size and importance. They are the preponderance of communism among the intellectual elites, with the rallying of leading figures such as Chen Duxiu and Li Dazhao; and the support of the USSR, a major power. However, as we have pointed out, communism was not the be-all and end-all for intellectuals during this period, and at no time did it arouse strong passions. The rallying at the very end of the period reflects a rejection of the Guomindang, not a surge of enthusiasm for Marxism. On the second point, it must be stressed that the CCP was never the only card played by the USSR in China, that the support given remained limited, and that on several occasions the Comintern imposed strategic choices with disastrous consequences.

In 1949, the swinging of a quarter of humanity into the communist camp was, of course, felt in the West as a geopolitical earthquake, which justified making of it a major rupture in Chinese history. Western historians rejoined communist historiography on this point – for whom, of course, the 'bourgeois' revolution of 1911 could only be a simple prelude to 1949's 'Liberation'.[3] The obvious haste with which an archive devoted exclusively to the period 1912–49 was organized in the early 1950s, as well as the choice of establishing it in Nanjing, testifies less to patrimonial concerns than to a desire to relegate the Guomindang regime to the past, and to set the 1949 break in stone. The model that hovers in the background when thinking about the division of Chinese history into periods is that of the cycle of dynasties, which also leads us to consider 1949 as *the* true rupture. In fact, the traditional scenario of a dynastic succession episode saw massive peasant revolts storming the cities. Now, the communist victory can be seen as the conclusion if not of a peasant revolt, at least of a long revolt drawing its forces overwhelmingly from rural China, sweeping the country with its trail of destruction and violence, to end in the tumult of the succession of decisive battles in 1948. In contrast, as we have pointed out, none of this happened in 1911: the revolution was an episode lasting a few months, with no bloodshed or major battles. In this respect, it turns its back completely on the traditional model.

Yet, unquestionably, the China we see today bears a familial resemblance to that of the 1930s. This is not only due to efforts to enhance the architectural heritage of that period or to television productions exploiting the supposed golden age of Shanghai in 1920–30. Much more fundamentally, as in the 1930s, China can be seen as a country inspired by the West, moving full steam ahead on the road to modernization and, ultimately, to power. We also observe a very pragmatic one-party state which (except in its rhetoric) has completely turned its back on its revolutionary origins, which exercises a power that is no longer totalitarian (as it had become between 1956 and 1976) but authoritarian. There is even a nationalistic and moralistic rhetoric, which increasingly leans towards a Confucianism reinvented in its own style.

In a particularly stimulating article, Joseph Esherick denounced the illusion of systematically opposing the Guomindang and the CCP. There is no doubt that they were bitter enemies, but this rivalry should not prevent us from seeing that one is, to a very large extent, the successor of the other.[4] Their ultimate goal, which has obsessed the political elites since the mid nineteenth century, was identical – the restoration of Chinese power. As we have seen, one of the main means of achieving this was the extension of the state's reach, which began in the early 1930s and has been pursued seamlessly by the CCP.

The fact that China is now heading in the same direction as it was in the 1930s is reflected in the place occupied by Shanghai. This city is the face of the republican period, the symbol of its openness, its intellectual and industrial dynamism. Undeniably, it is the focus for the dissemination of what must be called, for want of a more satisfactory term, modernity.[5] Like Rio de Janeiro for Brazil in the same period, it was the cultural centre, the main port open to the world, where publishers, film producers, artistic and literary avant-gardes were concentrated, and where political audacity was found (where the CCP was founded in 1921). It was the focus of new ideas, new values and, more prosaically, new ways of life. Of course, as we have seen in the course of this exposition, other cities (Beijing for the literary avant-garde, Hong Kong for the cinema, Guangzhou for painting) could occasionally rival it in certain fields. None could dispute Shanghai's global pre-eminence as capital of the intellectual avant-garde.

Marie-Claire Bergère wrote of Shanghai, in an ellipsis that hits the nail on the head, that it was 'the black sheep of the Maoist regime'. Slipping under the radar during the 1949–78 period, victim of abysmal underinvestment, fiscally bled dry, then forgotten during the first decade of the reform era launched in 1978, Shanghai regained some colour from the 1990s. At that time, Jiang Zemin realized that only Shanghai had the assets to give China a financial and services centre capable of competing with Hong Kong, Singapore and Tokyo.[6] More recently, since the 2000s, Shanghai has again become a major intellectual, scientific, cultural and artistic centre. The organization of the immense Expo 2010 was evidence of a clear political will to promote and accelerate this process.

China's posture of openness to the world is reflected not only in the rehabilitation of Shanghai, but also in the considerable number of

Chinese students on the benches of American universities and a particularly intense flow of translations of Western works into Chinese. It is also manifested in the restoration of close links with that other China, that of the overseas communities, whose importance during the republican period we have highlighted. After 1949, the overseas communities generally retained their allegiance to the Guomindang until the early 1970s. Although defeated on the mainland, the Guomindang made efforts from Taiwan to keep these communities in its orbit, with the complicity of the host countries, which were concerned that the Chinese would become a source of communist contagion. Mainland China has been ostensibly reaching out to the diaspora since the 1980s.[7] The first special economic zones (SEZs) created in the late 1970s (Shenzhen, Zhuhai, Xiamen and Shantou) are located in areas that are more than just maritime and peripheral. In a telling repetition of history, if we replace Shenzhen with Hong Kong and Zhuhai with Macao, we find the list of four ports from which almost all Chinese migrants left between 1860 and the First World War.[8] These ports were ideal bridgeheads for the return of diaspora investment.

If the elements of continuity beyond 1949 appear much more clearly now than they did, say, a quarter of a century ago, it is also because the leftist and Maoist wave of the years 1956–76 is further behind us. These twenty-odd years are increasingly seen as a parenthesis, a 'diversion', to use Rana Mitter's term, within a long-term process that began in the first decade of the twentieth century.[9] The change of name of the English-language journal that sets the tone for studies on the Republic is significant: since 1997 it has been called *Twentieth-Century China*, not *Republican China*. Another telling phenomenon is the publication of more and more studies spanning either side of the twenty years of Maoism.[10]

Despite all the evidence for significant continuity beyond 1949, the Republic is still largely accepted as a separate period in Chinese history, as evidenced by the monumental *History of the Republic of China* edited by Li Xin in 2011.[11] The *Cambridge History of China*, which remains the Western-language canon, devotes two volumes to it.

It may seem paradoxical to conclude a 350-page study of a period by refuting its relevance to a periodization of Chinese history. But that is what we will do to end this volume.

Let us be clear. The temptation to play the demiurge by questioning chronological limits and established periodizations is strong among historians. Thus, Peter Zarrow, one of the last historians to have published an ambitious synthesis of this period, chose 1895–1949 rather than the classic chronological limits, those that strictly echo institutional history: 1912–49.

It would also be possible to start the republican period in 1901 with the launch of the New Policies, or 1905, the year marked by the sociopolitical earthquake represented by the abolition of the imperial examination system, or even in 1909 when a new political cycle supposedly leading to a parliamentary monarchy began with the elections. Stopping at 1 October 1949 is just as arbitrary: one could extend it to 1950 (completion of the communist conquest with the fall of Hainan Island in April, and the beginning of the Korean War). It would even be possible to include the early years of the CCP government, which were marked by relative moderation. Didn't Mao Zedong praise the 'positive qualities of Chinese capitalism' at that time?

Why not stop, then, at the Five-Anti Campaign (1952), which conse-crated the break with the bourgeoisie, or even on the eve of the Great Leap Forward (1958)?

This little game is not very worthwhile, as you can see. What is important, however, is that the period 1912–49 is destined to become a mere subdivision of a period that opens with the profound rupture of the decade 1901–11. The importance of the Opium Wars of the mid nineteenth century has been exaggerated, particularly by Chinese histo-riography, which wishes to emphasize the starting point of imperialist encroachment. In fact, the Old Chinese Order only succumbed at the beginning of the twentieth century, with the New Policies. From 1901 onwards, the latter ratified a double dissociation: that of the social order based in particular on the system of imperial examinations, and that of the political system, characterized by the absolute pre-eminence of the emperor and a system of legitimacy of an imperial and cosmological nature. If the Old Order was dying in 1901, it was in 1912 that it was buried. Does this mean that the period 1912–49 remains strictly irrel-evant? If we accept that modernization is a much longer-term movement, and if we refuse to adhere to the teleology of the Communist Revolution, what unity does it retain?

The republican period has a real coherence, which emerges in the political field: it was *a time when a Western-style parliamentary democracy was a possibility*. In this sense, the use of the term 'republican' to designate it, on which our book opened, is fully justified.

Timeline

1901   January: launch of the New Policies
1905   20 August: founding of the United League in Tokyo
        September: abolition of the imperial examination system
1908   15 November: death of Empress Dowager Cixi
1911   10 October: Wuchang uprising (Hubei)
1912   1 January: proclamation of the Republic by Sun Yat-sen in
        Nanjing
        12 February: abdication of Puyi
        25 August: Guomindang founding congress
        December: parliamentary elections begin
1913   20 March: assassination of Song Jiaoren
        12 July: start of the 'Second Revolution' against Yuan Shikai
        November: Yuan Shikai dissolves the Guomindang
1914   10 January: dismissal of parliament by Yuan Shikai
1915   18 January: Japanese ultimatum of Twenty-One Demands
        September: founding of the magazine *New Youth*
        12 December: Yuan announces the restoration of imperial rule,
        to his own advantage
1916   22 March: Yuan renounces the restoration of the empire
        6 June: death of Yuan Shikai
1917   1 September: foundation of the Guangzhou military government
        June: attempted imperial restoration by Zhang Xun, dissolution
        of the parliament
1918   May–June: parliamentary elections
1919   4 May: student demonstration in Beijing against the transfer of
        German rights over Shandong to Japan
1920   July: Anhui/Zhili War, defeat of the Anhui clique
        November: Sun Yat-sen regains a foothold in Guangdong
1921   23 July: foundation of the CCP
1922   April–May: First Zhili/Fengtian War, defeat of the Fengtian clique

June: Sun is expelled from Guangzhou by his former ally Chen Jiongming

1923 January: reconquest of Guangzhou by mercenary troops from Yunnan and Guangxi on behalf of Sun Yat-sen

1924 20–30 January: 1st Guomindang Congress, beginning of the first Guomindang/CCP United Front

16 June: inauguration of the Huangpu Military Academy

September–November: Second Zhili/Fengtian War: defeat of the Zhili clique

15 October: Sun Yat-sen crushes merchant militias in Guangzhou

1925 12 March: death of Sun Yat-sen in Beijing

30 May: bloody repression of an anti-imperialist demonstration by the Shanghai International Concession police

June 1925 – November 1926: Great Hong Kong Strike

30 August: assassination of Liao Zhongkai

1926 July: start of the Northern Expedition (*Beifa* 北伐)

7 September: capture of Wuhan

1927 12 April: Chiang Kai-shek's *coup de force* against the communists; end of the first United Front

18 April: creation of a central government in Nanjing dominated by Chiang Kai-shek

1928 4 June: assassination of Zhang Zuolin

8 June: capture of Beijing, end of the Northern Expedition

1929 March–May: successive revolts by former Guomindang allies (Guangxi clique, Feng Yuxiang)

1930 May–November 1930: Central Plains War

1931 28 February: Hu Hanmin is placed under house arrest by Chiang Kai-shek

May: founding of a dissident government in Guangzhou

18 September: Mukden incident; Japan seizes Manchuria

1932 28 January: Japan goes on the offensive in Shanghai, strong Chinese resistance

1 March: founding of Manchukuo

1933 31 May: Tanggu Truce between China and Japan

25 October: Song Ziwen resigns as Finance Minister

1934 February: launch of the New Life Movement

October: start of the Long March

1935　January: Zunyi conference (Guizhou); Mao becomes head of the CCP
October: end of the Long March
1 November: attempted assassination of Wang Jingwei
1936　July: failure of the revolt of the two Guangs: Guangdong returns to the fold of central power
12–25 December: Xi'an incident
1937　7 July: Marco Polo Bridge incident, beginning of the Sino-Japanese War
August–November: Battle of Shanghai
December: Nanjing Massacre
1938　6 April: victory of Taierzhuang
5 June: destruction of the dykes of the Yellow River at Huayuankou in the hope of slowing the Japanese advance
27 October: fall of Wuhan
18 December: defection of Wang Jingwei
1939　July–August: Battle of Nomonhan between Japanese and Soviet troops
1940　January: Mao puts forward the theses of the 'New Democracy'
30 March: proclamation of the 'reorganized national government' by Wang Jingwei in Nanjing
August–December: communist offensive in Shanxi and Hebei (known as the Hundred Regiments)
1941　January: New 4th Army incident between CCP and Guomindang troops
October: end of Soviet aid
7–8 December: Japanese attack on Pearl Harbor, and simultaneous invasion of Hong Kong, Guam, British Malaysia and the Philippines
1942　February–May: victorious Japanese offensive in Burma
February–June: rectification campaign within the CCP
1943　January: Japan (on 9th) and then the Allies (on 11th) renounce their concessions and the privilege of extraterritoriality, putting an end to the system of unequal treaties
23–26 November: Cairo Conference
1944　April–December: Japanese Ichigō offensive
10 November: death of Wang Jingwei

1945   August: bombing of Hiroshima (6th) and Nagasaki (9th),
Japanese surrender

8 August: USSR enters the war against Japan

28 August – 10 October: negotiations between Mao and Chiang
in Chongqing

1946   5 January: China recognizes the independence of Northern
Mongolia

May: communist defeat of Siping in Manchuria

1947   1 January: promulgation of the Constitution

28 February: start of the Taiwan revolt

1948   April: capture of Luoyang by the communists, reflecting the
reversal of military power in north China

November: capitulation of the last nationalist divisions in
Manchuria

November 1948 – January 1949: Battle of Huaihai

1949   21 April: People's Liberation Army (PLA) crosses the Yangtze
River

25 May: PLA enters Shanghai

1 October: proclamation of the People's Republic of China

1950   April: capture of Hainan

Appendixes

Appendix 1 Sun Yat-sen's Last Will (yizhu 遺囑)

余致力國民革命，凡四十年，其目的在求中國之自由平等。積四十年之經驗，深知欲達到此目的，必須喚起民眾及聯合世界上以平等待我之民族，共同奮鬥。

現在革命尚未成功，凡我同志，務須依照余所著《建國方略》、《建國大綱》、《三民主義》及《第一次全國代表大會宣言》，繼續努力，以求貫徹，最近主張開國民會議及廢除不平等條約，尤須於最短期間，促其實現，是所至囑。

For forty years, I have devoted myself to the cause of the national revolution, the objective of which is to restore to China its liberty and equality [among nations]. The accumulated experience of those forty years has convinced me that to attain this goal it is necessary to rouse the popular masses and associate ourselves with those peoples of the world who treat us on a footing of equality so as to pursue the common fight.

The Revolution is not yet achieved. May all my comrades be guided by my writings, *The Plan for National Reconstruction*, *The Fundamentals of National Reconstruction*, *The Three Principles of the People* and *The Manifesto of the First National Congress*, and continue to do their utmost to realize these. Above all, the convocation of a People's Convention and the abolition of unequal treaties, which I have recently advocated, should be accomplished with the least possible delay. These are my instructions.

[Translated from the original by Xavier Paulès.]

Appendix 2 Comparison of China's population with that of other major countries (in millions of inhabitants)

	1913	1950
China	410	540
United Kingdom	45	50
Germany	65	68
France	41	41
Western Europe (total)	261	305
United States	97	152
World population	1,791	2,524

Sources: for China, Ge J. (ed.), *Zhongguo renkou shi*, vol. VI, p. 281; for other countries: A. Maddison, *The World Economy*, p. 241.

Appendix 3 Comparison of the length of China's rail network with that of other countries (in kilometres)

	1913	1950
China	9,854	22,238
France	40,770	41,300
Italy	18,873	21,550
United Kingdom	32,623	31,352
Japan	10,570	27,401
United States	401,977	360,137
Argentina	33,478	42,864

Source: A. Maddison, *L'économie mondiale 1820–1992*, p. 66.

Appendix 4 The Song family simplified family tree

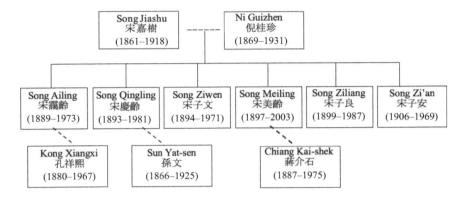

---------- Matrimonial link

Source: Nihon Shanhaishi Kenkyūkai 日本上海史研究會 (ed.),

Shanhai jinbutsushi 上海人物誌, Tokyo: Tōhō Shoten 東方書店, 1997, p. 153.

Maps

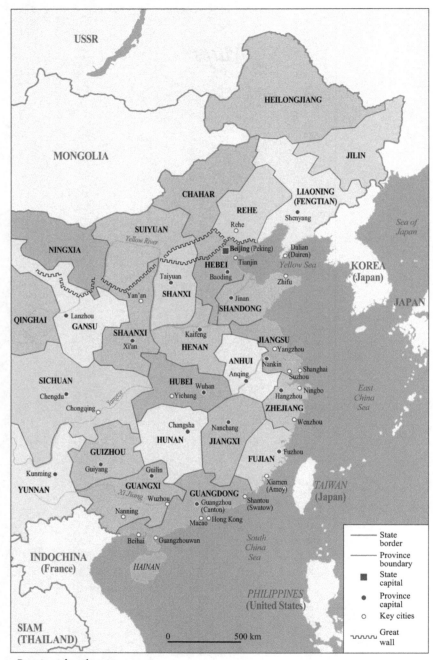

1 Province borders in 1912

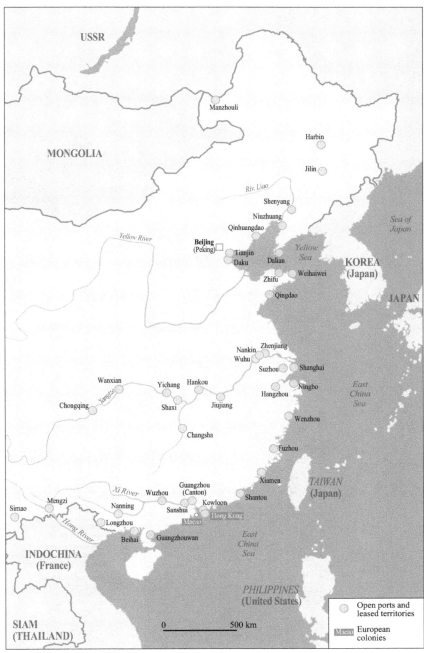

2 Open ports, leased territories and European colonies in 1926

RUSSIAN EMPIRE

HEILONGJIANG

M A N C H U R I A

JILIN

MONGOLIA

JEHOL

FENGTIAN

Sea of Japan

KOREA
(Japan)

JAPAN

Beijing
(Peking)

Taiyuan
SHANXI
(29 oct.)

ZHILI

Jinan
SHANDONG

Yellow
Sea

QINGHAI

Lanzhou
GANSU

SHAANXI
(22 oct.)

Kaifeng

Xi'an
HENAN

JIANGSU
(5 nov.)

Zhenjiang

Nankin

ANHUI
(8 nov.)

Shanghai

SICHUAN
(7 nov.)

Chengdu

10 oct. 1911

HUBEI
(10 oct.)

Wuhan

Hangzhou

ZHEJIANG
(5 nov.)

East
China
Sea

Changsha

Nanchang

HUNAN
(22 oct.)

JIANGXI
(31 oct.)

GUIZHOU
(4 nov.)

Guiyang

Guilin

FUJIAN
(11 nov.)

Fuzhou

Kunming
YUNNAN
(31 oct.)

GUANGXI
(7 nov.)

GUANGDONG
(9 nov.)

TAIWAN
(Japan)

Guangzhou
(Canton)

Hong Kong

Macao

South
China
Sea

■   Capital of the Empire

Starting point
of the revolution

Principal massacres
of both Manchu garrisons
and civilian populations

10 oct.   Provinces acquired
in the revolution
at the end of 1911
(date of proclamation
of independence)

Provinces remaining
loyal to the Qing dynasty
at the end of 1911

INDOCHINA
(France)

HAINAN

SIAM
(THAILAND)

0   500 km

3 The revolution

4 Principal warlords' zones in 1922

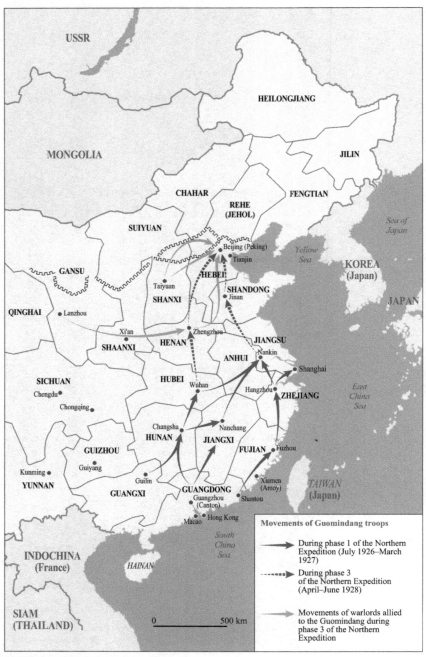

5 The Northern Expedition

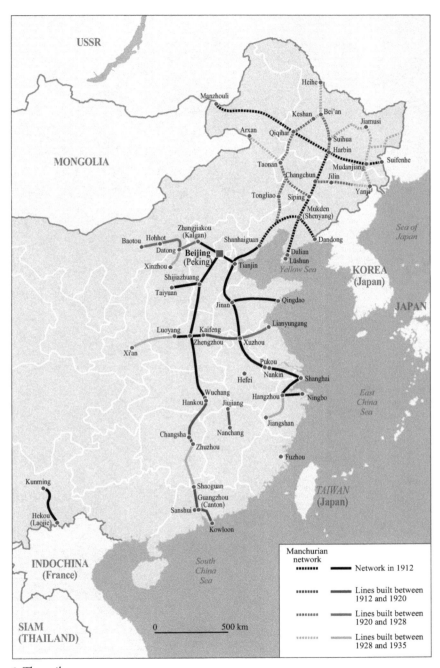

6 The railways

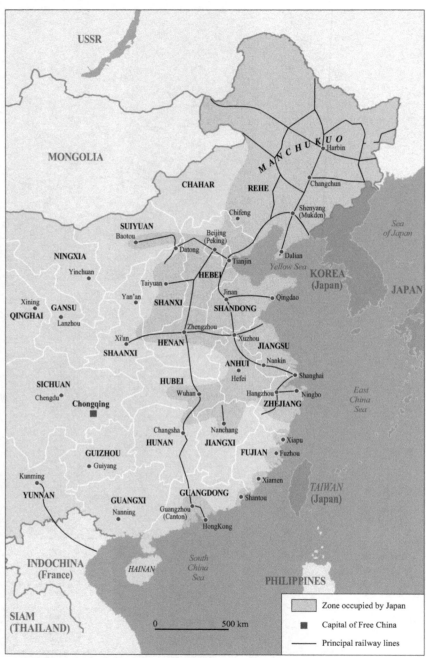

7 Zone occupied by Japan between 1938 and 1944

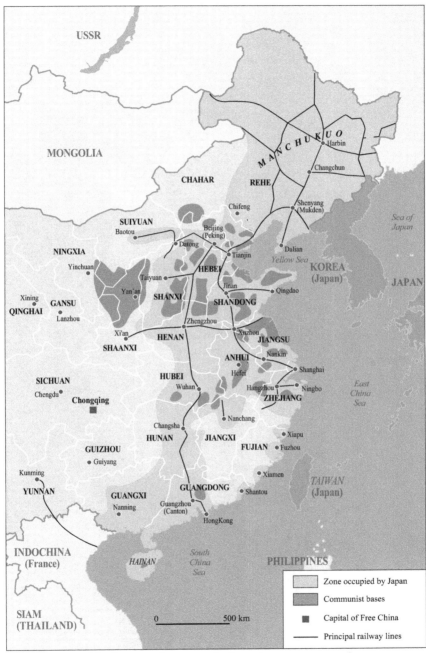

8 Zone occupied by Japan and communist bases between 1944 and 1945

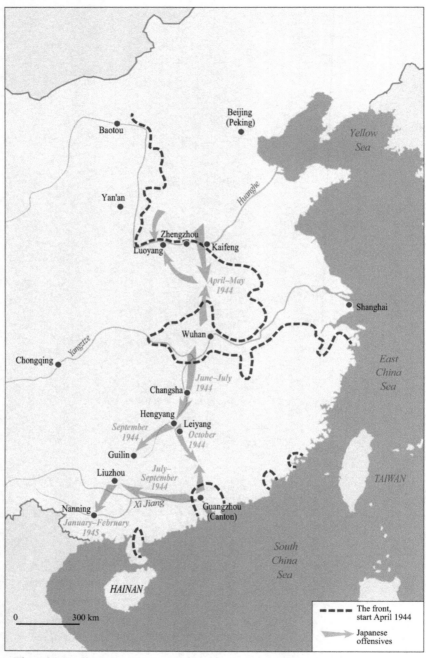

9 The Ichigō offensive

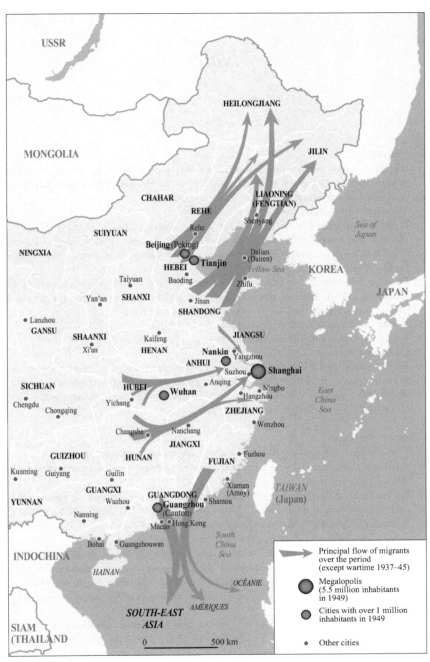

USSR

MONGOLIA

HEILONGJIANG

JILIN

CHAHAR

REHE

LIAONING
(FENGTIAN)

SUIYUAN

Rehe

Shenyang

Sea of
Japan

NINGXIA

Beijing (Peking)

HEBEI Tianjin

Dalian
(Dairen)

KOREA

Taiyuan

Baoding

Yellow Sea

JAPAN

Yan'an

SHANXI

Zhifu

Lanzhou

Jinan

GANSU

SHANDONG

SHAANXI

Kaifeng

JIANGSU

Xi'an

HENAN

Nankin

Yangzhou

ANHUI

Suzhou

Shanghai

SICHUAN

HUBEI

Anqing

Ningbo

Chengdu

Yichang

Wuhan

Hangzhou

East
China
Sea

Chongqing

ZHEJIANG

Wenzhou

Changsha

Nanchang

JIANGXI

GUIZHOU

HUNAN

Fuzhou

Kunming

Guiyang

Guilin

FUJIAN

GUANGXI

Xiamen
(Amoy)

TAIWAN
(Japan)

YUNNAN

Wuzhou

GUANGDONG
Guangzhou
(Canton)

Shantou

Nanning

Macao Hong Kong

Bohai

Guangzhouwan

South
China
Sea

INDOCHINA

HAINAN

OCÉANIE

SOUTH-EAST
ASIA

AMÉRIQUES

SIAM
(THAILAND)

0   500 km

Principal flow of migrants
over the period
(except wartime 1937–45)

Megalopolis
(5.5 million inhabitants
in 1949)

Cities with over 1 million
inhabitants in 1949

• Other cities

10 Migrations during the Republic

299

Notes

Introduction

1 It is often overlooked that most historians are also teachers. As such, they must produce in their courses a synthetic and accessible account of the period they specialize in, an exercise which influences their approach to research.
2 Translator's note: also known as the Kuomintang.
3 E. Wilkinson, 'How Do We Know What We Know about Chinese History?' p. 24.
4 Three of the most notable successful works in this area are: Hua L. and I. Thireau, *Enquête sociologique sur la Chine 1911–1949*; J. Strauss, *Strong Institutions in Weak Polities*; Lu H., *Beyond the Neon Lights*.
5 In an oral history survey that I conducted in 2005–6 in old people's homes in the Cantonese region, most of the witnesses, first and foremost, took the precaution of singing the praises of the CCP for showering them with benefits.
6 X. Paulès, 'Les *wenshi ziliao*', *Encyclopédie des historiographies*.
7 P. Perdue, 'China and Other Colonial Empires', pp. 85–103.
8 J. Lawson, 'Warlord Colonialism', p. 300.
9 See the fine study by F. Jagou, *Le 9e Panchen Lama (1883–1937), enjeu des relations sino-tibétaines*, pp. 10, 166–70 and 192–4; H. Lin, *Modern China's Ethnic Frontiers*, pp. 71–2.
10 Translator's note: now officially known as the Xinjiang 新疆 Uygur Autonomous Region.
11 D. Brophy, *Uyghur Nation*, especially ch. 7, pp. 204–32.

1 The 1911 Revolution

1 D. Reynolds, *China, 1898–1912: The Xinzheng Revolution and Japan*, pp. 2–4.
2 Translator's note: a censal vote is a system based on suffrage assessed according to wealth and tax paid.
3 For example, in Sichuan, tax revenues increased from 8.72 million in 1900 to 18.36 million in 1909: S. A. M. Adshead, *Province and Politics in Late Imperial China*, p. 123.
4 E. Rhoads, *Manchus & Han, Ethnic Relations and Political Power in Late Qing and Early Republican China, 1861–1928*, pp. 187–204.
5 S. A. M. Adshead, *Province and Politics in Late Imperial China*, pp. 98–101 and 121.
6 A penetrating analysis of the reasons for the particularly marked radicalization of the Wuhan troops can be found in J. Esherick, 'Founding a Republic, Electing a President', pp. 145–50. The very clear and detailed account of the events at Wuchang is on pp. 178–98 in the same volume.
7 The Xiaohong Xiao-Planes' chapter, 'Constitutions et constitutionnalisme', is an indispensable source of information on institutional reforms in the last years of the Qing and the first years of Republican rule.
8 Ch'en J., *Yuan Shih-k'ai*, pp. 84–9.

9   J. Esherick, *Reform and Revolution in China*, pp. 228–9.

10 E. Rhoads, *Manchus & Han, Ethnic Relations and Political Power in Late Qing and Early Republican China, 1861–1928*, pp. 187–204.

11 Zhou Y., *Historicizing Online Politics*, pp. 26–38.

12 Li X. (ed.), *Zhonghua minguo shi*, vol. II; a convenient map summarizing the various dates of declaration of secession is shown on p. 765.

13 E. McCord, *The Power of the Gun, the Emergence of Modern Chinese Warlordism*, pp. 33–9.

14 For an overview of the role played by secret societies in the 1911 Revolution: J. Lust, 'Les sociétés secrètes, les mouvements populaires et la révolution de 1911', pp. 360–92.

15 J. Esherick, 'Founding a Republic, Electing a President', pp. 129–52.

16 D. Strand, *An Unfinished Republic*, pp. 26–9.

17 An excellent overview of this debate can be found in C. Musgrove, *China's Contested Capital*, pp. 30–5.

18 D. Strand, *An Unfinished Republic*, pp. 39–50, 199–201 and 245–54.

19 X. Xiao-Planes, *Éducation et politique en Chine*, pp. 325–36.

20 M.-C. Bergère, *Shanghai*, pp. 139–40.

21 E. McCord, *The Power of the Gun, the Emergence of Modern Chinese Warlordism*, pp. 165–6.

22 M.-C. Bergère, *Sun Yat-sen*, pp. 258–9.

23 E. Young, *The Presidency of Yuan Shih-k'ai*, pp. 147–8.

24 E. McCord, *The Power of the Gun, the Emergence of Modern Chinese Warlordism*, pp. 177–84.

25 H. van de Ven, 'Public Finance and the Rise of Warlordism', pp. 841–7.

26 W. Kirby, 'The Internationalization of China', pp. 442–3.

27 P. Zarrow, *After Empire*, pp. 243–9.

2 Cliques and Warlords (1916–1928)

1   A. Nathan, *Peking Politics*, pp. 60–4 and 78–80.

2   G. McCormack, *Chang Tso-lin in Northeast China 1911–1928*, pp. 33–42.

3   A lineage is a social group that theoretically includes all individuals who descend in patrilineal line from a common ancestor. Lineages were one of the main forms of collective organization in South China. For more on this subject, see Chapter 8 on society.

4   Wou O., *Militarism in Modern China*, pp. 263–5.

5   These complex events are very clearly summarized in L. Pye, *Warlord Politics*, pp. 17–19.

6   Wou O., *Militarism in Modern China*, pp. 20–4.

7   This is suggested by a French diplomat, based on confidential documents he recovered when he offered asylum to Zhang Xun's chief of staff after Zhang's debacle: MAE [Ministry of Foreign Affairs] Nouvelle série, sous-série Chine, dossier no. 61, Conti report of 24 July 1917.

8   To follow the twists and turns of these elections, the most dependable guide (on which I rely heavily) is A. Nathan, *Peking Politics*, pp. 91–113.

9   L. Pye, *Warlord Politics*, p. 30.

10 A. Waldron, *From War to Nationalism*, pp. 229–39.

11 Ch'i H., *Warlord Politics in China 1916–1928*, pp. 139–40.

12 D. Sutton, *Provincial Militarism*, p. 229.

13 Wou O., *Militarism in Modern China*, pp. 95 and 118.

14 W. Rowe, *Crimson Rain, Seven Centuries of Violence in a Chinese County*.

15 A. Waldron, 'The Warlord', pp. 1080 and 1085.

16 Ch'en J., 'Defining Chinese Warlords and Their Factions', pp. 563–600. This article is still very valuable in describing the variety of *junfa*.

17 Translator's note: Vietnam, Laos and Cambodia, united as French colonial territories prior to 1950.

18 Translator's note: modern-day Shenyang.

19 J. Sheridan, *China in Disintegration*.

20 See, especially, L. Pye, 'Public Relations and Propaganda', in *Warlord Politics*, pp. 113–31.

21 Michael Tsin's masterful study shows the emergence of this political line in Guangzhou of the early 1920s: M. Tsin, *Nation, Governance, and Modernity in China, Canton 1900–1927*.

22 M.-C. Bergère, *Sun Yat-sen*, pp. 276–86 and 304–11.

23 Translator's note: former name for the northern area of Vietnam.

24 G. McCormack, *Chang Tso-lin in Northeast China 1911–1928*, pp. 64–8 and 131–42.

25 D. Barthélemy, *Nouvelle histoire des Capétiens (987–1214)*, p. 24.

26 A. Nathan, *Peking Politics*, pp. 212–13, and A. Waldron, *From War to Nationalism*, pp. 190–6.

27 These are the brothers of the following warlords: Cao Kun, Long Jiguang, Chen Jitang and Liu Xianshi.

28 For an excellent analysis of loyalty networks surrounding the warlords, and their fragility, see J. Sheridan, *China in Disintegration*, pp. 78–80.

29 G. McCormack, *Chang Tso-lin in Northeast China 1911–1928*, pp. 151–87.

30 H. Harrison, *The Making of the Republican Citizen*, pp. 105–14.

31 W. Kirby, *Germany and Republican China*, p. 24.

32 F. Lanza, *Behind the Gate*, p. 123; T. Weston, *The Power of Position*, pp. 156–7.

33 M.-C. Bergère, *Shanghai*, pp. 178–81.

34 T. Weston, *The Power of Position*, p. 156.

35 I have borrowed this rather neat encapsulation (which, of course, echoes the Nanjing decade, the subject of Chapter 3) from Chan M. K., 'A Turning Point in the Modern Chinese Revolution', pp. 224–41.

36 M.-C. Bergère, *Sun Yat-sen*, p. 296. This is a rebuilding of the Guomindang because the 'first' one was, as we saw in Chapter 1, the party founded in 1912 with the aim of winning the parliamentary elections of the winter of 1912–13.

37 Wang Q., *Dangyuan, dangquan yu dangzheng*, pp. 13–14.

38 E. Fung, *In Search of Chinese Democracy*, p. 30.

39 Translator's note: the Three Principles of the People.

40 Wang Q., *Dangyuan, dangquan yu dangzheng*, pp. 39–41.

41 D. Jordan, *The Northern Expedition*, remains indispensable concerning this operation.

42 A. Waldron, *From War to Nationalism*, pp. 119–40.

43 Wou O., *Militarism in Modern China*, pp. 123–44.

44 M.-C. Bergère, *The Golden Age of the Chinese Bourgeoisie, 1911–1937*, p. 237.

45 For a precise account of this takeover by force, which inspired André Malraux's novel *La condition humaine*, see A. Roux, *Grèves et politique à Shanghai*, pp. 64–9.

46 Iriye A., *After Imperialism*, p. 193.

47 Translator's note: also known as the Kwantung Army.

48 Iriye A., *After Imperialism*, pp. 195–214.

49 R. Mitter, *The Manchurian Myth*, pp. 51–2.

3 The Nanjing Decade (1928–1937)

1 This war is too often neglected by Western historiography. One must turn to the monumental history of the Republic edited by Li Xin for sufficient details: Li X. (ed.), *Zhonghua minguo shi*, vol. V, pp. 316–48.

2 Li X. (ed.), *Zhonghua minguo shi*, vol. V, pp. 339–48.

3 D. Jordan, *China's Trial by Fire*, pp. 4–6.

4 Li X. (ed.), *Zhonghua minguo shi*, vol. V, p. 474.

5 L. Eastman, *The Abortive Revolution*, pp. 85–139.

6 J. Fitzgerald, 'The Irony of the Chinese Revolution', pp. 18–23.

7 M. Zanasi, *Saving the Nation*.

8 On the Cotton Control Commission, see M. Zanasi, *Saving the Nation*, pp. 103–32.

9 On the subject of this assassination attempt, see F. Wakeman, *Spymaster*, pp. 182–4.

10 P. Coble, *The Shanghai Capitalists*, p. 172.

11 F. Wakeman, *Spymaster*, pp. 36–45 and 253.

12 J. Strauss, *Strong Institutions in Weak Polities*, p. 157.

13 P. Coble, *The Shanghai Capitalists*, p. 125.

14 On this issue, see P. Duara, *Sovereignty and Authenticity*, pp. 49–59.

15 P. Lorge, 'The Great Wall', p. 31.

16 J. Strauss, *Strong Institutions in Weak Polities*, pp. 133–9.

17 P. Coble, *The Shanghai Capitalists*, pp. 172–92; B. Martin, *The Shanghai Green Gang*, pp. 194–9.

18 T. Shiroyama, *China during the Great Depression*, pp. 183–7.

19 L. Pye, *Warlord Politics*, pp. 163–4.

20 For a concise overview of the appalling confusion of the weights and measures system at the end of the imperial period, see L. Eastman, *Family, Fields, and Ancestors*, pp. 107–8.

21 D. Jordan, *China's Trial by Fire*.

22 On Manchukuo, see Yamamuro S., *Manchuria under Japanese Dominion*.

23 P. Coble, *Facing Japan*, p. 209.

24 On this state of affairs, please see R. Mitter, *The Manchurian Myth*.

25 P. Coble, *The Shanghai Capitalists*, pp. 133–6.

26 R. Mitter, *The Manchurian Myth*, pp. 157–88.

27 Chen Jitang is the only great warlord not to have the honour of a biography in a European language. The best synthesis in Chinese about him remains: Zhong Z., *Chen Jitang*.

28 H. Boorman, *Biographical Dictionary of Republican China*, vol. II, pp. 62–3.

29 J. Sheridan, *China in Disintegration*, p. 184.

30 R. Kapp, *Szechwan and the Chinese Republic*, pp. 24–38 and 87–98. A valuable map of the areas controlled by the various warlords in this province around 1932 can be found on page 34.

31 D. Buck, *Urban Change in China*, pp. 169–70.

32 See the Shanxi case: D. Gillin, *Warlord*, pp. 135–6.

33 R. Kapp, *Szechwan and the Chinese Republic*, p. 117.

34 Thus, at the end of 1930, Chiang Kai-shek forced the two great warlords he had just defeated, Feng Yuxiang and Yan Xishan, to go abroad.

35 For example, between 1927 and 1935, the authorities of Zhejiang province managed to maintain a resolutely anti-opium policy, thus opposing the will of Chiang Kai-shek,

who sought instead to integrate the province into the lucrative opium circuits that he controlled: A. Baumler, *The Chinese and Opium under the Republic*, pp. 146–9.
36 J. Strauss, *Strong Institutions in Weak Polities*, pp. 60–105 and 127–33.
37 D. Buck, *Urban Change in China*, p. 167.
38 A. Roux and Wang X., *Qu Qiubai (1899–1935)*, pp. 12–13.
39 S. Averill, *Revolution in the Highlands*, pp. 81–166.
40 Hu Chi-hsi, *L'Armée rouge et l'ascension de Mao*, pp. 54–75.
41 Yang B., *From Revolution to Politics*, pp. 47–51.
42 Zhang E., 'The Long March' in Wang Ban (ed.), *Words and Their Stories*, pp. 40–9. Propaganda even went as far as to represent the Long March as a manoeuvre to counter Japanese aggression in the North.
43 Yang B., *From Revolution to Politics*, pp. 2–3.
44 T. Saich, *The Rise to Power of the Chinese Communist Party*, pp. 656–7.
45 This is the subject of the excellent book by G. Benton, *Mountain Fires*.
46 Yang B., *From Revolution to Politics*, p. 255. There is a very useful table charting the evolution of the CCP and its armed forces from 1921 to 1949 on p. 307.
47 For an excellent point on the issue, see P. Coble, *Facing Japan*, pp. 342–61.

4 The War against Japan (1937–1945)
1 W. Kirby, *Germany and Republican China*, pp. 124–5 and 220–3.
2 Yang T., 'Chiang Kai-shek and the Battles of Shanghai and Nanjing', p. 145.
3 Fu P., *Passivity, Resistance, and Collaboration*, pp. 2–5.
4 For a concise and dispassionate analysis of the reasons for the massacre, see P.-F. Souyri, *Nouvelle histoire du Japon*, pp. 523–5.
5 J. Garver, *Chinese–Soviet Relations, 1937–1945*, pp. 155–6.
6 E. Fung, *In Search of Chinese Democracy*, pp. 144–82.
7 This phase of the war is masterfully depicted in chs. 2 and 3 of S. MacKinnon, *Wuhan, 1938*, pp. 18–43.
8 H. van de Ven, *War and Nationalism in China, 1925–1945*, pp. 217–24.
9 D. Pietz, *The Yellow River*, pp. 105–8.
10 S. MacKinnon, *Wuhan, 1938*, pp. 35–7 and 41.
11 A. Cherepanov, *As Military Adviser in China*, p. 330. This data reflects the situation in June 1939.
12 A. Roux, *Chiang Kaï-shek*, pp. 305–6.
13 S. MacKinnon, *Wuhan, 1938*, pp. 20–2.
14 Ch'i Hsi-sheng, 'The Military Dimension, 1942–1945' in Hsiung and Levine (eds.), *China's Bitter Victory*, pp. 157–8.
15 On this struggle in Shanghai at the beginning of the war, see F. Wakeman, *The Shanghai Badlands*.
16 This was one of my main surprises during a series of interviews with elderly Cantonese in 2006 and 2008: a significant number of people told me that, after fleeing the Japanese advance, they had returned to the occupied zone after a few years.
17 See, for example, in the case of Guangzhou, a report by the British consul on 18 November 1938 (CO 129 571/11).
18 Wu J., *Jiehou tiantang*, p. 83.
19 K. Schoppa, *In a Sea of Bitterness*, pp. 14–31.
20 W. Churchill, *Memoirs of the Second World War*.

21 M. Lohanda, *Growing Pains*, pp. 164–5. The studies that mention aid from overseas suffer from three major flaws: they tend to exalt the attachment of overseas Chinese to their country of origin; they 'forget' to mention that some of the donations flowed not to Chongqing but to the occupied zone; finally, the figures they give are both very partial and not very reliable. It is not possible to discern the order of magnitude of all the aid that came from overseas during the entire war and therefore to know whether it played a really significant role. It is probable that it did not.

22 L. Eastman, *Seeds of Destruction*. Eastman does, however, give the nationalist army credit for not collapsing.

23 M. Muscolino, *The Ecology of War in China*, pp. 87–119.

24 Shen T., 'Food Production and Distribution for Civilian and Military Needs in Wartime China, 1937–1945', pp. 167–91.

25 E. Perry, *Rebels and Revolutionaries in North China, 1845–1945*, pp. 234–7.

26 C. Johnson, *Nationalisme paysan et pouvoir communiste*.

27 A. Roux, *Le Singe et le tigre*.

28 J. Taylor, *The Generalissimo*, p. 256. Returning to China after the conference, Chiang Kai-shek jubilantly wrote in his diary that it was 'the greatest success of all time for China's foreign policy'.

29 P. Short, *Mao Tsé-toung*, pp. 342–4.

30 The expression 'Mao Zedong Thought' (*Mao Zedong de sixiang*) dates from an article by Zhang Ruxin in February 1941.

31 J. Boyle, *China and Japan at War, 1937–1945*, pp. 88–92 and 110–16.

32 T. Weston, *The Power of Position*, pp. 126–7.

33 D. Serfass, 'Résister ou négocier face au Japon', pp. 121–32.

34 For a detailed account of the Ichigō offensive, see T. Hara, 'The Ichigo Offensive', pp. 392–402.

35 WO106/3588.

36 Ge J. (ed.), *Zhongguo renkou shi*, vol. VI, pp. 581–2. Some historians argue for much higher estimates. Many people died indirectly (due to famine and epidemics, in particular). The official figure currently put forward by the Chinese government is 35 million.

37 Translator's note: a population deficit in certain social strata due to increased mortality and natal deficit.

38 K. Schoppa, *In a Sea of Bitterness*, pp. 285–301.

39 W. Kirby, 'The Chinese War Economy' in J. Hsiung and S. Levine (eds.), *China's Bitter Victory*, pp. 185–6 and 204–5.

40 See, for example, the case of the Tianjin water supply system, studied by D. Spicq, *L'avènement de l'eau courante à Tianjin, Chine, 1900–1949*, pp. 177–93.

41 Sun Y., *China and the Origins of the Pacific War 1931–1941*, pp. 16–17 and 42–3; M. Zanasi, *Saving the Nation*, pp. 207–9; J. Boyle, *China and Japan at War, 1937–1945*, pp. 351–2 and 358–9.

5 Civil War (1945–1949)

1 In the last decades of the nineteenth century, the Qing exercised a political tutelage, particularly in relation to Korea, that was less akin to traditional suzerainty than to outright imperialist rule: K. Larsen, *Tradition, Treaties, and Trade*.

2 Fang X. (ed.), *Shanghai jindai minzu juanyan gongye*, p. 240.

3 Wang J., 'Le troisième âge d'or de l'industrie cotonnière de Shanghai (1946–1947)', p. 437.

4 More generally, the dearth of statistics on what I have called the 'little statistical golden age of the Nanking decade' explains why these two years of vigorous economic growth are overlooked: X. Paulès, 'Le petit age d'ôr statistique de la décennie de Nankin (1928–1937)'.

5 Y. Cheng, *Foreign Trade and Industrial Development of China*, pp. 166–70 and 268.

6 B. Sheehan, *Industrial Eden: A Chinese Capitalist Vision*, p. 153.

7 Wang J., *Jindai Shanghai mianfangye de zuihou huihuang*, pp. 42–57.

8 S. Levine, *Anvil of Victory*, pp. 77–82.

9 C. Atwood, 'Sino-Soviet Diplomacy and the Second Partition of Mongolia', in S. Kotkin and B. Elleman (eds.), *Mongolia in the Twentieth Century*, pp. 137–58.

10 This is, in any case, one of the conclusions of Alain Roux's fine biography of Chiang Kai-shek: A. Roux, *Chiang Kaï-shek*, pp. 480–1.

11 J. Boyle, *China and Japan at War, 1937–1945*, pp. 332–3.

12 The chapter 'The Losing Battle with Inflation' in J. Spence's book provides an excellent summary of these efforts: *The Search for Modern China*, pp. 445–51.

13 S. Pepper, *Civil War in China*, pp. 118–21.

14 O. Westad, *Decisive Encounters*, pp. 151–2.

15 F. Wakeman, *Spymaster*, pp. 242–319.

16 L. Eastman, *Seeds of Destruction*, p. 166; Chen L., *The Storm Clouds over China*, p. 211.

17 L. Bianco, *Origins of the Chinese Revolution, 1915–1949*.

18 WO 208/4569: secret report dated 8 April 1948.

19 D. Lary, *China's Civil War*, pp. 62–3 and 122–7.

20 A. Roux, 'Le syndrome de Ye Gong: le Parti Communiste chinois et les ouvriers à la veille de la prise de Shanghai', pp. 512–32; F. Wakeman, 'Liberation', pp. 463–80.

21 L. Eastman, *Seeds of Destruction*, p. 129.

22 Li C., *The Bitter Sea*, pp. 98–100.

23 S. Pepper, *Civil War in China*, pp. 156–7.

24 Chen L, *The Storm Clouds over China*, p. 213.

25 L. Eastman, *Seeds of Destruction*, pp. 108–29.

26 J. Taylor, *The Generalissimo's Son*, pp. 99–115 and 131–82.

27 E. Fung, *In Search of Chinese Democracy*, pp. 291–2.

28 X. Xiao-Planes, 'Constitutions et constitutionnalisme', p. 290.

29 Tong, T. and Li T., *The Memoirs of Li Tsung-jen*, pp. 491, 504 and 509–13.

30 F. Wakeman, 'Liberation', p. 511.

31 A. Dirlik and R. Prazniak, 'The 1911 Revolution', p. 224. On the ambiguity of 'democracy' as put forward by the CCP from the 1920s onwards, see M. Bonnin, 'Servante, épouvantail ou déesse, la démocratie dans le discours du pouvoir et dans celui de la dissidence en Chine', in Delmas-Marty and Will, *La Chine et la démocratie*, pp. 493–8.

32 Arquivo histórico-diplomático (Lisbon, Portugal), *Consulado de Portugal em Cantao*: Dossier 162 (Processo no. 6), Relatório consular 1946, pp. 5–7.

33 E. Fung, *In Search of Chinese Democracy*, pp. 294 and 315–16.

34 O. Westad, *Decisive Encounters*, pp. 38–40, 116–37 and 279.

35 O. Westad, *Decisive Encounters*, p. 10.

36 S. Levine, *Anvil of Victory*, pp. 98–100.

37 E. Fung, *In Search of Chinese Democracy*, pp. 230–2 and 289–93.

38 Lin H., *Accidental State*, pp. 40–5.

39 V. Louzon, 'Une révolte postcoloniale entre Chine et Japon', pp. 85–97.

40 J. Taylor, *The Generalissimo*, pp. 362–3 and 397.

41 C. Vidal, 'D'un régime à l'autre', pp. 41–60.
42 X. Paulès, 'The Afterlife of Sun Yat-sen during the Republic (1925–1949)', pp. 165–79.
43 Although the individual appropriation of power was not part of Sun's directives, it is true that he himself was already exercising strong leadership, which he constantly sought to institutionalize and strengthen.

6 Overview of the Chinese Economy

1 T. Rawski, *Economic Growth in Pre-war China*; A. Feuerwerker, 'Economic Trends, 1912–1949', in J. Fairbank and A. Feuerwerker (eds.), *Cambridge History of China*, pp. 28–127.
2 W. Kirby, 'The Internationalization of China', pp. 447–8.
3 J. Fewsmith, *Party, State and Elites in Republican China*, pp. 46–8.
4 T. Wright, 'Distant Thunder', pp. 697–748.
5 P. Richardson, *Economic Change in China*, pp. 43–4.
6 A. Maddison, *The World Economy*, p. 363.
7 K. Gerth, *China Made*, pp. 102–5.
8 Translator's note: an arrangement between individuals buying a property in common.
9 Cheng L., *Banking in Modern China*, pp. 10–39.
10 Eng R., *Economic Imperialism in China*, pp. 77–80.
11 D. Faure, *China and Capitalism*, pp. 42–3.
12 K. Pomeranz, *A Great Divergence*, pp. 178–81. Pomeranz tries to put forward arguments to explain why this high level of interest rates might not have been too great a brake on economic development. This is one of the few weak points in this brilliant book. One of the reasons why his demonstration is unconvincing is that it is based mainly on the idea – highly questionable in itself – that peasants who borrowed against land as collateral were encouraged to do so (despite, therefore, the high rates) because 'it was extremely hard in China to seize land used as a collateral'. Moreover, this last point hardly fits in with the picture Pomeranz presents to his reader a few chapters earlier (pp. 70–3) of a remarkably free and fluid market in agricultural land.
13 Ma D., 'Economic Growth in the Lower Yangzi Region of China in 1911–1937', p. 367.
14 R. Myers, *The Chinese Peasant Economy*, pp. 75 and 179–83.
15 L. Bianco, 'La société rurale' in M.-C. Bergère, L. Bianco and J. Domes (eds.), *La Chine au xxe siècle*, pp. 264–7. L. Bianco's chapter remains unsurpassed in its clarity and brilliant synthesis.
16 Translator's note: sericulture.
17 Li L., *China's Silk Trade*, pp. 72–138.
18 X. Paulès, *L'Opium, une passion chinoise*, pp. 84–6.
19 Eng R., *Economic Imperialism in China*, pp. 137–47.
20 T. Wright, *Coal Mining in China's Economy and Society, 1895–1937*, pp. 23–4, 35–76 and 200–1.
21 Lim T., 'Oil for the Center from the Margins'. The Yumen oilfields are noteworthy for another reason: their development is one of the very few examples of successful collaboration between the CCP and the Guomindang.
22 Wang D., *The Teahouse*, p. 86.
23 T. Rawski, *Economic Growth in Pre-war China*, pp. 70–5.
24 C. Henriot, Z. Zheng, O. Barge and S. Caquard, *Atlas de Shanghai*, p. 125.
25 T. Rawski, *Economic Growth in Pre-war China*, pp. 74 and 81. The data is from 1933.

26 Yeh W., *Shanghai Splendor*, pp. 84–100 (curiously, the chapter of the book entitled 'Enlightened Paternalism' hardly addresses this issue).

27 S. Cochran, *Encountering Chinese Networks*, p. 175.

28 M.-C. Bergère, *The Golden Age of the Chinese Bourgeoisie, 1911–1937*, pp. 154–9.

29 See the cases of Nanyang Cigarettes or Desheng Spinning Mills: S. Cochran, *Big Business in China*, pp. 163–9; E. Köll, *Cotton Mill to Business Empire*, pp. 256–64.

30 L. Eastman, *Family, Fields, and Ancestors*, p. 186.

31 X. Xiao-Planes, 'Marché, capital et pouvoir entrepreneurial en Chine', pp. 47–92.

32 M.-C. Bergère, *The Golden Age of the Chinese Bourgeoisie, 1911–1937*, p. 49.

33 S. Cochran, *Chinese Medicine Men*, pp. 118–26.

34 S. Cochran and A. Hsieh, *The Lius of Shanghai*.

35 Zhang J., *Coping with Calamity*, pp. 155–80.

36 Fei H., 'Peasant Life in China', p. 119.

37 Lu H., *Beyond the Neon Lights*, p. 217.

38 F. Dikötter, *Things Modern*, pp. 118–19.

39 Ma D., 'Economic Growth in the Lower Yangzi Region of China in 1911–1937', p. 367.

40 T. Rawski, *Economic Growth in Pre-war China*, pp. 208–9.

41 D. Strand, *Rickshaw Beijing*, p. 26; A. Roux, *Le Shanghai ouvrier des années trente*, pp. 87–8.

42 Wang D., *The Teahouse*, pp. 85–6.

43 Feng Y., 'The Sound of Images', pp. 111–42.

44 *Photographies du père Joseph de Reviers de Mauny*, pp. 188–95 and 211–21.

45 W. Kirby, 'Engineering China', pp. 137–60.

46 L. Bianco, *La récidive*, pp. 161–7.

47 On these issues, see the important article by M. Bian, 'Building State Structure', especially pp. 61–7.

7 Building the State

1 H. Harrison, *The Making of the Republican Citizen*, pp. 14–20 and 33.

2 C. Musgrove, *China's Contested Capital*, pp. 104–19.

3 Feng X., 'Counterfeiting Legitimacy', pp. 214–17.

4 J. Fitzgerald, 'From County Magistrate to County Head', pp. 268–70.

5 Xu X., *Trial of Modernity*, pp. 26–83 and 96–8.

6 X. Xiao-Planes, 'Constitutions et constitutionnalisme'.

7 L. Pye, *Warlord Politics*, p. 138.

8 A. Nathan, *Peking Politics, 1918–1923*, pp. 8–13 and 72–3.

9 Chen H., 'Last Chapter Unfinished'.

10 Zhai T., 'Étude comparative des monographies locales de la préfecture de Hui et du district de She', pp. 313–17.

11 Cheng M., *Diyu wenhua yu guojia renting*, pp. 261–3.

12 M. Bian, 'Building State Structure', p. 46. Xi'an had been elevated to the rank of secondary capital since 1932 and renamed Xijing 西京, 'the capital of the West': Fayolle Lussac, H. Hoyem and P. Clément (eds.), *Xi'an, an Ancient City in a Modern World*, pp. 59–60.

13 P.-É. Will, 'Bureaucratie officielle et bureaucratie réelle à la fin de l'Empire', pp. 99 and 118.

14 P.-É. Will, 'Le contrôle de l'excès de pouvoir sous la dynastie des Ming', p. 115.

15 Sun was simply the most important political ancestor Chiang gave himself; he also appropriated other important historical figures, such as Lin Zexu and Zeng Guofan: see X. Paulès, 'La lutte contre l'opium', p. 208; H. van de Ven, *War and Nationalism in China, 1925–1945*, pp. 230–2.

16 A. Morris, *Marrow of the Nation*, p. 204.

17 R. Bedeski, *State-Building in Modern China*, pp. 82–7.

18 M. Zanasi, *Saving the Nation*, p. 83.

19 L. Eastman, *The Abortive Revolution*, p. 164.

20 Wang Q., *Dangyuan, dangquan yu dangzheng*, pp. 162–3, 203–4, 222–3 and 315–32.

21 Li Z., *Fazhi yu dangzhi, guomindang zhengquan de sifa danghua*.

22 Wang Q., *Dangyuan, dangquan yu dangzheng*, pp. 195–9.

23 M. Zanasi, *Saving the Nation*, pp. 19–20.

24 L. Eastman, 'The Kuomintang in the 1930s', pp. 196–200.

25 A. Kerlan, *Hollywood à Shanghai*, pp. 169–70 and 184–6.

26 L. Eastman, *Seeds of Destruction*, pp. 89–107.

27 Yip K., *Health and National Reconstruction in Nationalist China*, p. 44.

28 J. Strauss, *Strong Institutions in Weak Polities*.

29 Wang C., 'Intellectuals and the One-Party-State in Nationalist China', pp. 1769–1807.

30 E. Fung, *The Intellectual Foundations of Chinese Modernity*, pp. 61–95.

31 R. Nedostup, *Superstitious Regimes*, pp. 196–7 and 207–8.

32 Yeh W., *The Alienated Academy*, pp. 167–82.

33 For a remarkable portrait of the Beijing police in a few pages, see D. Strand, *Rickshaw Beijing*, pp. 67–96. At the start of the Republic, Beijing had a very high ratio of 13 policemen per 1,000 inhabitants, compared to 2 or 3 at the same period in Paris, Berlin or London.

34 P. Carroll, *Between Heaven and Modernity*, pp. 90–4. Chengdu converted to a similar medium-term solution: Wang D., *Street Culture in Chengdu*, pp. 128–9.

35 Wang L., 'Tourism and Spatial Change in Hangzhou (1911–1927)', pp. 113–16.

36 Dong M., *Republican Beijing*, pp. 73–5.

37 K. Gerth, *China Made*, p. 93.

38 A publication that presents a selection of excellent articles offering a fairly exhaustive overview of the very extensive research conducted on this subject in the 1980s is M. Rankin and J. Esherick, *Chinese Local Elites and Patterns of Dominance*.

39 K. Bernhardt, *Rents, Taxes, and Peasant Resistance*, pp. 182–8.

40 J. Ch'en, *The Highlanders in Central China*, pp. 162–3.

41 Mao Y., 'Muslim Education Reform in 20th Century China', pp. 154–5.

42 R. Huenemann, *The Dragon and the Iron Horse*, pp. 94–5.

43 R. Kapp, *Szechwan and the Chinese Republic*, pp. 57–8.

44 D. Serfass, 'L'occupation japonaise comme objet pour l'histoire de l'État chinois', pp. 123–37.

45 Zhong Z., *Chen Jitang*, pp. 173–5.

46 X. Paulès, 'Le petit âge d'or statistique de la décennie de Nankin (1928–1937)'.

8 Changes in Society

1 Ge J. (ed.), *Zhongguo renkou shi*, vol. VI, p. 281. The first modern systematic census – and, as such, considered reliable by demographers – was organized in 1953. It counted 580 million inhabitants.

2 C. Henriot, *Scythe and the City*, pp. 17 and 41–2.

3 Ge J. (ed.), *Zhongguo renkou shi*, vol. VI, pp. 11–12 and 576–610.

4 M. Elvin and Zhang Y., 'Environment and Tuberculosis in Modern China', pp. 520–41.

5 C. Henriot, *Shanghai, 1927–1937, élites locales et modernisation dans la Chine nationaliste*, pp. 116–17 and 238–49.

6 X. Paulès, *L'Opium, une passion chinoise*, pp. 47–8.

7 P. Fuller, *Famine Relief in Warlord China*, pp. 1–2 and 19–21; Li L., *Fighting Famine in North China*, pp. 284–5 and 303–5.

8 M.-C. Bergère, *The Golden Age of the Chinese Bourgeoisie, 1911–1937*, pp. 38 and 99–101.

9 See an excellent review of the Chinese diaspora: A. McKeown, 'Conceptualizing Chinese Diasporas, 1842 to 1949'.

10 In Europe, which, it should be remembered, was then a region of emigration (with the notable exception of France), Chinese communities were negligible.

11 V. Purcell, *The Chinese in Southeast Asia*, pp. 82, 175, 232–4, 386 and 504–5.

12 Dong M., *Republican Peking*, pp. 131–41.

13 J. Chesneaux, *Le mouvement ouvrier chinois de 1919 à 1927*, p. 89.

14 E. Perry, *Shanghai on Strike*, see ch. 7.

15 G. Hershatter, *The Workers of Tianjin*, pp. 144–50.

16 A. Roux, *Le Shanghai ouvrier des années trente*, pp. 13–120.

17 R. Porter, *Industrial Reformers in Republican China*, pp. 24–5 and 184–202.

18 Yeh W., *Shanghai Splendor*, pp. 196–204.

19 M. Bastid, *L'évolution de la société chinoise à la fin de la dynastie des Qing, 1873–1911*, pp. 19–29.

20 M.-C. Bergère, *The Golden Age of the Chinese Bourgeoisie, 1911–1937*.

21 A. Roux, *Grèves et politique à Shanghai*, p. 190.

22 A. Roux, *Grèves et politique à Shanghai*, pp. 257–338 (the quotation is on p. 258).

23 L. Bianco, *Jacqueries et révolution*, pp. 415–20.

24 K. Schoppa, *Chinese Elites and Political Change*, pp. 50–2.

25 Liu Y., *Confucian Rituals and Chinese Villagers*, pp. 147–55.

26 Huang H., *Zai chengshi yu xiangcun zhi jian*.

27 T. Lam, *A Passion for Facts*, pp. 152–3.

28 The question has already been answered in an excellent, concise chapter of Jack Potter's book, *Capitalism and the Chinese Peasant*, pp. 174–203.

29 L. Eastman, *Family, Fields, and Ancestors*, p. 83.

30 K. Bernhardt, *Rents, Taxes, and Peasant Resistance*.

31 L. Eastman, *Family, Fields, and Ancestors*, pp. 76–8 and 83.

32 L. Bianco, *Jacqueries et révolution*, pp. 201–2.

33 L. Bianco, 'La société rurale' in M.-C. Bergère, L. Bianco and J. Domes (eds.), *La Chine au xxe siècle*, pp. 274–5.

34 L. Bianco, *Origins of the Chinese Revolution*, pp. 111–12.

35 Li L., *China's Silk Trade*, pp. 90–193.

36 P. Billingsley, *Bandits in Republican China*, pp. 21–3.

37 X. Paulès, *L'Opium, une passion chinoise*, pp. 198–200.

38 Cited in D. Courtwright, *Forces of Habit*, p. 4.

39 D. Buck, *Urban Change in China*, pp. 154 and 230–1.

40 Shao Q., *Culturing Modernity*, pp. 88–91.

41 Y. Imaeda, 'The Provenance and Character of the Dunhuang Documents', *Memoirs of the Research Department of the Toyo Bunko* (2008), p. 82.

42 S. Cochran, *Big Business in China*, pp. 34–5 and 234.

43 C. Benedict, *Golden-Silk Smoke, a History of Tobacco in China, 1550–2010*, pp. 149–77.

44 F. Dikötter, *Exotic Commodities*, 2006, pp. 233–5.

45 F. Sabban, 'The Taste of Milk in Modern China, 1865–1937', pp. 182–202.

46 C. Henriot, *Scythe and the City*, pp. 97–9 and 317–29.

47 Lu H., *Beyond the Neon Lights*.

48 S. Cochran, *Encountering Chinese Networks*, p. 39.

49 Hua L. and I. Thireau, *Enquête sociologique sur la Chine 1911–1949*, p. 166.

50 J. Judge, *The Precious Raft of History*, pp. 190–3 and 201.

51 Hua C., *La condition féminine et les communistes chinois en action, Yan'an, 1935–1946*.

52 K. Bernhardt, 'Divorce in the Republican Period', p. 191.

53 E. Perry, *Shanghai on Strike*, pp. 58–9.

54 S. Glosser, *Chinese Visions of Family and State, 1915–1953*, pp. 128–33.

9 Cultural Renewal

1 F. Dikötter, *The Age of Openness*.

2 A summary of the many works on this issue, especially in the 1980s, can be found in R. Suleski, *Daily Life for the Common People of China*, pp. 52–3.

3 A very concise description of *sishu* can be found in E. VanderVen, 'It's Time for School', pp. 67–71.

4 T. D. Curran, *Educational Reform in Republican China*, pp. 230–40.

5 Regarding this, Kouo Mo-jo's childhood recollections can be referred to with profit and pleasure, although they depict a slightly earlier period: Kouo Mo-jo, *Autobiographie: mes années d'enfance*, 1970.

6 Yeh W., *Shanghai Splendor*, p. 36.

7 Shao Q., *Culturing Modernity*, pp. 32–3.

8 É. Guerassimoff, *Chen Jiageng et l'éducation*.

9 É. Allès, *Musulmans de Chine, une anthropologie des Hui du Henan*.

10 T. Weston, *The Power of Position*, pp. 242–4.

11 Cheng M., *Diyu wenhua yu guojia renting*, pp. 228–9.

12 C. Reed, *Gutenberg in Shanghai*.

13 X. Paulès, 'Xishen xinwen jishi', pp. 341–2.

14 See, for example Ting L., *Government Control of the Press in Modern China 1900–1949*.

15 S. MacKinnon, 'Toward a History of the Chinese Press in the Republican Period', p. 7.

16 P. Link, 'Traditional-Style Popular Urban Fiction', pp. 327–49.

17 A. Kerlan, *Hollywood à Shanghai*.

18 Archives du Ministère des affaires étrangères, Série Asie Océanie 1944–55. Sous-série Chine, dossier no. 154, report by Roux, interim chargé d'affaires in Guangdong with the MAE, 21 December 1949.

19 J. Wasserstrom, 'Locating Old Shanghai', p. 193.

20 See, in particular, the special issue of the journal *Twentieth-Century China*, 37, 1 (January 2012).

21 A. Field, *Shanghai's Dancing World*, p. 163.

22 Fu P., *Between Shanghai and Hong Kong, the Politics of Chinese Cinemas*, pp. 56–61.

23 M. Bian, *The Making of the State Enterprise System in Modern China, the Dynamics of Institutional Change*, p. 154.

24 Zhang Y., *Le monde romanesque chinois au XXe siècle*, p. 19.

25 E. Levich, *The Kwangsi Way in Guomindang China, 1931–1939*, pp. 43–4.

26 He F., *Zhongwai wenhua jiaoliu shi*, vol. II, p. 871.

27 M.-C. Bergère, *Sauvons la Patrie!*, pp. 103–10.

28 This title is a reference to the great book by C. Digeon, *La crise allemande de la pensée française*.

29 F. Dikötter, *The Discourse of Race in Modern China*, pp. 101–4; P. Zarrow, 'Citizenship in China and the West', in J. Fogel and P. Zarrow (eds.), *Imagining the People*, p. 15.

30 M. Ozouf, *La fête révolutionnaire, 1789–1799*, pp. 336–7.

31 M. Bastid, 'Official Conceptions of Imperial Authority at the End of the Qing Dynasty', pp. 183–5.

32 T. Chow, *The May 4th Movement*, p. 183.

33 D. Strand, *An Unfinished Republic*, pp. 57–9.

34 Translator's note: two varieties of the same language.

35 See, for example, Anne Cheng's scholarly and amusing article, 'Si c'était à refaire ... ou: de la difficulté de traduire ce que Confucius n'a pas dit', pp. 205–17.

36 V. Schwarcz, *The Chinese Enlightenment*, pp. 77–85 and 207–10.

37 C. Maréchal, 'Trois mille ans de simplification des caractères chinois', pp. 61–2.

38 'The main cause of China's decline is its neglect of aesthetic education', quoted by L. Galy, 'Le Guomindang et ses relais dans la société shanghaienne en 1923', p. 245.

39 Liu X., *Daoist Modern*.

40 K. Dean and Zheng Z., *Ritual Alliances of the Putian Plain* (2 vols.), vol. I, pp. 139–43.

41 R. Nedostup, *Superstitious Regimes*, pp. 30–1.

42 J. Jammes, *Les oracles du Cao Dai*, pp. 48–117 and 201.

43 *Shenbao*, 28 February 1934, quoted in Chen X., 'Cong madiao dao majiang, xiaowanyi yu da chuantong jiaozhi de yi duan lishi yinyuan', p. 170.

44 See various contributions to the collective work by V. Alleton and M. Lackner (eds.), *De l'un au multiple*.

45 Quoted in P. Brocheux and D. Hémery, *Indochine, la colonisation ambiguë*, p. 221.

46 C. Salmon, *Literary Migrations, Traditional Chinese Fiction in Asia*, p. 42; He F., *Zhongwai wenhua jiaoliu shi*, pp. 338–40 and 443–4.

47 C. Goscha, 'Pour une histoire transnationale du communisme asiatique', pp. 21–46.

48 He F., *Zhongwai wenhua jiaoliu shi*, vol. I, p. 275.

49 P. Brocheux and D. Hémery, *Indochine, la colonisation ambiguë, 1858–1954*, p. 223.

50 B. De Beer-Luong, 'Les tribulations d'un journaliste chinois dans les mers du Sud', p. 110.

51 Yan B., 'The Influence of Chinese Fiction on Vietnamese Literature', pp. 278–84; C. Salmon, 'Malay Translations of Chinese Fiction in Indonesia', pp. 423–6.

52 Translator's note: an ethnic group descended from the first waves of southern Chinese settlers in maritime South East Asia.

53 D. Lombard, *Le carrefour javanais*, pp. 276–9.

54 L. Candelise, 'Georges Soulié de Morant'.

55 See, for example, the case of Surabaya, East Java: C. Salmon, 'La communauté chinoise de Surabaya', pp. 161–7.

56 Chen Y., *Chinese San Francisco, 1850–1943*, pp. 206–7.
57 M. Yap and D. Leong Man, *Colour, Confusion and Concessions*, pp. 255–74.

Conclusion and Epitaph

 1 A wealth of detail can be found in T. Saich's massive volume, *The Rise to Power of the Chinese Communist Party.*
 2 Even the very comprehensive *Cambridge History of China* devotes only three short pages to these decisive movements: J. Fairbank and A. Feuerwerker (eds.), *Cambridge History of China*, vol. XIII, no. 2, pp. 125–8.
 3 Could there be a more inappropriate term for 1949 than 'Liberation'? China had been free of foreign control since the end of the Second World War. And, domestically, the Guomindang's hold on society and individuals was slight compared to that which the CCP would bring.
 4 J. Esherick, 'Ten Theses on the Chinese Revolution', pp. 45–76.
 5 On the extreme difficulty of defining this notion, and the eminently problematic nature of its use, see B. Schwartz, *China and Other Matters*, pp. 35 and 60–1.
 6 See, on this subject, the chapter 'Hong Kong, Shanghai, Pékin, où se situera le centre financier international de la Chine?' in F. Gipouloux, *La Méditerranée asiatique*, pp. 281–306.
 7 Zhuang G., 'China's Policies on Chinese Overseas', pp. 36–7.
 8 Hong Kong and Macao were at the time under British and Portuguese sovereignty. As such, they obviously could not become SEZs. But Shenzhen and Zhuhai border these two territories.
 9 Rana Mitter talks about a 'diversion' on the road of Chinese history; R. Mitter, *A Bitter Revolution*, p. 104.
10 E. Remick, *Building Local States*; S. Billioud and J. Thoraval, *Le Sage et le peuple*, pp. 54–5. However, one should not take this too far: the notion of a 'parenthesis' is dangerously convenient, and to understand China today it is inappropriate to write off the two decades of hard-line Maoism.
11 Li X., *Zhonghua minguo shi.*

Bibliography

This bibliography brings together the works cited in the notes as well as recent complementary works, mainly in Western languages.

Twelve books considered particularly crucial are distinguished by an asterisk. These are the books to which the novice should turn to begin his or her dive into the historiography of this period.

Adshead, Samuel Adrian M., *Province and Politics in Late Imperial China: Viceregal Government in Szechwan, 1898–1911*, London: Curzon Press, 1984.

Allès, Élisabeth, *Musulmans de Chine, une anthropologie des Hui du Henan*, Paris: Éditions de l'EHESS, 2000.

Alleton, Viviane and Lackner, Michael (eds.), *De l'un au multiple: traductions du chinois vers les langues européennes*, Paris: Éditions de la MSH, 1999.

Arkush, David, *Fei Xiaotong and Sociology in Revolutionary China*, Cambridge, MA: Harvard University Council on East Asian Studies, 1981.

Averill, Stephen, *Revolution in the Highlands: China's Jinggangshan Base Area*, Lanham: Rowman & Littlefield, 2006.

Barmé, Geremie, *An Artistic Exile: A Life of Feng Zikai (1898–1975)*, Berkeley: University of California Press, 2002.

Barnes, Nicole, *Intimate Communities: Wartime Healthcare and the Birth of Modern China*, Stanford: University of California Press, 2018.

Barthélemy, Dominique, *Nouvelle histoire des Capétiens (987–1214)*, Paris: Seuil, 2012.

Bastid, Marianne, *L'évolution de la société chinoise à la fin de la dynastie des Qing, 1873–1911*, Paris: Éditions de l'EHESS, 1979.

—, 'Official Conceptions of Imperial Authority at the End of the Qing Dynasty', in Stuart Schram (ed.), *Foundations and Limits of State Power in China*, London: School of Oriental and African Studies, 1987, pp. 147–85.

Baumler, Alan, *The Chinese and Opium under the Republic: Worse than Floods and Wild Beasts*, Albany: State University of New York Press, 2007.

Bedeski, Robert, *State-Building in Modern China: The Kuomintang in the Prewar Period*, Berkeley: University of California, Berkeley, Center for Chinese Studies, 1981.

Benedict, Carol, *Golden-Silk Smoke, a History of Tobacco in China, 1550–2010*, Berkeley: University of California Press, 2011.

Benton, Gregor, *Mountain Fires: The Red Army's Three-Year War in South China, 1934–1938*, Berkeley: University of California Press, 1992.

Bergère, Marie-Claire, *Sauvons la Patrie! Le nationalisme chinois et le mouvement du 4 mai 1919*, Paris: Publications orientalistes de France, 1977.

—, *The Golden Age of the Chinese Bourgeoisie, 1911–1937*, trans. Janet Lloyd, Cambridge University Press, 1989.

*—, *Sun Yat-sen*, trans. Janet Lloyd, Stanford University Press, 1998.

—, *Shanghai: China's Gateway to Modernity*, trans. Janet Lloyd, Stanford University Press, 2009.

Bergère, Marie-Claire, Bianco, Lucien and Domes, Jürgen (eds.), *La Chine au xxe siècle*, vol. I: *D'une révolution à l'autre, 1895–1949*, Paris: Fayard, 1989.

Bernhardt, Kathryn, *Rents, Taxes, and Peasant Resistance*, Stanford University Press, 1992.

—, 'Divorce in the Republican Period', in Kathryn Bernhardt and Philip Huang, *Civil Law in Qing and Republican China*, Stanford University Press, 1994, pp. 187–214.

—, *Women and Property in China, 960–1949*, Stanford University Press, 1999.

Bian, Morris, 'Building State Structure: Guomindang Institutional Rationalization during the Sino-Japanese War, 1937–1945', *Modern China*, 31, 1 (January 2005), pp. 35–71.

—, *The Making of the State Enterprise System in Modern China, the Dynamics of Institutional Change*, Cambridge, MA: Harvard University Press, 2005.

Bianco, Lucien, *Origins of the Chinese Revolution, 1915–1949*, trans. Muriel Bell, Stanford University Press, 1971.

—, *Jacqueries et révolution dans la Chine du xxe siècle*, Paris: Éditions de la Martinière, 2005.

—, *La récidive: révolution russe, révolution chinoise*, Paris: Gallimard, 2014.

Bianco, Lucien and Chevrier, Yves (eds.), *Dictionnaire biographique du mouvement ouvrier international: la Chine*, Paris: Éditions ouvrières et Presses de la Fondation nationale des sciences politiques, 1985.

Bickers, Robert, *The Scramble for China: Foreign Devils in the Qing Empire, 1832–1914*, London: Allen Line, 2011.

Billingsley, Phil, *Bandits in Republican China*, Stanford University Press, 1988.

Billioud, Sébastien and Thoraval, Joël, *Le Sage et le peuple: le renouveau confucéen en Chine*, Paris: CNRS Éditions, 2014.

Bonnin, Michel, 'Servante, épouvantail ou déesse, la démocratie dans le discours du Pouvoir et dans celui de la dissidence en Chine', in Mireille Delmas-Marty and Pierre-Étienne Will (eds.), *La Chine et la démocratie*, Paris: Fayard, 2007, pp. 493–516.

Boorman, Howard, *Biographical Dictionary of Republican China*, New York: Columbia University Press, 1967.

Boyle, John, *China and Japan at War, 1937–1945: The Politics of Collaboration*, Stanford University Press, 1972.

Brocheux, Pierre and Hémery, Daniel, *Indochine, la colonisation ambiguë*, Paris: Éditions la Découverte, 2010.

Brook, Timothy, *Collaboration: Japanese Agents and Local Elites in Wartime China*, Cambridge, MA: Harvard University Press, 2005.

Brophy, David, *Uyghur Nation: Reform and Revolution on the Russia–China Frontier*, Cambridge, MA: Harvard University Press, 2016.

Buck, David D., *Urban Change in China: Politics and Development in Tsinan, Shantung, 1890–1949*, Madison: University of Wisconsin Press, 1978.

Cadart, Claude and Cheng Yingxiang, *Mémoires de Peng Shuzhi: l'envol du communisme en Chine*, Paris: Gallimard, 1983.

Campo, Daniela, *La construction de la sainteté dans la Chine moderne: la vie du maître bouddhiste Xuyun*, Paris: Les Belles Lettres, 2013.

Candelise, Lucia, 'Georges Soulié de Morant, le premier expert français en acupuncture', *Groupe de travail sur l'Histoire des techniques 2004–2008, Revue de Synthèse*, 131, 3 (2010), pp. 373–97.

Carroll, Peter, *Between Heaven and Modernity: Reconstructing Suzhou, 1895–1937*, Stanford University Press, 2006.

Chan Ming Ku, 'A Turning Point in the Modern Chinese Revolution: The Historical Significance of the Canton Decade, 1917–1927', in Gail Hershatter, Emily Honig, Jonathan N. Lipman and R. Stross (eds.), *Remapping China: Fissures in Historical Terrain*, Stanford University Press, 1996, pp. 224–41.

Cheek, Timothy (ed.), *A Critical Introduction to Mao*, Cambridge University Press, 2010.

Chen Hsi-yuan, 'Last Chapter Unfinished', *Historiography East and West*, 2 (2006), pp. 173–204.

Chen, Janet, 'Republican History', in M. Szonyi (ed.), *A Companion to Chinese History*, Chichester: John Wiley & Sons, 2017, pp. 168–78.

Chen, Janet, Cheng Pei-kai and Lestz, Michael (eds.), *The Search for Modern China: A Documentary Collection*, New York: W. W. Norton, 3rd edn, 2014.

Ch'en, Jerome, 'Defining Chinese Warlords and Their Factions', *Bulletin of the School of Oriental and African Studies*, 31, 3 (1968), pp. 563–600.

—, *Yuan Shih-k'ai*, Stanford University Press, 2nd edn, 1972.

—, *The Military–Gentry Coalition: China under the Warlords*, Toronto: University of Toronto – York University Joint Centre on Modern East Asia, 1979.

—, *The Highlanders in Central China: A History 1895–1937*, London: M. E. Sharpe, 1992.

Chen Lifu 陳立夫, *The Storm Clouds over China*, Stanford: Hoover Institution, 1994.

Chen, Yong, *Chinese San Francisco, 1850–1943*, Stanford University Press, 2000.

Chen Xiyuan 陳熙遠, 'Cong madiao dao majiang, xiaowanyi yu da chuantong jiaozhi de yi duan lishi yinyuan' 從馬吊到麻將, 小玩意與大傳統交織的一段歷史因緣, *Bulletin of the Institute of History and Philology Academia Sinica* 中央研究院歷史語言研究所集刊, 80 (2009), pp. 137–96.

Chen Yung-fa, *Making Revolution: The Communist Movement in Eastern and Central China, 1937–1945*, Berkeley: University of California Press, 1986.

Cheng, Anne, *Histoire de la pensée chinoise*, Paris: Seuil, 1997.

—, 'Si c'était à refaire … ou: de la difficulté de traduire ce que Confucius n'a pas dit', in V. Alleton and M. Lackner (eds.), *De l'un au multiple: traductions du chinois vers les langues européennes*, Paris: Éditions de la MSH, 1999, pp. 205–17.

Cheng, Yu-Kwei, *Foreign Trade and Industrial Development of China: An Historical and Integrated Analysis Through 1948*, Melbourne: Hassell Street Press, 2021.

Cheng Linsun, *Banking in Modern China: Entrepreneurs, Professional Managers and the Development of Chinese Banks, 1897–1937*, Cambridge University Press, 2003.

Cheng Meibao 程美寶, *Diyu wenhua yu guojia rentong: wan Qing yilai 'Guangdong wenhua' guan de xingcheng* 地域文化與國家認同:晚清以來 '廣東文化' 觀的形成, Beijing: Sanlian shudian, 2006.

Cherepanov, Aleksandr, *As Military Adviser in China*, Moscow: Progress, 1982.

Chesneaux, Jean, *Le mouvement ouvrier chinois de 1919 à 1927*, The Hague: Mouton, 1962.

Chevrier, Yves, 'Mort et transfiguration: le modèle russe dans la révolution chinoise', *Extrême-Orient, Extrême-Occident*, 2 (1983), pp. 41–108.

Ch'i Hsi-sheng, *Warlord Politics in China 1916–1928*, Stanford University Press, 1976.

Chow Tse-tsung, *The May 4th Movement: Intellectual Revolution in Modern China*, Cambridge, MA: Harvard University Press, 1960.

Churchill, Winston, *Memoirs of the Second World War*, Boston: Houghton Mifflin, 1987.

Coble, Parks, *The Shanghai Capitalists and the Nationalist Government, 1927–1937*, Cambridge, MA: Harvard University Press, 1980.

—, *Facing Japan: Chinese Politics and Japanese Imperialism, 1931–1937*, Cambridge, MA: Harvard University Press, 1991.

—, *Chinese Capitalists in Japan's New Order: The Occupied Lower Yangzi, 1937–1945*, Berkeley: University of California Press, 2003.

Cochran, Sherman, *Big Business in China 1890–1930*, Harvard Studies in Business History, Cambridge, MA: Harvard University Press, 1980.

—, *Encountering Chinese Networks: Western, Japanese and Chinese Corporations in China, 1880–1937*, Berkeley: University of California Press, 2000.

—, *Chinese Medicine Men: Consumer Culture in China and Southeast Asia*, Cambridge, MA: Harvard University Press, 2006.

Cochran, Sherman and Hsieh, Andrew, *One Day in China: May 21, 1936*, New Haven and London: Yale University Press, 1983.

—, *The Lius of Shanghai*, Cambridge, MA: Harvard University Press, 2013.

Cochran, Sherman and Pickowicz, Paul (eds.), *China on the Margins*, Ithaca, NY: Cornell University Press, 2010.

Cornet, Christine and Verdier, François, *Paysans de l'eau, Chine, 1932: photographies du père Joseph de Reviers de Mauny*, Arles: Actes Sud, 2004.

Courtwright, David, *Forces of Habit: Drugs and the Making of the Modern World*, Cambridge, MA: Harvard University Press, 2001.

Curran, Thomas D., *Educational Reform in Republican China: The Failure of Educators to Create a Modern Nation*, Chinese Studies 40, New York: Edwin Mellen Press, 2005.

De Beer-Luong, Brigitte, 'Les tribulations d'un journaliste chinois dans les mers du Sud', *Archipel*, 23 (1982), pp. 109–18.

Dean, Kenneth and Zheng Zhenman, *Ritual Alliances of the Putian Plain*, Leiden: Brill, 2010.

*Delmas-Marty, Mireille and Will, Pierre-Étienne (eds.), *La Chine et la démocratie*, Paris: Fayard, 2007.

Denton, Kirk, *The Columbia Companion to Modern Chinese Literature*, New York: Columbia University Press, 2016.

Dikötter, Frank, *The Discourse of Race in Modern China*, London: Hurst, 1997.

—, *Exotic Commodities: Modern Objects and Everyday Life in China*, New York: Columbia University Press, 2006.

—, *Things Modern: Modern Material Culture and Everyday Life in China*, London: Hurst, 2006.

—, *The Age of Openness: China before Mao*, Hong Kong University Press, 2008.

Dirlik, Arif and Prazniak, Roxann, 'The 1911 Revolution: An End and a Beginning', *China Information*, 25, 3 (November 2011), pp. 213–31.

Dong, Madeleine, *Republican Beijing: The City and Its Histories*, Berkeley: University of California Press, 2003.

Drea, Edward, Peattie, Mark and van de Ven, Hans, *The Battle for China: Essays on the Military History of the Sino-Japanese War of 1937–1945*, Stanford University Press, 2011.

Drège, Jean-Pierre, *La Commercial Press de Shanghai, 1897–1949*, Paris: IHEC, 1978.

Duara, Prasenjit, *Culture, Power and the State: Rural North China*, Stanford University Press, 1988.

—, *Rescuing History from the Nation: Questioning Narratives of Modern China*, London and Chicago: The University of Chicago Press, 1995.

—, *Sovereignty and Authenticity: Manchukuo and the East Asian Modern*, Lanham: Rowman & Littlefield, 2003.

Duby, Georges, *Rural Economy and Country Life in the Medieval West*, Philadelphia: University of Pennsylvania Press, 1998

Duus, Peter, Myers, Ramon and Peattie, Mark (eds.), *The Japanese Informal Empire in China, 1895–1937*, Princeton University Press, 1989.

*Eastman, Lloyd, *The Abortive Revolution: China under Nationalist Rule 1927–1937*, Cambridge, MA: Harvard University Press, 1974.

—, 'The Kuomintang in the 1930s', in Charlotte Furth (ed.), *The Limits of Change: Essays on Conservative Alternatives in Republican China*, Cambridge, MA: Harvard University Press, 1976, pp. 191–210.

—, *Seeds of Destruction: Nationalist China in War and Revolution 1937–1949*, Stanford University Press, 1984.

—, *Family, Fields, and Ancestors: Constancy and Change in China's Social and Economic History, 1550–1949*, Oxford University Press, 1988.

Elvin, Mark and Zhang Yixia, 'Environment and Tuberculosis in Modern China', in Mark Elvin and Liu Ts'ui-jung (eds.), *Sediments of Time: Environment and Society in Chinese History*, Cambridge University Press, 1998, pp. 520–42.

Eng, Robert, *Economic Imperialism in China: Silk Production and Exports, 1861–1932*, University of California, Berkeley, Center for Chinese Studies, 1986.

Esherick, Joseph, 'Founding a Republic, Electing a President: How Sun Yat-sen Became *Guofu*', in Joseph Esherick (ed.), *Reform and Revolution in China: The 1911 Revolution in Hunan and Hubei*, Berkeley and Los Angeles: University of California Press, 1976, pp. 129–52.

—, 'Ten Theses on the Chinese Revolution', *Modern China*, 21, 1 (January 1995), pp. 45–76.

*—, *Remaking the Chinese City: Modernity and National Identity, 1900–1950*, Honolulu: Hawaii University Press, 2000.

Eto Shinkichi and Schiffrin, Harold (eds.), *The 1911 Revolution in China: Interpretative Essays*, University of Tokyo Press, 1984.

—, *China's Republican Revolution*, University of Tokyo Press, 1995.

Eyferth, Jacob, *Eating Rice from Bamboo Roots: The Social History of a Community of Handicraft Papermakers in Rural Sichuan, 1920–2000*, Cambridge, MA: Harvard University Press, 2009.

Fairbank, John and Feuerwerker, Albert (eds.), *The Cambridge History of China*, vols. XII and XIII: *Republican China 1912–1949*, Cambridge University Press, 1983 (vol. XII) and 1986 (vol. XIII).

Fang Xiantang 方惠堂 (ed.), *Shanghai jindai minzu juanyan gongye* 上海近代民族卷煙工業, Shanghai shehui kexueyuan chubanshe, 1989.

Faure, David, *The Rural Economy of Pre-Liberation China: Trade Expansion and Peasant Livelihood in Jiangsu and Guangdong, 1870 to 1937*, New York: Oxford University Press, 1989.

—, *China and Capitalism: A History of Business Enterprise in Modern China*, Hong Kong University Press, 2006.

Fayolle Lussac, Bruno, Hoyem, Harald and Clément, Pierre (eds.), *Xi'an, an Ancient City in a Modern World: Evolution of the Urban Form 1949–2000*, Paris: Éditions Recherches, 2007.

Fei Hsiao-Tung, 'Europe and Asia: Peasant Life in China', *American Anthropologist*, 42, 1 (1940), p. 154.

Feng Xiaocai, 'Counterfeiting Legitimacy: Reflections on the Usurpation of Popular Politics and the "Political Culture" of China, 1912–1949', *Frontiers of History in China*, 8, 2 (June 2013), pp. 202–22.

Feng Yi, 'The Sound of Images: Peddlers' Calls and Tunes in Republican Peking', in Christian Henriot and Wen-hsin Yeh, *History in Images: Pictures and Public Space in Modern China*, University of California, Berkeley, Center for Chinese Studies, 2012, pp. 111–42.

Fewsmith, Joseph, *Party, State and Elites in Republican China: Merchant Organizations and Politics in Shanghai, 1890–1930*, Honolulu: University of Hawaii Press, 1985.

Field, Andrew, *Shanghai's Dancing World: Cabaret Culture and Urban Politics, 1919–1954*, Hong Kong: The Chinese University Press, 2010.

Fitzgerald, John, 'The Irony of the Chinese Revolution', in J. Fitzgerald (ed.), *The Nationalists and Chinese Society, 1923–1937: A Symposium*, History Department, University of Melbourne, 1989, pp. 18–23.

*—, *Awakening China: Politics, Culture and Class in the Nationalist Revolution*, Stanford University Press, 1996.

—, 'From County Magistrate to County Head: The Role and Selection of Senior County Officials in Guangdong Province in the Transition from Empire to Republic', *Twentieth-Century China*, 38, 3 (October 2013), pp. 254–79.

Freedman, Maurice, *Lineage Organization in Southeastern China*, London: Athlone Press, 1958.

Fu, Poshek, *Passivity, Resistance, and Collaboration: Intellectual Choices in Occupied Shanghai, 1937–1945*, Stanford University Press, 1997.

—, *Between Shanghai and Hong Kong: The Politics of Chinese Cinemas*, Stanford University Press, 2003.

Fuller, Pierre, *Famine Relief in Warlord China*, Cambridge, MA: Harvard University Press, 2019.

Fung, Edmund, *In Search of Chinese Democracy: Civil Opposition in Nationalist China, 1929–1949*, Cambridge University Press, 2000.

—, *The Intellectual Foundations of Chinese Modernity: Cultural and Political Thought in the Republican Era*, Cambridge University Press, 2010.

Fung Chi Ming, *Reluctant Heroes: Rickshaw Pullers in Hong Kong and Canton, 1874–1954*, Hong Kong University Press, 2005.

Galy, Laurent, 'Le Guomindang et ses relais dans la société shanghaienne en 1923', *Études chinoises*, 17, 1–2 (printemps–automne 1998).

Garver, John, *Chinese–Soviet Relations, 1937–1945: The Diplomacy of Chinese Nationalism*, Oxford University Press, 1988.

Ge Jianxiong 葛劍雄 (ed.), *Zhongguo renkou shi* 中國人口史, vol. VI: *1910–1953*, ed. Hou Yangfang 侯楊方, Shanghai: Fudan daxue chubanshe, 2001.

Gerth, Karl, *China Made: Consumer Culture and the Creation of the Nation*, Cambridge, MA: Harvard University Press, 2003.

Gillin, Donald, *Warlord: Yen Hsi-shan in Shanxi Province, 1911–1949*, Princeton University Press, 1967.

Gilmartin, Christina, *Engendering the Chinese Revolution: Radical Women, Communist Politics, and Mass Movements in the 1920s*, Berkeley: University of California Press, 1995.

Gipouloux, François, *La Méditerranée asiatique: villes portuaires et réseaux marchands en Chine, au Japon et en Asie du Sud-Est, XVIe–XXIe siècles*, Paris: Éditions du CNRS, 2009.

Glosser, Susan, *Chinese Visions of Family and State, 1915–1953*, Berkeley and Los Angeles: University of California Press, 2003.

Goossaert, Vincent and Palmer, David, *The Religious Question in Modern China*, University of Chicago Press, 2011.

Goscha, Christopher, 'Pour une histoire transnationale du communisme asiatique: les chevauchements sino-vietnamiens dans les mers du Sud', *Communisme*, 2013, pp. 21–46.

Grand dictionnaire Ricci de la langue chinoise (6 vols.), Paris: Institut Ricci / Desclée de Brouwer, 2001.

Guerassimoff, Éric, *Chen Jiageng et l'éducation*, Paris: L'Harmattan, 2003.

Guillermaz, Jacques, *Une vie pour la Chine: mémoires (1937–1989)*, Paris: R. Laffont, 1989.

Gunn, Geoffrey, *Encountering Macau: A Portuguese City-State on the Periphery of China 1557–1999*, Boulder: Westview Press, 1996.

Hara Takeshi, 'The Ichigo Offensive', in M. Peattie, E. Drea and H. van de Ven (eds.), *The Battle for China: Essays on the Military History of the Sino-Japanese War of 1937–1945*, Stanford University Press, 2011, pp. 392–402.

*Harrison, Henrietta, *The Making of the Republican Citizen: Political Ceremonies and Symbols in China, 1911–1929*, Oxford University Press, 2000.

—, *The Man Awakened from Dreams: One Man's Life in a North China Village, 1857–1942*, Stanford University Press, 2005.

Hartford, Kathleen and Goldstein, Steven (eds.), *Single Sparks: China's Rural Revolutions*, London: Routledge, 1989.

He Fangchuan 何芳川 (ed.), *Zhongwai wenhua jiaoliu shi* 中外文化交流史, Beijing: Guoji wenhua chuban gongsi, 2008.

Henriot, Christian, *Shanghai 1927–1937, élites locales et modernisation dans la Chine nationaliste*, Paris: Éditions de l'EHESS, 1991.

—, *Prostitution and Sexuality in Shanghai: A Social History, 1849–1949*, Cambridge University Press, 2001.

—, *Scythe and the City: A Social History of Death in Shanghai*, Stanford University Press, 2016.

Henriot, Christian and Macaux, Ivan, *Scènes de la vie en Chine: les figurines de bois de T'ou-Sè-Wè*, Paris: Équateurs, 2014.

Henriot, C., Zheng, Z., Barge, O. and Caquard, S., *Atlas de Shanghai: espace et représentations de 1849 à nos jours*, Paris: CNRS Éditions, 1999.

Hershatter, Gail, *The Workers of Tianjin, 1900–1949*, StanfordUniversity Press, 1986.

—, *Women in China's Long Twentieth Century*, Berkeley and Los Angeles, University of California Press, 2007.

Ho Virgil, *Understanding Canton: Rethinking Popular Culture in the Republican Period*, Oxford University Press, 2005.

Howard, Joshua, *Workers at War: Labor in China's Arsenals, 1937–1953*, Stanford University Press, 2004.

Hsia, C. T., *A History of Chinese Fiction*, New Haven and London: Yale University Press, 2nd edn, 1971.

Hsiung, J. and Levine, S. (eds.), *China's Bitter Victory: The War with Japan, 1937–1945*, New York: Routledge, 1993.

Hu Chi-His, *L'armée rouge et l'ascension de Mao*, Paris: Éditions de l'EHESS, 1982.

Hua Chang-ming, *La condition féminine et les communistes chinois en action, Yan'an, 1935–1946*, Paris: Éditions de l'EHESS, 1981.

*Hua Linshan and Thireau Isabelle, *Enquête sociologique sur la Chine 1911–1949*, Paris: Presses universitaires de France, 1996.

Huang Haiyan 黄海妍, *Zai chengshi yu xiangcun zhi jian: Qingdai yilai Guangzhou hezuci yanjiu* 在城市與鄉村之間: 清代以來廣州合族祠研究, Beijing: Sanlian shudian, 2008.

Huenemann, Ralph, *The Dragon and the Iron Horse: The Economics of Railroads in China, 1876–1937*, Cambridge, MA: Harvard University Press, 1984.

Iriye Akira, *After Imperialism: The Search for a New Order in the Far East, 1921–1931*, Cambridge MA: Harvard University Press, 1965.

—, *China and Japan in the Global Setting*, Cambridge, MA: Harvard University Press, 1992.

Jagou, Fabienne, *Le 9e Panchen Lama (1883–1937), enjeu des relations sino-tibétaines*, Paris: Éditions de l'EFEO, 2004.

Jammes, Jérémy, *Les oracles du Cao Dai: étude d'un mouvement religieux vietnamien et de ses réseaux*, Paris: Les Indes savantes, 2014.

Jaschok, Maria, *Concubines and Bond Servants: The Social History of a Chinese Custom*, London: Zed Books, 1988.

Ji Zhaojin, *A History of Modern Shanghai Banking*, Armonk and London: M. E. Sharpe, 2003.

Johnson, Chalmers, *Nationalisme paysan et pouvoir communiste*, Paris: Payot, 1969 [1st edn 1962].

Jordan, Donald, *The Northern Expedition: China's National Revolution of 1926–1928*, Honolulu: Hawaii University Press, 1976.

—, *China's Trial by Fire: The Shanghai War of 1932*, Ann Arbor: University of Michigan Press, 2001.

Judge, Joan, *The Precious Raft of History: The Past, the West, and the Woman Question in China*, Stanford University Press, 2008.

Kapp, Robert, *Szechwan and the Chinese Republic: Provincial Militarism and Central Power*, New Haven and London: Yale University Press, 1973.

Karl, Rebecca, *Staging the World: Chinese Nationalism at the Turn of the Twentieth Century*, Durham: Duke University Press, 2002.

Kaske, Elisabeth, *The Politics of Language in Chinese Education, 1895–1919*, Leiden: Brill, 2008.

Keating, Pauline, *Two Revolutions: Village Reconstruction and the Cooperative Movement in Northern Shaanxi, 1934–1945*, Stanford University Press, 1997.

Kerlan, Anne, *Hollywood à Shanghai: l'épopée des studios Lianhua, 1930–1948*, Presses universitaires de Rennes, 2015.

Kirby, William, *Germany and Republican China*, Stanford University Press, 1984.

—, 'Continuity and Change in Modern China: Economic Planning on the Mainland and on Taiwan, 1943–1958', *Australian Journal of Chinese Affairs*, 24 (July 1990), pp. 121–42.

—, 'The Chinese War Economy: Mobilization, Control, and Planning in Nationalist China', in J. Hsiung and S. Levine (eds.), *China's Bitter Victory: The War with Japan, 1937–1945*, New York: Routledge, 1993, pp. 185–213.

—, 'The Internationalization of China: Foreign Relations at Home and Abroad in the Republican Era', *China Quarterly*, 150 (June 1997), pp. 433–58.

—, 'Engineering China: Birth of the Developmental State, 1928–1937', in W. Yeh (ed.), *Becoming Chinese: Passages to Modernity and Beyond*, Berkeley: University of California Press, 2000, pp. 137–60.

Kirby, William and Lin Manhoung, *State and Economy in Republican China: A Handbook for Scholars*, Cambridge, MA: Harvard University Asia Center, 2001.

Köll, Elisabeth, *From Cotton Mill to Business Empire: The Emergence of Regional Enterprise in Modern China*, Cambridge, MA: Harvard University Press, 2003.

—, *Railroads and the Transformation of China*, Cambridge, MA: Harvard University Press, 2019.

Kotkin, Stephen and Elleman, Bruce A. (eds.), *Mongolia in the Twentieth Century: Landlocked Cosmopolitan*, Armonk: M. E. Sharpe, 1999.

Kouo Mo-jo, *Autobiographie: mes années d'enfance*, Paris: Gallimard, 1970.

Kuhn, Philip, *Chinese among Others: Emigration in Modern Times*, Lanham: Rowman & Littlefield, 2008.

Lam Tong, *A Passion for Facts: Social Surveys and the Construction of the Chinese Nation-State*, Berkeley: University of California Press, 2011.

Lanza, Fabio, *Behind the Gate: Inventing Students in Beijing*, New York: Columbia University Press, 2010.

Larsen, Kirk, *Tradition, Treaties, and Trade: Qing Imperialism, 1850–1910*, Cambridge, MA: Harvard University Press, 2008.

Lary, Diana, *Warlord Soldiers: Chinese Common Soldiers 1911–1937*, Cambridge University Press, 1985.

—, *China's Republic*, Cambridge University Press, 2007.

—, *China's Civil War: A Social History, 1945–1949*, Cambridge University Press, 2015.

Lawson, Joseph, 'Warlord Colonialism: State Fragmentation and Chinese Rule in Kham, 1911–1949', *Journal of Asian Studies*, 72, 2 (May 2013), pp. 299–318.

Lee Ou-fan, *Shanghai Modern: The Flowering of a New Urban Culture in China, 1930–1945*, Cambridge, MA: Harvard University Press, 1999.

Leung, Angela, *Leprosy in China, a History*, New York: Columbia University Press, 2009.

Levich, Eugene, *The Kwangsi Way in Kuomintang China, 1931–1939*, New York: M. E. Sharpe, 1993.

Levine, Steven, *Anvil of Victory: The Communist Revolution in Manchuria, 1945–1948*, New York: Columbia University Press, 1987.

Li, Charles, *The Bitter Sea: Coming of Age in China before Mao*, New York: HarperCollins, 2008.

Li, Lillian, *China's Silk Trade: Traditional Industry in the Modern World, 1842–1937*, Cambridge, MA: Harvard University Press, 1981.

—, *Fighting Famine in North China*, Stanford University Press, 2007.

Li Xin 李新 (ed.), *Zhonghua minguo shi* 中華民國史 (16 vols.), Beijing: Zhonghua shuju, 2011.

Li Zaiquan 李在全, *Fazhi yu dangzhi, Guomindang zhengquan de sifa danghua* 法治與黨治, 國民黨政權的司法黨化 *(1923–1948)*, Beijing: Shehui kexuewenxian chubanshe, 2012.

Lien Ling-ling, 'From the Retailing Revolution to the Consumer Revolution: Department Stores in Modern Shanghai', *Frontiers of History in China*, 4, 3 (2009), pp. 358–89.

Lim Tai Wei, 'Oil for the Center from the Margins', in S. Cochran and P. Pickowicz (eds.), *China on the Margins*, Cornell East Asia Series, Ithaca: Cornell University Press, 2010, pp. 117–34.

Lin Hsiao-ting, *Modern China's Ethnic Frontiers: A Journey to the West*, London and New York: Routledge, 2011.

—, *Accidental State: Chiang Kai-shek, the United States and the Making of Taiwan*, Cambridge, MA: Harvard University Press, 2016.

Link, Perry, 'Traditional-Style Popular Urban Fiction', in Merle Goldman (ed.), *Modern Chinese Literature in the May Fourth Era*, Cambridge, MA: Harvard University Press, 1977, pp. 327–49.

Liu Shoulin 劉壽林,Wan Renyuan 萬仁元, Wang Yuwen王玉文 and Kong Qingtai 孔慶泰 (eds.), *Minguo zhiguan nianbiao* 民國職官年表, Beijing: Zhonghua shuju, 1995.

Liu Xun, *Daoist Modern: Innovation, Lay Practice, and the Community of Inner Alchemy in Republican Shanghai*, Cambridge, MA: Harvard University Press, 2009.

Liu Yonghua, *Confucian Rituals and Chinese Villagers: Ritual Change and Social Transformation in a Southeastern Chinese Community, 1368–1949*, Leiden: Brill, 2013.

Lohanda, Mona, *Growing Pains: The Chinese and the Dutch in Colonial Java, 1890–1942*, Jakarta: Yayasan Cipta Loka Caraka, 2002.

Lombard, Denys, *Le carrefour javanais, essai d'histoire globale*, Paris: Éditions de l'EHESS, 1990.

Lorge, Peter, 'The Great Wall', in N. Standen (ed.), *Demystifying China: New Understanding of Chinese History*, Lanham: Rowman & Littlefield, 2013, pp. 25–32.

Louzon, Victor, 'Une révolte postcoloniale entre Chine et Japon: legs impériaux dans le soulèvement taiwanais de 1947', *Vingtième siècle: Revue d'histoire*, 136 (2017), pp. 85–97.

Lu Hanchao, *Beyond the Neon Lights: Everyday Shanghai in the Early Twentieth Century*, Berkeley: University of California Press, 1999.

—, *Street Criers: A Cultural History of Chinese Beggars*, Stanford University Press, 2005.

Lust, John, 'Les sociétés secrètes, les mouvements populaires et la révolution de 1911', in Jean Chesneaux, Feiling Davis and Nguyen Nguyet Ho (eds.), *Mouvements populaires et sociétés secrètes en Chine aux xixe et xxe siècles*, Paris: F. Maspero, 1970, pp. 360–92.

Ma Debin, 'Economic Growth in the Lower Yangzi Region of China in 1911–1937: A Quantitative and Historical Analysis', *Journal of Economic History*, 68, 2 (June 2008), pp. 355–92.

Mackinnon, Stephen, 'Toward a History of the Chinese Press in the Republican Period', *Modern China*, 23, 1 (January 1997), pp. 3–32.

—, *Wuhan, 1938: War, Refugees and the Making of Modern China*, Berkeley, Los Angeles and London: University of California Press, 2008.

Maddison, Angus, *L'économie mondiale 1820–1992: analyse et statistiques*, Paris: Organisation for Economic Cooperation and Development, 1995.

—, *The World Economy: A Millenium Perspective*, Paris: Development Centre of the Organisation for Economic Cooperation and Development, 2002.

Mao Yufeng, 'Muslim Education Reform in 20th Century China: The Case of the Chengda Teachers Academy', *Extrême-Orient, Extrême-Occident*, 33 (2011), pp. 143–70.

Maréchal, Chrystelle, 'Trois mille ans de simplification des caractères chinois – du processus spontané aux mesures normatives', *Études chinoises*, 32, 2 (2013), pp. 41–66.

Martin, Brian, *The Shanghai Green Gang: Politics and Organized Crime, 1919–1937*, Berkeley: University of California Press, 1996.

Mathews, Robert, *Mathews' Chinese–English Dictionary*, Cambridge, MA: Harvard University Press, 1944.

McCord, Edward, *The Power of the Gun: The Emergence of Modern Chinese Warlordism*, Berkeley: University of California Press, 1993.

McCormack, Gavan, *Chang Tso-lin in Northeast China 1911–1928: China, Japan and the Manchurian Idea*, Stanford University Press, 1977.

McKeown, Adam, 'Conceptualizing Chinese Diasporas, 1842 to 1949', *Journal of Asian Studies*, 58, 2 (May 1999), pp. 306–37.

—, *Chinese Migrant Networks, and Cultural Change: Peru, Chicago, Hawaii, 1900–1936*, University of Chicago Press, 2001.

Mitter, Rana, *The Manchurian Myth: Nationalism, Resistance, and Collaboration in Modern China*, Berkeley: University of California Press, 2000.

—, *A Bitter Revolution: China's Struggle with the Modern World*, Oxford University Press, 2004.

—, *Forgotten Ally: China's World War II, 1937–1945*, Boston and New York: Houghton Mifflin Harcourt, 2013.

Mittler, Barbara, *A Newspaper for China? Power, Identity and Change in Shanghai's News Media (1872–1912)*, Cambridge, MA: Harvard University Press, 2004.

Morris, Andrew, *Marrow of the Nation: A History of Sport and Physical Culture in Republican China*, Berkeley: University of California Press, 2004.

Muscolino, Micah, *The Ecology of War in China: Henan Province, the Yellow River and Beyond, 1938–1950*, Cambridge University Press, 2015.

Musgrove, Charles, *China's Contested Capital: Architecture, Ritual, and Response in Nanjing*, Honolulu: University of Hawaii Press, 2013.

Myers, Ramon, *The Chinese Peasant Economy*, Cambridge, MA: Harvard University Press, 1970.

Nathan, Andrew, *Peking Politics, 1918–1923: Factionalism and the Failure of Constitutionalism*, Berkeley: University of California Press, 1976.

Nedostup, Rebecca, *Superstitious Regimes: Religion and the Politics of Chinese Modernity*, Cambridge, MA: Harvard University Press, 2009.

Nishikawa, Yoshihiro, *The Formation of the Chinese Communist Party*, New York: Columbia University Press, 2013.

Ozouf, Mona, *La fête révolutionnaire, 1789–1799*, Paris: Gallimard, 1988.

Palmer, David and Liu Xun (eds.), *Daoism in the Twentieth Century: Between Eternity and Modernity*, Berkeley and Los Angeles: University of California Press, 2012.

Paquet, Philippe, *Madame Chiang Kai-shek: un siècle d'histoire de la Chine*, Paris: Gallimard, 2010.

Paulès, Xavier, 'La lutte contre l'opium, panacée politique pour le Guomindang?' *Vingtième siècle*, 95 (July–September 2007), pp. 193–217.

—, *L'opium, une passion chinoise, 1750–1950*, Paris: Payot, 2011.

—, 'Xishen xinwen jishi: *Yuehuabao* yu Guangzhou richang shenghuo 細審新聞記事：《越華報》與廣州日常生活 (1927–1938)', in L. Lien 連玲玲 (ed.), *Wanxiang xiaobao: jindai Zhongguo chengshi wenhua, shehui yu zhengzhi* 萬象小報：近代中國城市的文化、社會與政治, Taipei: Zhongyang yanjiuyuan jindaishi yanjiusuo, 2013.

—, *Living on Borrowed Time: Opium in Canton, 1906–1936* [trans. Noel Castelino], China Research Monograph, no. 74, University of California, Berkeley, Center for Chinese Studies, 2017.

—, 'The Afterlife of Sun Yat-sen during the Republic (1925–1949)', in A. Baumler (ed.), *Routledge Handbook of Revolutionary China*, London and New York: Routledge, 2019, pp. 165–79.

—, 'Le petit âge d'or statistique de la décennie de Nankin (1928–1937)', in N. Kouamé, É. Meyer and A. Viguier (eds.), *Encyclopédie des historiographies (Afriques, Amériques, Asies)*, Paris: Presses de l'Inalco, 2020, pp. 1330–4: https://books.openedition.org/pressesinalco/27790.

—, 'Les *wenshi ziliao* 文史資料', in N. Kaoumé, É. Meyer and A. Viguier (eds.), *Encyclopédie des historiographies (Afriques, Amériques, Asies)*, Paris: Presses de l'Inalco, 2020, pp. 1150–6: https://books.openedition.org/pressesinalco/27130.

Pepper, Suzanne, *Civil War in China: The Political Struggle, 1945–1949*, Berkeley: University of California Press, 1978.

Perdue, Peter, 'China and Other Colonial Empires', *Journal of American – East Asian Relations*, 16, 1–2 (Spring–Summer 2009), pp. 85–103.

Perry, Elisabeth, *Rebels and Revolutionaries in North China, 1845–1945*, Stanford University Press, 1980.

—, *Shanghai on Strike: The Politics of Chinese Labor*, Stanford University Press, 1993.

Pietz, David, *The Yellow River: The Problem of Water in Modern China*, Cambridge, MA: Harvard University Press, 2015.

Pomeranz, Kenneth, *The Great Divergence: China, Europe, and the Making of the Modern World Economy*, Princeton University Press, 2000.

Porter, Robin, *Industrial Reformers in Republican China*, Armonk: M. E. Sharpe, 1994.

Potter, Jack, *Capitalism and the Chinese Peasant: Social and Economic Change in a Hong Kong Village*, Berkeley: University of California Press, 1968.

Prusek, Jaroslav, *My Sister China*, Prague: The Karolinium Press, 2002 [1st edition in Czech, 1940].

Purcell, Victor, *The Chinese in Southeast Asia*, London: Oxford University Press, 2nd edn, 1965.

Pye, Lucian, *Warlord Politics: Conflict and Coalition in the Modernization of Republican China*, New York: Praeger, 1971.

Rankin, Mary and Esherick, Joseph (eds.), *Chinese Local Elites and Patterns of Dominance*, Berkeley: University of California Press, 1990.

*Rawski, Thomas, *Economic Growth in Pre-War China*, Berkeley: University of California Press, 1989.

Reed, Christopher, *Gutenberg in Shanghai: Chinese Print Capitalism, 1876–1937*, Vancouver: University of British Columbia Press, 2004.

Reinhardt, Anne, *Navigating Semi-colonialism: Shipping, Sovereignty and Nation-Building in China, 1860–1937*, Cambridge, MA: Harvard University Asia Center, 2018.

Remick, Elizabeth, *Building Local States: China during the Republican and Post-Mao Eras*, Cambridge, MA: Harvard University Asia Center, 2004.

Reynolds, Douglas, *China, 1898–1912: The Xinzheng Revolution and Japan*, Cambridge, MA: Harvard University Press, 1993.

Rhoads, Edward, *Manchus & Han, Ethnic Relations and Political Power in Late Qing and Early Republican China, 1861–1928*, Seattle and London: Washington University Press, 2000.

Richardson, Philip, *Economic Change in China, c. 1800–1950*, Cambridge University Press, 1999.

Rogaski, Ruth, *Hygienic Modernity: Meanings of Health and Disease in Treaty-Port China, 1860–1937*, Cambridge, MA: Harvard University Asia Center, 2018.

Roux, Alain, *Le Shanghai ouvrier des années trente: coolies, gangsters et syndicalistes*, Paris: L'Harmattan, 1993.

—, *Grèves et politique à Shanghai: les désillusions (1927–1932)*, Paris: Éditions de l'EHESS, 1995.

—, 'Le Guomindang et les ouvriers de Shanghai (1938–1948): la déchirure', *Le Mouvement social*, 173 (October–December 1995), pp. 69–95.

—, *Le singe et le tigre: Mao, un destin chinois*, Paris: Larousse, 2009.

—, 'Le syndrome de Ye Gong: le Parti communiste chinois et les ouvriers à la veille de la prise de Shanghai', in Y. Chevrier and X. Xiao-Planes (eds.), *Citadins et citoyens dans la Chine du xxe siècle*, Paris: Éditions de la MSH, 2010, pp. 455–96.

*—, *Chiang Kaï-shek: le grand rival de Mao*, Paris: Payot, 2016.

Roux, Alain and Wang Xiaoling, *Qu Qubai (1899–1935: des mots de trop* (duoyu de hua), *l'autobiographie d'un intellectuel engagé chinois*, Paris and Louvain: Éditions Peeters, 2005.

Rowe, William, *Crimson Rain: Seven Centuries of Violence in a Chinese County*, Stanford University Press, 2007.

Sabban, Françoise, 'The Taste of Milk in Modern China, 1865–1937', in J. Klein and A. Murcott (eds.), *Food Consumption in Global Perspective*, Basingstoke: Palgrave Macmillan, 2014, pp. 182–202.

Saich, Tony, *The Rise to Power of the Chinese Communist Party: Documents and Analysis*, London and Armonk: M. E. Sharpe, 1997.

Saich, Tony and van de Ven, Hans (ed.), *New Perspectives on the Chinese Communist Revolution*, London and New York: M. E. Sharpe, 1995.

Salmon, Claudine, 'Malay Translations of Chinese Fiction in Indonesia', in C. Salmon (ed.), *Literary Migrations: Traditional Chinese Fiction in Asia (17th–20th Centuries)*, Singapore: Institute of Southeast Asian Studies, 2013 [1st edn 1987], pp. 248–76.

—, 'La communauté chinoise de Surabaya: essai d'histoire, des origines à la crise de 1930', *Archipel*, 53 (1997), pp. 121–206.

—, *Literary Migrations: Traditional Chinese Fiction in Asia (17th–20th Centuries)*, Singapore: Institute of Southeast Asian Studies, 2013 [1st edn 1987].

Sanjuan, Thierry, *Atlas de la Chine: les nouvelles échelles de la puissance*, Paris: Autrement, 2018.

Schoppa, Keith, *Chinese Elites and Political Change: Zhejiang Province in the Early Twentieth Century*, Cambridge, MA: Harvard University Press, 1982.

—, *Blood Road: The Mystery of Shen Dingyi in Revolutionary China*, Berkeley: University of California Press, 1995.

—, *In a Sea of Bitterness: Refugees during the Sino-Japanese War*, Cambridge, MA: Harvard University Press, 2011.

—, *Twentieth Century China: A History in Documents*, Oxford University Press, 2011.

Schram, Stuart (ed.), *Mao's Road to Power: Revolutionary Writings, 1912–1949*, Armonk: M. E. Sharpe, 1999.

Schwarcz, Vera, *The Chinese Enlightenment: Intellectuals and the Legacy of the May Fourth Movement of 1919*, Berkeley: University of California Press, 1986.

—, *Time for Telling Truth Is Running Out: Conversations with Zhang Shenfu*, New Haven: Yale University Press, 1992.

Schwartz, Benjamin, *China and Other Matters*, Cambridge, MA: Harvard University Press, 1996.

Selden, Mark, *The Yenan Way in Revolutionary China*, Cambridge, MA: Harvard University Press, 1971.

—, *China in Revolution: The Yenan Way Revisited*, Armonk: M. E. Sharpe, 1995.

Serfass, David, 'Résister ou négocier face au Japon: la genèse du gouvernement de collaboration de Nankin (janvier 1938 – avril 1939)', *Vingtième siècle, Revue d'histoire*, 125 (January–March 2015), pp. 121–32.

—, 'L'occupation japonaise comme objet pour l'histoire de l'État chinois: l'exemple de la campagne de pacification rurale du gouvernement de Wang Jingwei, 1941–45', *Études chinoises*, 35, 2 (2016), pp. 123–37.

Shan, Patrick, *Yuan Shikai: A Reappraisal*, Vancouver: University of British Columbia Press, 2018.

Shao Qin, *Culturing Modernity: The Nantong Model, 1890–1930*, Stanford University Press, 2004.

Sheehan, Brett, *Industrial Eden: A Chinese Capitalist Vision*, Cambridge, MA: Harvard University Press, 2015.

Shen Tsung-han, 'Food Production and Distribution for Civilian and Military Needs in Wartime China, 1937–1945', in Paul Sih (ed.), *Nationalist China during the Sino-Japanese War, 1937–1945*, Hicksville, NY: Exposition Press, 1977, pp. 167–91.

Sheridan, James, *Chinese Warlord: The Career of Feng Yü-hsiang*, Stanford University Press, 1966.

—, *China in Disintegration: The Republican Era in Chinese History, 1912–1949*, New York: Free Press, 1975.

Shiroyama, Tomoko, *China during the Great Depression: Market, State, and the World Economy*, Cambridge, MA: Harvard University Press, 2008.

Short, Philip, *Mao Tsé-toung*, Paris: Fayard, 2005 (first published in English as *Mao, A Life*, London: Hodder & Stoughton, 1999).

—, *Mao: The Man Who Made China*, London: I. B. Tauris, 2017.

Souyri, Pierre-François, *Nouvelle histoire du Japon*, Paris: Perrin, 2010.

Spence, Jonathan, *The Search for Modern China*, New York and London: Norton & Co., 2013 [1st edn in English 1990].

Spicq, Delphine, *L'avènement de l'eau courante à Tianjin, Chine, 1900–1949*, Sarrebruck: Éditions universitaires européennes, 2012.

Stapleton, Kristin, *Civilizing Chengdu: Chinese Urban Reform, 1895–1937*, Cambridge, MA: Harvard University Asia Center, 2000.

—, 'Chinese Cities, 1900 to the Present', in P. Clark (ed.), *The Oxford Handbook of Cities in World History*, Oxford University Press, 2013, pp. 522–41.

Strand, David, *Rickshaw Beijing: City People and Politics in the 1920s*, Berkeley: University of California Press, 1989.

*—, *An Unfinished Republic: Leading by Word and Deed in Modern China*, Berkeley: University of California Press, 2011.

Strauss, Julia, *Strong Institutions in Weak Polities: State Building in Republican China, 1927–1940*, Oxford: Clarendon Press, 1998.

Suleski, Ronald, *Daily Life for the Common People of China: Understanding* Chaoben *Culture*, Leiden and Boston: Brill, 2019.

Sun Youli, *China and the Origins of the Pacific War 1931–1941*, New York: St Martin's Press, 1993.

Sutton, Donald S., *Provincial Militarism and the Chinese Republic: The Yunnan Army, 1905–25*, Ann Arbor: University of Michigan Press, 1980.

Tagliacozzo, Eric and Chang Wen-Chin (ed.), *Chinese Circulations: Capital, Commodities, and Networks in Southeast Asia*, Durham: Duke University Press, 2011.

Tan Chee-Beng (ed.), *Routledge Handbook of the Chinese Diaspora*, London and New York: Routledge, 2013.

Taylor, Jay, *The Generalissimo's Son: Chiang Ching-kuo and the Revolutions in China and Taiwan*, Cambridge, MA: Harvard University Press, 2000.

—, *The Generalissimo: Chiang Kai-shek and the Struggle for Modern China*, Cambridge, MA: Harvard University Press, 2009.

Teiwes, Frederick, 'From a Leninist to a Charismatic Party: The CCP's Changing Leadership, 1937–1945', in T. Saich and H. van de Ven (eds.), *New Perspectives on the Chinese Communist Revolution*, London and New York: M. E. Sharpe, 1995, pp. 339–87.

Ting Lee-hsia, *Government Control of the Press in Modern China 1900–1949*, Cambridge, MA: Harvard University Press, 1974.

Tong Te-kong and Li Tsung-jen, *The Memoirs of Li Tsung-jen*, Boulder: Westview Press, 1979.

Tsang, Steve, *A Modern History of Hong Kong*, London: I. B. Tauris, 2004.

Tsin, Michael, *Nation, Governance, and Modernity in China: Canton 1900–1927*, Stanford University Press, 1999.

Van de Ven, Hans, *From Friend to Comrade: The Founding of the Chinese Communist Party, 1920–1927*, Berkeley: University of California Press, 1992.

—, 'Public Finance and the Rise of Warlordism', *Modern Asian Studies*, 30, 4 (October 1996), pp. 829–68.

—, *War and Nationalism in China, 1925–1945*, London: Routledge, 2003.

VanderVen, Elizabeth, 'It's Time for School: The Introduction of the New Calendar in Haicheng County Primary Schools, North-East China, 1905–1919', *Twentieth-Century China*, 32, 2 (2007), pp. 67–71.

Vannière, Antoine, *Kouang Tchéou-wan, colonie clandestine: un territoire à bail français en Chine du Sud, 1898–1946*, Paris: Les Indes savantes, 2019.

Veg, Sebastian, *Fictions du pouvoir chinois: littérature, modernisme et démocratie au début du xxe siècle*, Paris: Éditions de l'EHESS, 2009.

Vidal, Christine, 'D'un régime à l'autre: les intellectuels ralliés au pouvoir communiste, 1948–1952', *Études chinoises*, 28 (2008), pp. 41–85.

Wakeman, Frederic, *Spymaster: Dai Li and the Chinese Secret Service*, Berkeley: University of California Press, 2003.

—, 'Liberation: The Shanghai Police, 1942–1952', in Y. Chevrier and X. Xiao-Planes (eds.), *Citadins et citoyens dans la Chine du xxe siècle*, Paris: Éditions de la MSH, 2010, pp. 497–540.

Wakeman, F., Jr, *The Shanghai Badlands: Wartime Terrorism and Urban Crime, 1937–1941*, Cambridge University Press 1996.

— (ed.), *Reappraising Republican China*, Oxford University Press, 2000.

Waldron, Arthur, 'The Warlord: Twentieth-Century Chinese Understanding of Violence, Militarism and Imperialism', *American Historical Review*, 96, 4 (October 1991), pp. 1073–1110.

—, *From War to Nationalism: China's Turning Point 1924–25*, Cambridge University Press, 1995.

Wang Chen-Cheng, 'Intellectuals and the One-Party-State in Nationalist China: The Case of the Central Politics School (1927–1947)', *Modern Asian Studies*, 48, 6 (November 2014), pp. 1769–1807.

* Wang Di, *Street Culture in Chengdu: Public Space, Urban Commoners, and Local Politics, 1870–1930*, Stanford University Press, 2003.

—, *The Teahouse: Small Business, Everyday Culture, and Public Politics in Chengdu, 1900–1950*, Stanford University Press, 2008.

Wang Ju, *Jindai Shanghai mianfangye de zuihou huihuang, 1945–1949* 近代上海棉紡業的最後輝煌 1945–1949, Shanghai shehui kexueyuan chubanshe, 2004.

—, 'Le troisième âge d'or de l'industrie cotonnière de Shanghai (1946–1947)', in Y. Chevrier and X. Xiao-Planes (eds.), *Citadins et citoyens dans la Chine du xxe siècle*, Paris: Éditions de la MSH, 2010, pp. 425–54.

Wang Liping, 'Tourism and Spatial Change in Hangzhou (1911–1927)', in J. Esherick (ed.), *Remaking the Chinese City: Modernity and National Identity, 1900–1950*, Honolulu: University of Hawaii, 2000.

Wang Qisheng 王奇生, *Dangyuan, dangquan yu dangzheng* 黨員，當權與黨爭, Shanghai shudian chubanshe, 2nd edn, 2009.

Wasserstrom, Jeffrey, *Student Protests in Twentieth-Century China, the View from Shanghai*, Stanford University Press, 1991.

—, 'Locating Old Shanghai: Having Fits about Where It Fits', in J. Esherick (ed.), *Remaking the Chinese City: Modernity and National Identity*, Honolulu: University of Hawaii Press, 1999, pp. 192–210.

— (ed.), *Twentieth-Century China: New Approaches*, London and New York: Routledge, 2003.

Westad, Odd Arne, *Decisive Encounters: The Chinese Civil War, 1946–1950*, Stanford University Press, 2003.

Weston, Timothy, *The Power of Position: Beijing University, Intellectuals, and the Chinese Political Culture, 1898–1929*, Berkeley: University of California Press, 2004.

Wieger, Léon, *Chine moderne* (10 vols.), Hien-hien: Imprimerie de la mission catholique, 1921–32.

Wilkinson, Endymion, 'How Do We Know What We Know about Chinese History?' in M. Szonyi (ed.), *A Companion to Chinese History*, Chichester: John Wiley & Sons, 2017, pp. 11–27.

—, *Chinese History, a New Manual*, Cambridge, MA: Harvard University Asia Center, 5th edn, 2018.

Will, Pierre-Étienne, 'Bureaucratie officielle et bureaucratie réelle à la fin de l'Empire', *Études chinoises*, 8, 1 (1989), pp. 69–142.

—, 'Le contrôle de l'excès de pouvoir sous la dynastie des Ming', in M. Delmas-Marty and P.-É. Will (eds.), *La Chine et la démocratie*, Paris: Fayard, 2007, pp. 111–56.

—, 'La génération 1911: Xi'an, 1905–1930', in Y. Chevrier and X. Xiao-Planes (eds.), *Citadins et citoyens dans la Chine du xxe siècle*, Paris: Éditions de la MSH, 2010, pp. 353–424.

Woon Yuen-fong, *Social Organization in South China, 1911–1949: The Case of the Kuan Lineage in K'ai-p'ing County*, Ann Arbor: Centre for Chinese Studies, 1984.

Wou, Odoric, *Militarism in Modern China: The Career of Wu P'ei-Fu, 1916–39*, Canberra: Australian National University Press, 1978.

—, *Mobilizing the Masses: Building Revolution in Henan*, Stanford University Press, 1994.

Wright, Tim, *Coal Mining in China's Economy and Society, 1895–1937*, Cambridge University Press, 1984.

—, 'Distant Thunder: The Regional Economies of Southwest China and the Impact of the Great Depression', *Modern Asian Studies*, 34, 3 (July 2000), pp. 697–748.

Wu Jen-shu 巫仁恕, *Jiehou tiantang: kangzhan lunxian hou de Suzhouchengshi shenghuo* 劫後天堂：抗戰淪陷後的蘇州城市生活, Taipei: Taida chuban zhongxin, 2017.

Wu Sufeng, 'The Nationalist Government's Attitude towards Post-War Japan', in H. van de Ven, D. Lary and S. MacKinnon (eds.), *Negotiating China's Destiny in World War II*, Stanford University Press, 2015, pp. 133–204.

Xiao-Planes, Xiaohong 蕭小紅, *Éducation et politique en Chine: le rôle des élites du Jiangsu, 1905–1914*, Paris: Éditions de l'EHESS, 2001.

—, Marché, capital et pouvoir entrepreneurial en Chine – Fan Xudong et l'édification de l'industrie sel-soude-acide (1914–1945)', *Études chinoises*, 22 (2003), pp. 47–92.

—, 'Constitutions et constitutionnalisme: les efforts pour bâtir un nouvel ordre politique (1908–1949)', in M. Delmas-Marty and P.-É. Will (eds.), *La Chine et la démocratie*, Paris: Fayard, 2007, pp. 259–95.

—, 'Zhanshi qiye yu zhengfu: cong minying changkuang neiqian kan dui minzu guojia mubiao de rentong 戰時企業與政府: 從民營廠礦內遷看對民族國家目標的認同 (1937–1939)', *Minguo yanjiu* 民國研究, 19 (Spring 2011), pp. 118–45.

Xu Dixin 許滌新 and Wu Chengming 吳承明 (eds.), *Zhongguo zibenzhuyi fazhan shi* 中國資本主義發展史, Beijing: Renmin chubanshe, 2003.

Xu Xiaoqun, *Trial of Modernity: Judicial Reform in Early 20th Century China*, Stanford University Press, 2008.

Yamamuro Shin'ichi, *Manchuria under Japanese Dominion*, Philadelphia: University of Pennsylvania Press, 2006 [1st edn in Japanese 1993].

Yan Bao, 'The Influence of Chinese Fiction on Vietnamese Literature', in C. Salmon (ed.), *Literary Migrations: Traditional Chinese Fiction in Asia (17th–20th Centuries)*, Singapore: Institute of Southeast Asian Studies, 2013 [1st edn 1987], pp. 163–95.

Yang, Benjamin, *From Revolution to Politics: Chinese Communists on the Long March*, Boulder: Westview Press, 1990.

Yang Tianshi, 'Chiang Kai-shek and the Battles of Shanghai and Nanjing', in M. Peattie, E. Drea and H. van de Ven (eds.), *The Battle for China: Essays on the Military History of the Sino-Japanese War of 1937–1945*, Stanford University Press, 2011, pp. 143–58.

Yap, Melanie and Leong Man, Dianne, *Colour, Confusion and Concessions*, Hong Kong University Press, 1996.

Yeh Wen-hsin, *The Alienated Academy: Culture and Politics in Republican China, 1919–1937*, Cambridge, MA: Harvard University Press, 1990.

—, *Shanghai Splendor: Economic Sentiments and the Making of Modern China 1843–1949*, Berkeley and Los Angeles: University of California Press, 2007.

Yip Ka-che, *Health and National Reconstruction in Nationalist China: The Development of Modern Health Services, 1928–1937*, Monograph and Occasional Papers Series, Association for Asian Studies, 50 (1996).

Young, Arthur, *China's Nation-Building Effort, 1927–1937: The Financial and Economic Record*, Hoover Institution Press, Stanford University, 1971.

Young, Ernest, *The Presidency of Yuan Shih-k'ai: Liberalism and Dictatorship in Early Republican China*, Ann Arbor: The University of Michigan Press, 1977.

Zanasi, Margherita, *Saving the Nation: Economic Modernity in Republican China*, University of Chicago Press, 2006.

*Zarrow, Peter, *China in War and Revolution, 1895–1949*, London: Routledge, 2005.

—, *After Empire, the Conceptual Transformation of the Chinese State, 1885–1924*, Berkeley and Stanford: University of California Press, 2012.

Zhai Tunjian, 'Étude comparative des monographies locales de la préfecture de Hui et du district de She', in M. Bussotti and J.-P. Drège (eds.), *Imprimer sans profit? Le livre non commercial dans la Chine impériale*, Geneva: Droz, 2015, pp. 289–337.

Zhang Enhua, *Words and Their Stories: Essays on the Language of the Chinese Revolution*, Leiden: Brill, 2010.

Zhang Jiayan, *Coping with Calamity: Environmental Change and Peasant Response in Central China, 1736–1949*, Vancouver: University of British Columbia Press, 2014.

Zhang Xiaohui 張曉輝, *Minguo shiqi Guangdong shehui jingji shi* 民國時期廣東社會經濟史, Guangzhou: Guangdong renmin chubanshe, 2005.

Zhang Yinde, *Le monde romanesque chinois au XXe siècle: modernités et identités*, Paris: Honoré Champion, 2003.

Zhang Yongguang 張永廣, *Jindai Zhong–Ri jidujiao jiaoyu bijiao yanjiu* 近代中日基督教教育比較研究, Shanghai shehui kexueyuan chubanshe, 2012.

Zhong Zhuoan 鐘卓安, *Chen Jitang* 陳濟棠, Guangzhou: Guangdongsheng dituchubanshe & Jinan daxue chubanshe, 1999.

Zhou Yongming, *Historicizing Online Politics: Telegraphy, the Internet, and Political Participation in China*, Stanford University Press, 2006.

Zhuang Guotu, 'China's Policies on Chinese Overseas: Past and Present', in Tan Chee-Beng (ed.), *Routledge Handbook of the Chinese Diaspora*, London and New York: Routledge, 2013, pp. 31–41.

Index

Page numbers in *italic* refer to illustrations. References to notes are in the form '303 n. 27'.

Guomindang and, 46
interest in China, 92
as model for China, 180
post-war role in China, 126, 132,
  133–4
respect status quo, 107
Second World War, 125
transmission of ideas, 254

Versailles Conference (1919–20), 49,
  51, 53
Viet Minh, 130
Vietnam, 268, 269, 270
von Glahn, Richard, 153
voting rights, 17, 23, 300 n. 2

walls, city, 170, 206
Wang Chonghui 王寵惠, 197, 199
Wang Di, 165, 175
Wang Jialie 王家烈, 90
Wang Jingwei 汪精衛, 55, 65–6, 78–9,
  122, 126
  Chiang Kai-shek and, 58, 73, 75, 208
  death, 123
  Executive Yuan president, 195, 199
  fall and defection, 97, 119, 120–1
  Sun Yat-sen and, 11, 25, 76
  trips to Europe, 255
Wang Kemin 王克敏, 120
Wang Ming 王明, 93, 114, 119, 120
Wang Qisheng, 8
Wang Shiwei 王實味, 115
Wang Yongjiang 王永江, 188
Wang Zhengting 王正廷, 266
warlords, cliques and, 32–71, 71, 72,
  75, 79, 88–92, 103, 130, 159, 193,
  198–200, 211–13, 234, 293
Warring States period, 246
wars, 10–11
See also individual wars
Washington Conference/Treaty
  (1921–2), 50, 81
water supply, 207, 237

waterway network, 174–5, 176, 219
weavers, 170–1, 173
Wedemeyer, Albert, 124
Wei Lihuang 衛立煌, 137
Weihaiwei 威海衛, 81
Wen Yiduo 聞一多, 135
Weng Wenhao 翁文灝, 199, 208
Wen-hsin, Yeh, 167
wenshi ziliao ('historical and cultural
  materials'), 4
wenti ('a question which poses a
  problem'), 262–3
wenyan (classical language), 260–1
Western crisis, 258–60
Westernization, 237–41
wheat, 160, 232, 233, 234
Wilbur, Martin, 4
Wilkinson, Endymion, 3
Will, Pierre-Étienne, 203
Wilson, Woodrow, 50–1
women, 241–4, 262–3
  famous, 225
  feminism, 23, 64
  feminization, 221, 223, 243, 244
  gender studies, 216
  migration and, 220
  political activism, 105
  social groups, 221, 223
  status of, 263
working class see proletariat
writers, public, 248
Wu Chaoshu 伍朝樞, 76
Wu Han 吳晗, 147
Wu Jinglian 吳景濂, 22
Wu Peifu 吳佩孚, 33, 37, 38, 39, 40,
  42, 47, 61–4, 120
Wu Tiecheng 吳鐵城, 85
Wu Tingfang 吳廷芳, 187
Wu Zhongxin 吳忠信, 6
Wuchang 武昌, 13, 184, 219
Wuhan 武漢, 11–15, 16, 17, 64–7, 70,
  105–6, 126, 166
Wuxi 無錫, 163, 167